Chinese Discourse and Interaction

Chinese Discourse and Interaction

Theory and Practice

Edited by
Yuling Pan and Dániel Z. Kádár

Published by Equinox Publishing Ltd.

UK: Unit 6, The Village, 101 Amies St., London SW11 2JW
USA: ISD, 70 Enterprise Drive, Bristol, CT 06010

www.equinoxpub.com

First published 2013

British Library Cataloguing-in-Publication Data
A catalogue record for this book is available from the British Library.

ISBN-13   978-1-84553-632-9   (hardback)

Library of Congress Cataloging-in-Publication Data

Chinese discourse and interaction: theory and practice / edited by Yuling Pan and Dániel Z. Kádár.
      p. cm.
   Includes bibliographical references.
   ISBN 978-1-84553-632-9
   1. Chinese language—Discourse analysis. 2. Intercultural communication. I. Pan, Yuling.
II. Kádár, Dániel Z., 1979-
   P302.15.C4C55 2012
   306.440951—dc23
                              2011022530

Typeset by S.J.I. Services, New Delhi
Printed and bound by Lightning Source UK Ltd., Milton Keynes

Contents

Contributors

Angela Chan is a senior research fellow at the City University of Hong Kong. She has published on leadership discourse, identity construction, humour and politeness in the *Journal of Pragmatics, Journal of Politeness Research* and *Journal of Asia Pacific Communication.*

Anna Yukyee Chan is a research social scientist in the Center for Survey Measurement at the US Census Bureau. Her publications include *Complex Ethnic Households in America* (edited with L. Schwede and R. Blumberg, 2006); book chapters in *American Families: Issues in Race and Ethnicity* (edited by C. K. Jacobson, 1995); *Resiliency in Ethnic Minority Families* (edited by H. I. McCubbin et al., 1995); and articles in the *Journal of Field Methods* and *Sociological Imagination.*

Wei-Lin Melody Chang is a doctoral student in the School of Languages and Linguistics at Griffith University. She has published papers in the *Journal of Pragmatics* and *Intercultural Pragmatics.*

Xinren Chen is Professor of English and Linguistics at Nanjing University, China. His major publications include *The Pragmatics of Interactional Overinformativeness in Conversation* (2004), *Contemporary Pragmatics* (with Ziran He, 2004), *Foreign Language Education and National Identity in the Context of Globalization* (2008) and *A New Coursebook in Pragmatics* (2009).

Winnie Cheng is Professor of English and Director of the Research Centre for Professional Communication in English at the Hong Kong Polytechnic University. Her books include *Exploring Corpus Linguistics: Language in Action* (2011) and *A Corpus-Driven Study of Discourse Intonation* (2008).

Tomoko Endo is a postdoctoral research fellow at the Japan Society for the Promotion of Science, affiliated with the Department of Linguistics in Kyoto University. Her publications include book chapters in *Studies of Chinese Linguistics: Functional Approaches* (edited by Janet Xing, 2009) and *Construction and Meaning* (in Japanese, edited by Harumi Sawada, forthcoming).

Yueguo Gu is a Research Professor and Head of the Contemporary Linguistics Department in the Chinese Academy of Social Sciences. He has authored and edited several series of textbooks on linguistics, pragmatics, discourse analysis, rhetoric, ELT methodology, action research, cross-cultural communication and teaching English to Chinese learners. He is a co-chief editor of the *Journal of Contemporary Linguistics* and on the advisory editorial boards of ten international journals.

Michael Haugh is a senior lecturer in Linguistics and International English at Griffith University. His books include *Situated Politeness* (edited with Bethan Davies and Andrew John Merrison, 2011) and *Face, Communication and Social Interaction* (edited with Francesca Bargiela-Chiappini, 2009).

Agnes Weiyun He is Associate Professor of Applied Linguistics and Asian Studies at Stony Brook University. A 2011 Guggenheim Fellow, she has authored *Reconstructing Institutions through Talk* (1998) and served as co-editor of *Talking and Testing* (1998) and primary editor of *Chinese as a Heritage Language* (2008).

Dániel Z. Kádár is Research Professor of English Language and Linguistics at the University of Huddersfield. His recent books include *Politeness in East Asia* (ed. with Sara Mills, 2011), *Politeness in Historical and Contemporary Chinese* (with Yuling Pan, 2011), *Politeness in China and Japan* (with Michael Haugh, John Benjamins, forthcoming), and *Politeness and Rituality* (Palgrave Macmillan, forthcoming).

Kenneth Kong is Associate Professor of Linguistics in the English Department of Hong Kong Baptist University. He has published extensively in the areas of discourse analysis, multi-modal communication and intercultural communication. He is currently working on two book projects, one on professional discourse and the other on the history of professions in China and the West and their influence on personal identities.

Cher Leng Lee is Deputy Head and Associate Professor in the Department of Chinese Studies, National University of Singapore. Her works include 'Compliments and responses during Chinese new year celebrations in Singapore' *Pragmatics* (2009) and 'Motivations of code-switching in Singapore Mandarin' *Journal of Chinese Linguistics* (2003).

Yuling Pan is Principal Researcher and Senior Sociolinguist at the US Census Bureau. Her books include *Politeness in Chinese Face-to-Face Interaction* (2000), *Professional Communication in International Settings* (with Suzanne Scollon and Ron Scollon, 2002), and *Politeness in Historical and Contemporary China* (with Dániel Kádár, 2011).

Stephanie Schnurr is Associate Professor at the Centre for Applied Linguistics at the University of Warwick. She has published widely on leadership discourse, (im)politeness, gender, and humour at work. Her most recent book-length publication is *Leadership Discourse at Work: Interactions of Humour, Gender and Workplace Culture* (2009).

Hao Sun is Associate Professor of Linguistics in the English and Linguistics Department at Indiana-Purdue University. Her publications include *It's the Dragon's Turn: Chinese Institutional Discourses* (co-edited with Daniel Z. Kádár, 2008) as well as several articles published in journals including *Language in Society, Journal of Pragmatics, Pragmatics, Pragmatics and Language Learning, Reflections on English Language Teaching* and *Journal of the Chinese Language Teachers Association*.

Virginia Wake Yelei is a researcher at Georgetown University Medical Centre. Her publications have appeared in the journal *Survey Practice and in Pragmatics of Chinese as Native and Target Language* (1995) edited by Gabriele Kasper.

Olga Zayts is Research Assistant Professor at the School of Humanities, and the Leader of Health Communication Research Cluster, the University of Hong Kong. Her publications have appeared in *Research on Language and Social Interaction, Journal of Politeness Research* and *Sociology of Health and Illness* among many others. She has co-edited (with M.A. Kang) Medical Communication in the Asia Context, a special issue of the *Journal of Asian Pacific Communication*.

Wei Zhang is Assistant Professor at the City University of Hong Kong. She has published on repair, turn continuation, conversational code-switching and patient participation in genetic counselling in journals such as *Chinese Language and Discourse, Pragmatics, Journal of Pragmatics* and *Journal of Asia Pacific Communication*.

1

Introduction

Yuling Pan and Dániel Z. Kádár

Objectives and background

This edited volume has two closely related goals: first, to contribute to the field of discourse and interaction, and secondly, to fill a knowledge gap in Chinese discourse studies by providing a series of empirical research on Chinese language use in various social contexts.

The linguistic study of discourse, discourse analysis in a wider sense, is a huge field – one may even wonder whether it is a single 'field' at all. Even strict-sense linguistic inquiries into discourse have differing views and approaches (Paltridge 2006; Schiffrin 1994). Other disciplines, such as communication, cognitive psychology, social psychology, and artificial intelligence, have applied, and thus extended, the analytical model and method of discourse analysis to their specific problems (see Schiffrin et al. 2001). The complexity and vagueness of what linguists call 'discourse analysis' is well illustrated by the description of Ron and Suzanne Scollon (2001) who summarised four groups of linguists involved in 'discourse analysis': first is the group of analysts who focus on the logical relations among sentences in texts and conversations. The second group of analysts focuses more on the processes of interpretation that people use in understanding discourses. A third group is concerned with discourse(s) which take place over many years or across many societies, such as the discourse of medicine and the discourse of the law. Finally, a group of analysts focus on studying the ways in which discourses are used to establish and reinforce ideological positions in society (Scollon and Scollon 2001: 60). Given this vastness and diversity of discourse analysis in a wider sense, it is important for us to first define the scope of the research reported in the current volume, and then explicate the position that we take in the realm of discourse analysis.

Our collection of 13 articles reflects diverse analytical models and methods in discourse analysis. Nevertheless, it has a clear focus on *linguistics* and incorporates various approaches in linguistic tradition, including speech act theory, interactional sociolinguistics, the ethnography of communication, pragmatics, conversation analysis, historical sociolinguistics and variation analysis. This choice is not self-evident because 'discourse' is at least as much a sociological as a linguistic notion (cf. Foucault 1970). The motivation for adopting a linguistic approach in this collection is that we apply discourse analytic notions and methods in order to understand the rules and characteristics of Chinese linguistic interactions. As China gains an increasing importance in the current world events, understanding the Chinese, without making them 'cultural others' (Spivak 1988), has become pivotal to many. As a result, the linguistic analysis of Chinese discourse interactions has gained momentum in the fields of cross-cultural and intercultural communication. What makes a project dedicated to Chinese discourse analysis particularly timely is the (perhaps) somewhat surprising fact that Chinese remains a lesser-studied language in the field of discourse analysis, despite increasing contact between the Chinese and people of other nations. Taking a linguistic perspective, we were able to identify Chinese-specific instances of language use, which greatly enrich our understanding of what we define as 'Chinese discourse.'

It should be noted that the present work fills an important knowledge gap in the field. Although many studies have been published, which describe certain aspects of Chinese discourse, no work to date has attempted to describe Chinese discourse and interaction in a wider sense. This is supposedly due to the fact that 'discourse and interaction' refers to a complex set of linguistic forms and practices – including both the micro and macro features of situated language use – and so there is not any single analytical methodology that could inquire into them in a comprehensive way. This problem manifests itself in the fact that, while many *papers* have been published on the various aspects of Chinese discourse,[1] few *books* have been devoted to this topic. Furthermore, volumes addressing Chinese discourse deal with its fairly specialised aspects, such as politeness (Pan 2000) or institutional communication (Sun and Kádár 2008). In other words, no attempt has been made to study Chinese discourse in a comprehensive way. This trend is quite different from sociological inquiries into Chinese discourse (e.g. Dikötter 1992; Li 2008). This volume hopes to fill this gap in linguistic studies by providing a series of contributions, applying a wide array of approaches and methodologies. It seems to us that by offering various data and frameworks we can at least illustrate the various segments of Chinese discourse.

To this end, we have included studies that are diverse in many ways: methods of analysis, data sources, Chinese used in different geographic locations, differing segments of Chinese population, interactional settings, and types of discourses. If we go back to the aforementioned categories of focus in discourse analysis by Scollon and Scollon (2001), we will see that the research reported here falls into all four groups. We believe that the diversity of this collection is its particular strength because it can contest theoretical standpoints and methodologies in discourse analysis and advance our knowledge and understanding of the function of discourse in human interaction in general, and in Chinese discourse in particular.

In order to provide uniformity for this diverse series of studies, there is a single principle that every study in the present volume shares: our goal is to comprehend the relationship between Chinese 'culture' and communication. In other words, every study in this volume (even grammar-based ones such as the chapters by Endo and He) approaches its linguistic data with the goal of revealing something about culturally situated language use in China and, in some cases, the intra-cultural diversity of certain discursive phenomena.[2] While not attempting to definitively summarise the relationship between Chinese language use and culture, we hope that the volume that the reader has in hand reveals the most important links between Chinese culture and discourse.

Theoretical stance and methodology

Apart from the wish of gaining a wide picture of Chinese discourse, a theoretical motivation for adopting diverse approaches in studying Chinese discourse and interaction was our desire to avoid taking an essentialist view of studying Chinese as a homogeneous cultural group, which can lead to creating stereotypes of the Chinese. Our own research on Chinese politeness (Mills and Kádár 2011; Pan 2000; Pan and Kádár 2011) has revealed that linguistic instances of Chinese politeness behaviour can change extensively, depending on the social setting of the interaction. Furthermore, linguistic presentation of politeness has changed over time. It is, therefore, crucial to tease out normative beliefs from the actual practice of language use in interaction, and to take into account social, interactional and situational effects on discourse practice. For example, we learn that while the concept of 'face' is important in Chinese culture, it has a distinct function in Taiwan business interactions (Chang and Haugh, this volume). The same goes for the notion of 'power'. The concept of power in the People's Republic of China is constructed through historical and political activities, unique to people in the People's Republic of China (Gu, this volume), and not necessarily found in other Chinese-speaking regions. So, while Chinese culture is often claimed to have an overarching, unifying Confucian ideology, the actual discursive practice of language use in interaction is constrained by and reflective of multifaceted, sociocultural and situational conditions of an action occurring at the moment. Mills and Kádár (2011) argue that no ideology can describe the socio-pragmatic features of a whole society. To (re)define Chinese-specific features of discourse, the analyst needs to consider all these factors, and observe situational constraints on the language instances under study. We believe this is both a challenge and a worthwhile endeavour for scholars involved in Chinese discourse studies.

Methodologically, in order to avoid forming sweeping, stereotypical accounts of Chinese discursive practices, we need to strike a balance between an inward and an outward pull towards discourse analysis. As Scollon (1998) maintains, there is a methodological tension between these two. Linguists and discourse analysts can be pulled down into the vortex of linguistic analysis and can sometimes lose sight of the ways in which texts are the tools of mediated action in social situations (Scollon 1998: 269). An outward pull tends to focus on a wide range of social forces and cultural spheres and can lose sight of the concreteness of the texts and the mediated actions in which texts are used to analyse the broader social forces at play.

> [T]he methodological trick is not to be thrown off balance in either direction. The trick is to maintain an interdiscursive tension between the fine-grained analysis of specific mediated actions and a socioculturally contextualized analysis of the historical and social production of the sites of engagement. (Scollon 1998: 269)

Taking this description as our guiding methodological framework, our two main approaches to Chinese discourse and interaction are Conversation Analysis and discourse analysis. These two methodologies have been chosen because the former addresses the micro-level (linguistic) and the latter the macro-level (social and socio-pragmatic) features of interaction. The joint application of these methodologies is not an unusual phenomenon (see Wooffitt 2005). We believe that their joint application makes it possible to widen the scope of research. Merging these approaches also helps keep our collection of studies interdisciplinary, that is, we are not obliged to put our analyses in the frame of a distinct 'school' or trend of research. In fact, the analyses not only merge micro-level and macro-level analytic elements but many contributions also make use of analytic frameworks that do not belong to discourse analysis in a strict sense, such as media studies. Thus, the methodology of the present volume is as diverse as its topics of research.

Special characteristics of data

Before we introduce the specific studies of this volume, a note on some special characteristics of the data collected for analysis is in order. Studies reported in this volume represent a wide spectrum of interactional domains, ranging from casual interpersonal communication to highly structured survey interviews. In others the social settings include business interaction, classroom interaction, medical counselling, institutional interviews, online forum discussion, in-clan discourse and the correspondence of a Community of Practice. Except the historical studies by Kádár and Chen, all chapters in this volume analyse data of naturally occurring interactions in varied situations rather than constructed language use. In fact, even the historical research includes *empirical* research in the sense that we analyse data retrieved from authentic native context. Our emphasis on the empirical analysis of *naturally occurring* data is reflective of the theoretical stance of viewing discourse as language use in action and in interaction (Gumperz 1999, 2001; Scollon 2001). Our analytical goal is to unfold the surrounding circumstances of the actual language instances and understand the linguistic, social and cultural constraints, as well as consequences of these constraints on language use.

Another reason for stressing the importance of studying naturally occurring interactional data is methodological concern. Data collection is a general issue for Chinese pragmaticians and Chinese discourse analysts because Chinese interactional data is difficult to obtain, due to the relatively closed society of China (see Kádár 2007; Sun and Kádár 2008). As a result, previous research on Chinese discourse and pragmatics made use of constructed language data such as questionnaires and discourse completion tasks (Chen 1993; Chen et al 1995; Zhang 1995), or adopted a cultural approach by relying on the emic (insider) view of the researcher (Gu 1990; Mao 1994). As we (Pan 2011) argue elsewhere, these methodological approaches generally elicit data reflecting group members' views of language behaviour. While these approaches provide a valuable insight into the ways in which cultural values or ideologies of a cultural group impact language use, analysts should be aware that the actual linguistic behaviour of individual group members does not always conform to the group members' assumptions. The limitations of such a methodological approach thus include a lack of contextual elements in the analysis and a heavy focus on the idealised use of language. Our objective in this volume is to contribute to Chinese pragmatic and discourse studies by introducing a wide variety of authentic language data.

In addition, the data collected for analysis covers a wide time span from historical (late imperial) Chinese communication to contemporary times, and includes major dialects in the Chinese language such as Cantonese, Shanghai dialect and Minnan 閩南 (Hokkienese) dialect. Some studies (Sun this volume) take a diachronic approach to examining the changing discursive practices that resulted from the shift in social practice and ideology in recent China. Last but not least, our research on Chinese discourse is not restricted to one particular Chinese-speaking region. This volume reports studies of Chinese discourse and interaction in all major Chinese-speaking regions, including mainland China, Taiwan, Hong Kong, Singapore, and the Chinese community in the United States.

Structure

The structure of the volume follows the two major methodological approaches adopted in data analysis. Part I includes studies that make use of conversation analytic methodology and Part II includes chapters that use discourse analysis as a major research approach to Chinese discourse and interaction. Within these two parts we arrange chapters on a thematic basis, in the following way:

Part I, 'Conversation analytic and linguistic approaches to Chinese discourse', consists of four chapters that focus on the micro-linguistic analysis of discourse features by investigating the constraints of grammatical properties of the Chinese language in discourse, and the ways in which the constraints manifest themselves in situated interactions. They examine four specific language instances of expression of epistemic stance, self-repair and other repair strategies, and loan words.

Endo's chapter examines the sentential positions and functions of a Chinese expression *wo juede* 我覺得 ('I think') and its relation to the epistemic stance that speakers take in conversation. By analysing two major interactional features of Chinese communication, namely, the ways in which the Chinese express personal views and in which they take epistemic stances in interaction, Endo demonstrates how Chinese speakers modulate social relation with their interlocutors by alternating the positions of *wo juede* 我覺得 ('I think') in conversation.

The next two studies are engaged in the Chinese-specific analysis of repair and self-repair, which is one of the fundamental topics for Conversation Analysis. Both studies show that the grammatical structure of a language can pose certain constraints on discourse and interaction. Zhang and Chan's research examines the structural particle *de* 的 in Mandarin and its counterpart *ge* 嘅 in Cantonese, and explores their position and frequency of occurrence in a particular repair strategy in daily conversation and news interviews. This analysis shows that linguistic differences between two varieties of Chinese, namely Mandarin and Cantonese, can affect self-repair patterns. In addition, sociolinguistic factors, such as domains, have an effect on repair behaviour as far as frequency is concerned.

Repair in conversation also serves the function of imparting social meanings encoded in modal verbs. The third study, by He, shows that both teachers and learners of Chinese used repair strategies through sequential organisation of turn-taking to reinforce the understanding and acquisition of modal meanings, such as volition, social obligation, responsibilities, constraints, and cultural and moral values.

Finally, Lee's contribution examines the ways in which loan words are used in Chinese interaction through a case study of the interactional application of the English loan-word *then* in Singaporean Chinese. Lee's study provides insights into the intercultural aspects of Chinese conversation, and so it forms a 'bridge' between micro-level and macro-level research, that is, the two parts of the present volume.

Part II, 'Discourse analytic and social approaches to Chinese discourse', is a collection of studies of discourse and interaction in various domains and professions. Thematically, this part consists of three 'sets'. The first set has a research focus on theoretical and methodological issues in studying key concepts for Chinese interaction, such as power, face, and communication style. The second set discusses discourse and interaction in various professional settings, including business, counselling, and online public discourse. Finally, this set of chapters ends with two studies on historical Chinese discourse, which is a neglected albeit important domain of Chinese interaction research.

The first four studies of part II aim to explore new perspectives and new methodologies in capturing characteristics of Chinese discourse and interaction and the interface of language and culture. The concept of power is central to understanding human interaction in general, and the characteristics of Chinese communicative practice in particular. The chapter by Gu introduces the ways in which power relations can be modelled in Chinese situated interactions. Gu's study is illuminating in that it strives to abstract the power relation in interaction to models that can predict power relation and its impact on discourse and interaction. This study presents an interesting methodological inquiry into how to examine power relations in situated discourse.

The notion of 'face' has been a key concept in linguistic politeness research since the seminal work of Brown and Levinson (1987), however, the construct of 'face' has been contested in recent studies (Bargiela-Chiappini and Haugh 2009). Chang and Haugh's chapter introduces an emic (insider) perspective of face in Taiwanese business interactions, but argues that the analysis of face needs to focus not only on how insiders talk about face (i.e. as an emic concept), but also on how face arises in interaction, i.e. emic practices. Chang and Haugh's study uses two types of research methods – recordings of naturally occurring business transactions and ethnographic interviews – to demonstrate how face is perceived as a concept and how it is deployed in practice by interactants in business interactions.

The next two chapters, by Pan and Anna Chan, examine Chinese discourse in the setting of survey interviews conducted in the United States with monolingual Chinese speakers. As the Chinese interviews analysed represent a hierarchical setting (the interviews were conducted by researchers from a federal government agency) and were conducted outside China, they are apt to focus on the hierarchical features of Chinese discourse behaviour on the one hand and its cross-cultural features on the other. The difference between these two chapters is that the first one aims to develop a method that can capture the features of Chinese communication style in survey interviews, while the second uses statistical research methods to compare these features with that of the English language group, and to link a discourse strategy to the socio-demographic characteristics of a large sample size. These two chapters have a running theme of searching for a method that combines discourse analysis and survey research. With a focus on investigating the effect of Chinese communication style on survey data quality, Pan's chapter opens with an empirical question of whether Chinese speakers are always indirect in providing responses to interview questions. She argues for the adoption of a methodology in the examination of Chinese communication style(s), that will avoid any imbalance between complexity and stereotyping. Chan's work is a 'continuation' of Pan's research in the sense that she applies the same coding scheme developed by Pan in classifying survey interview questions. However, Chan takes things a step further by applying a quantitative approach in examining a larger sample size and using a statistical model to predict the correlation between demographic characteristics. The application of quantitative research in the analysis of macro-level issues is a most welcome contribution to discourse studies.

The second set of chapters is united by the authors' focus on the ways in which the discourse participants' roles and power relations are manifested through discursive practices.

Sun's chapter traces the change of discursive practices within the business community (or, perhaps more accurately, various Communities of Practice engaged in business) in Shanghai, China across two time spans. Through the examination of telephone interactions between customers and business employees, Sun identified significant differences in the crucial segments of an interaction: opening, closing, and outcome of the interaction. Adopting this diachronic approach, Sun shows that discursive practice is not a static entity but rather it is fluid and reflective of social change.

The next chapter by Zayts, Wake Yelei and Schnurr presents an analysis of discourse in prenatal genetic counselling. Genetic counselling is a profession originated in Western discursive culture and it is mediated and modified in the context of Hong Kong. Zayts, Wake Yelei and Schnurr highlight the challenges of adhering to the guiding principle of non-directness in the genetic counselling practice in Hong Kong due to differences in patients' expectations and social and cultural norms of communication in medical encounters. These challenges manifest themselves in the emerging discourse between the patients and the healthcare providers.

The third chapter in this set of studies is by Cheng, who investigates discourse and interaction in a broader scope: online public discourse. The challenge of studying public discourse of this nature is that there are two types of competing audience in such interactions. One is the immediate audience such as news reporters in Cheng's study. The other is the assumed audience of the wider world. Cheng's study shows the tension between the immediate audience (reporters) and the assumed audience (wide public audience) and the ways in which tension is manifested in the response pattern.

Finally, the last two chapters analyse Chinese discourse and interaction in historical contexts. In the first chapter in this section Dániel Kádár sets out to examine the relationship between group identity formation and discourse in a late imperial Chinese Community of Practice (Wenger 1998). Relying on recent theorisations of linguistic formations of group identity, Kádár introduces the most important tools of linguistic identity formation in the Community of Practice studies. As the chapter argues, politeness – more precisely, meta-messages sent by polite utterances – had particular significance in identity formational practices. By showing these linguistic practices the chapter contributes not only to discourse and politeness studies, but also to recent research on communities of practice, by drawing data from a closed community. Chen's chapter is related to Kádár's research on politeness through its topic: both studies explore formal manifestations of politeness. By analysing self-referring deictic forms in the Chinese novel *A Dream of Red Mansions*, Chen's chapter provides a noteworthy introduction into discursive tools of self-reference in historical Chinese communication. Apart from its thought-provoking data, a special merit of the chapter is that it gives the reader a taste of the profound mainland Chinese research tradition of literary analysis devoted to *A Dream of Red Mansions*.

The present collection of chapters is closed by an epilogue by Kenneth Kong, which reflects on the arguments of the authors in a critical way and suggests future directions of research.

With studies of Chinese discourse employing diverse methods, analytic frameworks, and data sources, the present edited volume hopes to present a relatively comprehensive view of Chinese discourse and interaction. Again, 'comprehensive' needs to be slightly modulated as in our opinion no study on Chinese discourse can be comprehensive enough. We hope and believe that the present volume will contributes not only to Chinese discourse studies but also to other fields such as intercultural pragmatics and intercultural studies.

Notes

1. These include Gu (1990), Ma (1996) and Chan et al. (2000).
2. Without getting involved in the controversial question of what 'culture' is. See more on this in Bargiela-Chiappini and Kádár 2011.

References

Bargiela-Chiappini, F. and Haugh, M. (eds) (2009) *Face, Communication and Social Interaction.* London: Equinox.

Bargiela-Chiappini, F. and Kádár, D. Z. (eds) (2011) *Culture and Politeness.* Basingstoke: Palgrave Macmillan.

Brown, P. and Levinson, S. C. (1987) *Politeness: Some Universals in Language Usage.* Cambridge: Cambridge University Press.

Chan, et al. (2000) Mining discourse markers for Chinese textual summarization. *NAACL-ANLP-AutoSum '00 Proceedings of the 2000 NAACL-ANLP Workshop on Automatic Summarization,* Vol. 4.

Chen, R. (1993) Responding to compliments: A contrastive study of politeness strategies between American English and Chinese speakers. *Journal of Pragmatics* 20: 49–75.

Chen, X., Ye, L. and Zhang, Y. (1995) Refusing in Chinese. In G. Kasper (ed.) *Pragmatics of Chinese as Native and Target Language* 119–164. Honolulu: University of Hawaii Second Language Teaching and Curriculum Center.

Dikötter, F. (1992) *The Discourse of Race in Modern China.* London: Hurst & Co.

Foucault, M. (1970) *The Order of Things.* New York: Pantheon.

Gu, Y. (1990) Politeness phenomena in modern Chinese. *Journal of Pragmatics* 14: 237–257.

Gumperz, J. J. (1999) On interactional sociolinguistic method. In S. Sarangi and C. Roberts (eds) *Talk, Work and Institutional Order: Discourse in Medical, Mediation and Management Settings* 453–471. Berlin: Mouton de Gruyter.

Gumperz, J. J. (2001) Interactional sociolinguistics: A personal perspective. In D. Schiffrin, D. Tannen and H. E. Hamilton (eds) *The Handbook of Discourse Analysis* 215–228. Malden, MA: Blackwell Publishing.

Kádár, D. Z. (2007) *Terms of (Im)politeness – On the Communicational Properties of Historical Chinese Terms of Address.* Budapest: Eötvös Loránd University Press.

Li, C. (ed.) (2008) *China's Changing Political Landscape: Prospects for Democracy.* Washington: Brookings.

Ma, R. (1996) Saying 'yes' for 'no' and 'no' for 'yes': A Chinese rule. *Journal of Pragmatics* 25: 257–266.

Mao, L. (1994) Beyond politeness theory: 'Face' revisited and renewed. *Journal of Pragmatics* 21: 451–486.

Mills, S. and Kádár, D. Z. (2011, in press) Culture and politeness. In D. Z. Kádár and S. Mills (eds) *Politeness in East Asia.* Cambridge: Cambridge University Press.

Paltridge, B. (2006) *Discourse Analysis.* London: Continuum.

Pan, Y. (2000) *Politeness in Chinese Face-to-face Interaction.* Stamford: Ablex.

Pan, Y. (2011) Methodological issues in East Asian politeness research. In D. Z. Kádár and S. Mills (eds) *Politeness in East Asia* 71–97. Cambridge: Cambridge University Press.

Pan, Y. and Kádár, D. Z. (2011) *Politeness in Historical and Contemporary Chinese.* London: Continuum.

Schiffrin, D. (1994) *Approaches to Discourse.* Cambridge, MA: Blackwell.

Schiffrin et al. (2001) Introduction. In D. Schiffrin, D. Tannen and H. E. Hamilton (eds) *The Handbook of Discourse Analysis* 1–10. Malden, MA: Blackwell Publishing.

Scollon, R. (1998) *Mediated Discourse as Social Interaction.* Harlow: Longman.

Scollon, R. (2001) *Mediated Discourse: The Nexus of Practice.* London: Routledge.

Scollon, R. and Scollon, S. W. (2001) *Intercultural Communication: A Discourse Approach.* 2nd ed. (1st ed. 1995). Oxford: Blackwell.

Spivak, G. C. (1988) Can the subaltern speak? In C. Nelson and L. Grossberg (eds) *Marxism and the Interpretation of Culture* 271–313. Urbana, IL: University of Illinois Press.

Sun, H. and Kádár, D. (eds) (2008) *It's the Dragon's Turn: Chinese Institutional Discourses.* Berne: Peter Lang.

Wenger, E. (1998) *Communities of Practice. Learning, Meaning, and Identity.* Cambridge: Cambridge University Press.

Wooffitt, R. (2005) *Conversation Analysis and Discourse Analysis.* Thousand Oaks/London: Sage.

Zhang, Y. (1995) Strategies in Chinese requesting. In G. Kasper (ed.) *Pragmatics of Chinese as Native and Target Language* 23–68. Honolulu: University of Hawaii Second Language Teaching and Curriculum Center.

2

Epistemic stance in Mandarin conversation: The positions and functions of *wo juede* (I feel/think)

Tomoko Endo

Introduction

Conversation is rarely if ever a mere transmission of objective information. People engaging in conversation often reveal varying subjective attitudes regarding the contents, topics, and addressee(s) of their utterance. These positions are called 'stances' and the act of taking them is called 'stance-taking'. Because stance-taking is ubiquitous in interaction, it has come to attract attention from scholars in various fields concerning with the study of discourse (Englebretson 2007). Sociolinguistic studies of stance tend to focus on the social positioning of the speaker revealed by style and stylisation (Jaffe 2009). Such studies are directly related to the culture and society to which the speakers belong, as styles of speech can index the speaker's social identity. As Du Bois (2007: 163) says, however, stance is inherently a public act by a social actor: taking a stance presupposes the presence of another subject, and the act of stance-taking is a dialogical phenomenon. If we accept this view, a study of stance must necessarily be study of social action.

While it is extremely hard to set a unitary classification of the kinds of stances people may take in interaction, most of the studies that have proposed a taxonomy of kinds of stance list epistemic stance as one of the types of stance (Biber et al. 1999; Du Bois 2007; Goodwin 2007). By 'epistemic stance', I refer to the speaker's indication of his or her positioning with respect to what he or she is saying, regarding how he or she comes to have the idea or how committed he or she is regarding the factuality of the idea that he or she is conveying. Various kinds of grammatical devices, such as judgmental adverbs, verbs of cognition or sensation and modal verbs, can be used to mark a speaker's epistemic stance (see Biber et al. 1999; Nuyts 2001 for grammatical categories in English). Complement-taking verbs such as verbs of cognition, especially used with the first person subject, can often be used as the source for epistemic stance marking. It is also argued that only a limited number of expressions are employed as marker of epistemic stance. For example, American English speakers routinely use I think to mark their epistemic stance (Thompson 2002; Kärkkäinen 2003).

In Mandarin conversation, *wo juede* (I feel/think) is comparable with *I think* in English conversation in terms of its overwhelmingly high frequency.[1] It has already been pointed out in previous studies that *wo juede* is by far the most frequent epistemic expression in Mandarin conversation and that it is becoming 'grammaticalised' as an epistemic stance marker (Huang 2003; Fang 2005). Lim (2009) conducted a study in the Conversational Analytic framework in which he characterised *wo juede* as an invitation for joint-assessment. However, considering the fact that *wo juede* is so frequent that it can be used in various positions in conversation, a more detailed analysis needs to be done in order to capture the various functions of *wo juede*. The purpose of this chapter is to demonstrate that by using *wo juede*, which marks a speaker's epistemic stance that the speaker is saying is his or her personal view, conversation participants position themselves in consideration of other interlocutors, and that the detailed function of *wo juede* differs depending on the position of the conversation sequence in which *wo juede* is used. In so doing, I aim to describe the way Mandarin speakers modulate social relations with their interlocutors in casual conversations.

Data and methodology

Data: natural conversation between friends

The data for this study come from two corpora. One is the CALPER corpus (Center for Advanced Language Proficiency Education and Research) compiled by Prof. Hongyin Tao at UCLA, recoded in Los Angeles. A total of 27 groups participated (each group consisted of two to six participants), and the transcript amounts to approximately 909,000 characters. The other is the BEIF corpus (Beijing Interaction between Friends), which was collected by the author and videotaped in Beijing, Los Angeles and Tokyo. In total, 20 pairs participated and the total length of recorded material is about 15 hours. In both corpora, the participants were asked to come to the recording site and to talk freely. For the most part the participants were familiar with each other. Even when they were not, they became quite friendly during the recording.

Methodology: interactional linguistics

The research framework adopted is interactional linguistics (Ochs et al. 1996; Selting and Couper-Kuhlen 2001; Ford et al. 2002; Hakulinen and Selting 2005). Interactional linguistics is generally characterised as the intersection of linguistics, Conversation Analysis and anthropology. It aims to understand the process and mechanism in which language is shaped by interaction, as well as the constraints that languages may pose on the interaction of their speakers. Interactional linguistics differs from other approaches to language in that it adopts, from Conversation Analysis, a methodology for micro-analysis of conversation sequences while focusing on the actions performed by the participants in the ongoing activity rather than the meanings of linguistic expressions.

A total of 1,636 tokens of *juede* were found in the CALPER corpus. Of those, 1,163 tokens, which accounts for 77.6 per cent of the all the *juede* tokens, were used with the first person subject *wo*. Tokens of *wo juede* were then coded in terms of its position in a turn. I use the term 'turn' as a string of utterances produced by a single speaker. In other words, utterances between speaker changes are treated as a turn. Reactive tokens such as *n* or *dui* (right) are not counted as a turn. In order to examine the distribution of *wo juede* in a turn, I classified tokens of *wo juede* into four types based on the position of a clause that contains *wo juede*: turn-initial, turn-medial, turn-final and single-unit turn. A clause is turn-initial if it occurs first in a turn, turn-medial if it occurs neither first nor last in a turn, and turn-final if it is last in a turn. These three types are for multi-unit turns (turns consisting of multiple clauses). If the clause that contains *wo juede* is the only clause in a turn, it is coded as single-unit turn. The results are shown in Table 2.1 below.

Table 2.1 Position of wo juede in a turn

Turn-initial	Turn-medial	Turn-final	Single-unit turn	Total
428	610	63	62	1163
36.8%	52.5%	5.4%	5.3%	100%

Turn-initial and turn-medial positions are the two major positions of *wo juede* in a turn.

These positions in a turn are relevant to, though not identical to, the sequential positions of *wo juede*. As Schegloff says, the sequential position of an item is crucial for understanding what a speaker is doing in conversation. For example, 'It's raining' will be understood as an answer, rather than as a description of weather, when it is produced in response to a question 'Are we going to the game?' (Schegloff 2007: 20–21). Similarly, the actions that the speaker performs using *wo juede* need to be analysed separately depending on the position in conversation.[4] Using *wo juede*, speakers perform different actions in different positions in a turn: at the beginning of a turn, in the middle of a turn, and at the end of a turn. In analysing the above data, I have sorted the tokens based on the positions in a turn, and analysed the data in detail focusing on the flow of the conversational sequence. In the next section, I show the typical cases and discuss the functions of *wo juede* at each position.

Analysis

Mitigating conflict: at the beginning of a turn

In this section, I examine the function of *wo juede* in a position where a participant starts stating her opinion, which is often, but not limited to, the beginning of a turn. The beginning of a turn is a significant position for interaction, as it often projects the shape and type of the turn that it initiates (Schegloff 1987). What kind of projection, then, does *wo juede* make? I argue that *wo juede* projects that what the speaker is going to say is actually or potentially conflicting with the co-participant's opinion, and that *wo juede* functions to mitigate a conflict between participants.

In the example below, participants are having conflicting views about the rarity of 2007's level of snowfall. Li did not have the chance to see the heavy snow in that year because she was out of town. Ming says that it was a pity that Li missed the heaviest snow in 50 years, but Li thinks she will have another chance.

(1) Prefacing disagreement

EXTRACT 2.1

1	Li:	所以–...特别大的雪的时候我–我–我没有看见过。
2	Ming:	哎呀太遗憾了。
3	Li:	对呀。但是我发现 [今年
4	Ming:	[五十年一遇的大雪你都没看上。
5 →	Li:	但是我觉得这个不是..五十年一遇的问题。
6	Ming:	什么问题？@

    ((10 lines omitted))

17	Li:	所以我相信今年还是会这么样的@。
18	Ming:	是吗

19	Li:	嗯:
20	Ming:	应该没那么容易的吧。
21 →	Li:	我觉得应该还是这样子的。@@@
22	Ming:	我相信...二零零八年肯定不会再有那种雪了
23		(0.5)
24	Li:	我相信...会的。
25	Ming:	°哎呀算了吧°

1	Li:	So, … when it snowed especially heavily, I did not see (the snow).
2	Ming:	Oh, that's a pity.
3	Li:	Yeah. But I found [this year
4	Ming:	[You didn't see the once-in-50-years big snowfall.
5 →	Li:	But **I think** this is not a matter of once in 50 years.
6	Ming:	(Then) what kind of matter (is it)?

((10 lines omitted))

17	Li:	So I believe this year will be the same.
18	Ming:	Really?
19	Li:	mm hm
20	Ming:	(It) shouldn't be that easy.
21 →	Li:	**I think** (it) should be the same.
22	Ming:	I believe … the year 2008 definitely won't see that much snow.
23		(0.5)
24	Li:	I believe … (it) will.
25	Ming:	Ah, okay whatever.

Ming characterises the snow that Li missed as *wushi nian yi yu de daxue* (once-in-50-years big snowfall). Li disagrees with this, saying *danshi wo juede zhege bushi..wushi nian yi yu de wenti* (but I think this is not a matter of once in 50 years). Ming displays doubt about Li's opinion by saying *shi ma* (really?) in line 18 and *yingai mei name rongyi de ba* ([it] shouldn't be that easy) in line 20. Regarding Ming's conflicting opinion, Li maintains her claim in line 21, *wo juede yinggai haishi zheyangzi de* (I still think (it) should be the same). Neither of them yielding, they have one more exchange in lines 22 and 24, *wo xiangxin … erlinglingba nian kending bu hui zai you na zhong xue le* (I believe … the year of 2008 will never have that kind of snow) and *wo xiangxin..hui de* (I believe … (it) will). Ming then gives up, saying *aiya suan le ba* (Ah, okay whatever). Their conflict on whether the heavy snow was exceptional thus comes to an end without resolution. *Wo juede* is used when Li starts and maintains her opinion that conflicts with Ming's.

A similar situation can be found in the example below, in which the participants have conflicting opinions about a mutual friend's suitcase.

(2) Prefacing disagreement (l.17, l.21, l.24)/introducing an opinion (l.7, l.8)

EXTRACT 2.2

```
1     Fei:   而且她想带东西实在太多了。
2            (3.0)
3            [我
4     Jia:   [被子最后..带去了。
5     Fei:   x::- 想带吧。
6            (3.0)
7  →  Jia:   ((nods)) 我觉得他一个人那个箱子够呛。
8  →         而她箱子我觉得质量不太好。
9            =那天小月过来，
10           (0.2)摸了一把，也觉得，TSK，
11           而且[X
12    Fei:       [就那个大箱子？((gesture))
13    Jia:   ((nods)) 她的一百多。一百三？(0.8)一百三[[十五。
14    Fei:                                    [[在那个哪儿？XX
15    Jia:   zh- 质量不太好。
16           然后就是太大，不知道，到时候，是不是，
17 →  Fei:   =我觉得还行嘛，[还
18    Jia:                [超大。
19           (1.0)
20           就-你知道是那个大小超过吧。
21 →  Fei:   她那个尺寸我觉得应该没问题。
22           (0.2)
23    Jia:   是吗？
24 →  Fei:   嗯。我觉得没问题。
25    Jia:   ((nods))
26    Fei:   那个张三什么，那箱子比她还大呢。
27    Jia:   =^真的啊:
28    Fei:   而且大那个一号。(0.8)疯了。
29           她说要不然那个我的重量跟她重量合在一起。
30           那个呢。我的东西多少啊。后来她还超重呢。
```

```
1      Fei:   and she really wanted to bring too much stuff.
2             (3.0)
3             [I
4      Jia:   [The comforter, (she) finally brought it (with her).
5      Fei:   (she) wanted to bring.
6             (3.0)
7    → Jia:   I think her suitcase was too much for one person.
8    →        and her suitcase, I think the quality is not so good.
9             That day Little Yue came over,
10            (and she) touched it, (and she) also thought, TSK,
11            and [X
12     Fei:      [was it that big suitcase? ((gesture))
13     Jia:   ((nods)) Hers is over 100. 130? 1[[35?
14     Fei:                                    [[Where?
15     Jia:   The quality was not so good.
16            And it was too big. I don't know, whether eventually,
17 → Fei:     I think it is okay, [still
18   Jia:                         [oversized.
19            (1.0)
20   Jia:     You know that size was too big.
21 → Fei:     That size of hers, I think, should be no problem.
22            (0.2)
23   Jia:     Is it?
24 → Fei:     Yeah. I think it's no problem.
25   Jia:     ((nods))
26            That Zhang San, her suitcase was even bigger.
27   Jia:     Really!
28   Fei:     It was a whole size bigger. (0.8) (It's) crazy.
29            She wanted to put mine and hers together for the weight
              measurement.
30            Mine was much less. Then hers was still overweight.
```

At lines 7 and 8, Jia expresses her views that the suitcase was too big and
also that it was not of good quality, framing the views with *wo juede*. After
a short explanation, Jia goes on to express her suspicion that the suitcase
was too big (line 16). Fei then delivers her opinion about the suitcase, which
conflicts with Jia's: *wo juede hai xing ma* (I think it is okay) in line 17. Jia is
not convinced at first, but as Fei repeats that the weight of the suitcase is not

a problem in line 21 and line 24, Jia nods in line 25, which seems to indicate her accepting Fei's view of the suitcase. While the conflict was present, Fei used *wo juede* to frame her opinion.

First, I would like to focus on the uses of *wo juede* by Fei in lines 17, 21 and 24. These uses are similar to those by Li in example (1) in that she uses *wo juede* to start delivering an opinion that conflicts with the other interlocutor. The epistemic stance marker *wo juede* in these cases does not seem to mark their low degree of commitment. Rather, *wo juede* is used in the purpose of mitigating the disagreement. By prefacing the conflicting opinion with *wo juede*, the conflict between the participants becomes less incompatible, because it is presented as the speaker's personal opinion.

Of course, not all uses of *wo juede* are in disagreements. For instance, in example (2), lines 7 and 8, Jia uses *wo juede* before Fei takes any position with respect to the topic. These uses of *wo juede* may seem different from the ones that were just discussed. However, if we extend the notion of 'conflict' from actual conflict to anticipated or potential conflict, a uniform understanding of the function of *wo juede* emerges. That is, Jia is anticipating that her opinion might be in conflict with Fei's, and this anticipation of disagreement motivates the use of *wo juede*.

This is consistent with Lim's characterisation of the function of *wo juede* as "a pre-emptive hedging in anticipation of disalignment/disagreement from joint assessment" (Lim 2009: 340). *Wo juede* may introduce an opinion that is new and potentially conflicting with another participant's opinion. In this sense, *wo juede* works as a device for mitigating a possible conflict between participants.

The example below provides a similar case of *wo juede* produced in anticipation of a possible disagreement. The speaker introduces a new perspective into the discourse, and there is no obvious conflict in opinions. In the following example, participants discuss how children learn to use computers.

(3) Introducing a new perspective

EXTRACT 2.3

1   F1：我不知道怎么搞得，小孩就^天：然好像很喜欢计算机，

2   F3：啊啊，

3   F1：就是那种，就是-可能像这种东西更适合小孩的天性，

4   像计算机这种东西，^我就觉得很小的小孩子，

5   让他学计算机他很快就-

6 → F2：我觉[得这是很正常的]啊，

7   F1：[就上手了。]

8   F2: 因为他是-他-他-他这种年龄就是接触新的-东西，

9   就是很-就是很自然的就变成了是自己的本能，

10   本能样子去玩电脑，

11   而我们呢，一开始的时候并没有-一开始我们在那个-那个-

12   啊在那个成长过程中^并没有电脑出现，

13   F1: 是啊，

1   F1: I don't know why, children seem to like computers on their
          own accord.

2   F3: uh uh

3   F1: That is, probably this kind of stuff suits a child's nature,

4   like a computer, I think a very small child,

5   if you let him learn how to use a computer, he very quickly
          will get-

6 → F2: **I think** [this is very normal,

7   F1:   [very skillful.

8   F2: Because at his age, accessing a new thing,

9   it will very naturally become instinctual,

10   (he) instinctively plays with computers.

11   but we, at first there was no- at first when we-

12   while we were growing up, there was no computer,

13   F1: Right,

F2 gives her perspective on the topic, children's easy acquisition of computer skills, starting with *wo juede.* She first says that the situation is normal, and continues with *yinwei* (because), explaining that children become familiar with newer concepts much easier than adults do.

Introducing a new perspective can be risky because other participant(s) might have conflicting opinions. Also, providing a new perspective itself might be face threatening because it could imply that the other participant has not been aware of a particular possibility. Note that the preceding speaker (F1) has expressed her uncertainty with *wo buzhidao zenme gao de* (I don't know why). Saying that the situation is 'normal' may offend F1, as it denies the justifiability of F1's wonder. Starting her turn with *wo juede*, F3 marks what she is going to say as her personal view, thereby mitigating a possible conflict with F1.

To summarise, in this section, I showed that *wo juede* can be used to frame an opinion that is potentially or actually conflicting with the other participant's opinion. By framing the opinion with a use of the epistemic stance marker *wo juede,* the speaker mitigates an actual or potential conflict with other participants. Using *wo juede* before the introduction of an opinion, the speaker is able to warn the recipient that what she is going to say might be conflicting with the recipient's opinion.

Distancing self from own claim: in the middle of a turn

The next use of *wo juede* I examine is repeated uses of *wo juede* in the middle of formulating an opinion. By using *wo juede* in this way, the speaker distances herself from her own claim about an interactionally delicate issue.

In the example below, the participants are talking about their school. In lines 3 to 5, Rui utters *wo juede* four times in producing two points: that (i) their school is as good as Beijing Foreign Studies University (BFSU) and Second Beijing Foreign Studies University and that (ii) Beijing University (BU) is not as strong as BFSU.

(4) Distancing from own claim

EXTRACT 2.4

1 Rui: =但是也没有听说过–…保到日研中心。

2 An: 嗯，没有

3 → Rui: → 其实我觉得咱们，和人家北外– 北外– 北^二外：

4 →   我觉得– TSK–^可能还k–跟他们…势均力敌吧。

5 →   北外：我觉得和人–…我觉得北大都不如人家北外。

6 An: [嗯：

7 Rui: [每次是听什么：演讲会啊什么都觉得那边儿的人^太悍了哎唷。

8 An: 北外的学生？

9 Rui: 嗯：^太悍。

1 Rui: But I have never heard of …(anyone) recommended for the Japanese Study Centre.

2 An: yeah, no

3 → Rui: Actually **I think** we and BFSU–, the second BFSU,

4 →   **I think**, possibly (we) and they are … equally strong.

5 →   BFSU, **I think** with– … I think BU is not as good as BFSU.

6 An: [yeah

7 Rui: [Every time I go to a lecture or something, (I) think people there are great, oh.

8 An: Students at BFSU?

9 Rui: yeah, too great.

This example is different from the cases examined in the previous section in that the production of Rui's turn is not smooth. Lines 3 to 5 have features of repair such as repetition (*beiwai- beiwai-*), lengthening (*bei ^er wai::*) and tongue-clicking (represented by TSK). The production of the predicate is delayed by these disfluencies.

The delay of the production of the predicate seems to reveal the speaker's hesitation in making a claim about a delicate issue. In this example, the issue is delicate in the sense that the speaker is comparing schools including the one she goes to. The claim can be heard as self-praise, because Rui is claiming that her school is as good as BFSU and the second BFSU and that Beijing University is not as good as BFSU. These comparisons imply that her school is better than BU, which is generally regarded as one of the best universities in China. By framing her opinion with *wo juede*, her opinion is presented not as an objective fact but as her personal view, so it sounds less boastful. The speaker is distancing herself from the claim that her school is as good as the best schools.

In the example below, a participant states her view about a certain class of people. *Ta* (he) in line 1 refers to a so-called high-class person, while *ta* (he) from line 2 refers to a low-class person.

(5) Distancing from own claim

EXTRACT 2.5

1		Yan:	他就是完全，不论怎么样，他老看不起人家的那种。
2	→		但是我觉得还是，处于下面的那一种人，他就是，
3			他做的一些行为或是什么的，确实是，TSK
4			不能说是让人很鄙视，
5		Jie:	嗯
6		Yan:	就是觉得，唉呦，反正让人很看不起 [这种就是。
7		Jie:	[对
8			对对
9	→	Yan:	我觉得：就是- 我觉得：处于这种人，
10	→		他们可能- 我觉得就是素质比较低。
11	→		我觉得素质就是有点看不起人家的那种，
12			文化水平，...没的。
13			他没接受过那样的教育。
14			他就没觉得这种行为有多么多么地不好。

1   Yan: He is totally, whatever it may be, he always looks down
            on people.

2 →   But **I think**, that kind of person who is in the lower
            (rank), he is,

3   his action is actually,

4   cannot be said as making people contemptuous,

5   Jie: Uh-huh

6   Yan: It's just **(I) think**, Oh, making people look down [this
            kind anyway.

7   Jie: [Right

8   Right right.

9 → Yan: **I think** ... it's just-, **I think** ... belonging to this
            kind of people,

10 →   they possibly- **I think** (their) personal qualities are
            relatively lacking.

11 →   **I think** their personal qualities make people look down,

12   (They) are not ...very cultured.

13   They have not received any kind of education.

14   They just do not think their actions are that bad.

In this example too, Yan is epistemically qualifying her claim about a recognisably sensitive topic, a class of people that are *suzhi hen di* (lacking in redeeming qualities). Yan would sound arrogant if she characterised 'lower' class people as 'lacking in redeeming qualities' without hesitation. *Wo juede* is used as a hedge. By using *wo juede*, the speaker distances herself from her claim, thereby preventing the interlocutor from forming a negative impression of the speaker.

In this section, I examined cases in which the speaker is formulating an opinion about a delicate issue. Along with features of disfluency, *wo juede* marks a low degree of speaker commitment to a claim. In this way uses of *wo juede* may function to distance the speaker from her claim.

Marking closure and soliciting response: at the end of a turn

In this last section of analysis, I discuss the function of *wo juede* at the end of a turn, marking the closure of a turn and thereby soliciting a response from another participant. While the tokens of *wo juede* examined in above sections are in its canonical, clause-initial position, the tokens of *wo juede* discussed in the later part of this section (examples 7 to 9) are seen in a clause-final position.

Introducing a conclusion signals that the turn is approaching its closure. In the example below, the participants are talking about their housing arrangement. Prior to the excerpt, Wei complained about how expensive rent in her neighborhood is, and Xun suggested that the rent would be manageable if she shared her room with someone. In line 1, Wei responds to the suggestion saying that she does not mind (sharing a room). Xun then asks whether it is Wei's first time leaving home in line 2, which triggers Wei's recounting of a past experience of sharing a room.

(6) Introducing conclusion

EXTRACT 2.6

1	Wei:	我其实无所谓。　[以前XX,
2	Xun:	[嗯你是这第一次离开家吗?
3	Wei:	…嗯。
4	Xun:	[所以你以前住家里。
5	Wei:	[哦。　不是。
6		当然不是。
7		以前读大学，读硕士都是住学校啊。
8		住了六年。
9	Xun:	嗯。
10	Wei:	读-读本科的时候，一个房间^八个人。
11		读…硕士的时候一个房间四个人。　都过来。
12 →		所以我觉得现在两个人的话我也[能接受。
13	Xun:	[很舒服。
14		我知道。　我住宿舍的时候，一个房间四个人。
15	Wei:	嗯。

```
1    Wei: I really do not mind (sharing a room).[before XX
2    Xun:                                       [hm..Is it your first
                                                time to leave home?
3    Wei: yeah
4    Xun: [So you used to live at home before,
5    Wei: [Oh. No.
6         Of course not.
7         Before, in college, and in grad school, both (times I)
          lived on campus.
8         I lived (on campus) for 6 years.
9    Xun: uh-huh
```

```
10   Wei: When I studied as an undergrad, there were 8 people to a room.
11        When I studied as a master's student, 4 people to a room.
12 →      Therefore I think if (there are) 2 people now, I [can accept
          (it).
13   Xun:                                                   [very
                                                    comfortable.
14        I know. When I lived in a dorm, (there were) 4 people in a
          room.
15   Wei: uh-huh
```

After the detailed description of Wei's housing arrangements during college and her Master's programme, in lines 7 through 11, Wei makes a conclusive remark that living with another person is acceptable to her. Acknowledging Wei's turn with *wo zhidao* (I know), Xun starts talking about her experience sharing a dorm room in line 14. This indicates that line 12 is treated as the end of Wei's story. Xun becomes the speaker and Wei the recipient, which is evidenced by the continuer produced by Wei in line 15. This shift in the speakership occurs after line 12, where *wo juede* is used to introduce the conclusion.

It is important that the opinion framed by *wo juede* in line 12 is not new to the participants. Wei has already said that she does not mind (sharing an apartment with someone) in line 1. *Wo juede*, used with *suoyi* (therefore), projects that the speaker is going back to her point after the explanation of the details of her experience. In this way, *wo juede* indicates the closing of Wei's turn on this topic.

In the rest of this section, I examine the cases of *wo juede* attached to the end of a clause. Chinese has the basic word order of Subject-Verb-Object. The end of a clause therefore is not the canonical position for *wo juede*, if we take *wo* as the subject of the sentence and *juede* the verb and what precedes *wo juede* as the object complement of *juede*. The uncanonicality of clause-final *wo juede* is reflected in the distribution of its occurrence: among the 1,163 tokens of *wo juede*, only 57 tokens (4.9%) were found in clause-final position. Interestingly, however, 34 tokens, which accounts for 59.6 per cent of all clause-final tokens, were found at the very end of a turn: either at turn-final position in a multi-unit turn or single-unit turn. This percentage is much higher than *wo juede* at clause-initial or medial position: tokens in turn-final position and single-unit turn make up only 7.4 per cent of clause-initial and 17.6 per cent of clause-medial tokens. At the clause-final position in the final clause, *wo juede* works at the very end of a turn.

While occurrence in the clause-final position has been argued as one of the criteria of the grammaticalisation of *wo juede* into a pragmatic marker (Fang 2005), its position-specific function has not been fully investigated.

In what follows, I show that clause-final *wo juede* may function to solicit a response from another participant.

In the example below, the participants are talking about reunions. They agree that college reunions will not be held annually.

(7) Soliciting agreement

EXTRACT 2.7

```
1  → Li:    嗯：可能大学同学会，不会每年都召开我觉得。
2    Ming:  不可能：
3    Li:    对呀。可能，隔个五年呐，十年的那种xx.
```

```
1  → Li:    um, maybe college reunions won't be held annually I think.
2    Ming:  (It's) impossible.
3    Li:    Right. Maybe, every five years, every ten years or
            something like that.
```

Though Ming's response is very simple compared with Li's utterance in line 1, it works as an indicator of agreement with Li, as Ming upgrades Li's judgement from *keneng ... bu* (maybe ... not) to *bukeneng* (impossible). *Wo juede* at the end of Li's turn is soliciting an agreement by epistemically downgrading her claim at the end of her utterance.

The next example contains both clause-initial and clause-final uses of *wo juede*. The participants are talking about their friends who were going to work as volunteer staff for the Olympic Games in Beijing.

(8) Soliciting agreement

EXTRACT 2.8

```
1    Li:    呀真可惜。但是感觉通知的人，
2           工作做得真不到位啊。
3  → Ming:  我觉得他们根本就没把我们这种
4           ...没把我们这几个小-小语种的...考虑...进去。
5    Li:    嗯：。
6  → Ming:  我觉得-考，而且我们的那个英语就是和他们英语专业的人-..
7           一起考的。
8    Li:    嗯：
9  → Ming:  这-太不公平了我觉得。
10   Li:    对啊我们应该考自己的语言嘛。
```

```
11 → Ming: 就是啊。我觉得-我们日语的嘛肯定-…
12          应:应该肯定可以去为日本-日本队服务啊，什么的嘛。
13    Li:   对啊:。
1     Li:   oh it's really a pity. but (I) feel that those notifiers
            (of acceptance),
2            they aren't doing their job properly.
3 →   Ming: I think they don't take people like us
4            who study minor languages into consideration.
5     Li:   mm hm
6 →   Ming: I think- exam, and our English and those who major in
             English-
7            take the exam together.
8     Li:   mm hm
9 →   Ming: This- is too unfair I think.
10    Li:   Right, we should be tested on our own language.
11 →  Ming: Exactly. I think- we Japanese majors definitely-
12           definitely should be able to work for the Japanese team or
             something.
13    Li:   Right.
```

Lines 3, 6 and 11, in which Ming uses *wo juede* at the clause-initial position,
receive only minimal responses such as a continuer *n:* or an acknowledgment
token *dui* (right). In contrast, after line 9, where *wo juede* is produced at
the end of a clause, Li takes the floor and gives a substantial response by
paraphrasing Ming's preceding utterance. Thus it seems *wo juede*, added
after the assessment *tai bu gongping le* (it's too unfair), solicits the recipient's
response.

It is not only *wo juede* that triggers the recipient's reaction. Ming
expresses a strong evaluative stance toward the topic in line 9 with an
assessment *tai bu gongping le* (it's too unfair). *Wo juede* is added at the end
of assessment to epistemically qualify the assessment as a personal opinion.
By marking the epistemic stance, the speaker makes the assessment less
intrusive and thus easier to agree with. The end of a clause is a position that
provides the last opportunity for such modification.

Wo juede can even be strategically used to transfer the speakership after
the speaker reaches a Transition-Relevance Place (TRP), a point in which
speakership transition may occur (Sacks et al. 1974). Three participants,
Mei, Ying and Tao, are discussing food issues in China in the example below
(Tao only produces laughter in the excerpt). After Ying asks what the foreign
athletes would do if they don't know how to make dumplings, Mei answers

that they will make roasted stuff, and continues to act as the speaker for a considerable length of time explaining how to make a bagel. When her explanation is finished, however, neither Ying nor Tao starts talking. Then she adds *wo juede* to re-close her turn.

(9) Re-closing a turn after pause

EXTRACT 2.9

1	Ying:	你刚才说他要就是那个外国人运动员要带厨师,
2		他带来了想吃中国的饺子,
3		他不会做怎么办？@[@@
4	Mei:	[@@@
5		(1.0)
6	Ying:	我觉得-
7	Mei:	=反正他们做那些烤的东西。
8		你看他-我觉得类似他们做那种,
9		啊:: 好像是法式的那一个...叫什么？
10		就是那种, 那种面包圈儿的那种。
11		他-就擀了一半面, 擀了一个条儿,
12		然后呢, 弄弄弄, 然后, 弄好之后,
13		撒上点儿, 比如说, 撒上点儿那种,
14		芝麻呀或者什么东西, 酱之类的。
15		然后就搁烤箱里烤了。啊:::。
16		@非常简单。比蒸馒头简单多了。
17		(0.5)
18 →		我觉得。((shifting gaze to Ying))
19		(0.5)
20	Mei:	[但是
21	Ying:	[我XX那个..只是, 很早很早以前就是, 我听说一个故事。
22		就是那外国的, 就是那个人, 刚开始的时候,
23		不知道那个饺子是怎么做, 不知道那个馅是怎么在里面的。
24	Mei:	@@@

1	Ying:	You just said the foreign athletes want to bring their own chef,
2		What if they want to eat Chinese dumplings
3		but (the chefs) can't make (dumplings)?
4	Mei:	((laughter))

```
5            (1.0)
6    Ying: I think-
7    Mei:  They will cook that baked stuff anyway.
8          You see they- I think they cook something similar,
9          like French style stuff ... what's it called?
10         It's bagel or the like.
11         It's…knead the dough, knead into a strip,
12         and do it, and when it's done,
13         put some, for example, put some,
14         sesame or things like that, kind of sauce.
15         And then put into an oven and bake. Oh,
16         it's so easy. Much easier than steaming a Chinese bun.
17         (0.5)
18 →       I think. ((shifting gaze to Ying))
19         (0.5)
20   Mei:  [But
21   Ying: [I XX…just, long time ago, I heard a story.
22         That is, in a foreign country, a man, when he just started,
23         didn't know how to make dumplings. didn't know how the
           filling gets inside.
24   Mei:  ((laughter))
```

Mei's turn comes to its completion in line 16 when she concludes that
bagels are easier to make than Chinese buns. The end of line 16 is what Ford
and Thompson call CTRP, Complex Transition Relevance Place (Ford and
Thompson 1996: 154), as Mei's utterance is syntactically, intonationally and
pragmatically complete: *bi zheng mantou jiandan duo le* (to make a bagel is
much easier than steaming a Chinese bun) is syntactically complete because
nothing has to be added after it for it to be a syntactically sufficient unit. It
is intonationally complete because it has a falling intonation contour. It is
pragmatically complete because Mei's explanation of how to make a bagel is
finished. Other participants, however, do not take the floor. Mei then adds
wo juede in line 18 after a short gap of 0.5 seconds. As other participants
still do not initiate, Mei expands her turn with *danshi* (but) which overlaps
with Ying's turn.

Wo juede in line 18 is added to re-signal the end of Mei's turn so that other
participants may take the floor. As is argued in the literature on Conversation
Analysis, adding an epistemic stance marker is a way for a speaker to extend
her turn after its completion; by doing so she "may soften some claim

or communicate uncertainty, thus revising the context for agreement or disagreement" (Ford and Thompson 1996: 167; see also Schegloff 1996; Ford et al. 2002). By adding *wo juede*, Mei epistemically downgrades the assessment, thereby making the assessment easier for other participants to agree to.

It is also worth noting that in the video Mei shifts her gaze and looks at Ying as she says *wo juede*. With this shift of eye-gaze, Mei selects Ying as the next speaker.

Instead of agreeing with Mei, however, Ying starts telling a story. Note that the story that Ying starts telling in line 21 is not related to Mei's explanation of bagel making, but is directly related to her own question in line 1: what foreign athletes would do if they don't know how to make dumplings – and her story concerns a person who did not know how to make dumplings. By going back to her own question, Ying nullifies Mei's turn. This indicates that Ying treats Mei's turn as fully completed.

In this section, I examined the use of *wo juede* in soliciting a response from a co-participant such as an agreement or topic shift. Although this function of soliciting response may appear to differ significantly from the functions discussed in the previous two sections, it is also based on the speaker's consideration of the interlocutor: the speaker considers the interlocutor as the possible next speaker. This has significant implications for the grammaticalisation of *wo juede*. The end of a clause is a position where the other participant can start speaking. My observation suggests that the 'grammaticalised' use of *wo juede* at the end of a clause can result in, or even be motivated by the interactional need of marking closure and soliciting a response from a co-participant.

Concluding remarks

In this study, I have examined the interactional functions of the epistemic stance marker *wo juede* (I feel/think) in Mandarin casual conversation. I have shown that the function of *wo juede* varies depending on the environment in which it is used. When a speaker starts to state an opinion, marking of epistemic stance works to mitigate potential or actual disagreement between participants. When a speaker is in the middle of formulating an opinion, *wo juede* conveys his or her tentative commitment to the opinion, thereby distancing the speaker from it. When a speaker is about to come to, or has already arrived at, the completion of his or her turn, *wo juede* can signal the end of the turn and solicit a response. Although these functions differ in their detail, all of them can be regarded as a reflection of the speaker's various considerations regarding the other participants in conversation. Uses of *wo juede*, then, is a way of social coordination employed in Mandarin conversation.

Our findings concern the discursive behaviour of Chinese speaking people, and it is beyond the scope of this study to discuss whether this phenomenon is universal among cultures. I would like to note, however, that the structure of complementation is universally present in world languages (Noonan 1985) and that complement-taking verbs of cognition are mostly used with the first person subject to express the speaker's epistemic attitude (Givón 1980). It seems plausible that linguistic structures consisting of the first person subject and a cognition verb such as *I think* in American English or *wo juede* in Mandarin are universally used as an epistemic stance marker.

There are, of course, language-specific factors in epistemic stance markers. For example, the verb that is used as a part of the default epistemic stance marker is different from one language to another. While the combination of *wo juede* (I feel) is far more frequent than *wo xiang* (I think), in American English it is *think* that forms the most frequent epistemic stance marker *I think*. By contrast, in German, *glauben* (believe) is prototypically used for epistemic qualification (Nuyts 2001: 109). Also, epistemic stance markers may vary in their interactional functions. Some of the functions of English *I think*, which is among the most studied epistemic stance markers, seem to be similar to Mandarin *wo juede*, for example "bringing in a different slant in a second opinion sequence" and "pursuing a certain type of response" (Kärkkäinen 2003: 133, 147). By contrast, 'approximator' function of *I think* (e.g. *She is ... carrying a dark blue I think handbag*, Kaltenböck 2008: 109–110) is not observed in my Mandarin data. Of course, a more systematic and detailed analysis of the functions of epistemic stance markers is needed in order to make a legitimate comparison between languages.

In any culture or society, it is hard to imagine that a conversational participant does not take her interlocutor into consideration at all. In principle, when people talk, they coordinate with each other. What is counted as an action indicating coordination, however, may differ from one culture to another. As Pan (2008) showed, Mandarin speakers convey personal opinions in interviews using different strategies from English speakers. Even in the same culture, what is preferred in interaction varies according to the situation. In this study, I have shown that in Mandarin conversation *wo juede* can be used with interactional functions to coordinate between conversation participants. I hope my analysis of casual conversation between friends, which is arguably one of the most basic forms of interaction, can be compared with interaction in other settings, and contribute to a better understanding of Chinese culture and society.

Appendix: Transcription symbols

,	continuing intonation
₀	terminal intonation
[ ]	overlapping speech
X	uncertain hearing
^	stressed syllable
:	lengthening
...	short pause
(2.1)	long pause and its length in seconds
-	truncated speech
=	latching (no gap after the previous turn)
@	laughter or laughing quality
°	soft voice
TSK	tongue-clicking
.h	hearable inspiration

Acknowledgements

This work is supported by JSPS (Japan Society for the Promotion of Science) Grant-in-Aid for Scientific Research #21-3926, 'Stance expressions and syntactic status of complements in Mandarin conversation'. I am grateful to the anonymous reviewers for their truly helpful comments. I also thank Professor Hongyin Tao for his generosity in sharing his data and for his guidance throughout my graduate study at UCLA. Any remaining shortcomings are mine alone.

Notes

1. Other kinds of stance include: attitudinal and style of speaking stance (Biber et al. 1999); evaluation, alignment and affective stance (Du Bois 2007); instrumental, cooperative, moral and affective stance (Goodwin 2007).
2. This definition of epistemic stance does not itself differ radically from the definition of epistemic modality given by Palmer (2001) or Lyons (1977). However, by adopting the term *epistemic stance*, I intend to make what is achieved dialogically the primary point of focus. In other words, I intend to

focus on the interactional features of epistemic stance, which "emerges from dialogic interaction" (Kärkkäinen 2006: 699).

A relevant notion, epistemic authority, is explored by Heritage and Raymond (2005). Epistemic authority concerns the presumption of rights to evaluate topics of conversation, based on factors such as experience or knowledge about them. While Heritage and Raymond, as well as Clift (2006), examine how epistemic authority is indexed by various practices in interaction, my concern is with how marking, rather than indexing, of epistemic stance by *wo juede* may work in interaction.

3. According to Lü (1980), *juede* has two senses: (i) to have some feeling and (ii) to have some opinion. Since this study deals with *juede* in the second sense, I translate *juede* as *think* in the English translation of the examples, as *think* is most appropriate in English to convey the meaning of *wo juede* as the most frequent epistemic stance marker.

4. See Kärkkäinen (2003) for position-sensitive analysis of *I think* in American English conversation.

References

Biber, D., Stig, J., Leech, G., Conrad, S. and Finegan, E. (1999) *Longman Grammar of Spoken and Written English*. London: Longman.

Clift, R. (2006) Indexing stance: Reported speech as indexical evidentials. *Journal of Sociolinguistics* 10(5): 569–595.

Couper-Kuhlen, E. and Selting, M. (eds) (2001) Introducing interactional linguistics. In M. Selting and E. Couper-Kuhlen (eds) *Studies in Interactional Linguistics* 1–22. Amsterdam/Philadelphia, PA: John Benjamins.

Du Bois, J. (2007) Stance triangle. In R. Englebretson (ed.) *Stancetaking in Discourse* 139–182. Amsterdam/Philadelphia, PA: John Benjamins.

Ford, C. E. and Thompson, S. A. (1996) Interactional units in conversation: Syntactic, intonational, and pragmatic resources for the projection of turn completion. In E. Ochs, E. A. Schegloff and S. A. Thompson (eds) *Interaction and Grammar* 135–184. Cambridge: Cambridge University Press.

Ford, C. E., Fox, B. A. and Thompson, S. A. (eds) (2002) *The Language of Turn and Sequence*. Oxford: Oxford University Press.

Ford, C. E., Fox, B. A. and Thompson, S. A. (2002) Constituency and the grammar of turn increments. In C. E. Ford, B. A. Fox, and S. A. Thompson (eds) *The Language of Turn and Sequence* 14–38. Oxford: Oxford University Press.

Givón, T. (1980) The binding hierarchy and the typology of complements. *Studies in Language* 4(3): 333–377.

Goodwin, C. (2007) Participation, stance and affect in the organization of activities. *Discourse and Society* 18(1): 53–73.

Hakulinen, A. and Selting, M. (eds) (2005) *Syntax and Lexis in Conversation*. Amsterdam/Philadelphia, PA: John Benjamins.

Heritage, J. and Raymond, G. (2005) The terms of agreement: Indexing epistemic authority and subordination in talk-in-interaction. *Social Psychology Quarterly* 68(1): 15–38.

Huang, S. (2003) Doubts about complementation: A functionalist analysis. *Language and Linguistics* 4(2): 429–455.

Kaltenböck, G. (2008) Prosody and function of English comment clauses. *Folia Linguistica* 42(1): 83–134.

Kärkkäinen, E. (2003) *Epistemic Stance in English Conversation: A Description of its Interactional Functions, with a Focus on* I think. Amsterdam/Philadelphia, PA: John Benjamins.

Kärkkäinen, E. (2006) Stance taking in conversation: From subjectivity to intersubjectivity. *Text & Talk* 26(6): 699–731.

Lim, N-E. (2009) Stance-taking with Wo juede in conversational Chinese. In Yun Xiao (ed.) *Proceedings of the 21ˢᵗ North American Conference on Chinese Linguistics*, Vol. 2, 323–340. Smithfield, RI: Bryant University.

Lü, S. (ed.) (1980) *Xiandai Hanyu Babaici [Modern Chinese 800 words]*. Beijing: Shangwu Yinshuguan [Business Press].

Lyons, J. (1977) *Semantics*, Vol. 2. Cambridge: Cambridge University Press.

Noonan, M. (1985) Complementation. In T. Shopen (ed.) *Language Typology and Syntactic Description*, Vol. 2: Complex Constructions, 42–140. Avon: The Bath Press.

Nuyts, J. (2001) *Epistemic Modality, Language, and Conceptualization: A Cognitive-Pragmatic Perspective*. Amsterdam/Philadelphia, PA: John Benjamins.

Ochs, E., Schegloff, E. A. and Thompson, S. A. (eds) (1996) *Interaction and Grammar*. Cambridge: Cambridge University Press.

Palmer, F. R. (2001) *Mood and Modality*. 2ⁿᵈ ed. Cambridge: Cambridge University Press.

Pan, Y. (2008) Cross-cultural communicative norms and survey interviews. In H. Sun and D. Z. Kádár (eds) *It's the Dragon's Turn: Chinese Institutional Discourses* 17–76. Berlin: Peter Lang.

Sacks, H., Schegloff, E. A. and Jefferson, G. (1974) A simplest systematics for the organization for turn-taking in conversation. *Language* 50(4): 696–735.

Schegloff, E. A. (1987) Recycled turn beginnings: A precise repair mechanism in conversation's turn-taking organization. In G. Button and J. R. E. Lee (eds) *Talk and Social Organization* 70–85. Clevedon: Multilingual Matters.

Schegloff, E. A. (1996) Turn organization: One direction for inquiry into grammar and interaction. In E. Ochs, E. A. Schegloff and S. A. Thompson (eds) *Interaction and Grammar* 52–133. Cambridge: Cambridge University Press.

Schegloff, E. A. (2007) *Sequence Organization in Interaction: A Primer in Conversation Analysis*. Oxford: Oxford University Press.

Selting, M. and Couper-Kuhlen, E. (eds) (2001) *Studies in Interactional Linguistics*. Amsterdam/Philadelphia, PA: John Benjamins.

Thompson, S. A. (2002) "Object complements" and conversation: Towards a realistic account. *Studies in Language* 26(1): 125–164.

3

Self-repair in Mandarin and Cantonese: Delaying the next item due in casual conversation and news interviews

Wei Zhang and Angela Chan

Introduction[1]

In spontaneous talk-in-interaction, participants often need to attend to recurrent problems in speaking, hearing and understanding. Such recurrent problems are studied under the rubric of 'repair' (Schegloff et al. 1977). One frequent type of repair is 'same-turn self-repair' (hereafter self-repair) which refers to the situation where a current speaker indicates momentary 'difficulties' (called "trouble sources" or "repairables" in the literature on repair) during the construction of their own speaking turn and then repairs that difficulty through a number of means by him/herself. The following are two examples of self-repair in English.

Example from Schegloff et al. (1977: 363)

```
Ken: Sure enough ten minutes later the bell r- the doorbell rang …
```

Example from Fox and Jasperson (1995: 103)

```
A:    And generally the short versions I think are very (0.2)are
      very reasonable.
```

The process of self-repair (as in other types of repair) consists of three components: 1) the repairable, 2) the repair initiation, and 3) the repair outcome. Repairables are usually retrospectively recognised by the presence of the second and third components. They may or may not be obvious to participants other than the speaker who initiates the repair, and may or may not be an error. A repairable may be a word or phrase in the utterance just produced or a word or phrase due next. The second component is repair initiation. This includes a number of lexical and non-lexical "initiator techniques" (Schegloff et al. 1977: 367), through which the current speaker signals possible incipient repair.[2] The third component is the execution/operation of repair where the current speaker may produce a new item to replace the repairable, recycle some part prior to the repair initiation, restart with a new syntactic structure (abandoning the turn unit which is under construction up to the repair initiation), or to produce the next item which is delayed by word search.

The trajectory from repair initiation to repair completion may take either a backward or a forward orientation (Schegloff 1979). A backward-oriented repair works on some already produced part of the turn, for example replacing a word just said. For instance, an initiator (e.g. a mid-word cut-off) often disrupts the prosodic rhythm and syntactic progression of the turn-so-far in the service of launching a repair operation on an already produced part of the turn. In contrast, a forward-oriented repair looks ahead, for example searching for the next item due as projected by the turn-so-far. An initiator in such a repair, for example prolonging the sound of a word, or producing a filler such as 'uh', achieves the effect of standing in the place where the projected next item should be and thus delaying its production.[3]

The study reported here focuses on a forward-oriented repair practice taking place around the linking particle (LP) between a modifier and the head noun in a noun phrase with a [modifier + LP + noun] construction. The LP is DE (的, IPA symbol [tə]) in Mandarin and GE (嘅, IPA symbol [kɛ]) in Cantonese. Through studying the repair strategies used around DE/GE to delay a head noun when it is due, this chapter examines the relationship between syntax and social interaction, a major line of inquiry in the literature on self-repair. The chapter also explores the impact of interactional settings on repair practices by drawing on naturally occurring data collected from casual conversations and news interviews. The two settings differ in their degree of formality: the former is more relaxed and the latter more formal.

The chapter is organised as follows: we first review the existing literature on cross-linguistic studies of self-repair. This is followed by a report of our research findings on delaying the head noun in Mandarin and Cantonese. In a later section of the chapter, we explore possible reasons behind the differences observed in the two dialects and in two interactional settings.

Self-repair and syntax

Studies of self-repair have examined its organisational features, interactional functions, and especially its relevance to syntax (Fox et al. 1996, 2009; Fincke 1999; Goodwin 1979, 1987; Jefferson 1974; Laakso and Sorjonen 2010; Luke and Zhang 2001; Rieger 2003; Schegloff 1979, 1987; Uhmann 2001; Wouk 2005; Wu 2006; Zhang 1998, 2002, 2006; Zhang and Luke 2000). In one of the earliest studies on the relevance of repair to syntax-for-conversation Schegloff notes that "the occurrence of repair in a sentence can have consequences for the shape of the sentence and for the ordering of its elements beyond the consequences embodied by sheer inclusion of the repair element" (Schelgoff 1979: 263).

Further cross-linguistic studies confirm that strategies for self-repair are closely related to language-specific features. For instance, word replacement may be common in all languages but morpheme replacement is not, because the possibility of replacing a morpheme depends on the morphological structure of a given language. Studies have shown that it is possible for Japanese and Finnish speakers to replace a verb suffix because it is pronounceable as a unit on its own and is not agreement relevant (Fox et al. 1996; Kärkkäinen et al. 2007).[4] The procedure for delaying the next item due is another example. It is reported in Fox et al. (1996) that the delay of a noun, when it is due, is different in English and Japanese. While it is possible in English, to recycle the non-lexical material (e.g. preposition, article) before the noun to delay its production, such a strategy is not available in Japanese due to post-positioned case particles. Similar delaying procedures are also possible for languages with rich verbal prefixes which allow the speakers to recycle the prefixes as a way of delaying the verb root, as noted in a more recent cross-linguistic investigation on seven languages by Fox et al. (2009). Another study comparing conversations conducted, by bilingual speakers, in English and German, reveals different patterns for recycling as a self-repair strategy, and the differences are attributed to the linguistic structures of the two languages (Rieger 2003). For instance, recycling of pronoun-verb combination is found more frequently in English than in German because contracted pronominal subject and verb forms (e.g. 'it's', 'I'm', 'that's') are not grammatically possible in German. Therefore speakers take the combination as an inseparable unit in recycling when they are speaking English whereas they will either recycle the full form (e.g. *das ist das ist* 'that is that is') or the demonstrative pronoun only (e.g. *das das ist* 'that that is') when they are speaking German. The fact that the speakers in Rieger's study are bilinguals of English and German makes the role of syntax in different repair practices all the more clear.

These studies take the view that the organisation of self-repair is part of the organisation of language. They focus on the relationship between syntax and conversation in given languages with the aim of finding out to what extent syntax and social interaction mutually influence each other. The present study follows the same line of inquiry and looks at a repair strategy which is forward in orientation, namely delaying the head noun when it is due. For this, we identified the linking particles DE in Mandarin and GE in Cantonese in the construction of [modifier + DE/GE + noun] as a location where the noun due is delayed.

The existing literature shows that studies on repair have largely drawn on conversational data. Occasionally data in institutional settings such as medical consultations and social insurance offices are used (Laakso and Sorjonen 2010) but none of the studies have explored the use of repair strategies in different interactional settings. As noted above, self-repair strategies (e.g. scope of recycling) are practised differently in different languages. Moreover, Laakso and Sorjonen (2010) report that in Finnish some self-repair initiators (such as particle *Tai*) are employed more frequently than other self repair initiators (such as particles *eiku* and *siis*) for interactional reasons. It is reasonable to hypothesise that within a language certain repair strategies are preferred over others in certain interactional setting. To address this question, this chapter compares the frequency of a repair practice, that is, delaying the next item, in casual conversations and news interviews.

Data

This chapter draws on recordings of interaction in two Chinese dialects, Mandarin and Cantonese,[5] in two different interactional settings – casual conversations and news interviews.

The conversational data consist of recordings of face-to-face dyadic conversations. The participants were recruited via personal network, and most of them were postgraduate students or staff members in a university in Hong Kong when the data were collected. In order to ensure better sound quality and for ethics reasons, the participants, in pairs of two, were invited to carry out a conversation in a quiet room equipped with video and audio recorders[6] and the participants' consent was obtained prior to the recording. The participants were asked to behave as naturally as possible and they could freely introduce any topic they wanted to discuss. They were told to start and end their conversations as they pleased. This chapter draws on six Mandarin conversations and four Cantonese conversations and each conversation lasts for 20 to 30 minutes.

The media data used in the study are news interviews (speech of interviewees) extracted from evening news reports and financial reports from two Hong Kong-based television broadcasters. The Mandarin channel is a 24-hour news channel and is designed for the Mandarin-speaking communities all over the world while the Cantonese channel is targeted at the local audience who are mainly Cantonese speakers.[7] Interviews in news reports can bring out different voices to make the news "an interactional, dialogic discourse" (Montgomery 2008: 275; see also Hutchby 2006). Akin to casual conversations, talk in news interviews is usually unscripted and retains a certain degree of spontaneity.

Different styles of news interviews are deployed in the Mandarin and Cantonese news reports. In our Mandarin media data, news interviews are in the form of live interviews and are what Montgomery (2008) classifies as "expert interviews".[8] The guest speakers, who are usually experts or scholars and affiliated with a professional institution, are invited to provide information, explain concepts, and offer comments in connection with a news issue. This type of news interview is usually question-driven: the host questions and the guest speaker answers (Heritage and Roth 1995; Hutchby 2006). Only the interviewees' speech was extracted for study and each excerpt lasts from 24 seconds to 3 minutes 30 seconds). On the other hand, our Cantonese media data consist of pre-recorded interviews, excerpts of press conferences and, in two instances, live exchanges between a news presenter in the studio and another reporter at the scene. This set of data involves a wider range of speakers, including government officials, political figures, experts or scholars, and ordinary people (including witnesses) who are asked to provide information, explanations and/or comments in relation to the news event. The interviews (except the two instances of live exchanges) took place before the news reports and the reporters' questions (as well as part of the speakers' answers) were usually edited out. Consequently, these excerpts are much shorter than the ones in Mandarin, and range from 2 seconds to 55 seconds.

Table (3.1) shows the amount of each type of data examined.

Table 3.1 Sources of data

	Conversation	*News interview*
Mandarin	2h 03m 08s	2h 11m 24s
Cantonese	1h 41m 14s	2h 18m 59s

Forward-oriented repair initiation: delaying the next item in NP

As pointed out earlier, self-repair can take a backward or forward orientation (Schegloff 1979). The focus of forward-oriented repair is not on an already produced part of talk but on the next item due. Such repair is often initiated just before the next item, as projected by the syntax of the sentence-so-far. Initiation devices for delaying the next item include prolonging the sound of a word-in-production, inserting a filler or pause, recycling an already produced part of talk, or a combination of these. As such hitches and perturbations disrupt the flow of talk, they serve to hold the progression of the utterance-under-construction and effect a delay of the next item.

Our Cantonese and Mandarin data show that a site for delaying the next item, after a noun phrase is begun, is around the linking particle (DE/GE) that comes between the modifier and the head noun.

DE in Mandarin and GE in Cantonese

In Chinese grammar (both Cantonese and Mandarin) the elements in a noun phrase are organised in such a way that the modifying materials come before the head noun (Li and Thompson 1981 on Mandarin; Matthews and Yip 1994 on Cantonese) with the word order as illustrated below and in the following two made-up phrases:

Demonstrative – numeral – classifier – adjective – (DE/GE) – noun

(a) Mandarin

那	三 個	很	可愛	的	寶寶
na	san-ge	hen	ke'ai	de	baobao
that	three-CL	very	cute	DE	baby

those three adorable babies

(b) Cantonese

嗰	三個	好	得意	嘅	BB
go	saam-go	hou	dakji	ge	
that	three-CL	very	cute	GE	baby

those three adorable babies

We can see that the Mandarin DE and the Cantonese GE occur in the same syntactic position and serve a similar grammatical function in a noun phrase.

The 'modifier + DE/GE + noun' structure indicates that when the progression of the noun phrase comes to the particle DE/GE, the syntax would strongly project the next item to be a noun. When the progression of the noun phrase comes to the adjective before DE/GE, then a 'DE/GE + noun' string can be projected. With reference to this distinction in syntactic projection, a finer distinction can also be made for DE/GE as a site for delaying the next item inside a noun phrase. We have identified three locations around DE/GE where delay may start: (a) post-DE/GE, (b) on-site-of DE/GE and (c) pre-DE/GE. While the next item being delayed at positions (a) and (b) is often the head noun,[9] what an initiation at position (c) delays is not DE or GE alone, although the immediate next word after the delay is DE or GE. Rather, what is being searched for is the 'DE/GE + noun' string so that an already started noun phrase can be brought to completion.

Analysis of Mandarin data

In this section, we provide an analysis of the Mandarin data regarding the three locations around DE where repair is initiated. This is followed by a comparison of the frequency of repair initiation at the three locations between the conversation and news interview data sets.

Locations of delay

(a) Post-DE

Post-DE delay refers to the situation when the speaker has produced a 'modifier + DE' string, followed by a hitch such as a noticeable pause, audible in-breath, a filler, or a combination of these, after which the speaker carries the syntax of the utterance forward by producing the projected head noun. Examples 1 and 2 below are illustrations of this type.[10]

(1) Casual conversation

然後	我	的	(0.7)	office	的	另外	一個	同學
ranhou	wo	de			de	lingwai	yi-ge	tongxue
then	I	DE		office	DE	other	one-CL	fellow.student

他	就	做	DNA	的	那個
ta	jiu	zuo		de	na-ge
he	then	do	DNA	DE	that-CL

Then the other fellow student in my DE (0.7) office he is doing the one on DNA

(2) News interview

比如说		我们	知道	的,	英国	的 (0.3)	呃
birushsuo		women	zhidao	de	Yingguo	de	e
for.instance		we	know	DE	Britain	DE	uh

零六年		的	八月	十号		的	爆炸案。
lingliunian		de	bayue	shihao		de	baozhaan
zero.six.year		DE	August	the.tenth		DE	explosion.case

For instance as we know, Britain DE (0.3) uh explosion incident on the tenth of August 2006.

In (1), after the speaker has said *wo de* (literally 'I DE'), the production of the projected noun is delayed by a 0.7 second pause. In this case it turns out that the speaker has used the English word 'office' in the code-mixed noun phrase 'my office'. In (2), *Yingguo de* (Britain DE) also projects a next nominal expression, but a 0.3 second pause and the filler "uh" delays the production of *lingliunian de bayue shihao de baozhaan* "the explosion incident on the tenth of August 2006". In this case, the head noun *baozhaan* (explosion incident) is preceded by another 'modifier + DE' string and this part is delivered without a hitch.

(b) On site of DE

The search for the next noun may also start a little earlier, for example it may start when DE is still being uttered. The delay is achieved by the prolongation of DE which may be followed by other hitches. This can be seen in Examples 3 and 4 below.

(3) Casual conversation

兩年	前	我 (0.4)	我	算是	組織了	一個 (0.3)
liangnian	qian	wo	wo	suanshi	zuzhi-le	yi-ge
two.year	before	I	I	count.as	organize-PRT	one-CL

小學		的:	聚會
xiaoxue		de	juhui
primary.school		DE	party

Two years ago I (0.4) I sort of organized a primary school DE: (0.3) reunion (for my classmates)

(4) News interview

那麼:	把:	他們	這個	扣留	的:	(0.2)	啊-	員工	帶回來。
name	ba	tamen	zhege	kouliu	de		a	yuangong	daihuilai
then	BA	they	this-CL	detend	DE		ah	staff	bring.back

Then bring back the staff who had been detained by them.

The speaker in (3) is talking about a reunion she organised. The head noun *juhui* (party) does not follow immediately after the 'modifier + DE string' *xiaoxue de* (primary school DE). Instead, the search for it starts when DE is being prolonged and is followed by a further hitch of a 0.3 second pause. In (4) the head noun *yuangong* (staff) in the noun phrase "the staff who had been detained by them" is delayed by a combination of the prolongation of DE, a brief pause and a further filler "ah".

Recall that it has been reported in the literature that languages such as English provide for recycling pre-noun materials to delay the next noun due (Fox et al. 1996). This practice is also found in our Mandarin data. When an emerging noun phrase has progressed to the particle DE, the projected noun may be delayed by recycling the pre-noun material 'modifier + DE'. The recycling may be initiated either at location (a) or (b). The following is an example.

(5) Casual conversation

就	相當於:	那-	那-	初步	的: (0.2)	初步	的:
jiu	xiangdangyu	na	na	chubu	de	chubu	de
just	similar.to	that	that	preliminary	DE	preliminary	DE

(XX)	的	結果	嘛:
	de	jieguo	ma
	DE	result	PRT

It's similar to that- that- preliminary DE: (0.2) preliminary DE: (xx) result.

In (5), when the speaker has produced *chubu de* (preliminary DE) the first time, DE is prolonged and followed by a brief pause, after which *chubu de* (preliminary DE) is recycled and DE is prolonged again before the speaker goes on with another 'modifier + DE' string and the head noun.

The above examples show that, for Mandarin speakers, DE in a noun phrase is a site for starting the search of the head noun. Hitches may be produced right after DE or when DE is still being uttered, to delay the production of the noun which is projected by the 'modifier + DE' string. Pre-noun materials including DE may also get recycled to achieve a similar delaying effect.

(c) Pre-DE

Pre-DE delay refers to the situation where the immediate item produced after the delay is the particle DE, which is then followed by a noun. In other words, a 'DE + noun' string is separated from the modifier by the delay. Consider Examples 6 and 7.

(6) News interview

因此	他們	現在	(0.3)	沒有	辦法	把	(.)	正確	(0.7)
yinci	tamen	xianzai		meiyou	banfa	ba		zhengque	
so	they	now		no	means	BA		correct	

的	災情	(0.3)	向	外界	來	傳達。
de	zaiqing		xiang	waijue	lai	chuanda
DE	disaster.condition		to	outside	come	convey

So they now (0.3) have no means to convey the accurate (0.7) DE state of the disaster to the outside world.

(7) Casual conversation

…	你	收到	小花	嗯:	的	email	了	是	吧,
	ni	shoudao	Xiaohua	en	de		le	shi	ba
	you	receive-COMP	NAME	uhn	DE	email	PRT	be	PRT

you received Xiaohua: uh:n DE email, right,

When the speaker in (6) has produced the preposition BA, a nominal object is projected. And a noun phrase is indeed emerging upon the production of the adjective *zhengque* (correct); but the rest of it, that is, DE and the head noun, is delayed by a relatively long pause of 0.7 seconds. Similarly, when the verb *shoudao* (receive) in (7) projects an upcoming noun phrase, a repair is initiated with a prolonged filler "uhn" after the modifier thus delaying the part of the 'DE + noun' string. It can be seen from the above two examples that what is being delayed after the modifier is a 'DE + noun' string in an emerging noun phrase.

In this section, we have examined three locations around the linking particle DE where the progression of an already started noun phrase may be delayed by a repair initiation. When a delay occurs after DE in a 'modifier + DE' string or when DE is still being produced, the next item being searched for is often the head noun. When a delay occurs after a modifier, the next item being searched for is often a 'DE + noun' string (rather than DE alone) in order to bring the already started noun phrase to its completion. We have also shown that delay at these three locations may be achieved by brief pauses, fillers or recycling part of the pre-noun material. In the following a comparison is made between the two Mandarin data sets on the frequency of delay at each position.

Comparison 1: repair initiation around DE in Mandarin conversation and news interview

Table 3.2 below shows the frequency of repair initiation at the three locations around DE where delaying devices may be deployed.

Table 3.2 Location and frequency of repair initiation around DE in Mandarin

Initiation location	*Mandarin conversation*	*Mandarin news interview*
a. Post-DE	21 (54%)	69 (68%)
b. On site of DE	14 (36%)	26 (26%)
c. Pre-DE	4 (10%)	6 (6%)
Total	39 (100%)	101 (100%)

As we can see from Table 3.2, there are some similarities between the two data sets. For instance, post-DE is the most favoured location for delaying the next noun. This is true for both data sets. Table 3.2 shows that more than half of the delays start at this location (54% in conversations, 68% in news interviews). Likewise, the next favoured location in each set is on the site of DE (36% in conversation, 26% in news interview). The combined frequencies of the two locations indicate that the majority of delay occurs after the 'modifier + DE' string has been or is being produced (90% in conversation, 94% in news interview). In contrast, Mandarin speakers make much less frequent use of the pre-DE location for delay (10% in conversation, 6% in news interview).

Among locations (a) and (b), three cases in casual conversations and two cases in news interviews involve recycling of 'modifier + DE'. This indicates that recycling pre-noun material as a delaying device is used very infrequently by the Mandarin speakers in both settings (8% in conversations and 2% in news interviews) although, as reported in the literature, this is a possible means for delaying the next noun.

The main difference between the two data sets is the total amount of delaying initiated around DE. There are many more cases of delay in news interview (101) than in conversation (39). The findings from this comparison will be discussed later as a similar phenomenon is observed in the Cantonese data.

Analysis of Cantonese data

Like the Mandarin data, repair initiations around the corresponding Cantonese particle GE for delaying the next item are found in a post-GE, on-site-of-GE or pre-GE location. However, as shown below, a difference between the two dialects is observed in the recycling pattern.

Locations of delay

(a) Post-GE

Similar to the delay started after the 'modifier + DE' string in Mandarin, a post-GE delay refers to the situation when the speaker has produced a 'modifier + GE' string, followed by a hitch such as a noticeable pause, audible in-breath, a filler, or their combinations, after which the speaker carries the syntax of the utterance forward by producing the projected head noun. Examples 8 and 9 below are illustrations of delay initiated at this location.

(8) Casual conversation

```
但     同一      時間     呢    亦     都    係      瑪麗醫院
Daan  tungjat  sigaan  ne   jik   dou  hai   maalaijijyun
but   same     time    PRT  also  all  be    Queen.Mary.Hospital

嘅   誒  首-    誒   首席    法醫              嚟。
ge   e   sau   e    sauzik  faatji            leigaa
GE   eh  chie- eh   chief   forensic.doctor   PRT.PRT
```

but at the same time (he's) also Queen Mary Hospital GE eh chie- eh chief forensic doctor.

(9) Casual conversation

```
你    會         (.)   觸發起            人哋           某啲      嘅     (.)
nei  wui             zukfaathei       jandei         maudi    ge
you  would           trigger_COMP     other.people   some     GE

啫        思潮      喇
ze        siciu     laa
that.is   thought   PRT
```

You'd make others come up with certain (.) GE that is thought

In (8), after the 'modifier + GE' string *maalaijijyun ge* (Queen Mary Hospital GE) is produced, the head noun *sauzik faatji* (chief forensic doctor) is delayed by a filler "eh" (and further delayed by another repair attempt). In (9), the head noun *siciu* (thought) is delayed by a brief pause plus a lexical filler "ze".

(b) On the site of GE

Delay initiated on the site of GE is also found in Cantonese. In this situation the search for the next item is signalled by the prolongation of GE which may be followed by other hitches, as shown in Example (10) below.

(10) News interview

```
嗰個    使用  呢        一定  要        份量      啱,        服食
go-go   sijung  ne   jatding  jiu      funloeng  aam      fuksik
that-CL  usage   PRT  must          should  dosage    right    take

嘅::  次數    啱,      同埋      個   療程              都    啱。
ge    cisou   aam     tungmaai  go   liucing          dou   aam
GE    times   right   and       CL   treatment.period  all   right
```

As to its usage the dosage must be appropriate, the number of times of taking it must be appropriate, and the length of the treatment must also be appropriate.

The speaker in (10) is talking about the use of a medicine for treating H1N1 patients. In this extract he is emphasising the appropriate way of taking the tablets. The Cantonese equivalent of 'the number of times for taking tablets' is *fuksik ge cisou* (take GE times). Here a delay is signalled by the prolongation of GE before *cisou* (times) is produced.

    Recycling as a delaying device is also found at locations (a) and (b) but, unlike the Mandarin speakers, the Cantonese speakers simply recycle the particle GE itself rather than recycling the 'modifier + GE' string. Example (11) illustrates the GE-only recycling.

(11) News interview

```
我哋      係    好      少        有      咁    長        嘅:  (.)  嘅
ngodei   hai   hou    siu       jau    gam   coeng    ge        ge
we       BE    very   seldom    have   so    long     GE        GE

凍      嘅    時間      嘅。
dung    ge    sigaan    ge
cold    GE    time      PRT
```

We seldom experience such a long GE: (.) GE cold spell.

As shown in Example 11, after the 'modifier + GE' string, *gam coeng ge* (literally: so long GE) the expected next item is not produced immediately. Instead, there is first a very brief pause after which GE is recycled once before *dung ge sigaan* (literally: cold GE time) is produced. GE may also be recycled more than once as shown in Example (12).

(12) News interview

好	幾個		村民	呢,	係	我哋	疏散咗
hou	gei-go		cyunman	ne	hai	ngodei	sosaanzo
quite	several-CL		villager	PRT	BE	we	evacuate-ASP

去,	誒:	民政處			嘅:	嘅-	嘅-	庇護中心。
heoi	e	manzingcyu			ge	ge	ge	beiwuzungsam
to	eh	Home.Affairs.Department			GE	GE	GE	shelter.centre

Several residents were evacuated by us to, eh: Home Affairs
Department GE: GE- GE- shelter centre.

(c) Pre-GE

As in the Mandarin data, the corresponding pre-GE delay is also found in the Cantonese data. The immediate item produced after the repair initiation is the particle GE, which is then followed by a noun. In other words, a 'GE + noun' string is separated from the modifier by the delay. Example (13) is an illustration of delay initiated at this location.

(13) News interview

更加	多:	(0.4)	嘅	離島		居民	呢,	係
ganggaa	do		ge	leidou		geoiman	ne	hai
even	more		GE	outlying.island		resident	PRT	BE

承受唔到	哩	一個	嘅	(.)	政策	嘅	惡果	㗎。
singsau-m-dou	li	jat-go	ge		zingcaak	ge	okgwo	gaa
bear-NEG-COMP	this	one-CL	GE		policy	GE	bad.comsequence	PRT

even more (0.4) GE residents of the outlying island will be unable to bear this GE (.) policy's bad consequence.

The speaker in (13) is criticising a ferry company for reducing the ferry services for the residents of a Hong Kong outlying island, and points out that more residents would move away as a consequence. The repair initiation is started on site of *do* (more) of the modifier *ganggaa do* (even more); its prolongation delays the next 'GE + noun' string, *ge leidou geoiman* (GE outlying island residents).

Comparison 2: repair initiation around GE in Cantonese conversation and news interview

Table 3.3 below indicates that the Cantonese speakers in our data make use of all three locations around GE to initiate repair for delaying the next item in both conversation and news interview.

Table 3.3 Location and frequency of repair initiation around GE in Cantonese

Initiation location	Cantonese conversations	Cantonese news interviews
a. Post-GE	20 (83%)	42 (53%)
b. On site of GE	2 (8%)	31 (39%)
c. Pre-GE	2 (8%)	6 (8%)
Total	24 (100%)	79 (100%)

Consistent with our Mandarin data, the same major difference between conversations and news interviews is also found in Cantonese, that is, the total amount of repair initiations around the particle GE. There are more initiations in news interviews than in conversations: 24 instances in conversation and 79 in news interview.

Another similar finding is that the post-particle location is most favoured for both settings (83% in conversation and 53% in news interviews). Locations (a) and (b) make up the majority of repair initiations around GE (above 90% in both settings). Just like their Mandarin counterparts, the Cantonese speakers make very infrequent use of the pre-GE location for delaying the 'particle + noun' string.

Comparing the repair initiations in locations (a) and (b) in the two interactional settings, however, a difference is noticed: the percentage of initiations on site of GE in news interviews (39%) is considerably higher than that in casual conversations (8%). More interestingly, over half of the on-site GE initiations (17 out of 31) in news interviews are GE-only recycling where GE is cut off or prolonged before it is recycled. Cases of recycling are compared with Mandarin below.

Comparison 3: recycling pattern in Mandarin and Cantonese: scope and frequency

As noted above, recycling is a strategy to initiate repair on the site of the linking particle DE/GE. Two methods of recycling are observed in our data: the speaker may (1) go back to the modifier immediately preceding the particle, that is, what is recycled is a 'modifier + DE/GE' string (Example 5) or (2) simply recycle the particle by itself (Examples 11 and 12). Table 3.4 summarises the frequency of each method in our data.

Table 3.4 Scope and frequency of recycling involving DE/GE in Mandarin and Cantonese

	Mandarin		*Cantonese*	
Recycling pattern	*Conversation*	*News interview*	*Conversation*	*News interview*
Total initiations	39	101	24	79
Mod + DE/GE recycling	3 (8%)	2 (2%)	0	0
DE/GE-only recycling	0	0	6 (25%)	21 (27%)

Table 3.4 shows that while 'modifier + GE' recycling is absent in the Cantonese data, DE-only recycling is absent in the Mandarin data, suggesting that recycling involving the particles is different in the two dialects. This contrast raises an interesting issue which is explored in the following section.

Discussion

In this section, we discuss the differences observed from the above comparisons. Consistent with the objectives of this volume, we address the following two issues: 1) how interactional settings influence repair initiation; and 2) how the grammatical properties of DE and GE influence their repair practices.

Interactional settings and repair initiation

The comparisons shown in Tables 3.2 and 3.3 above indicate that both Mandarin and Cantonese speakers behave differently in casual conversations and news interviews with regard to the total amount of repair initiation issued around DE/GE for delaying the next noun. There are more initiations in news interviews than in conversations. We would like to explore possible reasons behind the phenomenon.

A possible explanation is a difference in the nature of the data sets along the dimension of formality. Talk in news interviews can be regarded as an example of formal institutional talk (Hutchby 2006) and is different from casual conversation in various aspects. One distinctive feature of news interviews is that the speaker not only talks to the interviewer or the immediate audience, but also talks to the overhearing audience (Heritage 1985). The speaker is "under pressure to style [his/her] talk" not just for the recipient(s) who is(are) present but also for those who are not, that is, the "imagined recipients" (Goffman 1981: 138). To some extent, the speaker is performing (Tolson 2006). Since the speech is to be broadcast to the public, the speaker tends to be careful with the choice of words in order to perform well in public and to talk "adequately for the public purposes" (Montgomery 2008: 260).

As Bell (2001) points out, speakers shift their speech styles in response to their audience (see also Giles and Powesland's (1975) Speech Accommodation Theory). In our study, the speakers in news interviews are aware of the fact that they speak not only to the immediate audience, who are often unfamiliar to them, but also to the overhearing audience because their speech is or will be broadcast to the public. It is likely for them to employ a style of speaking which is more formal than when they are in more relaxed casual conversations (Holmes 2008; see also Labov 1972; Trudgill 1974). In Cantonese, noun phrases with GE construction are more common in formal contexts while a classifier is used instead of GE in colloquial Cantonese, for example *nei go pangjau* (your CL friend) instead of *nei ge pangjau* (your GE friend) is preferred in colloquial settings (Matthews and Yip 1994: 108, 111).

In addition, in many cases, the speaker takes on an institutional identity, that is, representing an organisation more than him/herself when talking to the reporter. What is said in front of the camera for a TV audience is presumed to be more consequential. For these reasons, speakers facing a camera may be more careful in their choice of words, resulting in more frequent word searching and effecting the delay of the next item due. The locations for delay initiated around DE/GE, as described above, are likely among a number of locations where word searching would be found in more formal but unscripted talk. This speculation calls for further study on the general picture of forward-oriented repair in different types of talk-in-interaction.

Grammatical properties of DE and GE and their repair practices

As shown in Table 3.4, the scope of recycling involving DE/GE is different in Mandarin and Cantonese. While 'modifier + DE' recycling is found in the Mandarin data, GE-only recycling is found in the Cantonese data. It has been discussed in the literature that differences in repair practices are very often a function of syntax. Used to link the modifier and head noun, the particles DE and GE occur in the same syntactic position and serve a similar function in a noun phrase (although the two differ in other grammatical usages (Zhu 1980)). If DE and GE are syntactically similar in noun phrase construction but behave differently in repair it will be of interest to explore why this is so.

A possible explanation may be the phonetic properties of the two particles: tone and vowel quality. The structure of a Chinese syllable can be described in terms of consonant, vowel and tone (Li and Thompson 1981; Matthews and Yip 1994). As with consonant and vowel, DE consists of an unaspirated alveolar [t] and a schwa [ə] while GE is comprised of an unaspirated velar [k] and a mid-front vowel [ɛ]. With regard to tone, DE, like many Mandarin grammatical particles, takes a neutral tone while GE carries a mid-level lexical tone. A syllable with a neutral tone means the syllable is weak and unstressed; it "loses its contrastive relative pitch" and does not have a lexical tone (Li and Thompson 1981: 9). While the pitch of the neutral tone is not zero, its actual realisation is found to be determined by the lexical tone of the preceding syllable (Lee and Zee 2008). Our speculation is that these phonetic qualities may make it less likely for DE to be recycled on its own. On the other hand, it is easier for the schwa in DE to be prolonged and even developed into the common Mandarin filler [ə] for further prolongation. While GE can do the same with prolongation of its mid-front vowel and develop it into the common Cantonese filler [ɛ], its lexical tone also makes it possible for GE to be recycled on its own, in contrast to the neutral tone of DE.

Another difference shown in Table 3.4 is how frequently the speakers use recycling to delay the next item. The 'modifier + DE' recycling is used infrequently by the Mandarin speakers (8% in conversations, 2% in news interviews) whereas, in Cantonese, about a quarter of repair initiations around GE is GE-only recycling, in both settings. The figures for Cantonese need to be interpreted with caution though. The GE-only recycling appears to be similar in frequency in both interactional settings (25% in conversations, 27% in news interviews), but the six instances in the conversation set are all found in one conversation. Four are produced by one speaker who has had a lot of experience with the media, while the other two are produced by his conversational partner. GE-only recycling is not found in the other three conversations. This means GE-only recycling may not yet be a common repair strategy in conversation. But GE-only recycling is found across speakers in news interviews. As GE-only recycling is more common in news interviews, it is possible that the speaker has carried over his speech style in news interview to conversation. It is also possible that his conversational partner's two instances of GE-only recycling is a result of speech style accommodation (Giles and Powesland 1975). Whether this particular practice will be picked up in conversation remains to be seen.

Conclusion

This chapter has focused on a particular repair strategy in daily conversation and news interviews in Mandarin and Cantonese. The strategy is forward in orientation, that is, the repair initiation aims at delaying the next item when it is due but is still being searched for.

It is found that when the progression of a noun phrase has passed a modifier, a forward-oriented repair may be initiated around the structural particle DE in Mandarin and its counterpart GE in Cantonese. Three locations are identified: post-DE/GE, on-the-site-of-DE/GE and pre-DE/GE, where hitches such as fillers, brief pauses, sound stretches, cut-offs, or a combination of these may be deployed as signals for the upcoming repair. Recycling is also found in post- and on-the-site-of-particle locations, but the two dialects display different recycling patterns.

A general tendency is that in relation to the pre-DE/GE position, both Mandarin and Cantonese speakers, in both conversations and news interviews, favour the post-DE/GE and on-site DE/GE positions for repair initiation. This suggests that, for speakers of both languages, DE/GE is structurally closer to the modifying element preceding it than it is to the head noun following it.

A difference in conversation and news interviews is that there are more forward-oriented repair initiations for delaying the next noun in news interview than in conversation. This is true for both dialects. A difference found in Cantonese is that there seems to be more GE-only recycling in news interviews than in conversation. These findings suggest that the degree of formality of an interactional setting has an effect on the choice of repair strategies, and this issue is worth further investigation.

A major difference between Mandarin and Cantonese is the recycling pattern involving the particle DE/GE. The Mandarin speakers would go back to include the modifier and produce a recycled 'modifier + DE' string whereas the Cantonese speakers would produce a very local recycling of GE only. As the two particles are syntactically similar in a noun phrase with a 'modifier + DE/GE + noun' structure, this difference cannot be explained by syntax only. We have speculated that this may have to do with the phonetic shape of the two particles. While further studies are needed to confirm this, it will be useful to examine the relationship between repair and syntax with additional perspectives. In the existing literature which confirms the mutual influence of repair and syntax since Schegloff (1979) first proposed the idea of "syntax for conversation" (e.g. Fox et al. 1996 on English and Japanese; Fincke 1999 on Bikol; Uhmann 2001 on German; and Wouk 2005 on Indonesian), an assumption is that different syntax may explain differences in repair practice. Our investigation reported here provides some evidence that syntactically similar items may not always behave in the same way in repair. This implies that other linguistic aspects, in addition to syntax, may also be relevant in the organisation of repair.

Appendix: Transcription symbols

Notation   Meaning

\-   A sudden cut-off of the prior word or sound.

:   Lengthening of the prior sound. The more colons, the longer a lengthening is.

.   Final intonation.

,   Continuing intonation.

xxxx   Inaudible utterance.

(.)   Untimed brief pause.

(n)   Length of pause in seconds.

Notes

1. An earlier version of the chapter was presented at the 11th International Pragmatics Conference (IPrA), Melbourne, 12–17 July 2009. The authors are grateful for the comments from the audience, the reviewers and the editors. We also thank Li Bin for proofreading the manuscript. The study was supported by a Start-up Grant of City University of Hong Kong [No.7200091] and a CHASS Research Grant of the City University of Hong Kong [No.9610079].
2. Examples of lexical initiator techniques include explicit negation of a word or phrase just produced, for example the 'not X but Y' format, or expressions indicating word search. Examples of non-lexical initiator techniques include the use of sudden sound cut-offs, fillers, sound stretches, and so on or a combination of these.
3. However, Schegloff (1979: 273) also points out that there is not a fixed or "invariant" (his term) correspondence between the orientation of repair and a given initiator.
4. For details and other factors in morphological repair see Fox et al. (1996) on Japanese and Kärkkäinen et al. (2007) on Finnish.

5. While Mandarin refers to the standard dialect of China, Cantonese is a regional dialect mainly spoken in Guangdong Province and Hong Kong.
6. No obvious impact of the recorders on the participants was observed in our data.
7. In this study the Cantonese speakers and Mandarin speakers are not meant to be mutually exclusive groups. It is possible that a Cantonese/Mandarin speaker in our recording can speak Mandarin/Cantonese too.
8. News interviews are conducted for different reasons and can be delivered in different styles, as discussed in Montgomery (2008) and Tolson (2006). We do not intend to discuss the details here as they are not related to the focus of this chapter.
9. This does not exclude the possibility of another embedded 'modifier + DE' string before the head noun.
10. An attempt is made to indicate the position of DE/GE in free translation although this may render the translation a little unnatural in some cases.

References

Bell, A. (2001) Back in style: Reworking audience design. In P. Eckert and J. R. Rickford (eds) *Style and Sociolinguistic Variation* 139–169. Cambridge: Cambridge University Press.

Fincke, S. (1999) The syntactic organisation of repair in Bikol. In B. A. Fox, D. Jurafsky and L. A. Michaelis (eds) *Cognition and Function in Language* 252–267. Stanford: CSLI Publications.

Fox, B. A. and Jasperson, R. (1995) A syntactic exploration of repair in English conversation. In P. Davis (ed.) *Alternative Linguistics: Descriptive and Theoretical Modes* 77–134. Amsterdam: John Benjamins.

Fox, B. A., Hayashi, M. and Jasperson, R. (1996) Resources and repair: A cross-linguistic study of syntax and repair. In E. Ochs, E. A. Schegloff and S. A. Thompson (eds) *Interaction and Grammar* 185–237. Cambridge: Cambridge University Press.

Fox, B., Wouk, F., Hayashi, M., Fincke, S., Tao, L., Sorjonen, M-L., Laasko, M. and Hernandez, W. F. (2009) A cross-linguistic investigation of the site of initiation in same-turn self-repair. In J. Sidnell (ed.) *Conversation Analysis: Comparative Perspectives* 60–103. Cambridge: Cambridge University Press.

Giles, H. and Powesland, P. F. (1975) *Speech Style and Social Evaluation.* London: Academic Press.

Goffman, E. (1981) *Forms of Talk.* Philadelphia, PA: University of Pennsylvania Press.

Goodwin, C. (1979) The interactive construction of a sentence in natural conversation. In. G. Psathas (ed.) *Everyday Language: Studies in Ethnomethodology* 97–121. New York: Irvington.

Goodwin, C. (1987) Forgetfulness as an interactive resource. *Social Psychology Quarterly* 50: 115–131.

Heritage, J. (1985) Analyzing news interviews: Aspects of the production of talk for an overhearing audience. In T. A. Dijk (ed.) *Handbook of Discourse Analysis*, Vol. 3, 95–119. New York: Academic.

Heritage, J. and Roth, A. (1995) Grammar and institution: Questions and questioning in the broadcast news interview. *Research on Language and Social Interaction* 28: 1–60.

Holmes, J. (2008) *An Introduction to Sociolinguistics* (3rd ed.). Harlow: Pearson Longman.

Hutchby, I. (2006) *Media Talk: Conversation Analysis and the Study of Broadcasting*. Berkshire: Open University Press.

Jefferson, G. (1974) Error correction as an interactional resource. *Language in Society* 2: 181–199.

Kärkkäinen, E., Sorjonen, M. L. and Helasvuo, M. L. (2007) Discourse structure. In T. Shopen (ed.) *Language Typology and Syntactic Description*, Vol. II, 301–371. Cambridge/New York: Cambridge University Press.

Laakso, M. and Sorjonen, M. L. (2010) Cut-off or particle – devices for initiating self-repair in conversation. *Journal of Pragmatics* 42: 1151–1172.

Labov, W. (1972) *Sociolinguistic Patterns*. Philadelphia, PA: University of Pennsylvania Press.

Lee, W. S. and Zee, E. (2008) Prosodic characteristics of the neutral tone in Beijing Mandarin. *Journal of Chinese Linguistics* 36: 1–29.

Li, C. N. and Thompson, S. A. (1981) *Mandarin Chinese: A Functional Reference Grammar*. Berkeley, CA: University of California Press.

Luke, K. K. and Zhang, W. (2001) The relationship between conversational repair and syntactic structure. In Z. Dai and K. K. Luke (eds) *Problems in Linguistics*, Vol. 1, 171–185. Changchun: Jinlin People Publishers (In Chinese).

Matthews, S. and Yip, V. (1994) *Cantonese: A Comprehensive Grammar*. London: Routledge.

Montgomery, M. (2008) The discourse of the broadcast news in interview: A typology. *Journalism Studies* 9: 260–277.

Rieger, C. L. (2003) Repetition as self-repair strategies in English and German conversations. *Journal of Pragmatics* 35: 47–69.

Schegloff, E. A. (1979) The relevance of repair to syntax-for-conversation. In T. Givon (ed.) *Syntax and Semantics*, Vol. 12: *Discourse and Syntax*, 261–286. New York: Academic Press.

Schegloff, E. A. (1987) Recycled turn beginnings: A precise repair mechanism in conversation. In G. Button and J. R. E. Lee (eds) *Talk and Social Organisation* 70–85. Clevedon: Multilingual Matters.

Schegloff, E. A., Jefferson, G. and Sacks, H. (1977) The preference for self-correction in the organisation of repair for conversation. *Language* 53: 361–382.

Tolson, A. (2006) *Media Talk: Spoken Discourse on TV and Radio*. Edinburgh: Edinburgh University Press.

Trudgill, P. (1974) *The Social Differentiation of English in Norwich.* Cambridge: Cambridge University Press.

Uhmann, S. (2001) Some arguments for the relevance of syntax to same-sentence self-repair in everyday German conversation. In M. Selting and E. Couper-Kuhlen (eds) *Studies in Interactional Linguistics* 373–404. Amsterdam: John Benjamins.

Wouk, F. (2005) The syntax of repair in Indonesian. *Discourse Studies* 7: 237–258.

Wu, R. J. (2006) Initiating repair and beyond: The use of two repeat-formatted repair initiations in Mandarin conversation. *Discourse Processes* 41: 67–109.

Zhang, W. (1998) *Repair in Chinese Conversation.* PhD thesis, University of Hong Kong.

Zhang, W. (2002) Insertion as a self-repair device in Chinese conversation and its motivations. Paper presented at the 11th Annual Conference of the International Association of Chinese Linguistics (IACL 11), Aichi Prefectual University, Nagoya, 20–22 August 2002.

Zhang, W. (2006) Post-completion replacement: Data from Chinese conversation. Paper presented at the First International Workshop on Turn Continuation in Cross-Linguistic Perspective, The University of Hong Kong, 11–13 November 2006.

Zhang, W. and Luke, K. K. (2000) Sentence planning and execution in conversation: Evidence from item replacement in Chinese. Paper presented at the 7th International Pragmatics Conference, Budapest, 9–14 July 2000.

Zhu, D. X. (1980) Beijing hua, Guangzhou hua, Wenshui hua he Fuzhou hua li de 'DE' zi (DE in dialects of Beijing, Guangzhou, Wenshui and Fuzhou). *Fangyan* 3.

4

"Do I really have to?" The give-and-take of deontic meaning in Chinese

Agnes Weiyun He

Modality: a grammatical-interactional specification

Modality is commonly defined either as "the speaker's opinion or attitude towards the proposition that the sentence expresses or the situation that the proposition describes" (Lyons 1977: 452) or the source of information for a proposition (Bybee 1985). Some scholars think that the former indicates a broad sense of evidentiality and the latter a narrow sense (Chafe and Nichols 1986). Others consider "evidentiary strength, evidentiary source and evidentiary justification or knowledge" as integrated aspects of the same phenomenon (Givón 1982: 25). Literature indicates that children's exposure to and development of modality has important implications for learning in general (Bartsch and Wellman 1995; Dittmar and Reich 1993: Guo 1995; Halliday 1993; Willet 1988).

Specifically, Lyons (1977) further describes *epistemic modality* as relating to matters of knowledge or belief (p. 793), as in 那么阴的天, 等一会儿肯定下雨 *name yin de tian, deng yihuir kending xiayu* (It is such a cloudy day. It must rain in a little while), and *deontic modality* as relating to the necessity or possibility of acts performed by morally responsible agents (p. 823), as in 小朋友应该互相谦让 *xiaopengyou yinggai huxiang qianrang* (Little friends should yield to each other). Other linguists (Coates 1983; Leech 1971/1987; Palmer 1990) present alternative, more fine-grained categorisations of modal meanings. Palmer (1990) characterises deontic modality as "discourse-oriented" to reflect possible deontic sources it may be linked with, and dynamic modality as "subject-oriented" to portray the entity it may predicate about. On the other hand, Bybee and Fleischman use "agent-oriented" to mark deontic meanings which "predicate conditions on an agent with regard to the completion of an action referred to by the main predicate" (Bybee and Fleischman 1995: 6). The term "speaker-oriented" is left to deontic meanings that "represent speech acts through which a speaker attempts to move an addressee to action" (*ibid.*). In spite of the diversity in descriptions, the consensus is that there are broad epistemic and deontic types of meaning. Epistemic modality provides children with a resource for developing the capacity to infer, predict, generalise and hypothesise. Deontic modality provides a resource for children's exploration and understanding of social obligations, responsibilities, constraints, and cultural and moral values (Noveck and Sera 1996; Stephany 1986; Sweetser 1982).

As Fox (2001) points out, many studies from formal and functional linguistics have primarily looked at modality as a grammaticalised category expressed in verbal morphology. For example, there have been disputes over the matter of how to distinguish modal verbs from modal adverbs. Should the deontic modal expression 必须 *bixu* (must) be recognised as a verb or an adverb? Should evaluative modal expressions such as 难怪 *nanguai* (no wonder) be considered as a verb or an adverb? On the other hand, attempts to understand modality as a resource that constructs interlocutors as social and moral beings have been relatively few (but see He and Tsoneva 1998); Schieffelin 1996).

This study follows the interdisciplinary work spearheaded by Ochs et al. (1996). It draws upon three interrelated research traditions: functional linguistics – concerned with the role of language in communication and cognition, linguistic anthropology – focusing on cultural underpinnings of language, and conversation analysis – examining the interactional matrix of language structure and use. Specifically, this study focuses on how participants' deontic stances emerge, unfold and shift through conversational mechanisms such as repair organisation (Schegloff 1992, 1996; Schegloff et al. 1977) in naturally occurring interaction. It investigates how modal meanings such as obligation (最好 *zuihao*, 应该 *yinggai*, (非)得 *(fei)dei*, 必须 *bixu*, 要 *yao*) or permission (可以 *keyi*, 能 *neng*) in Chinese are elucidated, affirmed, modified, or negotiated through moment-by-moment interaction.

This study examines the following modal expressions as they are used by four teachers and 35 children (age 4.5–9) who are learning Chinese as their heritage language in the US:

最好 *zuihao* (had better)
应该 *yinggai* (should, ought to)
(非)得 *dei* (must, have to)

必须 *bixu* (must)

要 *yao* (should, must)

一定 *yiding* (must)

可以 *keyi* (may, can)

能 *neng* (can)

行 *xing* (may)

All of these expressions can, to varying degrees, denote deontic meanings, that is, the permitted, the obligatory, and the forbidden (Greek *deontos*: of that which is binding). Some of these expressions can have polysemous modal meanings and uses (e.g. 要 *yao* and 能*neng*). For example, 要 *yao* want/must can be used either to describe the volition of the subject in a sentence (我要喝水 *wo yao he shui* (I want to drink water)) or to express the obligation placed upon that subject by the speaker or a situation in the context (星期六我们要上中文学校 *xingqi liu women yao shang zhongwen xuexiao* (Saturdays we are to go to Chinese School)). The purpose of this study is to illustrate how the sequential organisation of classroom discourse ascertains deontic modal meanings such as obligation and permissibility, specifies the range of deontic meanings, and embodies the emergent and negotiated qualities of these meanings. It pays particular attention to how polysemous modal expressions are collaboratively interpreted by the participants through interaction.

Deontic modality: the sociocultural context

In the context of Chinese language and culture, the socialisation of deontic meanings takes on a particularly salient significance since fulfilling social obligations and responsibilities is conceptualised as the cornerstone of humanity and morality (Hsu 1981). At the heart of Confucian moral education are the five virtues: 仁 *ren* (benevolence, humanity), 伦 *lun* (relationship to others, associated duties and obligations), 礼 *li* (ritual, courtesy, proper behaviour), 忠 *zhong* (loyalty to one's leader, family and friends) and 孝 *xiao* (the greatest of all virtues, extreme respect for one's parents). Thus society must be ordered – everyone has a place and duty in accordance with his/her position in life. The society is governed by a code of ethics and follows the same moral principles, starting from the nucleus family and moving through the entire social hierarchy. Thus parents have their duties and obligations to the children and children in turn have to follow the ethical code of conduct and obligations towards the parents. Filial piety as well as responsibility to siblings according to the order of birth are moral precepts advocated by all Chinese families.

Diasporic communities of Chinese Americans have been teaching Chinese as a heritage language to their children since the very beginning of the Chinese immigration to America (Chang 2003; Chao 1997). As early as the 19th century, Cantonese classes were offered to children of early immigrants residing in Chinatowns in a number of larger US cities such as San Francisco and New York. Globally, data from the International Chinese Language Council, or Hanban in Chinese (http://english.hanban.org/), show that over several thousand higher education institutions in over a hundred countries worldwide have established programs to teach Chinese, putting the total number of students learning Chinese outside China at 40 million, including learners with a Chinese background. A vastly increasing number of students of Chinese descent are taking Chinese within the US educational system, from kindergarten to colleges and universities (He and Xiao 2008). A very important part of heritage language education concerns the socialisation of Chinese cultural norms and values in relation to social and familial responsibilities, obligations and constraints, which find their manifestation in language through the form of deontic modality.

Data presented in this chapter were collected in two Chinese heritage language schools in two different cities in the US where evening or weekend Chinese language classes are offered for children whose parents come from China or Taiwan and are pursuing professional careers in the US. These children were either born in the US or came to the US with their parents at a very young age. Most of them go to mainstream English-speaking schools on weekdays. While many of them are bilingual in Chinese and English in the oral form, some are already English-dominant and few have opportunities to learn how to read and write in Chinese. The reason that Chinese parents send their children to heritage language schools is so they can acquire literacy in the heritage language. As researchers have long noted, combining elements from family, community and school, heritage language schools like these function as an important vehicle for ethnic minority children to acquire heritage language skills and cultural values (Cummins 1992; Creeze and Martin 2006; Fishman 1964; He 2006). The corpus includes: (1) 30 hours of audio- and video-recorded class meetings involving four teachers in four different classes and a total of 35 children (aged 4.5 to 9); (2) classroom observations; and (3) interviews with parents, teachers and school administrators. Data transcription symbols can be found in Appendix 1, and a grammatical glossary in Appendix 2.

The role of conversational repair

As argued elsewhere (He 2003), children are not passive recipients of language and cultural socialisation. In the process of teaching and learning Chinese cultural values, there are clashes of ideas, goals, dispositions, expectations and norms of interaction between the teachers and the children. For socialisation to take place, the teacher and the children need to negotiate their differences through interaction. Even in idealised cases where the teacher and the children share the same goals, expectations and norms of behaviour, socialisation cannot be accomplished without the co-construction of the children. Any constitution of action, activity, identity, emotion, ideology or other culturally meaningful reality is inherently a joint achievement by all the participants (Jacoby and Ochs 1995). To understand and highlight this indispensable and important role of the children, we need to examine closely the reactions and responses of the children to attempts at socialisation, and see whether the values of responsibility, obligation and constraints promoted by the teachers are accepted, embraced, challenged, modified or rejected by the children. The structural mechanism of 'repair' in conversation affords the participants an excellent resource to negotiate deontic meanings, and provides the researcher with an empirically accountable anchor position to carry out such investigations.

When trouble such as mishearing, misunderstanding, or misspeaking in conversation occurs, it is noticed and then corrected, either by the party whose turn contains the source of trouble or by some other party. This sequence of 'trouble + initiation-of-correction + correction' is known as a *repair trajectory*. Repair occurs when one party corrects his or her own talk or that of another party, and it can be accomplished in a number of ways (Schegloff et al. 1977). Of particular relevance to our data are the following:

- *Self-initiated same turn repair.* This refers to the situation when the current speaker initiates and completes the repair within his/her current turn of talk and before coming to a possible completion of a complete grammatical, lexical, intonational and pragmatic unit, also known as the turn-constructional-unit (TCU) (Ford et al 1996). It is the earliest position in which repair can be undertaken. The repair is signalled by a number of speech perturbations such as cut-offs, hesitation markers, pauses and restarts. Schegloff et al. (1977) show that this is the most frequent and the most preferred type of repair. An example of this type of repair would be as follows:

(1) A: 我妈妈说我们今天去-今天要去rehearsal
Wo mama shuo women jintian qu-jintian yao qu *rehearsal*
My mother said we today go-today will go to *rehearsal*

• *Self-initiated repair in transition-relevant-space.* If the speaker whose utterance(s) are the source of the trouble does not perform repair during the turn in progress, he/she can repair the utterance in the transition-relevant-space, that is, at the end of a TCU, before another speaker takes a turn. Here is an example:

(2) A: 老师can you help me- 可以-可以帮忙(.)帮我吗?
Laoshi *can you help me* keyi keyi bangmang bang wo ma
Teacher *can you help me* can- can you help me?

• *Self-initiated third turn repair.* In this type of repair (Schegloff 1996) a speaker produces a turn and the hearer responds to it without showing any sign of breakdown in intersubjectivity. After the response by the hearer, the speaker uses the next turn to revise his/her previous turn, as in:

(3) A: 上次老师说了不要早交=
Shangci laoshi shuo le bu yao zao jiao
Last time Teacher said [work] should not be turned in early
     B: =那就给Kevin的妈妈
Na jiu gei Kevin de mama
Then give it to Kevin's mom
     A: 老师说了-上次老师说了可以提前交, 但是得有人看着
Laoshi shou le – shangci laoshi shuo le keyi tiqian jiao, danshi dei you ren kan zhe
Teacher said—last time Teacher said [it] can be turned in early, but there must be someone to watch it

• *Self-initiated third position repair.* While in the third turn repair the hearer provides an appropriate response which does not prompt repair of the speaker's first turn, in third position repair (Schegloff 1992) it is precisely the hearer's response that engenders the repair. In other words, the hearer's response enables the speaker to notice a problematic understanding of his/her prior turn. The following is a case in point:

(4) A: 快点快点啊, 草字头, 草字头, 一撇一横一点
Kuai dian kuai dian a, cao zi tou, zao zi tou, yi pie yi heng yi dian
Hurry hurry, grass radical top, grass radical top, one *pie* one *heng* one *dian*
     B: 怎么不像?
Zenme bu xiang
How come it doesn't look like it?

> A: 啊? 嗷, 竹字头, 竹字头, 老师说错了
> A ao zhu zi tou, zhu zi tou, laoshi shou cuo le
> What? Oh, bamboo radical top, bamboo radical top, Teacher said it wrong.

- *Other-initiated self-completed next turn repair.* This occurs when repair is initiated by a participant other than the speaker of the trouble source. When this happens, the repair initiation usually comes in the turn immediately subsequent to the trouble source turn (known as next turn repair initiation, or NTRI). See below for an example:

  (5) A: 在那个书里那个英雄=
       Zai na ge shu li na ge yingxiong
       In that [wrong classifier] book that hero
       B: =那个书?
       Na ge shu
       That [wrong classifier] book?
       A: 那本书里
       Na ben shu li
       In that [correct classifier] book.

- *Other-initiated other-completed repair.* This occurs when a participant other than the speaker of the trouble source both initiates and completes the repair. In adult conversation, it is usually preceded by discourse markers such as *well* or *uhm* and often takes the form of a proposed understanding with rising intonation characteristic of questions. This type of repair theoretically can occur in any turn or any position, as in (6).

  (6) A: 下面该 su-san 了
       Xiamian gai susan le
       Susan is next.
       B: Susie

Of the types of repair outlined above, the most preferred is self-initiated and self-completed in the same turn as the trouble source. Other initiation and other completion of repair can index a stance of disaffiliation with the interlocutor; and the farther the distance between the trouble source and the completion of the repair, the greater and the longer the miscommunication.

In the rest of the chapter, I will examine how the conversation structural resources described above enable the participants to navigate and negotiate deontic modal meanings – the indeterminacy between obligation and option, and the ambiguity between possibility and permissibility – and their associated cultural imports.

Data analysis

Negotiating obligations

Data segment (7) involves a case where self-initiated same turn repair and other-initiated third position repair serve to scaffold the process of ascertaining moral obligation versus practical option. The episode took place as the teacher was explaining the cultural connotations of a widely popular folk story titled "Kong Rong Yields Pears". The story is about a Chinese child prodigy in history called Kong Rong who insisted on giving up the big pears to both his older brothers and his younger brothers and picking the smallest one for himself. For generations, the Chinese have used this folk story to instill the notion of 'yielding to others' and 'putting others' interests first' in the minds of young children. Here the teacher at the Chinese heritage language school is doing precisely the same to her class.

(7) KongRong Rang Li '孔融让梨'

001老师: '孔融让梨'说的是小朋友应该互 (.) 相 (.) 谦 (.) 让'
'KongRong rang li'shou de shi xiaopengyou yinggai huxiang qianrang
'KongRong rang li' say NOM COP little friend should mutual yield

Teacher: What the story of 'Kong Rong Yields Pears' tells us is that little friends should yield (.) to (.) each (.) other.

002 要是你们在家跟弟弟妹妹玩，
Yaoshi nimen zai jia gen didi meimei wan
If you LOC home with younger brother younger sister play
If you are playing with your younger brothers and sisters at home,

003 你们 (.) 抢玩具 (.) 这样对不对啊？
Nimen xiang wanju zheyang dui bu dui a
You rob toy this way correct NEG correct Q
You (.) fight for toys (.) Is that right or not?

004 不好啊
Bu hao a
NEG good PRT
Not good ok

005 (.2)

006老师: 要把- 应该把玩具让::给弟弟妹妹
Yao ba yinggai ba wanju rang gei didi meimei
Should PTP-BA should PTP-BA toy yield to younger brother younger sister

Teacher: Should- Ought to yie::ld the toys to younger brothers and sisters

007Jason: 为什么要让给他？我们 share 就可以了。
    Wenshenme yao rang gei ta? Women share jiu keyi le
    Why should yield to he we share CONJ ok PRT
Jason: Why yield to him? We can share.

008老师: Share (.) 噢:: share 是不错
        Ao   shi bu cuo
        PRT   COP NEG wrong
Teacher: Share (.) uh:: share is not bad

009   (.2)

010老师: 可是能<u>让</u>就<u>更好</u>
    Keshi neng rang jiu geng hao
    But can yield CONJ even good
Teacher: But being able to YIELD will be EVEN better.

011Jason:Oh:: no::: Do I really have to?

012老师: 不是说非- 不是说<u>必须</u>得让
    Bushi shuo fei bushi shuo bixu dei rang
    NEG say must- NEG say must must yield
Teacher: I'm not saying you have to- not saying that you MUST yield

013   能让<u>最</u>:好啊
    Neng rang zui hao a
    Can yield most good PRT
    Being able to yield is THE BEST ok

014   让(.)就是就是做<u>别</u>人(.)不能(.)做的
    Rang jiu shi jiu shi zuo bier en bu neng zuo de
    Yield then COP then COP do other person NEG able do NOM
    Yielding means doing what others cannot do

015   别人做不<u>到</u>的(.)<u>好</u>事
    Bie ren zuo bu dao de hao shi
    Other person do NEG PRT good need
    The good deed that others cannot do

016   所以::最好::能让(.)啊
    Suoyi zuihao neng rang a
    Therefore best can yield PRT
    Therefore [you] had better yield.

Here, the teacher initially frames 'yielding' as obligation (001–004). In line 001, T clearly characterises yielding as a moral mandate (应该 *yinggai*). To reinforce this mandate, she carefully turns the modal verb 要 at the beginning of line 006 (want or should) which is ambiguous (as it can take either the volition or obligation sense) to a clear-cut deontic modal 应该 *yinggai* (要 把 *yao ba*-应该把 *yinggai ba*) through a same turn self-repair (006), thereby clarifying and enhancing the sense of 'obligation'. The child, however, challenges this obligation (为什么要 *weishenme yao*, line 007) and sets up a contrast between obligation (要 *yao* should) and option (可以 *keyi* can). To address this challenge, the teacher presents an alternative, better option (010), which is in turn taken by the student to mean 'obligation' (have to, 011). A consequent/subsequent third position repair by the teacher revises the 'obligation' interpretation (不是说必须得 *bu shi shuo bixu dei*, line 012) and reinforces the 'option' interpretation (能让最:好 *neng rang zuihao*, line 013). She then further proffers a definitional, categorical statement regarding what 'yielding' means (lines 014–015) with no modulation and concludes with a suggestion that has an obvious obligatory overtone (最好 *zuihao*, line 016). The segment shows that, even though in terms of quantity of input as measured by the number and length of speaking turns, the child contributes less to the interaction than the teacher, he nonetheless plays a pivotal role in the shaping of the deontic degree of 'yielding'. Figure 4.1 captures how the deontic degree evolves through moment-by-moment interaction.

001老师:	应该yinggai	Strong obligation
Teacher:	should/ought to	
005	(.2)	
006老师:	要把-应该 yao ba-ginggai	Ambiguous to strong obligation
Teacher:	Should/want- Ought to	
007 Jason:	为什么要wei shenme yao..?...可以keyi	Challenge to strong obligation; Introducing permissible options
Jason:	Why should? ...can	
009	(.2)	
010老师:	可是能..更好 keshi neng...geng hao	Weak obligation
Teacher:	But being able to ..EVEN better.	
011Jason:	Oh:: no::: Do I really have to?	Questioning weak obligation
012老师:	不是说非-不是说必须 bushi shuo fei- bushi shuo bixu	Revising strong obligation
Teacher:	not have to- not saying MUST	
013	能..最:好 neng...zui:hao Being able to .. is THE BEST	Proposing moderate obligation
014	让(.)就是就是 rang jiushi jiushi Yielding means	Non-modal, categorical statement
016	最好::能 zuihao neng Had better .. can	Revised moderate obligation

Figure 4.1

This data segment shows that each time the teacher revises her moral stance, it is in response to the child's challenge and question. It also shows that the socialisation of cultural knowledge and preference is not a unidirectional transaction. Instead, it involves expectations, counter-expectations, assertions, challenges, mitigations and modifications – all accomplished through a wide range of modals by all participants involved in situated interaction. As a result, 'yielding', an age-old Chinese cultural practice indicating proper etiquette and morality, becomes subject to discussion, negotiation and modification in a weekend community-based school in the US where Chinese is taught as a heritage language.

Delineating permissibility

In (8), the indeterminacy between what is permissible in the classroom and what is practically possible is teased out through third position self-repair. In this case, the teacher and the children are engaged in the activity of learning how to look up a Chinese word in the dictionary. The teacher has previously asked that students bring a Chinese dictionary to class. One of the students is flipping through her dictionary and complains that she cannot find what the teacher has asked the students to find. The teacher moves over to this student and picks up her dictionary.

(8) This is English dictionary '这是英文字典'

001老师:　　这是英文字典, 拿错了, 这不能用.
　　　　　　Zhe shi yingwen zidian na cuo le zhe bu neng yong
　　　　　　This COP English dictionary, take wrong PRT this NEG can use
Teacher:　　This is English dictionary. You took the wrong one. This cannot be used.

002学生:　　Chinese words (.2) here! 可以用!
　　　　　　　　　　Keyi yong
　　　　　　　　　　Can use
Student:　　It has Chinese words here! It can be used!

003老师:　　老师要你们用中文字典. 应该带中文字典. 下次-下次注意.
　　　　　　Laoshi yao nimen yong zhongwen zidian yinggai dai zhongwen zidian xia ci xia ci zhuyi
　　　　　　Teacher want you use Chinese dictionary should bring Chinese dictionary next time next time attention
Teacher:　　I want you to use Chinese dictionary. You should bring Chinese dictionary. Next time-next time pay attention.

When the teacher first points out that the dictionary cannot be used (不能 *bu neng*, line 001), the student takes the teacher to mean that the dictionary contains only English and therefore cannot be used for Chinese purposes (可以 *keyi*, line 002). In the third position, the teacher repairs her initial statement by specifying that it is a requirement to bring a Chinese dictionary (and not a dictionary that contains Chinese words), not a practical choice (要 *yao*, 应该 *yinggai*, line 003). In this case, 可以 *keyi* and 能 *neng* are both polysemous. Both can have either the deontic reference of permissibility or the ability/possibility reference. Where the student and teacher have different interpretations, the teacher resorts to a different set of modals 要 *yao* and 应该 *yinggai* to make unequivocal the permissibility-obligation deontic connotation.

Exploring abilities and constraints

If data segment (7) shows how a range of deontic modals are recruited by the participants to construct a negotiated, emergent sense of obligation, and segment (8) illustrates how a precise deontic meaning is delineated through the choice of an alternative set of deontic modal expressions, the next data segment, segment (9), tells us that the very same modal expression can evolve to have different meanings as an interaction unfolds. In this case, the class is engaged in the activity of reading aloud. The teacher invites volunteers to read in turns.

(9) Who can read? '谁能读?'
001老师:　好 (.)淑雨你来
　　　　　Hao Shuyu ni lai
　　　　　Good Shuyu you do
　Teacher:　Good (.) Shuyu you try it
002　　　　　((pause))
003老师:　你能读就大声读
　　　　　Ni neng du jiu da sheng du
　　　　　You can read CONJ big voice read
　Teacher:　If you can read, read loudly
004　　　　　别的同学好好听
　　　　　Biede tongxue haohao ting
　　　　　Other student well listen
　　　　　Other students listen well
005淑雨:　'它又-又-又 什么前走...'
　　　　　Ta you you you shenme qian zou
　　　　　It again again again what forward go
　Shuyu:　'It again-again-again something go forward...'

006小倩: '住:: [住前走'
          'Zhu zhu qian zou'
          Live live forward go
          Live go forward
Xiaoqian: live go forward

007波波: ['往'[那是'往'
          Wang that is wang
          'Toward' that is 'toward'
Bobo: ['wang'[That's 'wang'

008 S?:   [No:: wrong:::

009 Ss: [((inaudible))

010老师: 安静! 大家安静!
          Anjing dajia anjing
          Quiet everybody quiet
Teacher: Quiet! Everyone quiet!

011   (.4)

012   有人在读别人就不能读, OK?
          You ren zai du bieren jiu bun eng du
          Exist person DUR du other CONJ NEG can du
          When someone is reading others can't read, OK?

013   (.2)

014   淑雨再想想
          Shuyu zai xiangxiang
          Shuyu again think
          Shuyu think again

015淑雨: 我没学过
          Wo mei xue guo
          I NEG learn PERT
Shuyu: I didn't learn it.

016   (.2)

017淑雨: °我不会°
          Wo bu hui
          I NEG can
Shuyu: I can't

018老师: 没学过还是学了不会呀? 谁能读?
          Mei xue guo haishi xue le bu hui ya shui neng du
          NEG learn PERT or learn PRT NEG can Q who can read
Teacher: Didn't learn or learned but can't? Who can read?

019   好, Justin=
          Hao
          good
          Good, Justin=

020波波: =Me [me! 老师, 我! 我能读!
　　　　　Laoshi wo wo neng du
　　　　　Teacher I I can read

Bobo: =Me [me! Teacher, me! I can read!

021 Justin: ['它又((inaudible))'
　　　　　　　ta you
　　　　　　　it again

Justin: ['It again((inaudible))'

022老师: 安静!
　　　　　anjing
　　　　　quiet

Teacher: Quiet!

023波波: 我能! 我记得那个字!
　　　　　Wo neng wo jide na ge zi
　　　　　I can I remember that MSR word

Bobo: I can! I remember that word!

024老师: 等Justin读完
　　　　　Deng du wan
　　　　　Wait read COMP

Teacher: Wait until Justin finishes reading

025 °咱们不能影响别人 (.) 知道吧°?
　　　Zaimen bu neng yingxiang bieren zhidao ba
　　　We NEG can disturb other know Q
　　　We can't disturb others (.) Understand?

026 (.2)

027老师: 老师知道你能读
　　　　　Laoshi zhidao ni neng du
　　　　　Teacher know you can read

Teacher: I know you can read

028 (.2)

029老师: 但是你等- 你得- (.2)
　　　　　Danshi ni deng ni deng
　　　　　But you wait you must

Teacher: But you wait- you need to- (.2)

030波波: OK, 现在不能=
　　　　　Xianzai bu neng
　　　　　Now NEG can

Bobo: OK, I can't NOW=

031老师: =对了, 波波真懂道理!
　　　　　Dui le Bobo zhen dong daoli
　　　　　Right PRT Bobo EMP know principle

Teacher: =Right, Bobo is really sensible

This case concerns the dual function of 能 *neng* (can – possibility), 'ability' in 003 and permissibility in 012 (cf. He and Tsoneva 1998). In line 017, Shuyu first makes clear reference to ability (不会 *bu hui*). The next turn repair initiation NTRI by the teacher (018) (能*neng*=会*hui*) renders a sequential, local interpretation of 能 *neng* (can) as ability by association. After seeing the contrast between his 'possibility/ability' interpretation (020, 023) and the teacher's 'permission' interpretation (025), Bobo finally, through other repair (030), displays understanding of 能 *neng* (can) in its sense of permissibility. In this segment, the meaning and force of the same modal 能 *neng* (can) changes over interactional time and across interlocutors. What begins as an ability/possibility reference morphs into a permissibility/constraint reference and goes back and forth a number of times. What is possibility/ability to one interlocutor (Shuyu) becomes permissibility/constraint to another (Bobo). It is through the joint participation of both the children and the teacher that the duality in meaning is preserved and that all parties involved come to a shared understanding of the full range of modal meanings of 能 (can).

Conclusions and implications

This study has implications in several areas including language acquisition, language socialisation and the inherent properties of modality. While most acquisition studies on children's use of modal language have largely focused on the timing and frequency of isolated instances of usage, this study argues that it is not context-free frequency but rather the understanding of the interactional contingencies that indexes the learner's competence. It indicates that instead of a YES/NO question concerning whether a child has acquired a single, particular modal meaning, we should perhaps be asking whether a child has been socialised into a *range* of modal meanings and whether the child is able to negotiate and modulate modal meanings.

This study has highlighted the interactive, constructed, emergent, collaborative nature of the socialisation of cultural norms and values. Instead of viewing children as passive recipients of socialisation, this study has portrayed children as active collaborators in the process. Through this lens, even long held and deeply ingrained Chinese cultural ideals such as familial obligations before individual needs, societal permissibility before spontaneous action, and external constraints before internal desires cannot be treated as given or readily imparted to the younger generation. They must be enacted, assessed and negotiated.

This study also has implications for understanding modal meanings as inherently intersubjective and dynamic. It has shown that the clarification of modal meanings requires interaction between participants, and is not merely a matter of introspective grammatical judgement held by any one single speaker. And it is conversational structural mechanisms such as repair organisation that make the collaborative construction and clarification of meaning possible.

Appendix 1: Transcription symbols

CAPS	emphasis, signalled by pitch or volume
.	falling intonation
,	falling-rising intonation
°	quiet speech
[ ]	overlapped talk
-	cut-off
=	latched talk
:	prolonged sound or syllable
(0.0)	silences roughly in seconds and tenths of seconds (measured more according to the relative speech rate of the interaction than according to the actual clock time)
(.)	short, untimed pauses of one tenth of a second or less
( )	undecipherable or doubtful hearing
(( ))	additional observation
T:	at the beginning of a stretch of talk, identifies the speaker; T is for teacher
	(different teachers are represented by different small letters such as Ts or Tz), G for girl, B for boy, Ss for whole class.
->	speaking turns of analytical focus
< >	slow speech
> <	fast speech
____	code-switched components

Appendix 2: Grammatical glossary

COMP	directional or resultative complement of verb
CONJ	conjunction
COP	copula

DUR   durative aspect marker
EMP   emphatic marker
LOC   locative marker
MSR   measure
NEG   negative marker
PERT   perfective aspect marker
PRT   sentence, vocative or nominal subordinative particle
PTP   pre-transitive preposition
Q   question marker

Acknowledgements

This chapter is based on a presentation titled 'Conversational repair: Where modality and morality converge' which was given at the 21st NACCL (North American Conference on Chinese Linguistics) in June 2009 and the annual ACTFL Conference (American Council on Teaching of Foreign Languages) in November 2009. The original written version of the presentation appeared in the NACCL-21 Proceedings, pp. 138–148 (2009, published by Bryant University, Smithfield, Rhode Island). A related paper appeared in the journal *Chinese Language and Discourse* (He 2011). I thank the anonymous reviewers and the editors for insightful comments which helped me to highlight the cultural motivation and ramification of deontic modal usage. All remaining deficiencies are mine solely.

References

Bartsch, K. and Wellman, H. (1995) *Children Talk about the Mind*. New York: Oxford University Press.

Bybee, J. (1985) *Morphology: A Study of the Relation Between Meaning and Form*. Amsterdam: John Benjamins.

Bybee, J. and Fleischman, S. (eds) (1995) *Modality in Grammar and Discourse*. Amsterdam: John Benjamins.

Chafe, W. and Nichols, J. (eds) (1986) *Evidentiality: The Linguistic Encoding of Epistemology*. Norwood, NJ: Ablex.

Chang, I. (2003) *The Chinese in America*. New York: Penguin Books.

Chao, T. H. (1997) 'Chinese Heritage Community Language Schools in the United States.' *CAL Digest*, www.cal.org/resources/digest/chao0001.html.

Coates, J. (1983) *The Semantics of the Modal Auxiliaries*. London: Croom Helm.

Creeze, A. and Martin, P. (eds) (2006) *Interaction in Complementary School Contexts.* Special Issue of *Language and Education* 20.

Cummins, J. (1992) Heritage language teaching in Canadian schools. *Journal of Curriculum Studies* 24: 281–286.

Dittmar, N. and Reich, A. (eds) (1993) *Modality in Language Acquisition.* Berlin: de Gruyter.

Fishman, J. A. (1964) Language maintenance and language shift as a field of inquiry. *Linguistics* 9: 32–70.

Ford, C., Fox, B. and Thompson, S. (1996) Practices in the construction of turns: The 'TCU' revisited. *Pragmatics* 6: 427–454.

Fox, B. (2001) Evidentiality: Authority, responsibility and entitlement in English conversation. *Journal of Linguistic Anthropology* 11: 167–192.

Givón, T. (1982) Evidentiality and epistemic space. *Studies in Language* 6: 23–49.

Guo, J. (1995) Social interaction, meaning, and grammatical form: Children's development and use of modal auxiliaries in Mandarin Chinese. *Dissertation Abstracts International, B: Sciences and Engineering* 55(9), 4141-B-4142-B. (Available from UMI, Ann Arbor, MI. Order No. DA9504824.)

Guo, J. (1995) The interactional basis of the Mandarin modal *néng* 'can'. In J. Bybee and S. Fleischman (eds) *Modality in Grammar and Discourse* 205–238. Amsterdam: John Benjamins.

Halliday, M. A. K. (1993) Toward a language-based theory of learning. *Linguistics and Education* 5: 93–116.

He, A. W. (2003) Novices and their speech roles in Chinese heritage language classes. In R. Baley and S. Schecter (eds) *Language Socialization in Bilingual and Multilingual Societies* 128–146. Clevedon: Multilingual Matters.

He, A. W. (2006) Toward an identity theory of the development of Chinese as a heritage language. *Heritage Language Journal* 4: 1–28.

He, A. W. (2011) The role of repair in modulating modal stances in Chinese discourse. *Chinese Language and Discourse* 2(1): 1–22.

He, A. W. and Tsoneva, S. (1998) The symbiosis of choices and control: A discourse-based account of CAN. *Journal of Pragmatics* 29: 615–637.

He, A. W. and Xiao, Y. (eds) (2008) *Chinese as a Heritage Language: Fostering Rooted World Citizenry.* Honolulu, HI: University of Hawaii Press.

Hsu, F. (1981) *Americans and Chinese: Passages to Differences.* Honolulu: University of Hawaii Press.

Jacoby, S. and Ochs, E. (1995) Co-construction: An introduction. *Research on Language and Social Interaction* 28: 171–183.

Leech, G. N. (1971/1987) *Meaning and the English Verb.* London: Longman.

Lyons, J. (1977) *Semantics.* Cambridge: Cambridge University Press.

Noveck, I., Ho, S. and Sera, M. (1996) Children's understanding of epistemic modals. *Journal of Child Language* 23: 621–643.

Ochs, E., Schegloff, E. A. and Thompson, S. A. (eds) (1996) *Interaction and Grammar.* Cambridge: Cambridge University Press.

Palmer, F. R. (1979, 2nd ed. 1990) *Modality and the English Modals.* London/New York: Longman.

Palmer, F. R. (1979/1990) *Modality and the English Modals.* London/New York: Longman.

Schegloff, E. A. (1992) Repair after next turn: The last structurally provided place for the defense of intersubjectivity in conversation. *American Journal of Sociology* 95: 1295–1345.

Schegloff, E. A. (1996) Third turn repair. In G. R. Guy, C. Feagin, D. Schiffrin and J. Baugh (eds) *Towards a Social Science of Language. Papers in Honor of William Labov,* Vol. 2: Social Interaction and Discourse Structures, 31–40. Amsterdam: John Benjamins.

Schegloff, E. A., Jefferson, G. and Sacks, H. (1977) The preference for self-repair in the organization of repair in conversation. *Language* 53: 361–382.

Schieffelin, B. (1996) Creating evidence: Making sense of the written word in Bosavi. In E. Ochs, E. A. Schegloff and S. A. Thompson (eds) (1996) *Interaction and Grammar* 45–60. Cambridge: Cambridge University Press.

Stephany, U. (1986) Modality. In P. Fletcher and M. Garman (eds) *Language Acquisition: Studies in First Language Development.* 2nd ed. 375–400. Cambridge: Cambridge University Press.

Sweetser, E. (1982) Root and epistemic modality: Causality in two worlds. *Berkeley Linguistic Society Papers* 8: 484–507.

Willet, T. (1988) A cross-linguistic survey of the grammaticalization of evidentiality. *Studies in Language* 12: 51–97.

5

English 'then' in colloquial Singapore Mandarin

Cher Leng Lee

Introduction

Due to globalisation and the spread of English as an international language, Mandarin speakers in China, Taiwan and Singapore are code-switching with English to varying degrees. Mandarin in these places is not always spoken as a discrete language. There is an increasing research interest in how English is code-switched with Mandarin in China (Dong 2007). In Taiwan, although the focus is more on code-switching between Mandarin and Taiwanese (Su 2009), one can also expect to see code-switching between Mandarin and English. In Hong Kong, there is prevalent code-switching between Cantonese and English (Li 2000). In colloquial Singapore Mandarin (CSM), code-switching is the most common phenomenon. This chapter focuses on the English 'then' in CSM, the discourse-pragmatic functions of 'then' in CSM and the implication for bilingual speakers.

Singapore is a linguistically and ethnically diverse country with a population of about 3.2 million (2000 Census of Population). The racial composition is roughly 76.8 per cent Chinese, 13.9 per cent Malay, 7.9 per cent Indian, while the remaining 1.4 per cent are mainly Eurasians and Europeans. There are four official languages in Singapore: Malay, Mandarin, Tamil and English. Malay is also the national language. The largest ethnic community is Chinese. The Chinese community was for a long time charac-terised by a large number of sub-groups speaking mutually unintelligible Chinese dialects. In 1979, the government initiated the Speak Mandarin Campaign to encourage the Chinese community to use Mandarin instead of other dialects. By the end of the 1980s, census figures indicated that the campaign had been largely successful in its attempts to replace the other Chinese dialects with Mandarin. The 1990 census showed that the percentage of Chinese households where Mandarin is spoken rose from 13.1 per cent in 1980 to 39 per cent in 1990, while the percentage where other Chinese dialects are spoken dropped from 76.2 per cent in 1980 to 48.2 per cent in 1990. English is the main language of work in Singapore. Singapore's education system is a policy of English-knowing bilingualism; ethnic Chinese students are expected to learn English as well as Mandarin, the latter being taught as a second language. Since the nation's independence in 1965, the nation's founding Prime Minister Mr Lee Kuan Yew saw that English would be the language to provide individuals with skills needed for them to be economically independent and therefore had put a strong emphasis on learning English, giving it a dominant and prestigious status in the nation. As Lee puts it:

> The deliberate stifling of a language which gives access to superior technology can be stifling beyond repair. Sometimes this is done not to elevate the status of the indigenous language, so much as to take away a supposed advantage a minority in the society is deemed to have, because that minority has already gained a greater competence in the foreign language. This can be most damaging. It is tantamount to blinding the next generation to the knowledge of the advanced countries. (Lee Kuan Yew, 'The Twoin Hae Met', Dillingham Lecture, East-West Center, Honolulu, Hawaii, 11 November 1970)

Given this sociolinguistic context and history, students in Singapore have much more exposure to English than to Mandarin within the school curriculum. Students who are able to speak Mandarin are also able to speak English and it is not surprising that they are better in English than in Mandarin given the English-dominant environment.

Colloquial Singapore Mandarin (CSM; see Chen 1984) is a variety of Mandarin spoken among Singapore Chinese in informal everyday conversations. Characteristics of CSM, among others, include code-switching to English, code-switching to other southern dialects, and sometimes code-switching to Malay (Lee 2003). It also has a large percentage of discourse particles such as *lah, leh, lor* which are used in colloquial Singapore English (Gupta 1992; Platt and Ho 1989; Wee 2002; Wong 1994). In a study on the motivations of code-switching in Singapore Mandarin (Lee 2003), it is found that the word 'then' is the highest occurring English word in CSM. The equivalent of 'then' in Mandarin is *ranhou* 然后 (see Ong and Phua 2011). This is a common connector of events and time. However, whenever one speaks CSM, 'then' is used instead of *ranhou*. This is clearly not a case of culture borrowing when one language does not have an equivalent word.

According to Myers-Scotton's (1993) definition, it is a *core* borrowing word. Core borrowings do not show very obvious motivations for code-switching as they have presumably entered into the mental production of the matrix language. 'Then' often appears in sentences that are completely spoken in Mandarin such as the following:

Example extract

```
我  要  去  图书馆        THEN   去 吃 饭 THEN 回  家。
Wo yao qu  tushuguan          qu chi fan      hui jia
I  want go library           go eat rice   go  home
I want to go to the library then have a meal then go home.
```

This chapter aims to investigate 'then' in CSM by addressing the following questions:

1) What are the discourse-pragmatic functions of 'then' in CSM?
2) Why are there more discourse-pragmatic functions of 'then' in CSM than in Standard English?
3) Why do these bilingual speakers use 'then' instead of *ranhou* 然后?

By answering these questions we will understand the differences between how 'then' is used in Standard English and how it is used in CSM. Colloquial Singapore English (CSE) is examined to see if the discourse-pragmatic functions of 'then' in CSM have been influenced by those in CSE. We will also explore why 'then' behaves differently in CSM and why CSM speakers use 'then' instead of its Chinese equivalent.

The data in this chapter will show that the discourse-pragmatic functions in CSM are more extensive than those in Standard English. When bilinguals speak CSM, they use 'then' for a more general connector than when 'then' is used in Standard English. In other words, 'then' has become a core borrowing word in CSM and an important connecting word in this variety of Mandarin. The reason why 'then' is used instead of *ranhou* 然后 could be because firstly, 'then' is monosyllabic and so it is easier to articulate, but perhaps a more important reason is that these CSM speakers are in a sociolinguistic environment where English is the main working language in education, administration and the media. As such, English is a dominant language and a prestigious language in this sociolinguistic setting. Moreover, 'then' in CSM has many more functions than any other connecting word in Chinese. Such a phenomenon is not evident in China, Taiwan, or Hong Kong where the dominant language is Chinese.

Schiffrin's (1987) work serves as a benchmark to outline the standard functions of 'then' in English. It states that 'then' is mainly used at the simultaneous juncture between two coinciding units of talk – the episodes (successive in real time) and the topics (successive in discourse time). I argue that the functions of 'then' in CSM have gone beyond showing succession of time or topic to become more of a general connector. The functions of 'then' in CSM are also compared to colloquial Singapore English (CSE) to see if the discourse-pragmatic functions in CSM are different from those in CSE. The results show that 'then' has more functions in CSM than in CSE.

This chapter is organised as follows: an introduction; a review of the literature; an explanation of the data and methodology used; a discussion of relevant previous studies, notably Schiffrin's (1987) account of the functions of 'then' in English, and Biq's (1990) study of a similar discourse marker in Chinese *na(me)* '[since...] then...'; analysis of the extended functions of 'then' in CSM and a comparison of these with the functions of 'then' in CSE; a conclusion.

Review of literature

Code-switching and borrowing

In distinguishing code-switching (CS) and borrowing (B), Myers-Scotton (1992: 30) states "I will suggest that absolute frequency/relative frequency is the single criterion best linking B forms more closely with the ML (matrix language) mental lexicon than single CS forms." 'Then' in colloquial Singapore Mandarin has the highest frequency (60%) of all English discourse markers in the data in Lee (2003). According to Myers-Scotton's (1992) definition, 'then' is a B form rather than a CS form, although both categories fall along a process continuum. B forms are in turn made up of Cultural B forms and Core B forms. Cultural B forms stand for objects or concepts new to the matrix language culture. Once the lexeme encoding a new object/concept is used in the ML, it is predicted that those speakers who first used it will use it again when the need to signify the same referent comes up. Therefore, the claim is that Cultural B forms enter their ML lexicon abruptly and are unrelated to code-switching as a phenomenon (Myers-Scotton 1992: 29). In contrast, Core B forms are borrowed because certain types of contact situations promote the desire to identify with the EL (embedded language) or at least aspects of it (Myers-Scotton 1992: 29). Haugen says (1953: 373) "Borrowing always goes beyond the actual 'needs' of language." Examples of Core B forms include words such as 'twenty' and 'because' from the Zimbabwe corpus in Myers-Scotton's (1992) data.

Given this analysis, 'then' is clearly a Core B form. Another piece of evidence is how 'then' is pronounced; it is said that "most established B forms may well be phonologically integrated into the ML" (Myers-Scotton 1992: 31). 'Then' in CSM is usually not a dental fricative as is the norm in RP (received pronunciation) or General American, but is pronounced more like 'den'. Perhaps it is more economical to use a single word 'then' than to use the Mandarin *ranhou* (see Wee 2003 for 'know').

Bilingual discourse markers

Although 'then' is a connecting word of succession in time, events and actions, it is also a discourse marker. Bilingual conversations offer a unique perspective from which to examine discourse markers. Goss and Salmons' (2000) work on German-English bilinguals shows that those who use English discourse markers in the plays are inevitably heavy code-switchers. De Rooij (2000) attributes the presence of French discourse markers in Shaba Swahili discourse to highlighting contrast and thus maximising the saliency of the contextualisation cue (Gumperz 1982) these elements constitute. Matras (1998, 2000) attributes the motivation for switching at discourse markers to the reduction of cognitive pressure. Studies on the functions of discourse markers have been seen to segment or mark boundaries; or to show impatience in conversations in Maschler's (1994, 2000, 2003) work on Hebrew-English bilinguals.

This chapter addresses the extended functions of a discourse marker when used in another language. In the bilingual context, these high occurring words with new extended meanings usually belong to the dominant language. A similar phenomenon is seen in Tao and Thompson (1991) when Mandarin-English bilinguals in the US use English backchannels such as *yeah, aha, mm-hmm* (instead of using the Mandarin *dui*, right, yes) in Mandarin conversations as continuers or in order to signal understanding, confirmation and acknowledgement of agreement. In the language environment of these Mandarin speakers in the US, English is clearly the dominant language, hence the tendency to use English backchannels when they are speaking in Mandarin.

'Then' as a connector

In Schiffrin's analysis (1987) 'then' refers to prior discourse time to establish succession between events (the anaphoric property), as well as succession between other units of talk such as ideas, topics and actions. Schiffrin's analysis of 'then' is summarised in Table 5.1.

Table 5.1 Schiffrin's (1987) analysis of *'then'*

Functions of 'then' in Schiffrin (1987)	Examples of Functions
1) The successive function of *'then'* as successive ideas in discourse time (p.251).	a. *And uh I went on the beach with them.* b. *THEN when they went ho-off eh for their nap, I:-* c. *THEN I gave the younger son uh... attention.*
2) Units of talk which are not temporally successive events still succeed one another in discourse time (p.252).	a. *because down south they weren't makin' any kind of money.* b. *And THEN, the Southerners used t'give 'em carfare t'get'em the hell outa there.*
3) Introduces successive topics. In example (3a, 3b), the first episode introduces the first pair of toys which are the different colored buckets:	a. *So w-there's two big red buckets. One has a handle and one doesn't. And there was a green bucket, with a handle.* *After reporting the first episode, the speaker opens the second episode by introducing the second pair of toys:* b. *And THEN there was like a blue shovel with r-eh it was a rake. One had-there was only one :: like that. The other was an ordinary shovel.*
4) distal time deixis and *'then'*: *'Then'* creates a bridge within the flow of discourse time by pointing away from a current utterance to a prior utterance produced by either the current or prior speaker.	
5) a member not only of the proximal/ distal deictic pair, but of the conditional pair if/then.	

Biq (1990) discusses the Mandarin connective *na(me)*, (pronounced as/nah-mer/, roughly glossed as 'so, (given...) then (...)') in conversation. She has shown that there are three types of relationship manifested in units of talk marked by *na(me)*: conditional relation, topic succession and topic change. Although topic change appears to be the opposite of topic succession, she argues that the topic change marked by *na(me)*, in which continuation is anchored at the interactional dimension rather than at the textual/ideational dimension, is a sub-type of the distant topic succession. She suggests that the speaker-addressee interactions both motivate and constrain the frequent occurrences of *na(me)* in conversation. Although *na(me)* is not the exact equivalent of 'then', which is more accurately rendered by *ranhou* ('after that', 'subsequently'), they share the same function of topic succession. According to Biq, the speaker exploits the successive function of *na(me)* even in concession.

Data and methodology

The CSM data in this chapter is collected from 18 half hour audio-taped natural conversations among undergraduate students. They include 3212 turns of conversations and 1146 English words. These undergraduates major in Chinese and are effectively bilingual in Mandarin and English. These conversations are transcribed in terms of intonation units, each line in the transcription standing for one intonation unit, which is defined roughly as a stretch of speech uttered under a single coherent intonation contour (Du Bois et al. 1993: 47).

For purposes of comparison, I have obtained a set of colloquial Singapore English (CSE) data from the Grammar of Singapore English Corpus database (GSEC) which consists of about 20 speakers and a total of 60,000 words from 31 conversations of varying lengths, between ten minutes and half an hour. This data is transcribed from audio-taped conversations taken from undergraduates who spoke mainly in English. In this data, there are 339 occurrences of 'then'. Since the chapter focuses on CSM, the CSE data is used only as a reference for discussion.

Extended functions of *then* in CSM

When we analyse 'then' in CSM and CSE according to the standard functions in Schiffrin (1987), it is found that 'then' in CSE has 77 per cent of standard form functions whereas in CSM it has 65 per cent. This means that CSM has a higher percentage of extended meaning (35%) compared to CSE (23%). These extended functions include requesting information, marking consequence, showing concession, securing conversational floor and introducing quotation or action, summarised in Table 5.2 below. What is really interesting is that in CSE 'then' does not have the functions of marking concession and securing conversational floor. These two extra functions show that 'then' is more highly generalised as a connector in CSM than in CSE.

Table 5.2 Extended functions of *'then'*

Extended functions	CSM (%)	CSE (%)
1) **Generalised connector**		
Requesting for information	15	7
Consequence marker	7	3
Concessive marker	7	0
Securing conversational floor	1	0
2) **Metalinguistic function**		
Introduce quotation or action	5	13
Total	35	23

Request for information

One extended function of 'then' in CSM is to preface questions or to ask for further elaboration, such as 'then what happens next?' Even standing alone 'then?' is sufficient to prompt the hearer to provide more information of the topic under discussion. The basic meaning of 'then' is succession, and it has developed from succession to asking question. In Example (1), CL begins her question with 'then' to ask if SH is going alone to the fitness class or if someone else is going with her. Except for 'then', the rest of the question (line 12) is in Chinese. This function of 'then' in CSM makes up 15 per cent.

(1) C2 (32) (CL, a female student, and SH, a working female, are discussing the costs of various fitness classes.)

```
1 CL:   等     一下
        deng yixia,
        wait a while

2       wait, wait, wait,

3       我  很    confused,
        wo hen
        I very

4       how do you get your free,

5       you have to sign up, right?

6 SH:   Sign up card /lor/,
                    DP(obvious)

7       pay the subscriptions /lor/
                        DP (obvious)
```

8   不用　紧　的　啦
      buyong   jin   de   /lah/
      no need matter   POS   DP(assertive)

9   随便　　啦
      suibian /lah/
                anything DP(assertive)

10 CL: Wow

11 SH: 最多　　　三　六十　块
        zuiduo   san   liu shi kuai
        most more three   six ten dollars

12 CL: THEN 你　一　个　人　去，还是　有　　晓芬
              Ni   yi   ge ren   qu haishi you Xiaofen
              you one CL person   go or   have Xiaofen

    CL: Wait, wait, wait, wait, I am very confused, how do you get your free... you have to sign up, right?

    SH: Sign up for the card /lor/, pay the subscriptions /lor/ never mind /lah/ it's all right with me /lah/

    CL: Wow!

    SH: Thirty to sixty dollars at the most.

    CL: THEN are you going on your own, or together with Xiaofen?

Consequence marker

In the CSM data, 'then' also has the function of marking the consequence resulting from prior events. From its start as a temporal succession between prior and upcoming talk, 'then' later generalised to *leading to the final outcome of event*, having the meaning of *as a result ..., therefore..., in that case....* In Example (2) below, we see that the meaning of 'then' has been even more generalised. The speaker says that perhaps after having been washed many times, her pants feel looser and *as a result* she feels slimmer. 'Then' leads to a logical conclusion.

(2) C13 (112 B) (Two female friends are talking about the pants which they wear. LT mentions her jeans.)

1 LT: 我　那天　　　那天　　　　我那个　裤
      Wo natian natian   wo nage ku
      I that day that day   I   that pants

2   你不是　讲　　那个 金金　　　的 啰
      nibushi jiang nage jin jin de /lor/
      you not said that   gold gold POS DP(obvious)

3   我   起初   穿   也是   很   紧
    wo qichu chuan yeshi hen jin
    I at first wear also very tight

4   THEN after that 最近 穿   得   蛮   舒服
            zuijin chuan de man shufu
               recently wear ASP quite comfortable

5   可能   洗 比较   多   次，
    keneng xi bijiao   duo ci
    Maybe wash comparatively more times

6   或者   expand   了   啊
    huozhe   liao /ah/,
     Or   ASP   DP(assertive)

7   THEN 给 我 那个 错觉   我 瘦   了
        gei wo nage cuojue wo shou le
        give me that illusion I thin ASP

LT: That pair of pants which I (was wearing) that day, and didn't you say was 'gold-gold' in colour- when I wore them, they were also very tight. Then after that, they became quite comfortable when I wore them recently. Maybe it was because the pants were washed comparatively more often. Or (the pants) had expanded, 'then' giving me the false impression that I had become thinner.

Concessive meaning

There is an interesting tendency of temporal 'then' moving towards the concessive 'then' in CSM. Interestingly, the Chinese equivalent of 'then' – *ranhou* also displays this similar characteristic (Ong and Phua 2011). In Example (3) below, 'then' functions as a concessive marker. JR expresses his dismay that, though his friend was not bribed, he had reported on the rest who had been bribed and got himself into trouble as well.

(3) C16 (254) (Four students are talking about an incident involving the bribery of policemen. JR (male) offers his view.)

1 JR: 没有   I mean 哎呀
     Meiyou,   /aiyah/
     No   DP

2   大家   都 like 被 被   bribe 了
    dajia   dou   bei- bei   le,
    everyone also   get-get   ASP

3   THEN 你 没有   被 bribe,
       ni meiyou bei
      you never get

4   然后   你 还 去 告
      ranhou ni hai qu gao,
      after that you still go tell on (the others)

5   害到   我们   被   打
      haidao women bei da,
      cause   us   get beaten

6   然后   你 自己 也 被 打。
      ranhou ni ziji ye bei da
      Then you self also get beaten.

> JR: No, I mean.. /aiyah/ everyone was bribed, 'then' you were not bribed, and
> you still went to tell on (the others), and caused us to get beaten up, after
> that you would also get beaten up.

A similar pattern is observed in Biq's (1990) study of *na(me) since... then...*
whereby a successive connector is used to show topic change. She explains
that speakers exploit the connective function of *na(me)* to lead to a topic
change.

Secure conversational floor

In CSM, 'then' is used to secure the conversational floor or to restart a
conversation. In other words, the meaning of succession has been extended
to link the subsequent conversation to an earlier conversation, even when
the topics are unrelated. Biq (1990), when discussing a Chinese connective
na(me), states that it is used for topic transition by exploiting the interactional aspect of conversation. She argues that in cases where there is no clear
cohesiveness, by using *na(me)*, the speaker manages to get by the pressure
for topic cohesiveness in the conversation, that is, the speaker assumes
cohesiveness by using *na(me)*. *Na(me)*, in effect, makes conversation participants believe that there has not been any topic change but rather that the
upcoming talk is a continuation of what has been going on. In the same way,
'then' in CSM is also used to restart conversations when there is no apparent
connection in the topic.

In Example (4), one friend is telling the other about her travel experiences
(lines 1–6). After a long pause, LK uses 'then' to continue the conversation.
However, what follows is not a continued topic but a new topic (in line 7).
Thus, 'then' originally indicated continuation in content, but now it is used
to secure the conversational floor.

(4) C15 (107) (YY is telling LK about her travel experience.)

```
1 YY: But 那种      有时候      不是 很  好  啦
          na zhong youshihou bushihen hao /lah/,
          that type sometimes not very good  DP(assertive)

2         因为 like one country 它给
          yinwei              ta gei
          because             he give

3         你maybe 一一 天  两   天       这样,
          ni...    yi yi tian liang tian zhe yang
          you...   one one day two  day   like that

4         走  马    看  花          这样
          Zou ma    kan hua        zhe yang
          walk horse see flower    this sort

5         可是  要  很     贵        啦
          Keshi yao hen    gui      /lah/
          but   need very expensive DP(assertive)

6         嗯   所以 我 暂时    目标
          /umm/suoyi wo zanshi mubiao
               So   I temporary  target

7         是  台湾    比较 便宜
          shi Taiwan bijiao pianyi
          is Taiwan   more cheap

8         不过   我  妈妈   讲      那边   的
          buguo  wo mama  jiang nabian de
          but    my mother say    there  POS
          食物  很   贵,    东西   很  贵。
          shiwu hen  gui    dongxi hen gui
          food very expensive things very expensive

9 LK:     台湾
          Taiwan
          Taiwan

   ... (4.0)

10 LK:    /eh/ THEN 你.. 最近    好像
                    ni..zuijin haoxiang
                    you recently like

11        没有   看 你 在 ICQ /hor/?
          meiyou kan ni zai
          no     see you on   DP(question)
```

YY: But that type (of travel package) is not very good /lah/, because they give
you maybe like one- one or two days per country, just rushing from place to
place, but it is very expensive /lah/, /umm/ that's why.. at the moment my

target is Taiwan @ (it is) cheaper. @ But my mother said that the food there is more expensive, and the things are expensive (too).

LK: Taiwan

... (4.0)

LK: /eh/ THEN you...I don't seem to see you on ICQ recently /hor/?

Metalinguistic function: introduce quotations and actions

'Then' also introduces quotations, dialogues or act-out actions so as to present the situation more vividly for the hearer. This seems to be a common device used in other bilingual and multilingual conversations as well. In Schely-Newman's (1993) study of Hebrew-Arabic-French-Yiddish multilingual narrative, Arabic 'verbs of saying' segment the report of direct speech. In Woolard's (1987) study of Catalan-Castilian code-switching in Catalonia, the Catalan form *diu* (he says) in the midst of mostly Castilian speech indicates that speech is about to be reported. Auer (1998: 19) shows that in Italian-German bilingual conversation, the Italian perception verb *guardate* (look) is used in the midst of German discourse, beginning a quote, providing a contrast between the conversational context of the quote and the reported speech itself. Tannen (1989) states that perception verbs are used as a discourse marker beginning a new conversational action, constructing dialogue.

In Example (5) below, 'then' in line 3 introduces a self-quotation. SH is recounting how she tells another friend that she is not anxious about not having a boyfriend (line 3).

(5) C2 (61B) (SH is telling CL that she is not really worried about not being able to find a boyfriend.)

```
1 CL:    /han/ /nah/ 那是    可以, 对          呀
                     nashi keyi dui        /ya/
         (granted) That's fine correct   DP

2 SH     Then /oi/那时      Ah Leng  都 没 有
                     nashi            dou meiyou
              DP  that time Ah Leng also not have

3        没有     THEN我 就  '我 不 急,
         meiyou      wo_jiu wo bu ji
             no       I then I not anxious

4        你 比   我 还 要   急?
         ni bi   wo haiyao ji?
            you than me more anxious?
```

CL: /han/ /nah/ That is okay, right /ya/

SH: Then /oi/ that time Ah Leng also didn't have (a boyfriend), didn't have THEN I said 'I am not anxious, yet you are more anxious than me?'

In another example (6), 'then' introduces a hypothetical quotation. CL was telling SH about her intention to wear contact lenses the next day. SH says then people will ask about her glasses, and her answer would be *My glasses were damaged by my brother.* SH uses 'then' to introduce this hypothetical answer in Mandarin.

(6) C2 (114) (CL is telling SH about her intention to wear contact lenses the next day.)

```
1 CL:  哦  … (9.2)明天   戴 contacts      /huh/?
       /oh/    mingtian dai
       Oh        tomorrow wear contacts    DP (right?)

2 SH:  应该       高兴
       yinggai    gaoxing
       Should be happy

3 CL   /han/ /noh/
       DP(agree)

4 SH:  THEN人家      会     问
          renjia   hui    wen
          others   will   ask

5      ‘没有，我的 眼镜    给 我 brother弄 坏    了’
       meiyou wode yanjing gei wo      nong huai le’.
       No     my spectacles give my   make spoil ASP’
```

CL: /Oh/… Tomorrow wear contacts /huh/

SH: … (You) should be happy /hor/, [excuse /hor/]

CL: [/han/ noh/]

SH: THEN other people will ask, (and you say) 'no, my brother damaged my spectacles'.

Besides quotations, the data also shows that speakers use 'then' to introduce actions so as to re-enact a past action. In Example (7), two friends are talking about primary (or elementary) school days and how they interacted with boys in their class. When it reaches the part where little boys and girls hold hands, the speaker uses 'then' to lead to the action of how the boys let go of the girls' hands (line 3).

(7) C4 (288) (CL and NA are talking about primary school days.)

```
1NA  But 其实 他 不 需要 force 你 手 牵 手   的right?
         qishi ta bu xuyao        ni shou qian shou de
         actually he not need        you hand hold hand POS

3    是你    一直 拉    那些 男 的
     Shi ni  yizhi la   naxie nan de,
     Is you  always hold those boy POS

4    不要    放手，
     buyao   fangshou
     not want let hand

5    THEN他们    这样     放手<@@>
         tamen zheyang  fangshou.
         they  this way put hand
```

> NA: But actually he didn't need to force you to hold hands right? You were the one who held those boys, not wanting to let go, THEN they let go, like that.

Discussion and conclusion

This study has used Schiffrin's (1987) analysis of 'then' as a benchmark for how 'then' is used in Standard English. Schiffrin has shown that 'then' is basically a marker of succession of events and ideas, and a marker of succession of action. Analysis of 'then' in CSM and CSE in this study shows that there are more extended discourse-pragmatic functions of 'then' in CSM than in CSE. In particular, 'then' in CSM has the functions of concessive marker and securing the conversation floor while these functions are not present in CSE. This would seem to indicate that, once 'then' becomes a core borrowing word in CSM, its function as a connector gets generalised. It appears that when 'then' functions in the CSM environment, it develops more general functions of a connector.

Specific findings from this study include:

1) The extended discourse-pragmatic functions of 'then' in CSM beyond those in Standard English are: requesting information, marking consequence, marking concession, securing the conversational floor, and introducing a quotation or action.

2) When 'then' is fully integrated into CSM as a core borrowing it becomes a more generalised connector than in the English discourse context. As a result, 'then' in CSM has more discourse-pragmatic functions than in Standard English and CSE.

3) Speakers of CSM are Mandarin-speaking English-dominant bilinguals in an environment where English is the main working language for administration, finance and education. As such, English is the prestigious language in the speech community of these CSM bilinguals, and it is the dominant language in Singapore among the CSM speakers. This is why these CSM speakers use 'then' instead of *ranhou*.

4) 'Then' is monosyllabic, while its Chinese equivalent *ranhou* consists of two syllables, so, in terms of the economy of words, it is faster to say 'then' than *ranhou*.

5) 'Then' can function as a general connector which serves many connecting functions. So, out of convenience, 'then' is used instead of *ranhou*.

These findings have important implications for bilingual studies as they show that bilinguals code-switch as a result of language contact. Due to globalisation, and the status of English as an international language, spoken Mandarin in different parts of the world has absorbed/is absorbing words from English. Mandarin speakers in China or Taiwan also have their own form of code-switching variety.

Appendix: Transcription symbols

ASP   Aspect marker

POS   Possessive case

DP   Discourse particle (see Gupta 1992; Wee 2002)

@   laughter

Acknowledgements

I am grateful to the three anonymous reviewers who have given me invaluable suggestions. I would also like to thank Lisa Lim for granting permission to use the GSEC (Grammar of Singapore English Corpus) database. All disclaimers apply. This work is supported by the Academic Research Fund (AcRF) Tier 1 (R-102-000-0580112) of the Faculty of Arts and Social Sciences, National University of Singapore.

References

Auer, P. (ed.) (1998) *Code-Switching in Conversation*. London: Routledge.

Biq, Y. O. (1990) Conversation, continuation, and connectives. *Text* 10: 187–208.

Chen, C. Y. (1984) Certain lexical features of Singapore Mandarin. In B. Hong (ed.) *New Papers on Chinese Language Use* 93–104. Canberra: Contemporary China Centre, Australian National University.

De Rooij, V. A. (2000) French discourse markers in Shaba Swahili conversations. *International Journal of Bilingualism* 4: 447–67.

Dong, Ying 董颖 (2007) Zhongguo hanying shuangyu xianzhuang ji yuma hunhe zhuanhuan tanxi 中国汉英双语现状及语码混合转换探析 [A study of Chinese-English bilingualism and code-switching]. 现代语文（语言研究）*Modern Chinese* 7: 16–18.

Du Bois, J. W., Schuetze-Coburn, S., Cumming, S. and Danae, P. (1993) Outline of discourse transcription. In J. A. Edwards and M. D. Lampert (eds) *Talking Data: Transcription and Coding in Discourse Research* 45–89. Hillsdale, NJ: Lawrence Erlbaum Associates.

Goss, E. and Salmons, J. C. (2000) The evolution of a bilingual discourse marking system: Modal particles and English markers in German-American dialects. *International Journal of Bilingualism* 4: 469–94.

Gumperz, J. J. (1982) *Discourse Strategies*. Cambridge: Cambridge University Press.

Gupta, A. F. (1992) The pragmatic particles of Singapore Colloquial English. *Journal of Pragmatics* 18: 31–57.

Haugen, E. (1953) *The Norwegian Language in American: A Study in Bilingual Behavior.* 2 Vols. Philadelphia, PA: University of Pennsylvania Press.

Lee, C. L. (2003) Motivations of code-switching in multi-lingual Singapore. *Journal of Chinese Linguistics* 31: 145–76.

Li, David C. S. (2000) Cantonese-English code-switching research in Hong Kong: A Y2K review. *World Englishes* 19(3): 305–322.

Maschler, Y. (1994) Metalanguaging and discourse markers in bilingual conversation. *Language in Society* 23: 325–66.

Maschler, Y. (2000) What can bilingual conversation tell us about discourse markers? Introduction. *International Journal of Bilingualism* 4: 437–45.

Maschler, Y. (2003) The discourse marker nu: Israeli Hebrew impatience in interaction. *Text* 23: 89–128.

Matras, Y. (1998) Utterance modifiers and universals of grammatical borrowing. *Linguistics* 36(2): 281–331.

Matras, Y. (2000) Fusion and the cognitive basis for bilingual discourse markers. *International Journal of Bilingualism* 4: 485–504.

Myers-Scotton, C. (1992) Comparing codeswitching and borrowing. *Journal of Multilingual and Multicultural Development* 12: 19–40.

Myers-Scotton, C. (1993) *Duelling Languages: Grammatical Structure in Codeswitching*. Oxford: Clarendon Press.

Ong, F. P. and Phua, C. P. 王慧萍、潘秋平 (2011) Cong yuyi ditu tan ranhou 从语义地图谈'然后' [Ranhou: A Semantic Map Perspective], 吴福祥、张谊生编《语法化和语法研究(五). In Wu, F. and Zhang, Y. (eds.) Grammaticalization and Grammar Studies (5) 254–311, Peking: Commercial Press.

Platt, J. and Ho, M. L. (1989) Discourse particles in Singaporean English: Substratum influences and universals. *World Englishes* 8: 215–21.

Schely-Newman, E. (1993) *Ha'axer besi'ax shel yisra'elim yots'ey tunis* ('The 'other' in the discourse of Tunisian Israelis'). Paper presented to the Seminar of the Department of Communication and Jounalism, Hebrew University of Jerusalem, Israel, 15 November 1993.

Schiffrin, D. (1987) *Discourse Markers*. Cambridge: Cambridge University Press.

Su, H. Y. (2009) Code-switching in managing a face-threatening communicative task: Footing and ambiguity in conversational interaction in Taiwan. *Journal of Pragmatics* 37: 372–92.

Tannen, D. (1989) *Talking Voices: Repetition, Dialogue, and Imagery in Conversational Discourse*. Cambridge: Cambridge University Press.

Tao, H. Y. and Thompson S. A. (1991) English backchannels in Mandarin conversations: A case study of superstratum pragmatic 'interference'. *Journal of Pragmatics* 16: 209–223.

Wee, L. (2002) *Lor* in colloquial Singapore English. *Journal of Pragmatics* 34: 711–25.

Wee, L. (2003) The birth of a particle: *know* in colloquial Singapore English. *World Englishes* 22: 5–13.

Wong, J. O. (1994) A Wierzbickan approach to Singlish particles. MA Thesis, National University of Singapore.

Woolard, K. A. (1987) Codeswitching and comedy in Catalonia. *Papers in Pragmatics* 1: 106–22.

6

Approaching Chinese power in situated discourse: From experience to modelling

Yueguo Gu

Preliminaries

"Of all the concepts used by sociologists, few are the source of more confusion and misunderstanding than power" complains Lenski (1993: 61). There are "hundreds, perhaps thousands, of more recent definitions of social power" observes Wrong (1993: 9). In linguistics, power most recently is prototypically associated with critical discourse analysis (CDA). As Blommaert observes (2005: 1), "[i]t is a commonplace to equate 'critical approaches' with 'approaches that criticize power.'" Although this chapter has benefited significantly from sociological studies of power, the literature review will concentrate, for space considerations, on CDA's treatment of power in discourse analysis only. Basically the power that CDA has put to scrutiny is State power, or political power, or the governing party's power, or class power (e.g. Fairclough 1995, 2001; Hodge and Kress 1993; Wodak 1989; van Dijk 1988, 1993). In this chapter, however, the concept of power to be examined is based on mutual and reciprocal dependency relations between actors, as initially formulated by Emerson (1993). The reason for this option, as argued below, is that it is far more basic and ubiquitous, as far as everyday situated discourse is concerned.

The subtitle of the chapter signals the methodology adopted in examining power in situated discourse. In a nutshell, it looks at power in three successive stages: 1) power as it is experienced by laymen in everyday situated discourse; 2) power as it is modelled; and 3) power as it is simulated. The task in the first stage is to extract and make knowledge constructs about power. The second is to create data models of the power extracted in the first stage. The last is to produce computer simulation of the power on the basis of the data models drawn at the second stage. This chapter will focus on the first two, leaving the third for a different paper, for it goes far beyond the scope of this chapter.

The data for the chapter are drawn from the Spoken Chinese Corpus of Situated Discourse (SCCSD for short; see Gu 2002b and www.multimodalgu.com for details of this corpus).

In what follows, first we shall review CDA's treatment of power in discourse. We then examine analytically the notion of power as defined in terms of mutual dependency relations. This is followed by the introduction of situated discourse, another key concept of this chapter, and the modelling methodology. The power-exercising behaviours found in the Min Dialect Dictionary Launching Symposium, videotaped data lasting 120 minutes, are modelled as a case study. The chapter concludes with a brief discussion of theoretical implications and issues for future research.

Power: a critical review of CDA

As mentioned above, the interaction between power and discourse has been the primary concern of critical discourse analysis. 'The pros and cons of CDA' can be found in a very recent work by Blommaert (2005, see chapter 2 in particular for a thorough review). What is reviewed below will be the notion of power adopted in CDA and its methodology.

Power as a property of social class: Fairclough's early work

Mainstream CDA theorists' concern with the relation between discourse and State power (or the power of a governing party or a social class) is particularly apparent in Fairclough's early work (1995). This notion of power naturally generates its correlates such as domination/subordination, opposition/ struggle, ideology/resistance. Language via discourse in this connection becomes a tool used and abused by the powerful to rule the powerless. Discourse as a form of social practice is thus shaped by the dominating ideology of the party in power. What is extremely interesting and pertinent to this chapter is that Fairclough's early framework would offer a next-to-perfect critical tool to examine what I have called 'revolutionary discourse', namely discourse during the Great Cultural Revolution (Gu 2001). However, the practice of stratifying Chinese society by class was abandoned after the Cultural Revolution. Gone with it are the notions of class struggle, and the Proletariat Dictatorship. The State power, and the Party's power – the politically correct order in China should be: the Party's power and the State power – have to be redefined, legitimised and exerted. What is significant is that the open door policy and economical reforms have created undercurrents, anticipated or unanticipated by the authorities, that render the redefinition, legitimisation and exertion difficult and painful at times. Clearly Fairclough's early framework is no longer appropriate to the current situation of China. Moreover, his framework is built on viewing social institution as 'pluralistic', which assumes ample room for discursive practices, was alien even in the social-political context of that period in China.

Interestingly enough, reflecting upon the early writing, Fairclough himself makes the following observations:

> Another characteristic of this early work is *the centrality of social class in its view of power*. The later relative retreat from a classical left perspective focusing class, ideology and social reproduction is *comprehensible in view of political changes and the shifts in theoretical fashions in the 1980s, but I would now see it as rather too hasty.* (Fairclough 1995: 24; italics mine)

The "centrality of social class in its view of power" is reflectively found to be "rather too hasty" even in the British context, and perhaps also in the European context as well.

Power as domination

CDA's conceptualisation of power, or rather its adoption of such conceptualisation, has recently been challenged by Grillo (2005). He argues that "although the way in which power relations actually 'work' amounts to domination in many cases, it does not entail that power is to be reduced to domination" (Grillo 2005: 6). He continues:

> As Hannah Arendt (1972: 105–87) rightly pointed out, domination is far from constituting the very "core" of power: it merely amounts to what power relations become when considered within conflicting contexts or situations. Yes, as she (again rightly) emphasised, *human activity (including discursive practices as well) does not always take place within such contexts; obviously, there are also co-operative situations, which can hardly be accounted for by means of the "agonistic model" of power, for in such cases it just ceases to apply.* (Grillo 2005: 6; italics mine)

In those activities where the agonistic model of power ceases to apply, it does not mean that they are islands devoid of power. Power relations still exist and operate. What we need is an alternative conceptualisation of power that will do the job; a generic form of power with the agonistic model of power as its sub-type, so to speak. This is the direction Grillo attempts to advance, viz. power without domination, as the title of the book signals it.

Power and agency

Fairclough's early emphasis on the determination of action by structure is replaced by the increasing emphasis on agency and change:

> The chapter ... does take a dialectical view of the relationship between *structure and action*. But the emphasis, under the influence of Althusser and French discourse analysis (Althusser 1971; Pêcheux 1982), is upon the determination of action by structures, social reproduction, and the ideological positioning of subjects. Later chapters have increasingly emphasized *agency and change*, and ideology has in some cases become relatively backgrounded. (Fairclough 1995: 24; italics original)

The CDA's conceptualisation of power is characteristically made at the expense of *marginalising agency*. It is often borne out in such syntactic structure as "Text/discourse/language does such-and-such". For instance: "*Texts* in their ideational functioning *constitute* systems of knowledge and belief...", "*Texts negotiate* the sociocultural contradictions and more loosely 'differences' ..." (Fairclough 1995: 67; italics mine). I shall argue for an alternative agent-centred conceptualisation with human agency (human actors) playing a pivotal role. In other words, power in this chapter is always embodied. It is the power of the first order (see section below, *Power as defined in terms of mutual dependency relations*, for further discussion).

Hermeneutics of suspicion

In reviewing media studies, Scannel (1998) draws a distinction between two broad attitudes towards the reality of world and language:

> ... either to take it at face value or not. The former accepts and recognizes, in the first instance, reality as it is. The latter regards this reality with a principled suspicion. At the least, it wishes to put in question what appears as unquestionable from the former stance. Each attitude embodies a particular way of interpreting reality. We will call them the hermeneutics of trust and of suspicion, a distinction first suggested by Ricoeur ... (Scannel 1998: 254)

It is the hallmark of CDA to adopt the hermeneutics of suspicion. Its mission is to act like a detective sieving the surface of language use for power manipulation, ideological brainwashing, and so on. It is driven by the assumption that "an underlying structure that, when found, will serve to explain the form and content of things as they ordinarily appear to us" (Scannell 1998: 255).

The hermeneutics of suspicion used to be the dominating mode of stance in China during the so-called 'Great Cultural Revolution' (1966–1976). One of the distinctive features of revolutionary discourse then was to interpret almost any piece of language use, written or spoken, in terms of class struggle. This resulted in a great deal of witch-hunting and prosecutions based on sheer (mis)interpretations of verbal texts.

CDA's mission deserves respect and admiration. But as a linguist, one may very well take a more neutral stance by adopting a hermeneutics of trust. That is, trust the everyday phenomenological reality as data, and respect it as such in the first instance.

The Western and Chinese compared

In the Western context, the populace takes part in politics, either in macro-politics or in micro-politics, via activities such as voting, debating, policy-criticising in the mass media, demonstrating, lobbying, and so on. As we know, these activities are foreign in China. Voting is indeed occasionally reported in the official media, but it is rare and conducted with 'Chinese characteristics', a euphemistic term for ticking boxes without making genuine choices. Politics used to come into the everyday lives of the Chinese populace via what was called 'political studies', which is often characterised by Western scholars as brainwashing studies. This kind of brainwashing practice is dying out nationwide, and is only found occasionally in certain sections of government, but political activities in the Western sense account for a negligible part of people's everyday life in China. This however does not mean that Chinese people are not 'political animals'. We are! We play it in our own way, indeed, with Chinese characteristics. The notion of power defined in this chapter is the power played in the everyday lives of the Chinese populace. It is their politics with a small p, not a big P.

Power as defined in terms of mutual dependency relations

Emerson's theory of power

Emerson holds that "power resides implicitly in the other's dependency" (Emerson 1993: 49). The 'other's dependency' is entailed by social relations.

> A *depends* upon B if he aspires to goals or gratifications whose achievement is facilitated by appropriate actions on B's part. By virtue

of mutual dependency, it is more or less imperative to each party that he be able to control or influence the other's conduct. At the same time, these ties of mutual dependence imply that each party is in a position, to some degree, to grant or deny, facilitate or hinder, the other's gratification. Thus, it would appear that the power to control or influence the other resides in control over the things he values, which may range all the way from oil resources to ego-support, depending upon the relation in question. (Emerson 1993: 49)

Since human beings are social animals in the sense that any individual member has to form some social relations with others for his or her own survival, power relation is intrinsic to human life activities. This coincides with Hawley (1963: 422; re-quoted from Olsen and Marger 1993: 1): "Every social act is an exercise of power, every social relationship is a power equation, and every social group or system is an organization of power."

Emerson attempts to define power by first fixing the dependency relationship. "TWO variables appear to function jointly in fixing the dependence of one actor upon another" (Emerson 1993: 49).

Dependence (Dab). The dependence of actor A upon actor B is 1) directly proportional to A's *motivational investment* in goals mediated by B, and 2) inversely proportional to the *availability* to those goals to A outside of the A–B relation. (Emerson 1993: 49; italics original)

The dependence of one actor provides the basis for the power of the other. Thus power must be defined as a potential influence:

Power (Pab). The power of actor A over actor B is the *amount of resistance* on the Part of B which can be potentially overcome by A. (Emerson 1993: 49; italics original)

Power (Pab) is obviously relational and relative. It is relational in the sense that it makes little sense that actor A has such-and-such power without reference to the dependency relations between A and other actors. An emperor has no power while he is asleep. All he has is huge potential for power. Later we shall further clarify the power potential in terms of resources owned by an actor that can be transformed into power energy. The notion that power is relative refers to the fact that the amount of resistance changes from one situation to another, from one actor to another, and from one goal to another.

As social relations between actors A and B are reciprocal, the power-dependence relationship is a "pair of" equations: Pab = Dba; Pba = Dab (Emerson 1993: 50). Reciprocal social relations do not mean that the power-dependence relationship is always a balanced one. Pab can be weightier than Pba, or the other way round. This leads to inequality, due to the differences between Dab and Dba, the values of which depend, by definition, on 1) the goals; 2) "motivational investment" (Emerson's expression, and I use 'goal commitment'); and 3) the resources mobilised to be converted into usable power energy (see the next section for further discussion).

Resources and power energy

Etzioni likens power to energy: "Like energy, *power is directly observable only when used.* The power of a unit can be predicted by studying its assets, its total structure, and its past performances in this regard" (Etzioni 1993: 20; italics mine). This metaphor of power is totally compatible with the power-dependence relationship discussed above. A human actor's potential of power energy can be predicted by the resources that he/she has access to and that he/she is able to transform into power energy. The power energy potential of an institution can be studied in a similar fashion. Take for example a human actor in a Chinese social-cultural-political context. The resources that are transformable into power energy potential include the following (not meant to be exhaustive):

- *Resources being fairly stable and individually owned:* 1) knowledge; 2) expertise; 3) practical skills; 4) rhetorical skills; 5) wealth; 6) charisma; 7) familial relations; 8) age; 9) gender; and so on.

- *Resources being less stable and socially granted:* 1) political role (hierarchical); 2) social role (hierarchical); 3) academic role (hierarchical); 4) job role (hierarchical); 5) social network; 6) customs; 7) conventions; 8) deep-seated values; and so on.

Take a social institution for another example.[1] The resources that are transformable into power energy potential include (again not meant to be exhaustive):

- *Resources available to a governmental unit:* 1) Party structure (hierarchy); 2) State government structure (hierarchy); 3) People's Congress structure (hierarchy); 4) Army structure (hierarchy); 5) mass media (hierarchical), and so on.

- *Resources available to an organisation:* 1) industrial products; 2) agricultural products; 3) financial products; 4) commercial products; 5) educational services; 6) health services; 7) other resources; 8) customs; 9) conventions; 10) deep-seated values; and so on.

Thus *power-exercising behaviour is such behaviour that mobilises and transforms the resources into power energy that in turn generates power force in pursuit of goals in real-life discourses.* Everyday expressions such as

'Someone is very powerful', 'Zhang San is more powerful than Li Si', and so on. can be interpreted in two ways. One interpretation is made in terms of transformable resources. That is, to claim that 'Someone is very powerful' is interpreted as 'He/she has many resources, or some particular type of resource that can be transformed into powerful energy'. 'Zhang San is more powerful than Li Si' can be interpreted as the former has more transformable resources than the latter, or the former possesses some particular type of transformable resource that the latter lacks.

The other interpretation is made in terms of power-exercising behaviour. 'Being powerful' or 'more powerful than' will be construed as 'being skilful' or 'being more skilful in mobilising and transforming the resources into power energy'. These two interpretations are useful because they help distinguish those who possess transformable resources but do not make use or make only some limited use of them, from those who possess perhaps limited resources, but make the best out of them.

Strategies of power-exercising behaviour

Transformable power resources can be employed in various ways. The nature of power-generating resources, together with the manner in which they are being employed, define a power-exercising strategy. For instance, actor A gives actor B the money B needs. In return B helps achieve A's goal. We may call it *monetary strategy*. Actor A threatens to prevent actor B from accessing the desired resources unless B does what A demands. This can be called *coercive strategy*. Actor A may be extremely good at verbal skills and use them to persuade actor B to comply with his/her wishes. This can be called a *rhetorical strategy*. In the Chinese context, pupils are not supposed to dispute with or openly challenge their teacher, still less disobey him/her. The teacher seems to be given by custom or convention and by knowledge/ expertise a *dominance strategy* of exercising his/her role resource to achieve compliance.[2]

The concept of power-exercising strategy is fairly straightforward. It is an empirical matter to find out their total number and kinds.

Dynamic density of power-exercising behaviour

Power-exercising behaviour co-varies with actors and activities, that is, the variation with actors, and the variation with activities take place separately but simultaneously. The power-exercising strategy discussed above is one potential parameter of variation. The dynamic density is another important parameter. It can be assessed in terms of three attributes:

- *Extensiveness*: concerning the number of actors whose behaviour is affected by the power-exercising behaviour. For example, in a classroom activity the teacher's exercise of power may affect all students or only some of the students;
- *Comprehensiveness*: concerning the number of activities affected by the power-exercising behaviour;
- *Intensiveness*: concerning the number of options left open for the affected actors to choose from.[3]

The dynamic density of power-exercising behaviour can be used to classify discourses into types, for example from extremely high power density discourse to the least power density discourse, and with many intermediate ones in between. In the SCCSD, the meeting with the deputy prime minister is an example of extremely high power density discourse. The *extensiveness* is total, for all the participants' behaviour is affected; the *comprehensiveness* is complete: all the activities were carefully planned and executed; and the *intensiveness* is the widest: every move was scheduled to one minute accuracy without leaving any space for online negotiation.

Levels of power-exertion

Olsen (1993: 34–35) identifies three levels of 'power-exertion' as determined by its scope. The first level, often referred to as 'decision-making power', concerns the actors making decision and taking actions that affect others. The second level, often referred to as non-decision-making power, concerns the actors preventing decisions from being made or actions from being taken by others. The third highest level involves the power of agenda setting: some "actors shape the overall settings in which issues are defined and decisions are made and hence define the parameters for the exercise of power" (original italics removed).

Olsen's three levels of power-exertion are significant to discourse analysis. Although the distinctions are drawn primarily with the context of society as a whole in mind, they are equally applicable to 'mini-societies', such as a family, an organisation, a team, and so on. All the levels of power-exertion are mediated by discourse, and are all found in the SCCSD: there are situated discourses that are decision-making meetings, property owners protesting against the estate developers, and agenda-setting meetings.

A quick recap

Mainstream CDA focuses on the interaction between political/State power and discourse. The power is conceptualised in terms of dominance vs. subordination, control vs. struggle, and so on. I have argued for an alternative, namely conceptualisation of power in terms of mutual dependency relations between social agents, who mobilise and transform resources into power energy potential. In such conceptualisation, power is relational as well as dynamically relative to actors, goals and activities in question.

Situated discourse and power

The use of the terms *discourse, discourse analysis* and *text* invites problems and difficulties (see for example issues critically examined by Widdowson 2004, chapter 1 in particular). The best we can do here is to declare how they will be used in this chapter.

Language-in-action and situated discourse

"Discourse", writes Blommaert (2005: 2), "is language-in-action, and investigating it requires attention both to language and to action ..." I am on the same wavelength as Blommaert in extending discourse to include "all forms of meaningful semiotic human activity seen in connection with social, cultural, and historical patterns and developments of use". But I differ from Blommaert in my approach to this extended part of discourse. If his is semiotically oriented, mine is ecologically oriented. While both of us are interested in human activities, I am concerned with how human activities are first and foremost shaped by their ecological environments which include time, space, physical locale, body mobility, habitat, and the web of trajectories of our life path (see Gu 2002a, 2009, 2010, 2012). This leads to the notion of situated discourse.

The term *situated discourse* is used to refer to the face-to-face social interaction by real-life individual members of a speech community that takes place at a particular historical period of time and at a particular locale. It is 'discourse in flesh and blood' without abstraction. This is in contrast with the dominant research paradigm favouring abstraction, idealisation, and so on. In terms of human geography, it is a node on the web of the life-path trajectories of individual members who happen, by daily routine, by arrangement or by chance, to meet face-to-face. What is particularly pertinent to this chapter is the human agency of situated discourse. In whatever ways it is affected by power, by society, by ideology and so on, situated discourse is always conducted via face-to-face social interaction, by human agents. This holds true even in cases such as utterances performed by prisoners, who are deprived of some basic rights of a normal citizen.

In a word, situated discourse is always some people's discourse. It belongs to them in the following senses:

1) It is performed by them, that is, uttered by them in the case of verbal utterances, or carried out by them in the case of non-verbal 'utterances';

2) It is always associated with some capacity the actors possess and have activated while performing, such as age, gender, voice quality, emotion, social role, familial role, desired goals to achieve, and so on;

3) It is historically situated in the actors' temporal-spatial behaviour setting;

4) It is part of the actors' ongoing life activities.

These four qualities that 'belong' to situated discourse can easily be dismissed as performance contingencies, being too concrete to be of any value. My argument is this: such situated discourse is most of the time an essential part of daily routine activities, as Giddens observes:

> Time-space 'fixity' also normally means social fixity; the substantially 'given' character of the physical *milieux* of day-to-day life *interlaces with routine and is deeply influential in the contours of institutional reproduction.* (Giddens 1986: xxv; italics mine)

Giddens' "time-space 'fixity'" correlating with "social fixity" is captured in Barker (1968) as behaviour setting. "The routine (whatever is done habitually)", according to Giddens, "is a basic element of day-to-day social activity. ... The repetitiveness of activities which are undertaken in like manner day after day is the material grounding of what I call the recursive nature of social life" (Giddens 1986: xxiii).

Another important point associated with situated discourse is that, in situated discourse, it does not make much sense to say that discourse does this or that, or text does this or that, or power does this or that. *It is the discourse agents who do this or that.* In other words, text with a capital T or discourse with a capital D, or power with a capital P, if they have some effects on agents, and indeed they do, they do so through a process of individualisation and personalisation: *they are individualised and personalised by the acting agents. And through routinisation individualised and personalised practice of discourse not only reproduce, but also reshape the social life system, with power relations, of course, being a crucial part of the system.*

Power in situated discourse

As noted earlier, power is relational and relative, and it is defined in terms of mutual and reciprocal dependency relations between actors. This view of power fits perfectly well with the properties of situated discourse discussed above. In situated discourse, *power means a process in which actors mobilise and transform potential power resources into power energy to be spent in pursuit of goals*. This point is demonstrated below. Here a short illustration will serve our argument. My 11-year-old son once came to my study, saying: "Mum said I could watch TV after finishing my homework." My son had a goal that he would be allowed to watch TV. The attainment of his goal created a dependency relation with me, since I could transform my familial role of being his dad into power energy with which I could prevent him from attaining his goal. Being fully aware of my potential power energy, my son adopted a persuasive power-exercising strategy by mobilising and transforming Mum's authority to generate power energy that overpowered mine.

Agent, behaviour, eco-environment and affordance

Now we are ready to come to the very basics of situated discourse: 1) agent, 2) behaviour, 3) eco-environment and 4) affordance. The notion of agent has been demonstrated without being given a formal definition. I have adopted Giddens' conceptualisation of it. According to Giddens (1986: xxii–xxiii) a human agent has two essential qualities: knowledgeability and reflexivity:

> "Human agents or actors – I use these terms interchangeably [and so do I] – have, as an inherent aspect of what they do, the capacity to understand what they do while they do it. … What agents know about what they do, and why they do it – their knowledgeability *as* agents – is largely carried in practical consciousness. Practical consciousness consists of all the things which actors know tacitly about how to 'go on' in the contexts of social life without being able to give them direct discursive expression" (italics original).

Reflexivity, on the other hand, "should be understood not merely as 'self-consciousness' but as the monitored character of the ongoing flow of social life" (Giddens 1986: 3). "To be a human being", observes Giddens (1986: 3), "is to be a purposive agent, who both has reasons for his or her activities and is able, if asked, to elaborate discursively upon those reasons (including lying about them). … Human action occurs as a *durée*, a continuous flow of conduct, as does cognition."

Now let us look at the third basic term, eco-environment. It is adapted from Gibson's ecological theory of visual perception. Gibson uses *environment* to refer to the surroundings of animals, which include plants, inanimate things and of course other animals. Gibson emphasises that:

> [t]he fact is worth remembering because it is often neglected that the words *animal* and *environment* make an inseparable pair. Each term implies the other. No animal could exist without an environment surrounding it.
> (Gibson 1986: 8; italics original)

Gibson's conception of the animal/environment pair leads to an analysis of the animal's interaction with its environment and with other animals, in terms of affordance. In a dog's eye, the living room floor is a surface that affords him a surface on which he can behave in a certain way, such as walk or chase a cat. The same living room floor will offer a different affordance to a human animal. Hence the physical floor can be the same, but the dog's environment is certainly different from that of the human inhabitant. Elsewhere (Gu 2010: 460) I have used *ecological relativism* as a short-cut term to refer to Gibson's theory.

Gibson's ecological relativism, as spelt out in 1986, needs some amendments if it is applied seriously to the study of human animals and their environments. I have translated Gibson's affordance into two forms of potential behaviour of interaction: framing and enabling. That is, the environment both frames and enables the behaviour of the animal in question. The dog's behaviour in a living room is framed by the layout of the living room, and at the same time enabled by the layout. The human inhabitant's behaviour is equally framed and enabled by the living room. There is a limit which s/he cannot exceed, yet, while within that limit, s/he has the freedom to do certain things in the room.

Summary

Up to here we have attempted to restore power from its prototypical political arena to the mundane domain of everyday life activities, where mutual dependency relations for goal attainment are commonplace. The term *situated discourse* is used to refer to face-to-face social interaction, materialised in both verbal and non-verbal behaviours. In situated discourse, power is a process involving actors mobilising and transforming potential power resources into power energy in pursuit of their goals. Agents are part of one another's eco-environments, in which power-exercising behaviours both frame and enable agents' behaviours.

Modelling as a research methodology

Critical vs. modelling

Fairclough distinguishes between 'critical' and 'descriptive' goals in discourse analysis. "Adopting critical goals means aiming to elucidate" phenomena such as naturalisation of ideology in discourse, and "more generally to make clear social determinations and effects of discourse which are characteristically opaque to participants" (Fairclough 1995: 28). As mentioned earlier, the present study has adopted a hermeneutics of trust by treating everyday phenomenological reality as data, and has approached the data in three closely related stages: 1) knowledge construction (recall our definition of agent as knowledgeable and reflexive actor above), 2) modelling, and 3) simulation. The first stage can be put under Fairclough's descriptive category. The other two stages will go beyond it. The three stages in fact constitute the methodology found in Artificial Intelligence, that is, to understand the research object by building it (see Agre 1997: 10–11 for a review of it). Modelling plays a pivotal role in the building process.

The Chinese laymen's power-exercising behaviour in situated discourse is the research object we hope to understand by way of modelling. "A model", according to Blaha and Rumbaugh (2006: 15; italics mine), "*is an abstraction of something for the purpose of understanding it before building it.*" That is, the complexity of power-exercising behaviour can be analysed by modelling "a small number of important things to deal with at a time" (Blaha and Rumbaugh 2006: 16). What "a small number of important things" is depends on 1) the research objective and 2) the viewpoints from which the researcher looks at the system. Each 'important thing' in the system, being looked at from a particular perspective, constitutes a potential candidate for modelling. A set of models constructed for the complex system having been looked at from various perspectives will constitute an overall understanding of the system.

Elsewhere (Gu 2009) I have proposed conceiving of the world, real or unreal, as if it consists of agents of various kinds who interact with one another by way of exercising framing and enabling behaviours. It is a modelling metalanguage labelled as agent-oriented modelling (AOM for short).

The nature of agent construct

An agent in the AOM is a theoretical construct made to model an aspect of a real-life activity. It has two basic descriptors: attributes and behaviour.

Attributes are properties abstracted from the object of investigation *that are pertinent to the interaction of the agents involved*. For instance, we are not interested in all the attributes that a chair potentially possesses. We only abstract those attributes that are pertinent (e.g. to the approaching human agent who is pursuing the goal of sitting down on it) in order to achieve an even higher level of goals. In other words, attributes of agents are abstracted on the basis of the activity type and the goals that are being pursued by the agents (human or non-human). *Behaviour*, on the other hand, falls into two general types: *initiative* and *responsive*. In the real-life world, human agents prototypically will have both initiative and responsive behaviours, whereas non-human agents will exhibit responsive behaviour. In our modelling world, however, we can also construct non-human agents with the capacity of initiative behaviour (e.g. AI agents are given such capacity).

Power as mutual dependency and the AOM

Now we are ready to consider how power as mutual dependency relations fits into the picture. Emerson's formula Pab = Dba says that actor A's power over Actor B is determined by the extent to which actor B depends on actor A: whereas Pba = Dab says that actor B's power over actor A is determined by the extent to which actor A depends on actor B. In the ecological model, Emerson's reciprocal mutual dependency relation is reinterpreted in terms of mutually framing and enabling effects on each other's behaviour. In Emerson, actor A depending on B for the pursuit of the former's goal G generates actor B's power over actor A. This power relation, namely B's power over actor A, is dealt with, in the ecological model, in terms of actor B's framing and enabling effects on actor A's behaviour in pursuit of his goal G. Actor A's power over actor B will be dealt with in similar fashion. Emerson's theory is hence considerably enriched by the ecological model in that both actors A and B bring fresh resources to generate their own power energy to effect the power relationship as defined by Emerson. Note that the power energy freshly generated does not 'smuggle in' a new definition of power. The fresh power energy generates in essence new mutual dependency relations.

Figure 6.1 shows the two generic agent constructs representing the power dependency relation between actors A and B.

It is important to note that, although actors A and B in Figure 6.1 are generically speaking the same, their interactions in situated discourse will never be the same. For actor A's engagement with actor B generates an environment for each. Actor A's environment (with actor B as part of it) is different from actor B's environment (with actor A as part of it). They are different because the resources, strategies, framing and enabling functions

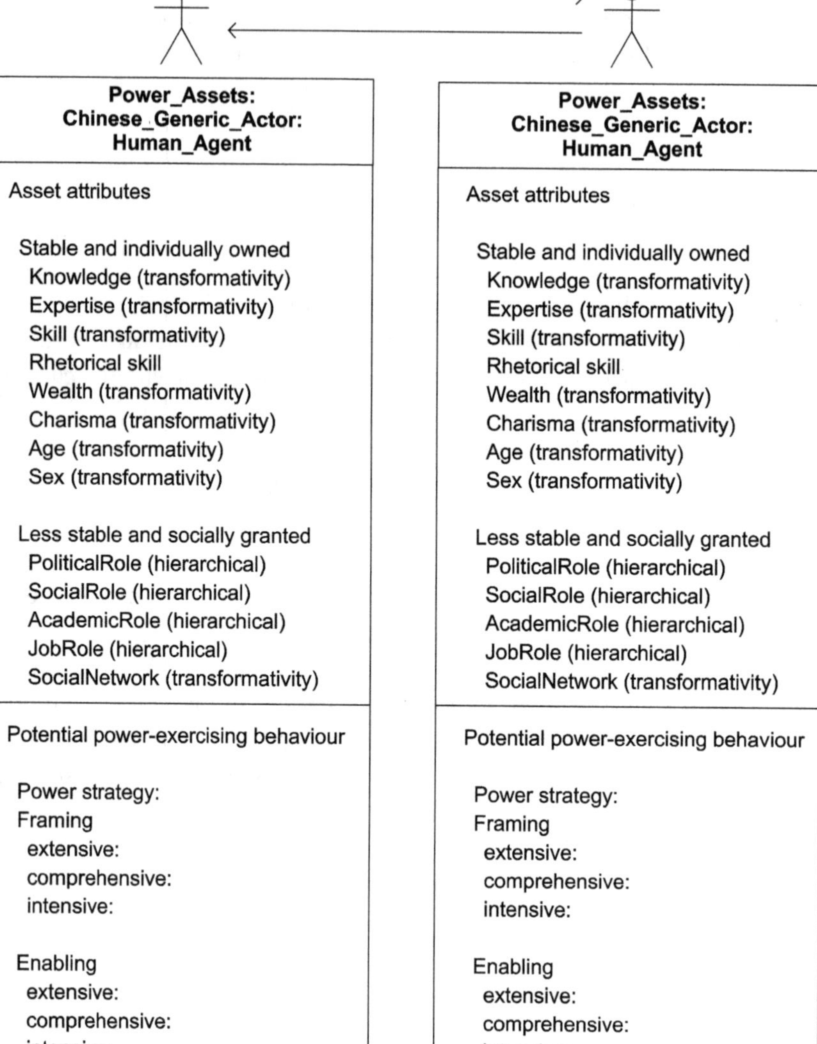

Figure 6.1 Two generic agent constructs

that are activated for instances of situated discourse are always different from each other.

Research procedure and meta-models

Agent construct is the key meta-language with which power-exercising behaviours of human agents can be modelled. The modelling uses a visual representation adapted from the UML (i.e. unified modelling language), and follows an iterative research procedure. The major advantage of using the modelling methodology is that the original data in real-life situated discourses get mined in a structured manner and achieve a high degree of computer processibility. Readers interested in knowing details of the research procedure and meta-models are referred to Gu (2009).

A case study: the Min Dialect Dictionary Launching Symposium

It is time to demonstrate the understanding of power-exercising behaviour by way of modelling. The sample is the Min Dialect Dictionary Launching Symposium held in Beijing on 8 February 2007, which was attended by 40 participants from 1) branches of central and local governments; 2) universities and research institutes; 3) publishers; and 4) the mass media. The whole process was videotaped, digitalised, and put to detailed analysis by using ELAN, an application that enables us to segment and annotate the video streams to millisecond accuracy.

Background of the situated discourse

Some background information about this situated discourse is in order. The Min dialect is one of the major dialects in China, widely spoken mainly in Fujian and Taiwan Provinces. The dictionary is compiled by the Min dialectologists, mainly from Xiamen University, and published by the Fujian People's Press. The fact that the publisher organised a launching symposium to publicise its dictionary is quite a normal practice. What makes this case particularly interesting to a discourse analyst is twofold. First, some linguists/ separatists campaigning for Taiwan independence argue that Min spoken in Taiwan is historically unrelated to Min spoken in Fujian. Second, the symposium venue was placed not in Xiamen, but in a much more costly city, Beijing. These two features have charged the launching activity with some extra political significance.

Since I have no access to the decision-making discourse – an important power-exercising behaviour – conducted by the organiser, I cannot comment on how and why these organisations/institutions and their representatives were chosen.

Modelling practice

Modelling practice in the AOM requires the spelling-out of 1) the research object/domain; 2) the viewpoints from which the object will be analysed;

3) the theoretical lenses, through which the object is to be analysed; and
4) the package structure of meta-models.

The research object, as alluded to above, is the power-exercising behaviour as found in the aforesaid symposium. It is modelled from three perspectives: 1) the perspective of the social system, as a piece of the current Chinese political-social-cultural behaviour; 2) the perspective of the organiser, as an organised collective behaviour; and 3) the perspective of participants, as an aggregate of individual participants' behaviours. Correspondingly, three generic agent constructs will be made:

1) System_Agent (Agent_sys for short);
2) Organising_Agent, (Agent_org for short);
3) Participant_Agent (Agent_act for short).

The theoretical lenses refer to the active assumptions the discourse analyst holds while the research object is being modelled from a particular perspective. In the current case, the active assumptions I hold include the following:

1) The behaviours of all the parties (i.e. the social system, the organisers and the individual participants) are goal-directed.
2) They all depend on one another's support in pursuit of their separate goals.
3) The situated discourse brings the three types of actors together in pursuit of shared as well as collaborative goals, thus engaging them in power-exercising behaviours between them.
4) They all have their own resources at their own disposal and can be mobilised to generate power energies to be expended in goal-directed discourse.

The package structure of meta-models, that is, agent constructs that are structured systematically to make an overall picture about the research object, is based on Giddens' structuration theory. As shown in Figure 6.2, situated discourses, as represented by the aforesaid symposium, are ongoing, continuous lived experiences of everyday life. They are the primary activities, being routinised and recursive, on which social systems/structures are produced, reproduced and maintained over space and time – the essential ingredient of Giddens' structuration theory. In the present chapter, situated discourses are also analysed as the interface bridging individuals and institutions/organisations. In other words, individuals' power-exercising behaviours, if targeted at an institution/organisation, are to be mediated through situated discourses. The reverse is also true – the institution/ organisation exercises its power via the mediation of situated discourses. The power of individuals is, in the final analysis, derivative, that is, derived from the situated discourses they are engaged in.[4]

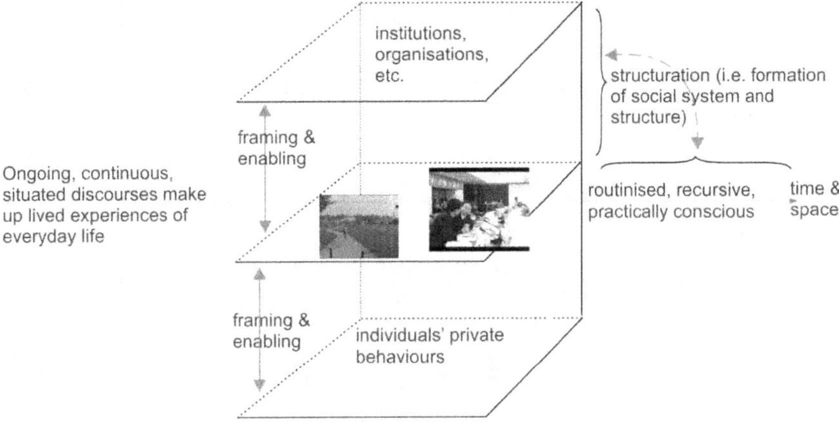

Figure 6.2 Modelling package and Giddens' theory of structuration

It would take enormous space to spell out the whole modelling package, which is not possible or necessary for the current purpose. Instead, some highlights are presented below.

Modelling the organisers' power-exercising behaviour

Analysis: The participants fall into two general categories: organisers, and non-organisers who are the goal mediators of the organisers. The organisers comprise the publishers and the dictionary compilers and, since they pursue joint goals, they have been treated in the previous text as a collective participant (Agent_org). On the other hand the non-organisers (goal-mediating participants) break into three types: political, academic and mass media. So from the organisers' perspective, there are three pairs of interaction, hence three pairs of power relations: organisers with 1) political mediators, 2) academic mediators, and 3) media mediators. They enter into power relations with the organisers because they depend on these three group mediators to achieve their own goals. That is, the three group mediators have power over the organisers. In order to make things happen, the organisers have to make the goal mediators depend on them. That is, they have to adopt appropriate power-exercising strategies – ways of mobilising and deploying power-transformable resources to generate enough power energy.

I have no direct access to the information about how the organisers designed their power-exercising strategies. For example, I have no information about how the organisers reached the two high-ranking politicians and made them accept the invitation. The only direct information

I have is about how I myself was invited, and why I accepted it. I was approached by a retired colleague of mine, who happened to be a good friend of the chief compiler. The mobilisation of contact persons in Beijing must be the organisers' important power-exercising strategy. In my own case, the organisers' power over me is generated through my dependence on my colleague for face maintenance and friendship renewal.[5] And my colleague, in turn, has dependence on the chief compiler for reasons I am unaware of. In my own case, the organisers have an extra power over me because I depend on them for a free copy of the dictionary!

Modelling: The modelling of the organisers' power-exercising behaviour consists of two phases: the power-exercising strategy and the activation of the power-transformable resources possessed by the three types of mediators. The modelling diagram is shown in Figure 6.3.

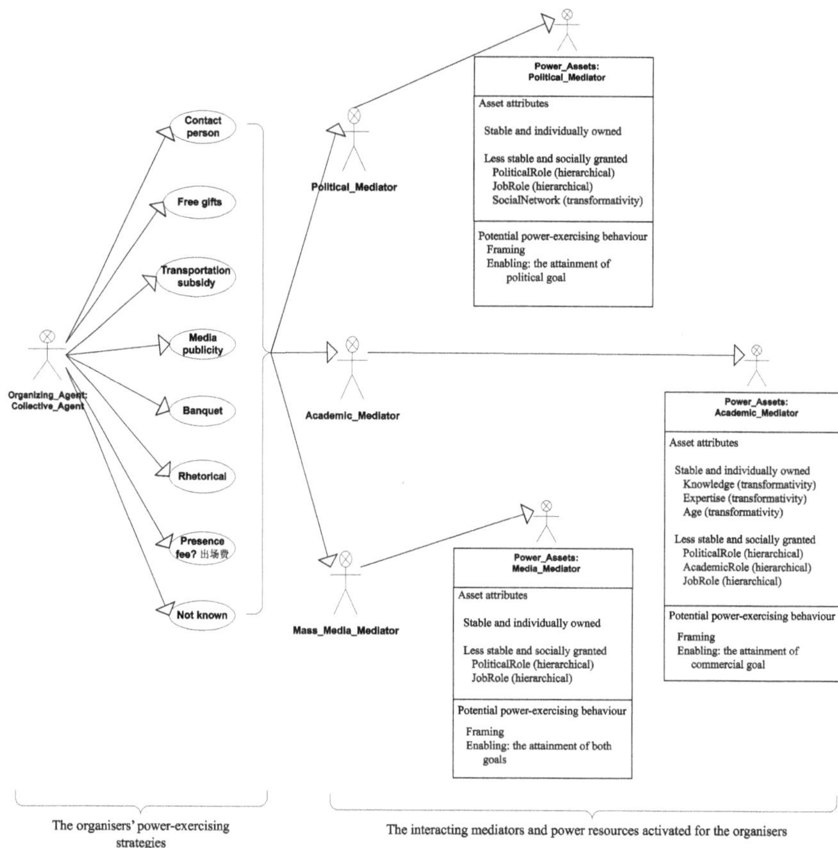

Figure 6.3 The organisers' power-exercising strategies and mediators' power resources

Modelling the goal-attaining process

Analysis: There is a stereotypical type of goal associated with dictionary-launching discourse, namely to publicise it so as to promote its sale. In the present case, there is an extra goal, a politically motivated one, namely to show the world that the Min dialect in Taiwan is historically derived from Fujian Min dialect, designed to counter-argue against the position held by some Taiwan dialectologists. The organisers therefore simultaneously pursue two goals, a commercial goal and a political goal. The attainment of the two goals requires the mediation of three types of participants, as shown above, namely the political, academic and mass media.

In the actual goal-attaining process, there were some pre-start activities, and a follow-up lunch banquet. The symposium proper lasted 164 minutes. The first 41 minutes were given to speeches by government officers. The remaining time was given to academics and mass media representatives. So the symposium was divided into two parts: the political part dedicated to the pursuit of the political goal, and the academic part to the pursuit of the commercial goal.

There are eight points that are particularly pertinent to the theme of this chapter.

1) In the political part, there were two politicians, Mr Luo and Mr Zhang, both deputy chairmen of the National People's Consultancy Congress, who were present only but did not say anything. There were five government officers, much lower in rank than the two politicians, who read their speeches. A recently retired government officer of ministerial rank sent her written speech which was read on her behalf. This part was very carefully planned in advance. The order of speeches was arranged according to the officers' rank. All but one of the speeches commenced by addressing the two senior politicians with the formula "Respectable + Surname + (Deputy) Chairman" (尊敬的 + 姓（名）（副）主席).

2) The academic part, in contrast, was given little advanced planning. After the presider declared that the floor was open to volunteers, all the turn-taking afterwards was self-selecting.

3) The mass media crew were busying themselves in the first part, but most of them left in the second part.

4) The coverage of the symposium by official mass media reported the presence of the two politicians with their names and titles. The academics were reported anonymously except for the chief compiler.

5) The politicians and government officers all left in the second part of the symposium with the excuse that they were too busy with their jobs to stay any longer.

6) It seems that the academics were only too happy to see the back of the politicians and government officers.

7) The speeches by government officers were categorised as *zhishi* (指示, instructions), the chief compiler's speech as *huibao* (汇报, reports), whereas the talks by academics as *fayan* (发言, talks). *Zhishi* implies that the speaker and the addressee hold a superior-to-inferior relationship; *huibao* implies that the speaker is inferior to the addressee; *fayan* signals a neutral value.

8) Although the academic part had no planned schema, and the floor was declared by the presider to be on a volunteering basis, a pattern of floor-taking according to seniority and closeness to the chief compiler emerged, that is, those senior white-headed academics or the chief compiler's former classmates 'volunteered' to speak. The younger black-headed academics knew their places, and 'volunteered' to be listeners.

Modelling: The political goal attaining process is modelled in Figure 6.4a, which can be contrasted with the model of the commercial goal-attaining process shown in Figure 6.4b.

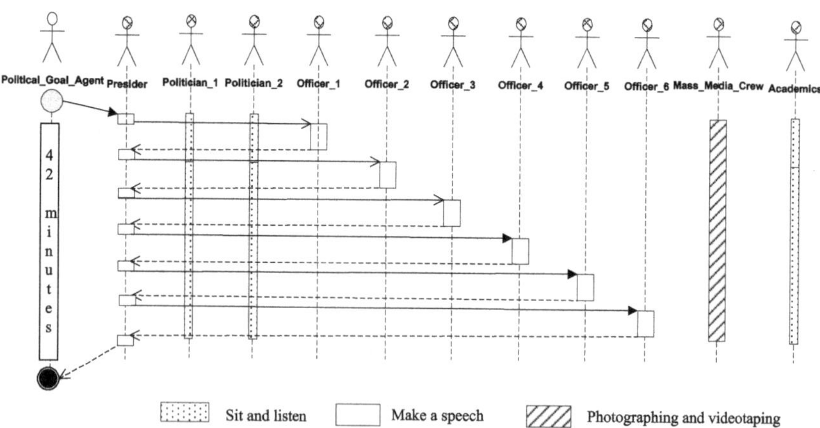

Figure 6.4a Political goal-attaining process

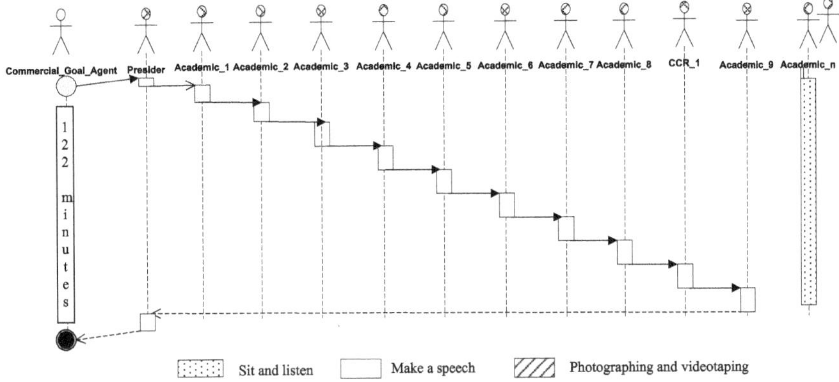

Figure 6.4b Commercial goal-attaining process

The differences in the interactive patterns of the two goal-attaining processes are clearly represented in the two figures. The presider in Figure 6.4a had strict control of turn-taking, while in Figure 6.4b all he did was declare the discussion open and closed.

A final note: readers may have little doubt that to the organisers the political goal was seen as far more important than the commercial goal. Its importance, however, does not match the time allocated to its attaining process – the commercial goal-attaining process lasted much longer than the political goal-attaining process. This seeming discrepancy between the importance and the time resource allocation can easily be explained. A political process is different from, say, a teaching process. In the former 'who is there' – just being present – tends to carry far more weight than any other factors, while in the latter the length of the process can play a decisive role in the outcome. Furthermore, in this case, the academics, and perhaps also the organisers, were killing time with free talks before the free lunch/banquet (literally) arrived.

Modelling individual participants' behaviour

In situated discourse, the relationship between the individual and the system is ideological. This holds true even for those who are the personae of the system, such as policemen, government officers, and so on. When an individual enters into a behaviour setting, s/he interacts ideologically with the system by accepting, or rejecting, or re-adjusting the behaviour pattern associated with the setting. The power relation only emerges between individuals who are engaged in interaction in pursuit of goals. Recall that job relation, familial relation, etc. do not generate power relation. They are *power-generating resources*, that is, they can be mobilised and transformed into power energy. It is the interpersonal goal relation that generates interpersonal power relation.

Now with those relationships in mind we are ready to model the symposium from the participant's perspective.

Analysis: The symposium is a node on the web of the life trajectories of 40 individuals, who converged at the symposium venue from two geographical locations: Xiamen, Fujian Province and Beijing. The convergence marks the commencement of power relations between the participants on the one hand, and the organisers on the other. The dispersion of the participants terminates the engagement of power relations.

Notice the power balance changing as the symposium proceeds. In the beginning the participants have more power than the organisers, for the latter depend more on the former's efforts in mediating the latter's goal attainment. By the end, this dependency diminishes to nil, and the balance of power reaches a state of equilibrium.

There are two points that smack of something particularly Chinese. Firstly, power is best understood and exercised without being openly talked about. What is to be talked about instead is *mianzi* (面子) or *lian* (脸). The presence of the two deputy chairmen, for example, is acknowledged and talked about in terms of *gei mianzi* (给面子, literally meaning 'give face' to the organisers). The symposium is consequently 'uplifted' to a very high level (*shang dangci*, 上当次).

Secondly, the equilibrium of power relationships at the end of the interaction does not mean that the interpersonal relationships have also reached an equilibrium. Either party may end up in positive debt, known as *renqing* (人情), or in negative debt, an offence known as *dezuiren* (得罪人) in Chinese. Take my own case for example. By the end of the symposium, my power energy over the organisers was exhausted. Their power energy over me – generated through friendship, recognition of my status, gifts, transportation subsidy, and a banquet – is considered by me as more or less equal to the power energy of mine. So I don't feel I owed *renqing* to the organisers. Nor do I feel offended, in spite of the fact that I was designated to a corner seat on the second row! This is because I know 'my place' relative to the rest of the participants. I had no resources to generate political power, as the politicians and government officers did. Nor did I have resources to generate mass media power, as the mass media crew did. The power energy I was able to generate was a kind of academic power, but not as strong as that of my fellow academics, for I am not an expert of the Min dialect! Had I been offered a handsome *chuchang fei* (出场费, fee for being present), I certainly would have owed the organisers a *renqing*.

Modelling: The highly abstract relationships discussed above can in theory be modelled, but it would take a great deal of space to work it out. I will instead focus on modelling the participants' behavioural contributions.

Generic participation diagram

Let us first make an agent construct for generic participation, Generic Participation_Agent (Agent_gp). The Agent_gp has three higher-level acts:{converge, attend, disperse}. The attend-act in turn has its own high-level sub-acts: (pre-activity, positioning, contributing, post-activity). The acts of positioning and contributing are fine-grained into sub-sub-acts. Figure 6.5 shows the modelling diagram.

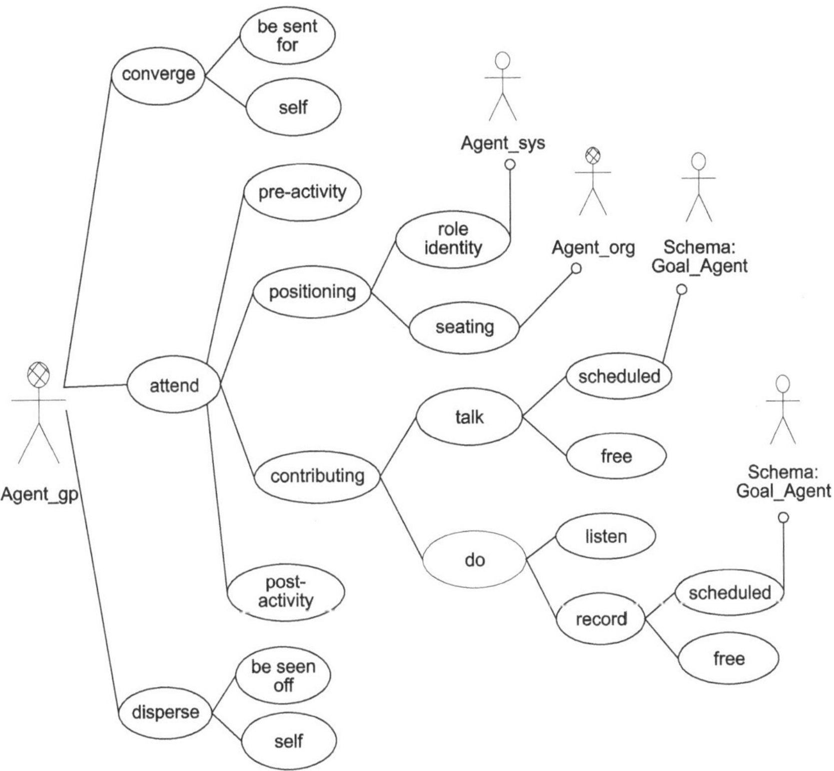

Figure 6.5 Generic participation diagram

It is important to note that Figure 6.5 includes *interface-nodes* indicating the interactions between agent constructs.

Modelling individuals

In modelling, the agent construct for individual participation inherits the generic participation framework, with modifications made to capture the individual characteristics. Three agent constructs for individual participation are demonstrated in Figures 6.6a–c.

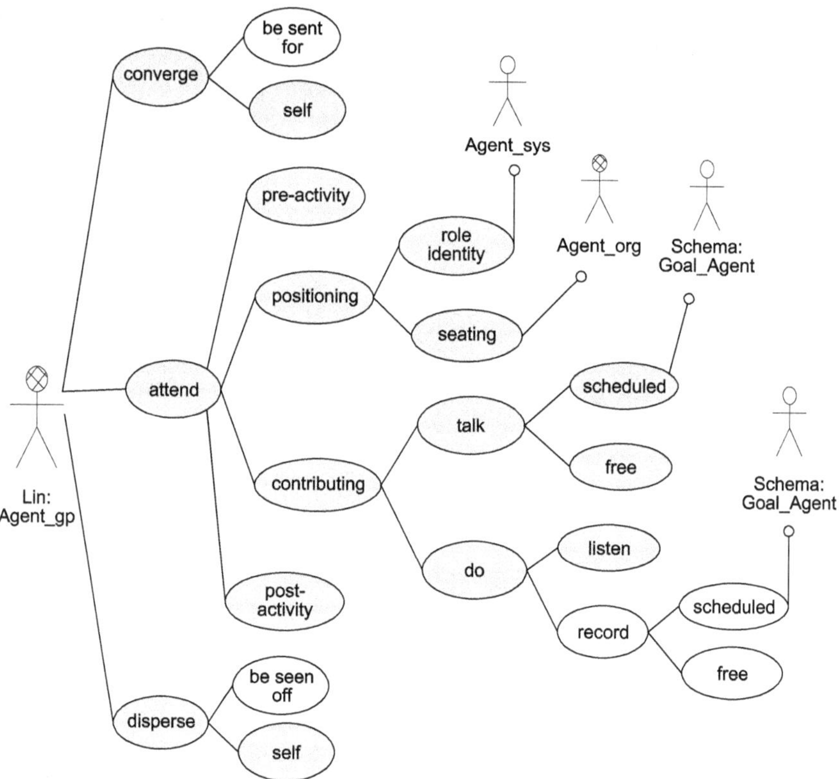

Figure 6.6a Behaviour configuration map for Lin: Participation_Agent

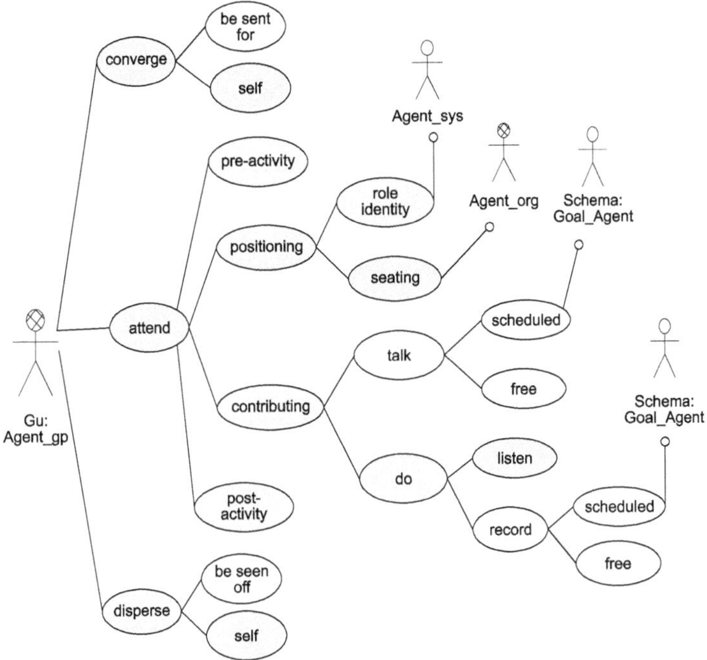

Figure 6.6b Behaviour configuration map for Gu: Participation_Agent

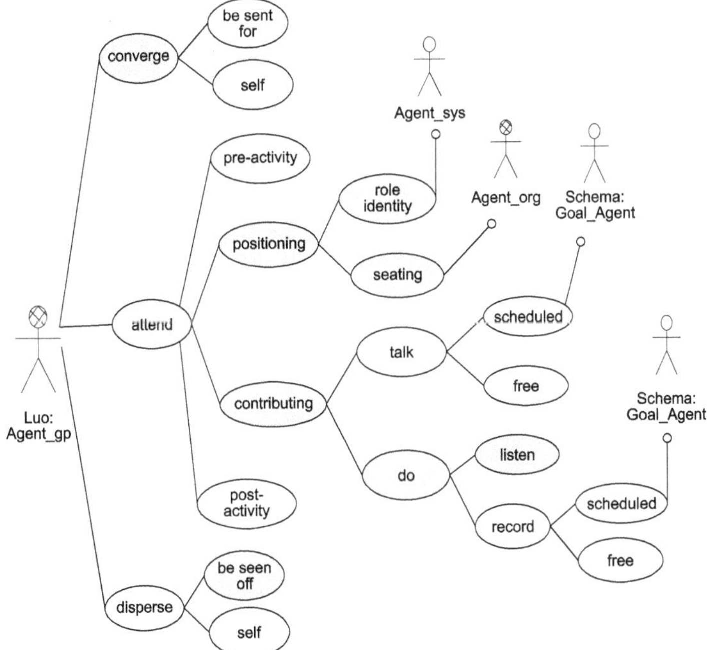

Figure 6.6c Behaviour configuration map for Luo: Participation_Agent

The following points are worth noting.

1) Figure 6.6c is the model showing the behavioural configuration of Luo, the deputy chairman, the highest ranked political figure in the symposium. The number of grey-highlighted ovals is much fewer than for the other two participants, but Luo has a feature that the other two do not have, namely he was sent for and seen off!

2) Figure 6.6b (modelling Gu) looks very similar to Figure 6.6a (modelling Lin). However, in Gu's model, the ovals for the scheduled talk and the free talk are not highlighted, as they are in Lin's model. Although in Gu's model, he has an extra highlighted oval, record, but it was not scheduled, that is, not on the official schema. It was self-initiated!

3) The first two points remind us of two crucial messages: (a) what is not present is equally important as what is absent; (b) the overall configuration of what is present against the background of what is absent carries a real message for power relation analysis concerning individual participants.

Implications and future research

Up to this point, we have carried out two main tasks. First, departing from the mainstream CDA notions of power (i.e. class power, State power, political power, etc.), we have argued for the adoption of Emerson's notion of 'power as mutual dependency relation', which is fundamental to human interaction in general, for humans depend on one another for survival. Our major goal has been to transform 'power as mutual dependency relation' into *a set of operational attributes* (i.e. assets that can be turned into power energy), and *behaviours* (i.e. framing and enabling the interacting actors) that are contingently activated and made use of in situated discourses. The transformation is primarily based on Gibson's ecological relativism and Giddens' structuration theory.

Our second task was to make the attributes and behaviours operational, which can be achieved by using the modelling methodology, specifically the AOM. To Figures 6.3–6.6, technically called *agent construct diagrams*, appear to be similar to the tree diagrams found in a generative grammar in terms of visualising concepts and relations. However, they differ from the latter in that the AOM diagrams are to the UML and Java (i.e. an object-oriented programming language in software engineering). In other words, the AOM diagrams can easily be translated into Java so that the attributes and behaviours can be 'computed' by the computer.

In a sense the first task was implemented more satisfactorily than the second, the full implementation of which requires a simulation application to show that the modelling actually works. As observed above, the simulation part goes far beyond the scope of the present chapter. This does not mean that readers cannot critically evaluate the AOM modelling practice by themselves. On this point we agree with Gilbert and Conte (1995: 2), who have made pioneering efforts in computer simulation of social life:

> Once the process of modelling has been accomplished, the model achieves a substantial degree of autonomy. It is an entity in the world and, as much as any other entity, it is worthy of investigation. Models are not only necessary instruments for research, they are themselves also legitimate objects of enquiry.

Finally, it is hoped that what has been outlined and demonstrated in this chapter, although only Chinese data were cited, is applicable to power and its discourse in other social-political-cultural contexts. The potential applicability to broader contexts is derived from three aspects: 1) Emerson's notion of power as mutual dependency relation (discussed above in Emerson's theory of power) is generic and ubiquitous; 2) our re-formulation of Emerson's power in terms of resources and transformation has not altered the essence of his conceptualisation, but made it operational; and 3) the AOM, though designed by us, is based on Gibson's ecological relativism, which we think is quite universal. Having said this, there are some features which are assumed to be culture-specific, notably 1) resources transformable to power energy, and 2) power-exercising strategies that are bound to vary from one culture to another.

Notes

1. An institution has a power potential, but it is embodied by the role incumbent. For instance, university is a higher education institution. It is embodied by many role incumbents such as Peking University and Tsinghua University among others.
2. Note that the teacher's dominance is derived from such power-generating resources as custom/convention and knowledge/expertise. It is treated as a strategy here since it is up to teachers to employ the resources or leave them dormant.
3. The three attributes are inspired by Wrong's (1993: 14) analysis of power resistance.

4. Private behaviours such as those carried out in private rooms, in our analysis, have no impact on the social system/structure. They have to be mediated via public channels such as situated discourse, to have any impact at all. This view is in complete harmony with our view of power as mutual dependency relation.
5. It is almost a standard practice for publishers to give free copies to participants of symposiums of this kind. In my own case, the organisers have an extra power over me because I depend on them for a free copy of the dictionary!

References

Agre, P. E. (1997) *Computation and Human Experience.* Cambridge: Cambridge University Press.

Barker, R. G. (1968) *Ecological Psychology: Concepts and Methods for Studying the Environment of Human Behaviour.* Stanford: Stanford University Press.

Blaha, M. and Rumbaugh, J. (2006) *Object-Oriented Modeling and Design with UML.* Beijing: Posts and Telecom Press.

Blommaert, J. (2005) *Discourse: A Critical Introduction.* Cambridge: Cambridge University Press.

Emerson, R. M. (1993) Power-dependence relations. In M. Olsen and M. N. Marger (eds) *Power in Modern Societies* 48–58. Boulder, CO: Westview Press, Inc.

Etzioni, A. (1993) Power as a societal force. In M. Olsen and M. N. Marger (eds) *Power in Modern Societies* 18–28. Boulder, CO: Westview Press, Inc.

Fairclough, N. (1995 [1985]) *Critical Discourse Analysis.* London: Longman.

Fairclough, N. (1998 [1992]) *Discourse and Social Change.* Cambridge: Polity Press.

Fairclough, N. (2001) *Language and Power.* 2nd ed. Harlow: Longman.

Gibson, J. J. (1986) *The Ecological Approach to Visual Perception.* Hillsdale, NJ: Lawrence Erlbaum Associates.

Giddens, A. (1986) *The Constitution of Society.* Berkeley, CA: University of California Press.

Gilbert, N. and Conte, R. (eds) (1995) *Artificial Societies: The Computer Simulation of Social Life.* London: UCL Press Limited.

Grillo, E. (ed.) (2005) *Power Without Domination.* Amsterdam: John Benjamins.

Gu, Y. (2001) The changing orders of discourse in a changing China. In H. Pan (ed.) *Studies in Chinese Linguistics*, Vol. 2, 31–58. Hong Kong: Linguistics Society of Hong Kong.

Gu, Y. (2002a) Towards an understanding of workplace discourse. In C. N. Candlin (ed.) *Research and Practice in Professional Discourse* 137–185. Hong Kong: The City University of Hong Kong Press.

Gu, Y. (2002b) Sampling and representativeness in compiling Chinese Spoken Corpus of Situated Discourse in the Beijing area (北京地区现场即席话语语料库的取样与代表性问题) 载于《全球化与 21 世纪》 In *Globalization and the 21st Century* 484–500. Beijing: Social Sciences Publisher.

Gu, Y. (2006) Multimodal text analysis: A corpus linguistic approach to situated discourse. *Text & Talk* 26: 127–167.

Gu, Y. (2009) From the real-life situation to video stream data-mining. *International Journal of Corpus Linguistics* 14: 433–66.

Gu, Y. (2010) The activity type as interface between langue and parole, and between individual and society. *Pragmatics and Society* 1: 74–101.

Gu, Y. (2012) Discourse geography. In J. P. Gee and M. Hanford, (eds) *The Routledge Handbook of Discourse Analysis*, 541–557. London: Routledge.

Hodge, R. and Kress, G. (1993) *Language as Ideology.* 2nd ed. London: Routledge.

Lenski, G. E. (1993) Power and distributive systems. In M. Olsen and M. N. Marger (eds) *Power in Modern Societies* 59–67. Boulder, CO: Westview Press, Inc.

Olsen, M. and Marger, M. N. (eds) (1993) *Power in Modern Societies.* Boulder, CO: Westview Press, Inc.

Olsen, M. E. (1993) Forms and levels of power exertion. In M. Olsen and M. N. Marger (eds) *Power in Modern Societies* 29–36. Boulder, CO: Westview Press, Inc.

Scannell, P. (1998) Media – language – world. In A. Bell and P. Garrett (eds) *Approaches to Media Discourse* 251–268. Oxford: Blackwell Publishers.

Van Dijk, T. A. (1988) *News as Discourse.* Hillsdale, NJ: Laurence Erlbaum Associates.

Van Dijk, T. A. (1993) *Elite Discourse and Racism.* Newbury Park, CA: Sage Publications.

Widdowson, H. G. (2004) *Text, Context, Pretext: Critical Issues in Discourse Analysis.* Oxford: Blackwell Publishing.

Wodak, R. (ed.) (1989) *Language, Power and Ideology.* Amsterdam: John Benjamins.

Wrong, D. (1993) Problems in defining power. In M. Olsen and M. N. Marger (eds) *Power in Modern Societies* 9–17. Boulder, CO: Westview Press, Inc.

7

'Face' in Taiwanese business interactions: From emic concepts to emic practices

Wei-Lin Melody Chang and Michael Haugh

Introduction

'Face' in the figurative sense of a positive social image, honour, prestige or good reputation is often closely associated with feelings of pride and satisfaction or, alternatively, embarrassment and humiliation. It is perhaps for this reason that it has been extensively studied and theorised over the past few decades, being increasingly applied to the analysis of communication and social interaction in a variety of disciplines. Yet while face has become firmly established as a means of explaining various social phenomena including politeness, impoliteness and offence, impression management, conflict management and the like (e.g. Arundale 2006; Bousfield 2008; Brown and Levinson 1987; Goffman 1967; Ting-Toomey 1988, 2005), it has also been long associated with East Asians, particularly the Chinese. This is not surprising as the use of face in both folk and academic discourse can be traced back to the Chinese term *mian* (originally meaning 'front of the head', and later being extended to mean 'surface' and 'appearance') (Haugh 2005: 213–215). Indeed, numerous studies of face in Chinese have appeared, many of which focus on explicating the notions of *mianzi* and *lian* and their related collocations, as these are invariably embedded in folk and academic discourse about Chinese language, culture and social practice (e.g. Gao 1998, 2009; Hinze 2005; Ho 1976, 1994; Hu 1944; Mao 1994; Yu 2003). These studies have largely drawn from analyses of metapragmatic data where cultural insiders describe *mianzi* and *lian* directly, or use these terms in discourse to describe particular incidents. Most studies of Chinese face have thus taken a largely emic perspective where they attempt to explicate the concepts of *mianzi* and *lian* "in terms of the conceptual schemes and categories regarded as meaningful and appropriate by native members of the culture whose beliefs and behaviours are being studied" (Lett 1990:130). In other words, these explications of the emic concepts of face are ultimately based on how people ordinarily talk about and conceptualise particular interpersonal and social aspects of what they are doing.

However, while studies of emic concepts of face have shed considerable light on Chinese culture and social practice, they do not necessarily help us better understand how face actually arises in the first place. As Arundale (2008) argues, "talk about how face is created does not itself create face" (note 1, p. 11). Instead, face emerges as contingent interpretings and evaluations of actions and meanings in interactions, which in most cases are not explicitly commented upon by participants. Consequently, in order to further our understanding of face in Chinese, we need to make recourse to actual interactional or discourse data. There have been, however, relatively few studies of face in Chinese from a discourse perspective that closely analyse how face is interactionally managed and achieved in actual Chinese social interactions (Chen 1990/1991; Pan 2000; Su 2009; Yang 2010). While emic concepts of face in Chinese have received considerable attention in the literature thus far, emic practices, whereby participants can be observed to be demonstrably orienting to and interactionally achieving face through particular linguistic and non-linguistic behaviour, have been relatively neglected by analysts.

The distinction between emic concepts and emic practices is made here because while we might expect some level of correspondence between particular emic face practices and their reflexive emic conceptualisations, they are ultimately of a different type or order of analysis.[1] While emic practices are recognisable to cultural insiders, they are recognisable through their doing in interaction, and so are not always explicated in folk ideologies of face. As Arundale (2008: 3) goes on to argue:

> [n]ot all emic practices are necessarily part of a culture's emic conceptualisation of face, and there are likely to be aspects of the emic conceptualisation that have no counterpart in the explanation of emic practices.

Since explicating emic concepts and emic practices involves a different order of analysis, conflating them introduces unnecessary conceptual confusion into our theorising of face. We therefore argue that, although emic concepts of face should inform the theorising of face, they are not in themselves a suitable basis for constructing a more general theory of face (Haugh 2009: 5). Instead, as Arundale (2006) argues, a theory of face should be framed by analysts as an explanatory set of concepts and principles that are sensitive to culture-specific construals of what is ultimately a culture-general phenomenon. In this chapter, it is proposed that face be examined through the lens of a pragmatics informed by methods and research in conversation and discourse analysis, in an attempt to adequately ground the ensuing interactional analysis in the perspective(s) of the participants, rather than imposing an etic framework that distorts or misrepresents how face is interactionally achieved (Arundale 2010; Chang and Haugh 2011; Haugh 2009, 2010; Haugh and Bargiela-Chiappini 2010). In doing so, we argue that research about face moves from a singular focus on emic concepts such as *mianzi* and *lian* to an approach that also considers emic face practices, in particular, how face arises in actual interactional discourse.

This chapter opens by first discussing the data and methodology which are employed in the subsequent analysis of emic face concepts and practices in Taiwanese business interactions. It is suggested that operationalising the distinction between emic concepts and practices requires recourse to different approaches to analysing discourse. This is followed by the analytical section which is divided into two parts. In the first part, transcripts of ethnographic interviews with business people are carefully examined to investigate how native informants of Taiwanese Chinese conceptualise face when doing business, drawing from these informants' knowledge and experiences in relation to face. These findings are related to previous research on Chinese face, highlighting the significance of the ways in which *mianzi* is conceptualised, in particular, in business settings. This analysis thus contributes to our understanding of what Taiwanese business people *say* about face, or what we have termed here emic face concepts. An analysis of the interactional achievement of face in an extended audiovisual recording of an authentic business negotiation then provides insight into how face may be strategically threatened in interaction, reflecting an example of what we have termed here emic face practices. This is followed by a brief consideration of the implications of this analysis for the role of theorising face in the analysis of discourse and social phenomena, more generally, and for future research on face in Chinese-speaking societies, in particular.

Data and methodology

We draw from two types of data in the analysis that follows. The first data set consists of 11 ethnographic interviews conducted with native informants who have an association with a particular insurance company in Taiwan. The informants were approached through the social network of the researchers' main contact in that company. They were asked if they would be willing to be interviewed on the topic of human communication in business. The audio recordings of these 11 interviews ranged from 12 to 30 minutes long. Five of the interviewees work in the insurance company, while the remaining six interviewees are clients of that company.[2] These clients all have their own businesses in that city in Taiwan. All of the interviews were conducted either in the insurance company itself or in the workplaces of the clients. The data from these ethnographic interviews were first directly transcribed from the audio recordings, and then all of the transcriptions were translated from Taiwanese/ Mandarin into English. The participants were interviewed in relation to their understandings of face (*mianzi*), in order to explore the concept of *mianzi* in business settings from the perspective of native speakers. A list of questions asked during the interview can be found in Appendix 1.

An interpretive approach was employed in analysing the ethnographic interview data. After repeated listenings to the audio recordings and examination of the transcripts, notes identifying key informant under-standings of *mianzi* were made. Four salient themes emerged upon careful examination of these notes, with sections from the interviews which best represented those themes then being identified. In order to contextualise this interpretive process, these emergent themes were carefully analysed as jointly formed understandings, which reflect the particular footings of the interviewer and interviewee that are interactionally achieved at those points in the interviews (Potter and Hepburn 2005). As Pan (2008, see also Pan in this volume) argues, interviews are interactional settings in and of themselves, where potential offence or face threats may arise although, in the case of these ethnographic interviews, this problem was somewhat alleviated by the existence of a social network between the researcher's main contact and the interviewees. These themes are discussed in further detail below, in the section *Emic face concepts*.

The second data set consists of audiovisual recordings of naturally occurring interactions between one agent from the insurance company and his various clients. Twenty-two interactions, ranging from 30 seconds to 35 minutes long, were recorded. The amount of audiovisual data recorded overall was approximately two hours. All of the participants in the recordings were the main participant's clients, with the interactions taking place either in the clients' homes or in their workplaces when the agent went to pass on the renewal forms for insurance, collect insurance fees, or deal with insurance cases. These interactions were all randomly selected. Through repeated viewings of the recordings in conjunction with the ethnographic interviews, interactions in which face emerged as salient were selected for close interactional analysis. These key incidents were then transcribed according to standard conversation analytic transcription practices (Jefferson 2004), and also translated into English.[3]

In order to explore how face (*mianzi*) is interactionally achieved in interactions in a business setting in Taiwan, a theoretical and analytical framework that conceptualises face as a joint accomplishment of interlocutors is drawn upon, namely Face Constituting Theory (Arundale 1999, 2006, 2010). Face Constituting Theory (FCT) provides an integrated explanation of face and facework as both relational and interactional, explaining how participants interactionally achieve actions and relationships coordinate with their producing and interpreting of the meaning(s) of sequences of utterances (Arundale 2010). A focus on the interactional achievement of face means, here, that the analyst's role is that of elucidating the participant's interpretings and evaluations of actions and meanings in interaction rather than imposing the analyst's own understandings (Arundale 2010; Chang and Haugh 2011; Haugh 2010). Consistent with Chen's (1990, 1991) earlier study of the accomplishment of *mianzi* in dinner-table interactions, this study focuses on the analysis of authentic interactional data, focusing on both linguistic and non-verbal dimensions of those interactions. This interactional analysis is grounded in the emic conceptualisations of *mianzi* that were identified through the ethnographic interviews, although it is not limited in scope to just these folk understandings of face.

Analysis

Emic face concepts

While the ethnographic interviews initially focused on both *mianzi* and *lian*, it became evident from the responses of the native informants that in (insurance) business contexts *mianzi* is regarded as more salient, particularly in regards to accomplishing business goals. The following analysis of the interview data thus provides an overview of native perspectives on the emic concept of *mianzi* that are most relevant to communication in business settings. Through this analysis four key themes emerged: (1) *mianzi* is a socially constructed image of persons or groups, (2) a close inter-relationship holds between *mianzi*, *guanxi* (關係 'relationship'), and *ganqing* (感情 'emotive quality'), (3) a dynamic tension exists between *mianzi* and pursuing *lizi* (裡子 'profit' or 'gain') which is likely to be specific to business negotiations, and (4) upholding *mianzi* and avoiding damage to it in business interactions is claimed to be crucial.

Mianzi was first of all characterised by informants as a socially constructed image of a person or a group of persons in a business network, as argued by Mao (1994: 460) in relation to face in Chinese more generally.

In other words, in the business context, *mianzi* is conceptualised as the positive value a person can claim for him/herself (or his/her group) through being acknowledged by others with a positive attitude, deference and approval during the flow of interaction (cf. Goffman 1967: 5). If they receive positive evaluations, such as compliments, respect, expressions of satisfaction, acknowledgements of superiority (including status and professional background) or trustworthiness when they do business with their clients, they interpreted this as *you mianzi* ('having *mianzi*' 有面子). This positive attitude and feeling of respect between people has a key impact on *mianzi*, although only if it is mutually understood and acknowledged by both parties. *Mianzi* is thus socially constructed rather than being merely a psychological construct as Ho (1976: 876) argues:

> a person's face is assessed in terms of what others think of him; the assessment does not include what a person thinks of himself, but may include what he thinks others think of him.

This emphasis on *mianzi* as relating to feelings of respect and positive attitude expressed through interactions emerged, for instance, in the following excerpt from one of the ethnographic interviews.

EXTRACT 7.1 [EI-W1: 2:30]

1   I: 為什麼會覺得有面子?
    Weishenme hui juede you mianzi
    'Why do you think [people] have *mianzi*?'

2   W: 面子...呃....面子這種問題，面子好像說你接受肯定的時
    候，你就覺得說我很有面子。
    Mianzi...er...mianzi zhe zhong wenti, mianzi
    haoxiang shuo ni jieshou kending de shihou ni
    jiu juede shou wo hen you mianzi.
    'Mianzi, well, it seems that when you are
    approved by people, then you will feel 'you
    have *mianzi*'.'

3   I: 嗯
    mm
    'hmm'

4   W: 你被稱讚的時候很有面子，被刮的時候就很沒有面子，我們簡單
    形容 大概就是這樣子的感覺
    Ni bei chengzan de shihou hen you mianzi, bei gua de shihou
    jiu hen meiyou mianzi, women jiandan xingrong dagai jiushi
    zhe yangzi de ganjue.
    'You would feel you have *mianzi* when you are praised; you
    would feel you lose *mianzi* when you are criticised. I think
    we can simply put it this way.'

5 I: 對

   dui

   'yes'

   ((section omitted))

6 W: 在人跟人之間的對待裡面，喔尊重，這種尊重的感覺度，台語）你有尊
   重我，我就有尊重你，喔我感覺是這個樣子。那還有一種是一種態度，那種所謂態
   度之間的感覺，也會找到面子，它不見得就是說，（台語）我稱讚你，那你就很有
   面子，有時候刮的也很有面子耶。（台語）我給你一些喔，呃，很不錯建議
   （台語）給你產生喔你可能會有正面的影響，會有另外一個光明面。

   *Zai ren gen ren zhijian de duidai limian, ou zunzhong,
   zhezhong zunzhong de ganjue du, ((Taiyu)) li tioh u tsuntiong
   gua gua tioh u bintsu, ou wo ganjue shi zhe ge yangzi, na
   haiyou yi zhong shi yi zhong taidu, na zhong suowei taidu
   zhijian de ganjue, ye hui zhao dao mianzi, ta bujiande jiu
   shi shuo, ((Taiyu)) gua ga li o-lo, a li do jioh u bin-tsu
   e, you shihou gua de ye hen you mianzi ye, ((Taiyu)) gua
   ga li gei ni yi xie ou, er, hen bucuo jianyi, ((Taiyu)) ho
   li, chansheng ou, ni keneng hui you zhengmian de yingxiang,
   huiyou lingwai yi ge guangming mian*

   '[*Mianzi* is generated] from the relationship between each
   other. It's a feeling of respect (*zunzhong*). If you respect
   me, then I have *mianzi*. *Mianzi* also refers to an 'attitude'.
   [You can] also find 'mianzi' from the so-called attitude
   [between each other]. It does not necessarily mean you have
   mianzi when I praise you; sometimes [you] will have *mianzi*
   when [you] are criticised [by someone]. I give you some good
   suggestions which may bring you some positive influence, that
   is, another promising aspect.'

Reflecting the way in which face in Chinese is often described in the literature, this informant characterises *mianzi* as involving approval from others (turn 2), and as involving both a feeling and an attitude which is generated in relationships between people (turn 6). Interestingly, while the informant initially says approval is shown through praise, and disapproval through criticism (turn 4), he later claims that being criticised does not automatically lead to loss of face. Indeed, criticism can also sometimes be recognised as 'having *mianzi*' in business settings (turn 6). In other words, when a person is criticised, he or she would not necessarily interpret this as face-threatening conduct if the criticism has a positive or beneficial influence for him or her.

The informant went on to explain this point further:

EXTRACT 7.2 [EI-W1: 4:07]

7　W：這個也是很有面子喔，因為人家願意傾囊相授嘛....。那總是有一些
關係嘛，呃，像老前輩看得起晚輩的話，像我前輩喔，他就會真的把他
所有以前曾經學過的東西，他經歷過的東西，　會教我們很多。

*Zhe yeshi hen you mianzi de ou, yinwei renjia yuanyi
qingnangxiang shou ma,.... na zong shi you yi xie guanxi de
ma, er xiang lao qianbei kan de qi wanbei de hua, xiang wo
qianbei ou, ta jiu hui zen de ba ta suoyou yiqien cengjing
xue guo de dongxi, ta jingli guo de dongxi, hui jiao women
hen duo.*

'This can be also [interpreted as] 'have *mianzi*' because the
person would like to 'empty one's pocket to give' (*qingnangxiangshou* 傾囊相授)..... [it indicates] there's a relationship
(*guanxi*) [between each other]. It's like a forerunner values
a junior. Like [one of] my superiors, he really teaches us
a lot about what he has learned and his experiences. [He]
teaches us a lot.'

Here, the informant uses the idiomatic expression *qingnangxiangshou*
(傾囊相授, lit. to empty one's pockets to give) to show how the person
making the criticism is actually giving everything he or she has, whether
material things, skills or ideas and so on, without hiding anything from
the person being criticised. This means that criticisms made in business
contexts, according to the informant, can be interpreted as *you mianzi*
('having *mianzi*' 有面子), since criticism illuminates the intimate *guanxi*
('relationship' 關係) between those two people. Gao and Ting-Toomey
(1998) also suggest that "in Chinese culture, criticism often is perceived as
affectively based and relational in nature" (cited in Gao 2009: 185). 'Having
mianzi' can thus involve an intimate attitude and positive feelings which are
indexed through criticism between people who have *guanxi* ('relationship').
The level of intimacy and interpersonal attitudes that are reflexively indexed
through evaluations from others are all crucial factors that impact on *mianzi*
in business networks.

Through this example, then, we can see that *guanxi* (relationship) is
a crucial element involved in the interactional achievement of *mianzi* in
business settings. The close link between *guanxi* and *mianzi* thus emerges
as the second salient theme in the emic conceptualisation of face. *Guanxi*
denotes the relationship, network or social capital that circulates in reciprocal
business relationships, as noted for Chinese interactions more broadly
(Hwang 1987).[4] The most common circumstance where *guanxi* relates to
mianzi is the use of such phrases as *kan wo de mianzi* ('to employ my *mianzi*',

看我的面子) or *gei mianzi* ('giving *mianzi*', 給面子), used either directly as appeals to *mianzi* in interactions, or reflexively to describe particular business interactions. Such direct appeals or reflexive uses of *mianzi* are only possible because the parties involved perceive that they have *guanxi*. In other words, *mianzi* is invoked when people ask someone with whom they have *guanxi* to help out or achieve some particular business aim. *Guanxi*, which encompasses both rights and obligations, is thus employed in establishing harmony and strengthening the reciprocal relationship through giving and/or saving *mianzi* (Pan 2000: 68–71). However, the employment of *guanxi* is not limited to those who are already directly acquainted. One can ask a favour of someone whom one does not know, for instance, as long as there is an intermediary who mediates the *guanxi* between oneself and the other party. The person gives the intermediary *mianzi* by agreeing to the request from the third party, thereby also giving the one who asked the favour *mianzi* in passing.

Another important factor involving *guanxi* is gangqing (emotive quality, 感情), which encompass either *renqing* (human emotion, 人情) or *jiaoqing* (friendly emotion, 交情). A number of scholars have proposed that the collective meanings of *mianzi*, *guanxi* and emotional components (*ganqing* and *renqing*) in Chinese social relations need to be investigated in terms of their interrelationships, as these components are inevitably involved in face practices in Chinese social relationships (Chang and Holt 1994; Gao et al. 1996; Hwang 1987; Yang 1994), echoing Chang and Holt's (1994) argument that "*mianzi*, human emotion and interpersonal relations must be understood as a whole" (p. 103). *Renqing* is always associated with the notion of *renqing zhai* (human emotion debt, 人情債), meaning *renqing* is something that is expected to be contributed or returned through *guanxi*, whereas *jiaoqing* (friendly emotion) indicates the quality of the friendship, and is normally under consideration when employing *guanxi*. According to the informants, then, *guanxi* is closely related to issues of *mianzi*, in particular, when conducting business negotiations. According to one informant, for instance:

EXTRACT 7.3 [EI-W1: 16:40]

8 I: 那覺得談保險或是談生意上面，你覺得我們常講關係或是靠關係
　　很 重要嗎?

> *Na juede tan baoxian huo shi tan shengyi*
> *shangmian ni juede women chang jiang guanxi huo*
> *shi kao guanxi hen zhongyiao ma?*

> '[Do you think] the common saying about
> guanxi/relying on guanxi is very important
> during insurance business negotiations?'

9   W:喔很重要而且是非常非常非常的重要。呃，專業領域喔，它只是
你工作必要的東西而已，專業是你的必要，因為那是你專門生財的器具嘛。不過這
個關係如果沒有的話，或者你連關係都靠不了的話，（台語）這樣不好意思，如果
你要在社會上生存，可能要比別人多百分之八十的努力。那今天如果有關係的話，
人家說（台語）若娶到一個千金小姐，少奮鬥三十年，一樣意思嘛。

Ou, hen zhongyao, erqie shi feichang feichang feichang de
zhongyao, er, zhuanye lingyu ou, ta zhi shi ni gongzhuo biyao
de dongxi eryi, zhuanye shi ni de biyao, yinwei na shi ni
zhuanmen shengcai de qiju ma. Buguo zhe ge guanxi, zhe ge
guanxi meiyou de hua, huo zhe ni lian guanxi dou kao bu liao
de hua, ((Taiyu)) na an-ne phainn-se, li na-be di sia-hue
sing-tsun, keneng yao bi bieren duo baifenzhi bashi de nuli.
Na jintian ruguo you guanxi de hua, renjia shuo, ((Taiyu)) na
tshua diu tsit ui tshian-kim sio-tsia, kiam hun tau sann tsap
ni, kang khuan i-su a.

```
'Oh, very important, and [it's] very very very important.
Hmm, [in] professional area, it is just a necessity of your
job. Your profession is the necessity because it is your
tool of making money. However, if you do not have any guanxi
or you do not know how to rely on guanxi, then I'm sorry.
If you live in this society, you may have to put 80 percent
more effort than others. If you have guanxi, [it's like]
what people say, "if you marry to a lady from a rich family,
you can work 30 years less than others." The meaning is the
same.'
```

In this excerpt the informant responds to a question about the importance of *guanxi* from the interviewer (turn 8). He emphasises that *guanxi* is indeed very important in business, implying that if one does not have *guanxi,* or know how to employ it, then one is unlikely to be very successful (turn 9). He goes on to emphasise the importance of *guanxi* by invoking a common Taiwanese saying, which in this context means that the better *guanxi* one has, the more likely one will be successful in business.

The third salient aspect raised by informants was the idea that *mianzi* is closely linked in dynamic tension with issues of profit or gain (*lizi* 裡子), which arise as a matter of course in business negotiations. *Lizi* literally denotes 'inside', and so contrasts with the literal meaning of *mianzi*, which is 'surface'. The connotations of *lizi* mentioned by the informants included that it involves substantive gains made through business negotiations, such as purchasing the commodity at a lower price, obtaining extra benefits or receiving additional services. Such gains can be interpreted as *you lizi* ('having *lizi*', 有裡子). While *mianzi* is characterised by informants as involving an intangible attitude and positive feeling, *lizi* involves tangible profits. From the perspective of clients, then, if one gets a lower-priced service than others, one would feel not only that one 'has *mianzi*', but also one 'has *lizi*', since a lower-priced service or product is what clients aim for. Thus, from the perspective of business people, it is extremely important to find a balance between *mianzi* and *lizi* during their negotiations.

One informant, for instance, talked about the need to strike a balance between maintaining the *mianzi* of the client as well as that of the company, and considerations of *lizi* in business negotiations.

EXTRACT 7.4 [EI-H3: 19:51]

10   I: 你覺得保持有面子很重要嗎?

     Ni juede baochi you mianzi hen zhongyao ma?

     'Do you think that it is very important to maintain 'having mianzi'?'

11   H: 對我們來講，我們談兩個部分一個面子一個裡子，彼此就是要賺到
錢嘛，我就是顧全我的面子不賺到錢沒關係，有時候我會去衡量說，如果這個單
（金額）很大，那有時候我會顧全裡子，不一定要面子，只要他不要太過分，那
如果太過分的時候我想可能任何人都受不了，那就會是不要裡子要面子。

     Dui women lai jiang, women tan liang ge bufen, yi ge mianzi, yi ge lizi, bici jiu shi yao zhuan dao qian ma, wo jiu shi guquan wo de mianzi bu zhuan dao qian meiguanxi. You shihou wo hui qu hengliang shuo, ruguo zhe ge dan (amount of money) hen da, na you shihou wo hui guquan lizi, bu yiding yao mianzi, zhiyao ta buyao tai guofen. Na tai guofen de shihuo, wo xiang renhe ren dou shoubuliao, na jiu hui shi buyao lizi yao mianzi.

     'For us, there are two aspects [of business negotiations], *mianzi* and *lizi*. We want to make a profit from each other. Sometimes I only care about my own *mianzi* rather than making money. However, sometimes I might weigh up [the situation and] if there's a lot of money involved, sometimes I only care about *lizi* not *mianzi*, as long as he [the customer] doesn't go too far. If he goes too far, I don't think anyone can put up with it. Then [I'll] choose *mianzi* rather than *lizi*.'

The informant responds here to the question of what 'having *mianzi*' means in the context of business by focusing on the balance she needs to find between maintaining *mianzi* and *lizi*. She points out that in business contexts making money (i.e. *lizi*) is clearly important, but this needs to be balanced with considerations of maintaining *mianzi*. In some cases she puts maintaining her *mianzi* first, over and above obtaining *lizi*, although if the *lizi* is potentially very large, then this may be favoured over maintaining her *mianzi*. However, she alludes to comments she made earlier in the interview claiming that she would favour maintaining her *mianzi* over even potentially large *lizi* in situations where she feels the client has "gone too far", for example, by being overly demanding or not showing appropriate consideration. The dynamic tension arising in business negotiations from the need to find a balance between the two sides of a coin, namely *mianzi* and *lizi*, is thus a key consideration in decisions about whether or not to place emphasis on maintaining *mianzi* in business negotiations.

A related theme that also emerged through the ethnographic interviews was that maintaining *mianzi* during business interactions is crucial for obtaining business cases. Maintaining *mianzi* (*'gu mianzi'* 顧面子) involves showing consideration for both one's own *mianzi* and the *mianzi* of others (Hinze 2002: 147). This means it is important to avoid *puhuai mianzi* ('damage *mianzi*'), particularly the *mianzi* of the clients, as claimed by one informant in the excerpt below.

EXTRACT 7.5 [EI-Lan6: 4:42]

7 I:　　你認為跟同事，客戶或上司洽談生意的時候，顧面子是很重要 的嗎？
　　　　Ni renwei gen tongshi, kehu huo shangsi qiatan
　　　　shengyi de shihou, gu mianzi shi hen zhongyao
　　　　de ma?

　　　　'Is it important to maintain *mianzi* when dealing with
　　　　business among your clients, colleagues or superiors?

8 Lan:　那當然你不能去傷害到破壞到別人的面子啊，你要破壞他的
　　　　面子，甚至生意會做不成啦！
　　　　Na dangran. Ni buneng qu shanghai dao puohuai
　　　　dao beiren de mianzi a, ni yao puohuai ta de
　　　　mianzi shenzhi shengyi hui zuo bu cheng la!

　　　　'Of course. You can't hurt or damage others' *mianzi*. If you
　　　　damage his *mianzi*, you will even lose your business.'

Here the informant responds to a question about the importance of maintaining *mianzi* in business negotiations by claiming that damaging the *mianzi* of others will result in losing business.

This theme of maintaining *mianzi* was expanded upon by another informant who outlined the importance of maintaining both the client's *mianzi* and that of the agent.

EXTRACT 7.6 [EI-C9: 3:40]

6 I:　　那你們在跟客戶解說你的產品的時候啊，會不會覺得顧自己的
　　　　面子跟顧客戶的面子很重要？
　　　　Na nimen zai gen kehu jieshao nimen de chanpin de shihou a,
　　　　hui bu hui juede gu ziji de mianzi gen gu kehu de mianzi
　　　　hen zhongyao? Zhe liang fangmian zenme nanie?

```
'When you introduce your products to your clients, do
you think that it is important to maintain your mianzi or
maintain your client's mianzi?'
```

7   C: 可能在業務方面處理這個會比較圓融性…就像我們台語所講
的 （台語）抹壁雙面光，…相同意思，公司的部分是一個面，客戶的部分也是
一個面，面子有的話裡子大家都有，…那今天你出去是代表公司，要把這個廠
免銷售出去，那你也要取得客戶的認同，要認同你的公司你的產品你才有辦法把
產品銷售出去，所以這個方面兩邊都要顧。

*Keneng zai yewu fangmian, chuli zhege hui bijiao
yuanrongxing, ((section omitted)) jiu xiang women taiyu suo
jiang de, ((Taiyu)) 'mua beia shen min goun', ((section
omitted)) xiang tong yisi. ((section omitted)) Gongsi
de bufen shi yi ge mian, kehu de bufen yeshi yi ge mian,
mianzi you de hua, lizi dajia dou you, ((section omitted))
na jintian ni chuqu shi daibiao gongsi, yao ba zhege
chanpin xiaoshou chuqu, na ni yeyao qu de kehu de rentong,
yao rengtong ni de gongsi ni de chanpin, ni cai you banfa
ba chanpin xiaoshou chuqu, suoyi zhege fanmian liang bian
dou yao gu.*

```
'Maybe in the aspect of marketing, while handling this, [we
try to be] more flexible. ((section omitted)) It's similar
to a Taiwanese saying, "mua beia shen min goun" (polishing
the wall furbishes two sides). ((section omitted)) The
meaning is the same. ((section omitted))The company is one
side [of mian], and the client is the other [side of mian].
If you have mianzi, everyone can have lizi. ((section
omitted)) If you are [acting] on behalf of the company to
sell this product today, you need to seek the client's
recognition first. To enable to sell this product, you need
to have your clients recognise your company. Therefore, you
need to maintain both sides [of mianzi].'
```

This informant responds to the same question, as in excerpt (7.5) above, by emphasising that in order to do business one needs to be 'recognised' by one's clients. This recognition is achieved through maintaining the *mianzi* of both sides in business negotiations. The Taiwanese expression mentioned by the informant, *mua beia shang min geng* ("polishing the wall furbishes two sides", 抹壁雙面光), implies that it is vital to maintain your own *mianzi*, as well as your client's *mianzi* and *lizi* at the same time. If a client does not obtain *lizi* (that is, his expectations in regards to the business negotiations), he may feel his *mianzi* is being threatened or even lose *mianzi*. Thus, even though obtaining *lizi* is of course a primary aim in business, the informants all emphasised the importance of building a good image by maintaining *mianzi* on both sides. In the following analysis of interactional data, however, we see an instance where both participants are not always oriented to maintaining each other's *mianzi,* and indeed at some points even threaten the other person's *mianzi.* Nevertheless, the agent ultimately gains the case (*lizi*) without damaging the long-term relationship between himself and the client.

Emic face practices: strategic face threatening

The analysis in this section focuses on the way in which threats to *mianzi* were interactionally achieved in an incident which took place at the client's (Chen) place of business when the insurance person (Lan) went to collect the annual insurance fee for Chen's property. Both participants spoke in Taiwanese for the entire conversation, except for one word at the end.[5] The key incident involving face occurs when Lan threatens the client's *mianzi* as he attempts to persuade Chen to transfer the insurance for his cars back to Lan's company. Since Lan and Chen have known each other for more than 15 years, they have established a long-term *guanxi* based on Chen buying insurance from Lan's company. Lan projects face-threats to his client in a number of sequences in the following conversation, despite previously claiming that agents should not damage the *mianzi* of their clients (Excerpt 7.5). Yet he also succeeds in persuading Chen to shift his car insurance cases from another company to Lan's company through these face threats. He does so by evoking their long-term business *guanxi,* which is deeply embedded in the Taiwanese conceptualisation of *mianzi* according to the ethnographic interviews discussed in the previous section. As both Lan and Chen are demonstrably orienting to these face threats in this interaction, we characterise this particular emic practice as 'strategic face threatening'.[6]

Extract 7.7 [IR-4: 1:44]

1 L:　*ah　li　tsuekin (.) e　　li　dan tshia si long puann　di*
　　　PRT you recently　 PRT you now car　is　to deal with CP
　　　to>wi ah khi °huh°<
　　　where PRT CP PRT
　　　"Ah where has your car [insurance] been dealt with recently?"

2 C:　*chia? (0.2) °chia↓ (0.1) huechia° hue-##wa ze do >giou<*
　　　car　　　　　car　　　　　van　　 van- me this is sedan-
　　　giouchia ok?
　　　sedan　　PRT
　　　"Car? car van va- this sedan, sedan's [insurance]?"

3 L: =*chia wa dan wa a bo bun tai ah*↑ ((swishing hand))>*lin*
       car   I   now I PRT N half C PRT   your
       mu   a   jihle kong beh hoo wa °*beh hoo wa*°-
       mum PRT once say want give me want give me
       "Now I don't [even] have half of [your] car [insurance]. Your mother just
       said she wants to give it [insurance case] to me."
       ((phone rings))

4 C: =>*ah chai*↑< ((looking away)) *e::: wa hi tai huechia*
       PRT car   PRT I that C van
       (1.0) *ah*↓ *wa hi dai huechia hoo wen giapboo-a*
               PRT I that C van   give our business agent[8]
       pan   la (.) *wen giapboo-a   pan   la*
       handle PRT   our business agent handle PRT
       "Er, that car, er, that van, ah, my van has been given to my business agent,
       [it's] being dealt with by my business agent."

5 L: *lin giapboo-a kan wu sami wu sami >hiro ah?<*
       your business agent could have what have what that PRT
       "Your business agent, what could, what does [he] have?"

6   (2.0)((chair squeaking))

7 C: ((looking into distance)) *ah: >tiu< tiu*[*::*] ((patting envelope))
                                   PRT that's that's
                                   "Ah, that's, that's..."

8 L: [*li*] *hi   tai tangshi kahki?*
                                         your that C when   due
                                         "When is that one (car insurance) due"

9 C: >*un hi ja< tangshi kahki?*
       our that C when   due
       "When is our one (car insurance) due?"
       ((chair squeaking))

10 L: °*kimni   tsuan dau tuan lai*°=
       this year shift   CP   back CP
       "Shift it (the insurance) back this year."

11 C: =[*ho   la*] *ho   la*
                                         alright PRT alright PRT
                                         "Alright, alright."

12 L: ((walking away))   >[*kaki*   ]*< tsia   e*
                                         ourself   this side ASSC
       [*bo ma*   ] *ka sittsai ::*
       N   also   more down-to-earth
       "It's more reliable to deal with people on your side."

13 C: [*ho   la   ho*]
       alright PRT alright
       "Alright, alright."

14 L: °*heh a°*
      right PRT
      "Right."

15 C: °*ho* [*a°*   ]
      okay PRT
      "Okay."

16 L: [*hon ho*] *ho   bo anne wa lai   zau=* ((walking away))
           okay right right N   then   I   come go
      "Okay? Okay okay. I'm leaving [now]."

17 C: =*in hya wushizun giam chia*
      their side sometimes inspect car
      sizun il ehyan kan ki >kan ki< ga un suahle   [ban]
      when he can take CP take CP give us in passing handle
      **"In their [company] they help you to take your car to do an
      inspection, and then they deal with your car [insurance] in passing straight
      after."**

18 L: [*men la*]
                                              no need PRT
      ((frowning)) *giam za kaki   ki (.) dan >dan< ki lang*
             inspect   CP oneself go   now now   go people
      do   ga   li   giam   ga hoosei ado go   ho li   ban
      then help you inspect CP okay   N   need give you handle
      **"[You] don't need it. You can go to do the car inspection by yourself. Once
      you go there, they will deal with your car inspection. You don't need to
      handle it."**

19 C: *il wu ga   un kanki giam   chia sooi za   sunsuah*
      he has help us take   inspect car so   then in passing
      ho   [ban-]
      give him handle
      **"He helps me take the car for inspection, that's why I have him deal with
      it."**

20 L: [*il*] *ga li   bo   da   zi king?*
               he   help you insure where C company
      "Which [insurance] company did he help you insure your car with?"

21 C: (1.5) ((looking into distance)) *il do-* (.)Toyota *laide=*
                              he just Toyota inside
                              "He's just- in the Toyota [company]"
      ((chair squeaking))

22 L: =>*he a< il ga li ban   daji king?*
          yes PRT he help you handle which C
      "Yeah, then which [insurance]company did he help you [insure with]?"

23 C: *un ma hmm tsaiya bo   daji   king=*
        I   also N   know insure which C
        "I don't know which company [he] insured with."

24 L: =*hoonn il ga   li   bo   daji   king li hmm zai*
        PRT   he help you insure which C   you N   know
        "You don't know which company he insured with?"
        ((looking away))

25 C: ((embarrassed laughing)) *wa tsingjai hmm zai a* (.)
                              I really N know PRT
        il gagi   kan le ban   e (.) *ganla   ma shi bei* (.)
        he oneself take CP handle PRT it's like also is want
        ganla   hmm zai   da (.) *wa hmm zai dazi   king* (.)
        it's like N   know where I N   know which C
        wa bo ga   khan wa hmm zai   daji   king
        I   N give it look I   N   know which C
        **"I really don't know. Ah, he took my car to ask the company for the
        insurance by himself. It seems like the one which sells, it seems I don't
        know which, I don't know which company. I didn't check, I don't know
        which company."**

26 L: ((nervous laughing)) °*hiou*°   *hola hola shigau za*
                          is that right? Okay okay until then
        lai   khan la
        come look PRT
        "Oh, alright, alright. Deal with it until then."

27 C: *ho   [la]*
        alright PRT
        "Alright"

28 L: [*ho*] xie xie
        okay thank you
        "Okay, thank you."

This excerpt begins after the insurance agent, Lan, has collected the insurance
fee from Chen, and suddenly brings up the topic of which company Chen
insures his car with at present. In doing so, a request sequence, to shift the
insurance case back to his company, is initiated. Lan's attempt to obtain the
car insurance case from Chen in turns 1 to 12 begins with the pre-request
"where is your car (insurance) being dealt with recently?" which establishes
the grounds for making a request later in the sequence (Rue and Zhang
2008). Through this pre-request, it is presupposed that Chen has given the
insurance cases to someone else instead of Lan, even though they have had
business *guanxi* for a long time. The interrogative is thus evoking a potential
threat to Lan's *mianzi* as a competent insurance person with whom Chen

has had a long-term *guanxi*, and thus a threat to Chen's face as well. From his hesitant and repetitive response in turn 2 it appears that Chen interprets Lan's question as face threatening (to both Lan and Chen).[7]

Lan then goes on to project another threat to Chen's *mianzi* by immediately responding that he has not been given any car insurance cases by Chen (turn 3), thereby implying a complaint that Chen did not keep his (previous) promise (to shift the insurance case to Lan) (Wu 2003). This utterance is also apparently interpreted by Chen as a face threat. Through his pausing and by cutting his line of gaze towards Lan (Heath 1988; Sandlund 2004; Yang 2010) Chen indicates his hesitation and *buhaoyisi* ('embarrassment') in answering the question at the beginning of turn 4. Then Lan continues on to ask what Chen's business person 'has' (turn 5) using the term *wu sami*, which implies either that Chen's business person must have some kind of ability or, more likely, a special *guanxi*. There is, thus, an implicature embedded in the question, namely, a complaint as to why Lan has not been given the insurance cases by Chen. In this way, Lan is drawing upon the *guanxi* between them once again. That the implied complaint is interpreted as face threatening by Chen is reflected in his next turn where, once again, his hesitance and reluctance to respond to the question is evident from him cutting his line of gaze towards Lan, and his nervous body language.

In turn 8, Lan returns to the request sequence with another pre-request asking when the insurance is due. Chen responds by repeating the question (in turn 9), perhaps to give himself time to think about the question. Lan then (in turn 10) directly asks Chen to shift the insurance back to him. However, there is no evidence from Chen that he is necessarily interpreting this as offensive or face threatening. Instead, Chen responds with immediate agreement. By immediately agreeing, the *guanxi* between the two participants, which allows Lan to enact authority and power over Chen, is evoked. Moreover, in turn 12, Lan employs the term *kaki* ('insider') to again emphasise the importance of *guanxi*. In turns 15 and 16, then, in response to Lan's request, which is framed in the imperative mood, Lan and Chen reach an agreement that Chen will shift his car insurance back, later in the year.

However, in the subsequent turn (17), Chen then goes on to project a potential threat to Lan's *mianzi* about the services offered by Lan's company. In giving the reason as to why he asked his business person to take over the case, Chen is implicitly complaining that Lan's company does not provide such services, thereby projecting a threat to Lan's *mianzi*. That Lan interprets this as a face-threatening becomes apparent from his subsequent response where he displays an uncomfortable facial expression, concomitant frowning, and increases the volume of his speech (turn 18). This threat continues on through to turn 19 in which Chen more clearly explains the reason why he asked someone else rather than asking Lan. Again this implies a complaint about Lan's service, and so once again Chen is projecting a potential threat to Lan's *mianzi*. However, rather than attending to Chen's implied complaint, which would necessarily presuppose his *mianzi* has been threatened, Lan asks which company Chen insures his cars with, thereby pushing Chen to take the next turn and answer Lan's question in turns 20 and turn 22. In not attending to Chen's implied complaints, Lan may be attempting to save his own *mianzi*.

However, Lan's interrogatives are also at the same time (inadvertently) projecting threats to Chen's *mianzi*, which is apparent from Chen's initial silence, cutting of his line of gaze towards Lan, and subsequent ambiguous response in which he does not provide the name of the insurance company, but instead only that of the car company (turn 21). After Chen next responds that he does not know which company he insures his own car with (turn 23), Lan continues by projecting a further threat to Chen's *mianzi*, using a doubtful tone when trying to clarify whether Chen really does not know where his own cars are insured (turn 24). In particular, Lan uses the particle *hoonn* to index his scepticism about Chen's preceding assertion in turn 23, as well as reformulating it from the declarative into the interrogative mood, thereby implying an accusation that Chen should know this information. That this is interpreted by Chen as a face threatening is evident from Chen's response in turn 25 where his *buhaoyisi* (embarrassed) facial expression and repetitive acknowledgement of unawareness about the matter indicates that Chen is somewhat uncomfortable about answering Lan's line of questioning. Lan finally accepts Chen's explanation (turn 26) with nervous laughter, showing he is *buhaoyisi* about continuing the face threatening sequence, and also projects the end of their conversation. More specifically, through the verbal token *hola* (alright), Lan indicates that he would like to end the discussion, which implies Lan is showing restraint in not continuing this face threatening sequence, thereby saving Chen's *mianzi*.

This incident involves the interactional achievement of face threats over a number of utterances in the sequence, including Lan's direct questions about Chen's insurance cases, and his request that Chen shift the insurance cases back to him. That this sequence involves the interactional achievement of face threats is apparent from the way Chen becomes defensive and embarrassed by the line of questioning from Lan. Those face threats, which are directed mainly towards Chen's *mianzi*, also invoke the *guanxi* between the participants which has been established over a number of years. The incident thus also shows the importance of taking *guanxi* into account when analysing Chinese/Taiwanese face-in-interaction, as it is through invoking *guanxi* that Lan is able to exercise power over Chen. In this analysis we have focused on just one type of emic practice, namely, strategic face-threatening, due to space limitations, but there are, of course, other types of emic practices salient to face in Taiwanese interactions as discussed in Chang and Haugh (2011).

Conclusion

In the course of this analysis it has emerged that divergences between emic concepts and emic practices can arise. In this case, while informants claimed that maintaining *mianzi* is important in business negotiations, in an analysis of an actual business interaction we can see the agent is threatening the *mianzi* of his client in order to obtain *lizi* (i.e. the insurance case). Both participants in the interaction are oriented to these face threats, and so this can be characterised as an emic practice or, more specifically, strategic face threatening.[9] It is argued that this shows the importance of including an interactional perspective in the analysis of face, as emic conceptualisations apparently do *not* always reflect actual emic practices. As we have argued, there was no recognition of this kind of face practice amongst native speaker informants in the ethnographic interviews, where the focus was on emic concepts of face. A theory of face should thus ultimately be informed by emic concepts, but not unduly constrained by them in explicating emic practices. This study also indicates the need to carefully analyse face as it arises in interactional data, as well as in ethnographic data, when attempting to tease out the subtleties of various emic practices in instances of actual communication. In this way, we can deepen our understanding of face and face practices in business contexts in Taiwan and other Chinese-speaking societies, and as a result studies of face in Taiwanese may contribute more to broader theories of face and facework employed across other sociocultural and situational settings.

Appendix 1: Ethnographic interviews

1. 你所認為的面子和臉是甚麼？
   Ni suo renwei de 'mianzi' he 'lian' shi shengme?
   'What do you think "*mianzi/lian*" are?'
2. 你認為跟同事/客戶/上司洽談生意的時候，顧面子是很重要的嗎？
   Ni renwei gen tongshi/kehu/shangsi qiatan shengyi de
   shihou, 'gu mianzi' shi hen zhongyao de ma?
   'Do you think that is it important to maintain '*mianzi*' between your clients/colleagues/superiors in business negotiations?'

3. 你所認為的丟臉和丟面子是甚麼？

   Ni suo renwei de 'diu lian' he 'diu mianzi' shi shengme?

   'What do 'losing *lian*' and 'losing *mianzi*' mean to you?'

4. 你有在生意場和丟臉或丟面的經驗嗎？請提供過去經驗。當你丟臉或丟
   面子的時候，你會怎麼做？

   Ni you zai shengyi changhe 'diu lian' huo 'diu mianzi' de jingyen ma? [You] qing tigong guoqu jingyen, dang ni diu lian hou diu mianzi de shi hou, ni hui zenme zuo?

   'Have you ever experienced 'losing *mianzi*' or 'losing *lian*'? [if yes:] Please talk about your past experiences [if no:] What would you do if you 'lost *mianzi*' or 'lost *lian*?'

5. 你覺得在生意洽談的場合，顧面子很重要嗎？請提供過去經驗。

   Ni juede zai shengyi qiatan de changhe, 'gu mianzi' hen zhongyao ma? Qing tigong guoqu jingyan.

   'Do you think is it important to 'maintain *mianzi*' in business contexts? Please talk about some past experiences.'

6. 你覺得關係或靠關係在生意洽談上很重要嗎？

   Ni juede 'guanxi' huo 'kao guanxi' zai shengyi qiatan shang hen zhongyao ma?

   'Do you think *guanxi* or relying on *guanxi* is very important in business contexts?'

7. 你有過需要靠別人的面子來達成某項工作的經驗嗎？或是別人曾經要用
   你的面子去達成某項工作嗎？

   Ni you guo xuyao kao beiren de mianzi lai dacheng mou xiang gongzhuo de jingyan ma? Huoshi beiren cengjing yao yong ni de mianzi qu dacheng mou xiang gongzuo ma?

   'Have you ever had an experience where you needed to 'rely on other's *mianzi*' to achieve a particular task? Or someone 'employed your *mianzi*' to achieve a particular task?'

8. 當你想要幫助你的客戶或同事的時候，你會說甚麼或做甚麼來表達出你
   的誠意？

   Dang ni xiangyao bangzhu ni de kehu huo tongshi de shihou, ni hui shuo shengme huo zuo shengme lai biaoda chu ni de chengyi?

   'When you want to help out your clients/colleagues, what would you do/say to express your sincerity?'

9. 你在生意洽談上你聽過或用過客氣這兩個字嗎？你怎麼用這個詞？

   Ni zai shengyi qiatan shang you tingguo huo yong guo 'keqi' zhe liang ge zi ma? Ni zenme yong zhege ci?

   'Have you heard or used the expression *keqi* in business contexts? How do you use this term?'

Appendix 2: Transcription symbols (Jefferson 2004)

(.)	micro-pause
(0.2)	timed pause
( )	uncertainty about transcription
-	cut-off of prior sound in a word
.hhh	hearable aspiration or laugh particles
CAPITALS	higher pitch volume
°	markedly soft speech
<u>underlining</u>	stressed word or part of word
↑↓	marked rises or falls in pitch
[ ]	overlapping talk
=	talk 'latched' onto previous speaker's talk
:	stretching of sound
?	rising intonation
(( ))	transcriber's description of non-verbal activity
> <	rushed or compressed talk

Appendix 3: Grammatical glossary

ASSC	Associative (-de)
CP	Complement
C	Classifier
N	Negation
PRT	Particle
Q	Question marker

Notes

1. The distinction between emic concepts and emic practices was first made by Arundale (2008). Haugh (2009: 5) makes an analogous distinction between emic perspectives (in the anthropological sense) and participant perspectives (in the conversation analytic sense).
2. There were three females and eight males, and the age range of the interviewees was between 32 and 55 years old.

3. While Chinese characters are used for transcription of excerpts from the interviews, which were conducted mainly in Mandarin Chinese, the transcription of the excerpt from the recording of the interaction, which was all in Taiwanese (apart from one word), features no Chinese characters since Taiwanese cannot be accurately represented in Chinese characters. Instead, the interaction was transcribed according to the Taiwanese Church Romanisation System (Ong 2007). Where there was code-switching into Taiwanese in the interview excerpts, the Chinese characters are actually translations into Mandarin Chinese from Taiwanese. In addition, to further assist readers, the English translation is accompanied by a morphological gloss in the case of the transcription of the excerpt from the interaction. See Appendix 2 for a list of transcription conventions and Appendix 3 for symbols used in the morphological gloss.

4. While Hwang (1987) translates *guanxi* as 'favour', we believe that 'favour' constitutes just one aspect of the complex emic notion of *guanxi*. In particular, we suggest that 'favours' are only expected because of presupposed *guanxi*, in other words, the relationship of mutual obligation that holds between parties.

5. Code-switching is thus not at issue in this particular interaction, although it can be exploited as a face practice in both business and interpersonal settings (Pan 2000: 60–68; Su 2009).

6. While we are in fact focusing on threats to *mianzi* in this analysis, there is no equivalent expression for face threats in either (Mandarin) Chinese or Taiwanese. We thus prefer to use the expression face threat over '*mianzi* threat' since the latter does not exist in Chinese.

7. See Chang and Haugh (2011) where the focus of the analysis is on face itself being inherently relational in nature.

8. 'Business agent' (translated from *giapboo-a* in Taiwanese) is a particular job which involves look after marketing and promoting products for a company or a shop.

9. It remains an open question, of course, whether this particular emic practice would be found in other settings both in Taiwan, and across Chinese-speaking societies more generally.

References

Arundale, R. (1999) An alternative model and ideology of communication for an alternative to politeness theory. *Pragmatics* 9: 119–154.

Arundale, R. (2006) Face as relational and interactional: A communication framework for research on face, facework, and politeness. *Journal of Politeness Research* 2: 193–216.

Arundale, R. (2008) Relating Japanese emic face concepts and face constituting theory. Unpublished manuscript, University of Alaska Fairbanks.

Arundale, R. (2010) Constituting face in conversation: Face, facework and interactional achievement. *Journal of Pragmatics* 42: 2078–2105.

Bousfield, D. (2008) *Impoliteness in Interaction*. Amsterdam: John Benjamins.

Brown, P. and Levinson, S. (1987) *Politeness. Some Universals in Language Usage*. Cambridge: Cambridge University Press.

Chang, H.-C. and Holt, R. (1994) A Chinese perspective on face as inter-relation concern. In S. Ting-Toomey (ed.) *The Challenge of Facework* 95–132. Albany, NY: State University of New York Press.

Chang, W. M. and Haugh, M. (2011) Strategic embarrassment and face threatening in business interactions. *Journal of Pragmatics* 43: 2948–2963.

Chen, V. (1990/1991) *Mien tze* at the Chinese dinner table: A study of the interactional accomplishment of face. *Research on Language and Social Interaction* 24: 109–140.

Gao, G. (1998) An initial analysis of the effects of face and concern for other in Chinese interpersonal communication. *International Journal of Intercultural Relations* 22: 467–482.

Gao, G. (2009) Face and self in Chinese communication. In F. Bargiela-Chiappini and M. Haugh (eds) *Face, Communication and Social Interaction* 175–191. London: Equinox.

Gao, G. and Ting-Toomey, S. (1998) *Communicating Effectively with the Chinese*. Thousand Oaks, CA: Sage.

Gao, G., Ting-Toomey, S. and Gudykunst, W. B. (1996) Chinese communication processes. In M. H. Bond (ed.) *Chinese Psychology* 280–293. New York: Oxford University Press.

Goffman, E. (1967) On face-work: An analysis of ritual elements in social interaction. In E. Goffman (ed.) *Interaction Ritual* 5–45. New York: Pantheon.

Haugh, M. (2005) What does 'face' mean to the Japanese? Understanding the import of 'face' in Japanese business interaction. In F. Bargiela-Chiappini and M. Gotti (eds) *Asian Business Discourse(s)* 211–239. Berne: Peter Lang.

Haugh, M. (2009) Face and interaction. In F. Bargiela-Chiappini and M. Haugh (eds) *Face, Communication and Social Interaction* 1–30. London: Equinox.

Haugh, M. (2010) Jocular mockery, (dis)affiliation, and face. *Journal of Pragmatics* 42: 2106–2119.

Haugh, M. and Bargiela-Chiappini, F. (2010) Face in interaction. *Journal of Pragmatics* 42: 2073–2077.

Heath, C. (1988) Embarrassment and interactional organization. In P. Drew and A. Wootton (eds) *Erving Goffman: Exploring the Interaction Order* 136–160. Cambridge: Polity Press.

Hinze, C. (2002) Re-thinking 'face': Pursuing an emic-etic understanding of Chinese mian and lian and English face. Unpublished PhD, University of Queensland, Brisbane.

Hinze, C. (2005) Looking into 'face': The importance of Chinese *mian* and *lian* as emic categories. In F. Bargiela-Chiappini and M. Gotti (eds) *Asian Business Discourse(s)* 169–210. Berlin: Peter Lang.

Ho, D. Y.-F. (1976) On the concept of face. *American Journal of Sociology* 81: 867–884.

Ho, D. Y.-F. (1994) Face dynamics: From conceptualization to measurement. In S. Ting-Toomey (ed.) *The Challenge of Facework* 269–285. Albany, NY: State University of New York Press.

Hu, X. (1944) The Chinese concept of face. *American Anthropologist* 46: 45–64.

Hwang, K.-K. (1987) Face and favour: The Chinese power game. *American Journal of Sociology* 92: 944–974.

Jefferson, G. (2004) Glossary of transcript symbols with an introduction. In G. Lerner (ed.) *Conversation Analysis: Studies from the First Generation* 13–23. Amsterdam: John Benjamins.

Lett, J. (1990) Emics and etics: Notes on the epistemology of anthropology. In T. Headland, K. Pike and M. Harris (eds) *Emics and Etics. The Insider/Outsider Debate* 127–142. Newbury Park, CA: Sage.

Mao, L. (1994) Beyond politeness theory: 'Face' revisited and renewed. *Journal of Pragmatics* 21: 451–486.

Ong, K. B. (2007) *Taiyin Zenzi Huibian (Taiwanese Romanisation version)*. Taipei: Avanguard Publishing House.

Pan, Y. (2000) *Politeness in Chinese Face-to-Face Interaction*. Stanford, CA: Ablex.

Pan, Y. (2008) Cross-cultural communication norms and survey interviews. In H. Sun and D. Kádár (eds) *It's the Dragon's Turn. Chinese Institutional Discourses* 17–76. Berne: Peter Lang.

Potter, J. and Hepburn, A. (2005) Qualitative interviews in psychology: Problems and possibilities. *Qualitative Research in Psychology* 2: 281–307.

Rue, Y.-J. and Zhang, G. Q. (2008) *Request Strategies. A Comparative Study in Mandarin Chinese and Korean*. Amsterdam: John Benjamins.

Sandlund, E. (2004) Feeling by doing: The social organization of everyday emotions in academic talk-in-interaction. Unpublished PhD thesis, Karlstad University.

Su, H.-Y. (2009) Code-switching in managing a face-threatening communicative task: Footing and ambiguity in conversational interaction in Taiwan. *Journal of Pragmatics* 41: 372–392.

Ting-Toomey, S. (1988) Intercultural conflict styles. A face-negotiation theory. In Y. Y. Kim and W. Gudykunst (eds) *Theories in Intercultural Communication* 213–238. Newbury Park, CA: Sage.

Ting-Toomey, S. (2005) The matrix of face: An updated face-negotiation theory. In W. Gudykunst (ed.) *Theorizing about Intercultural Communication* 71–92. Thousand Oaks, CA: Sage.

Wu, R. J. (2003) *Stance in Talk: A Conversation Analysis of Mandarin Final Particles*. Amsterdam: John Benjamins.

Yang, M. M.-H. (1994) *Gifts, Favours and Banquets: The Art of Social Relationships in China*. New York: Cornell University Press.

Yang, P. (2010) Managing *mianzi* in Mandarin Chinese talk-in-interaction: A nonverbal perspective. *Semiotica* 181: 179–223.

Yu, M. (2003) On the universality of face: Evidence from Chinese compliment response behaviour. *Journal of Pragmatics* 35: 1679–1710.

8

What are Chinese respondents responding to? A close examination of question-answer sequences in survey interviews

Yuling Pan

Introduction

The research reported in this chapter is part of an ongoing endeavour initiated by the author to introduce the theoretical notion and analytical tool of discourse analysis to examine Chinese speakers' linguistic behaviour in survey interviews (Pan 2008; Pan et al. 2010). Like any other type of interview, a survey interview consists of a series of question-answer sequences, but a survey interview question-answer sequence has a unique and crucial function. That is, statistical analyses and predictions depend on the quality of data collected through the question-answer sequence. If an answer to a question is not relevant or is unreliable, then the data are not valid. Therefore, it is vital, using some systematic method, to examine if survey questions can elicit the intended information, and discourse analysis seems a plausible approach to achieve this end.

My previous research on Chinese politeness (Pan 2000; Pan and Kádár 2011) and its impact on survey interviews (Pan, forthcoming) has shown that there are some unique challenges in conducting survey interviews with Chinese-speaking respondents. In particular, Chinese-speaking respondents, as a group, are more likely to provide indirect and ambiguous responses in survey interviews compared to their English-speaking counterparts (Chan and Pan 2009; Chan, this volume). Chinese-speaking respondents appear to respond to interview questions in a way that is (a) less direct; (b) restricted in the amount of information revealed; and (c) less likely to reveal very individualised or personal opinions (Pan 2008). These findings are related to research on Chinese communication patterns, highlighting the Chinese preferences for indirect and implicit expressions in communication (Gao 1998; Günthner 1993, 1994; Li 1999; Ma 1996; Young 1994). As a result of these communication characteristics, survey researchers often encounter difficulties in coding Chinese respondents' responses because many responses seem 'off track' or seem to include minimal information (Pan et al. 2010). While studies on Chinese discourse and communication have shed considerable light on Chinese indirect communication style, most of them focus on describing the phenomenon. They do not necessarily offer a clear measure of Chinese indirectness or a possible solution to bridge the communication gap. For example, when faced with practical problems of how to interpret or code the responses of Chinese-speaking respondents, researchers do not have an analytical framework to categorise Chinese indirectness and to analyse data from Chinese respondents.

This study aims to develop a method that can be used to capture the degree of Chinese indirectness in interview interaction and to identify when Chinese speakers do not fully address the questions asked in the interview. Starting with the functional approach (Schiffrin 1994) to question-answer sequences, I examine the function of interview questions and Chinese speakers' responses to these questions. By categorising Chinese speakers' responses in terms of the degree of indirectness and its relation to the types of questions asked, I show that Chinese speakers do not always provide evasive or indirect responses to interview questions, but they do tend to avoid direct answers to interview questions that ask for personal opinion (or volition) or evaluation. Results of this study helped develop a coding scheme that allows the application of quantitative analysis method (see Chan, this volume) to systematically code and analyse the quality of Chinese speakers' survey responses.

This chapter starts with a discussion of the theoretical framework that guides the development of a coding scheme for question-answer sequences in interviews. It argues for the need to systematically define and measure indirectness. The subsequent section (*Data and method*) describes the interview data and methodology for coding question types and response patterns. This methodology section is followed by the analytical section (*Findings and discussion*), which is divided into two parts: summary of findings and discussion. The analysis in this section focuses on two question types that elicit the most indirect responses and expounds the functions of indirect responses, followed by a discussion. The chapter concludes with a proposal for further study of this topic.

Theoretical framework

Indirectness has been a topic of interest for linguists for a long time and has been examined from many different perspectives. For example, it has been approached from a syntactic perspective, looking at how syntactic structure constitutes indirect speech acts (Paltridge 2006; Schiffrin 1994), and from a pragmatic perspective, examining the role of indirectness in discourse (Tannen 1981), in linguistic politeness (Brown and Levinson 1987; Watts 2003), or in cross-cultural pragmatics (Blum-Kulka et al. 1989). However, these analyses have a singular or monologic approach. That is, they all focus on utterances from the speaker, that is, one interlocutor. For analyses of interview interactions, the monologic approach presents some limitations because interview interaction consists of a series of question-answer sequences. Each utterance (e.g. an interview question) predetermines the one that follows it. Likewise, in the case of a response, each utterance is dependent upon the one that precedes it. This means the analysis cannot consider a single utterance as a meaningful unit to determine its degree of indirectness. The basic notion to start with is whether a response answers what a question asks in light of its semantic content. If a response deviates from what the question asks, it indicates some level of indirectness. Therefore the analysis needs to be dialogic, in that both the question and response must be analysed in conjunction with each other.

In line with this idea of dialogic methodology, I draw on three theoretical orientations to conceptualise the analytical framework for this study. The first one is the classic work of speech act theory (Austin 1962; Searle 1966), which views a question as the speech act of requesting information. The illocutionary act of asking requires the hearer (in our case, the respondent) to take the action of providing information by answering a question. Searle (1966) outlines the rules for questions, where 'S' is speaker and 'H' is hearer:

Table 8.1 Rules for questions

Types of rules	*Explanations*
Propositional content	Any proposition or propositional content
Preparatory	(a) S does not know 'the answer', i.e. does not know if the proposition is true, or in the case of the propositional function, does not know the information needed to complete the proposition truly
	(b) It is not obvious to both S and H that H will provide the information at that time without being asked
Sincerity	S wants this information
Essential	Counts as an attempt to elicit this information from H

Under this theoretical stance, interview questions in this study are treated as an illocutionary act which functions to elicit information from the respondent in an interview event. The interview questions are 'real questions' instead of 'exam questions' (Searle 1969) in the sense that the interviewer or the survey researcher really wants to know or find out the answer from the respondent.

The second theoretical orientation is the discursive notion of question-answer sequences in pragmatics (Brown and Yule 1983; Levinson 1983; Schiffrin 1994). It adopts a functional view of looking at a question and its answer. That is, there may not be an exact correlation between form and function in a question or an answer. The syntactic structure of a question can come in different forms, for example, a closed question format (i.e. yes/no questions), an open question format (i.e. wh-questions), or even a declarative sentence. Contextual cues such as intonation can satisfy the sincerity, preparatory, and essential conditions underlying questions, and help construct a declarative as a question (Schiffrin 1994). Similarly, an answer can be in different forms. An answer is determined by whether it provides information to verify the truth of the proposition in question or whether it provides enough information to complete the proposition.

In a similar line of argument, Huddleston and Pullum (2005) make a distinction between responses and answers. A response is an utterance produced "as a result of being asked some question" (*ibid.*: 162). The function of a response is tied to its discursive and sequential position in light of the preceding utterance, and not defined wholly by its semantic content. An answer, in comparison, provides the specific information in light of the question asked (see also Sun 2008). In other words, an answer provides information to the proposition or propositional function of a question. This notion is important in my analysis of Chinese interview data in this study because it will serve as a yardstick to examine the relevance of Chinese speakers' responses to interview questions.

The third theoretical orientation is cross-cultural pragmatics (Blum-Kulka et al. 1989; Schiffrin 1984; Tannen 1984; and Wierzbicka 1985, 2003) which argues for a cultural-script approach to pragmatics. Under this theoretical paradigm, people in different communities speak differently. The differences in speaking are profound and systematic as they reflect different cultural values and priorities. Pragmatics, or the use of language in social interaction, is largely based on a cultural script that frames a communicative event and pre-selects appropriate linguistic strategies for interaction. For example, in American English, a conventional response to a compliment is an acceptance of the compliment by saying "Thank you", while in Chinese, a conventional response is to decline the compliment by displaying modesty:

"No. I'm no good" (Chen 1993; Yu 2003). Wierzibicka (2003) contends that a cultural-script approach to pragmatics allows us to map the differences in communication styles and understand how and where miscommunication occurs.

These theoretical orientations guide the analysis of question-answer sequences in this study. First, interview questions were classified based on their intended function in an interview event, that is, the type of information that a question intended to elicit. Then, respondents' responses were categorised based on whether they performed the act of answering the proposition of a question. Finally, cross-cultural pragmatics helps explain Chinese respondents' linguistic behaviour based on an analysis of the response patterns of Chinese respondents.

I also draw on notions from conversation analysis and Discourse Analysis (Schiffrin 1994). One analytic concept in conversation analysis pertinent to the current study is the notion of adjacency pairs (Schegloff and Sacks 1973). In a survey interview such as the one under study, the question-answer sequence is an adjacency pair with predetermined roles and questions. When the interviewer asks a question, the respondent is expected to take up the next speaking turn in this adjacency pair. Schiffrin (1994) maintains that adjacency pairs have sociological as well as linguistic importance. Their sociological importance is that they provide a normative framework for expected actions in verbal exchange. Their linguistic importance is that they provide an environment for making inferences about relevance across utterances (Schiffrin 1994: 236–237). Using this analytical concept, I examined each question-answer sequence by looking at the types of question and the relevance of the response to the question to see if the response fulfilled the expectation in the question-answer adjacency pair.

Data and method

Data

Data for this study is drawn from two of 48 Chinese interviews that came from two large-scale multilingual research projects undertaken at the United States Census Bureau. The cognitive interviews for this study were conducted during 2006 and 2008 to pre-test the Chinese translation of the US Census Bureau American Community Survey advance letters and informational brochures. The goal of the pre-testing project was to evaluate the accuracy and appropriateness of these translated survey documents. Forty eight Chinese-speaking respondents were recruited for the project and they were asked to review and comment on the Chinese translation of the survey documents. The 48 Chinese respondents were monolingual and bilingual recent Chinese immigrants residing in the United States. They were recruited to reflect a range of characteristics, including age, gender, educational level, length of stay in the US and dialect preference.

Based on this large data set, two cases were selected for detailed analysis. The two cases were selected based on the differing demographic characteristics of respondents in terms of age, gender, educational level, length of stay in the US and dialect preference. To some degree, the two cases represent the general characteristics of the discourse pattern of the 48 interviews. However, it is not the goal of this study to make that generalisation. Instead, this study aims to develop a method of noting the linguistic features of Chinese indirectness in the question-answer sequence through a detailed analysis of these cases. The next study by Chan (this volume) is a continuation of this study, employing the method developed to examine the 48 interviews to identify the general pattern and to link these linguistic features with respondents' demographic characteristics[2].

Coding of question types and response patterns

Question types

Before I describe the categorisation of questions, a note on the purpose of the interview questions being examined is in order. The interview setting under study is one type of interview in survey research called cognitive interview, a technique used by survey questionnaire designers to pre-test survey questions. Cognitive interviewing is basically an in-depth one-on-one interview in which survey researchers use a series of questions to examine respondents' comprehension and interpretation of the survey questions and survey materials being pre-tested (see Willis 2005). Questions in this kind of interview focus on eliciting respondents' reactions and interpretations of the materials presented to them. It is highly important that respondents can articulate their thoughts and answer interview questions directly so that survey researchers can gather valid data to pinpoint the problems in survey instruments or survey documents.

Cognitive interview questions for this particular project are designed with the purpose of eliciting respondents' comprehension and reaction to the Chinese translation of survey letters and brochures. The interview questions, therefore, focus on four aspects: 1) whether the Chinese-speaking respondents have a good understanding of the general information conveyed in the translated materials; 2) whether the respondents understand some specific terms or the specific information included in the materials; 3) whether they would be motivated by these materials to participate in the survey; and 4) whether they have positive or negative reactions to the translated materials.

While there are many ways to code question types (see, for example, Cheng, this volume), the coding of question types in this study is based on the specific design and research requirements of the cognitive interviewing, so that the coding scheme can be easily applied to examine question-answer sequences in survey interviews. Therefore, based on the types of information being elicited, the interview questions were coded into four groups: 1) general information questions, which aim to obtain respondents' general impression or general understanding of the materials under review in a cognitive interview; 2) specific information questions, which are intended to *ascertain* respondents' understanding or interpretations of specific facts or specific terms included in the materials under review; 3) personal opinion questions, which ask about respondents' personal view of an issue under discussion or their volition to take or not to take certain actions, and 4) evaluation questions, which ask for respondents' reaction to the materials under review, either positive or negative.

Although a question can appear in various syntactic structures (for example, WH-question, or Yes/No question) or different formats, the main concern here is the pragmatic function of a question in the cognitive interviewing setting, and the pragmatic functions are decided based on the type of information that these questions are intended to elicit, as discussed above. In other words, each interview question is coded based on its pragmatic function, rather than on its format. Table 8.2 below is a brief summary of question types and examples.

Table 8.2 Question types and examples

Question type	*Example*
General information question	What do you think this letter is about?[3]
Specific information question	What does the term 'confidentiality' mean to you here?
Personal opinion question	If you were selected, would you participate in the survey?
Evaluation question	Is this brochure easy or difficult to understand?

Response types

The types of responses are categorised based on their relevance to the proposition of a question. It is assumed that each interview question has a proposition with a key question word, functioning to elicit a certain type of information. The expected answer is one which matches the semantic content or provides information to fully complete the proposition. Therefore, responses are categorised and coded on how closely they completed the proposition or matched what the question was asking. If a response fully answered the question, it was coded as 'match'. If a response only partly answered the question, it was coded as 'partial matching'. If a response was totally off track, or off topic, it was coded as 'off' or 'opt out'. 'Opt out' means a 'don't know' response or reluctance to provide any answer. Table 8.3 provides a summary of response types and examples with explanations to illustrate how responses are coded in the study.

Table 8.3 Response types and examples with explanations

Response type	Example with explanation
Matching	Q*: If you were selected, would you participate in the survey? R: Yes, I will participate because it is a good thing and it will benefit us all. **Explanation:** The response fully answers the semantic content of the question and provides information for the affirmative answer 'yes'.
Partial matching	Q: If you were selected, would you participate in the survey? R: I don't speak English. It is difficult for me to participate. **Explanation:** The response answers part of the question by mentioning the difficulty participating in the survey.
Off	Q: If you were selected, would you participate in the survey? R: It doesn't matter. **Explanation:** The response does not provide any information that the question asks for. It is irrelevant on the surface.
Opt out	Q: If you were selected, would you participate in the survey? R: I don't know. **Explanation:** The 'don't know' response is a way to opt out of answering this question.

*Q = question   R = response

The assumption is that if a response is coded as 'partial matching' or 'off/opt out' it is an indication of irrelevance or indirectness. In analysing survey interview data, researchers would like to see more matching responses because the analysis relies on the verbal report from respondents. If survey interview questions elicit mostly irrelevant or off-track answers, researchers do not have clear evidence to interpret the cognitive interview data and the conclusions drawn may not be valid.

In order to achieve a relatively high degree of objectivity, three researchers – two sociolinguists and one sociologist – coded the interview questions and responses independently using the coding scheme. The researchers then convened to review and discuss the coding to reach consensus. In what follows, I will first summarise findings of response patterns in the two cases respectively, and then discuss the function of questions and responses and how interactional elements play a role in Chinese response patterns.

Findings and discussion

As mentioned earlier, two cases were selected for analysis based on their differing demographic characteristics. Case #1 was a female in her early to mid forties. She had less than high school education and, at the time of the interview, had lived in the US for 2.5 years. Her dialect preference was Mandarin. Case #2 was a male in his fifties. He had a high school diploma. He came to the US in the 1980s and so was a long-time resident of the US. His dialect preference was Cantonese.

Response patterns in Case #1 and Case #2

A total of 62 questions and 46 questions were coded for Cases #1 and #2 respectively. Analysis shows that, despite their demographic differences, the two cases share very similar response patterns to different types of questions.

Figure 8.1 is a summary of the response pattern in Case #1. The first set of bars shows her responses to questions that asked for general information and the percentage of matching, partial matching, and off responses to these types of questions. The light grey bar shows that 67 per cent of responses matched the proposition of questions that asked for general information. The dark grey bar shows that 33 per cent of responses are partial matching responses. She had no off or opt out responses for the general information questions.

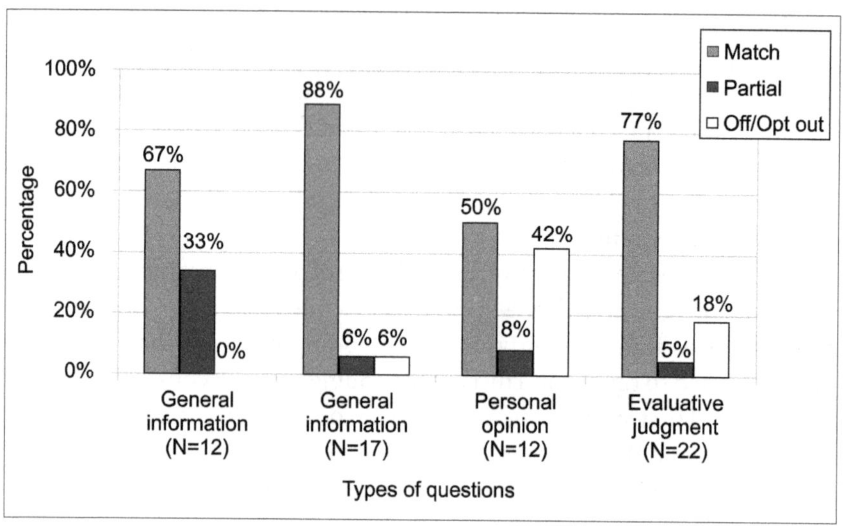

Figure 8.1 Response pattern in Case #1

The second set of bars indicates the response pattern to questions asking for specific information. As indicated by the data, the matching response rate for this type of question is the highest (88%). The percentages for partial matching and off/opt out responses are very low.

For questions asking for personal opinion, the matching responses are only 50 per cent, while off/opt out responses are 42 per cent, and partial matching responses are 8 per cent. This type of question generated the most indirect or irrelevant answers. For evaluation questions, matching responses are 77 per cent, off/opt out responses are 18 per cent, and partial matching responses make up 5 per cent.

Case #2 shows a similar response pattern to the various types of questions. That is, the most matching responses fall within the category of specific information questions (93%), followed by the general information questions (67%). The personal opinion questions generated the least matching responses (50%). They elicited 33 per cent partial matching responses and 17 per cent off/opt out responses. The evaluation questions had 60 per cent matching responses and 15 per cent off/opt out responses. Figure 8.2 summarises the response pattern of Case #2.

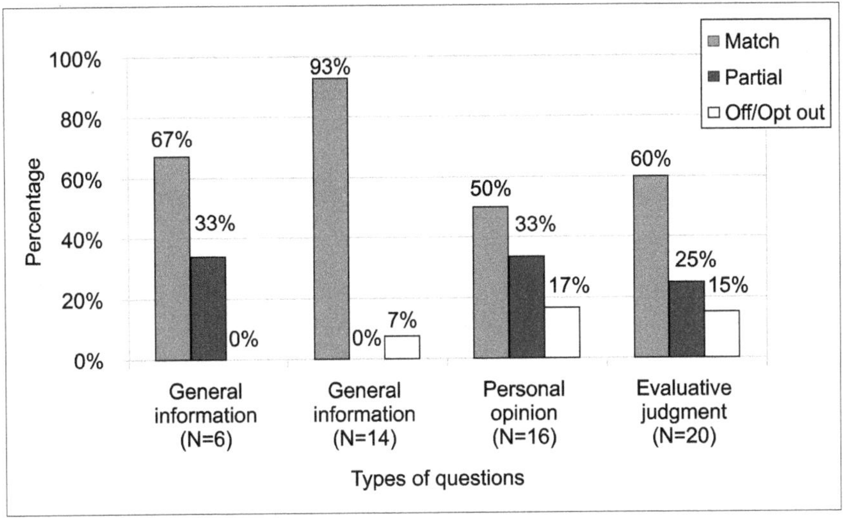

Figure 8.2 Response pattern of Case #2

Functions of questions and responses

The two cases show similar overall response patterns in how closely a response matches a question's proposition. Overall, specific information questions elicited the most matching responses for both respondents (88 to 93%). General information and evaluative type of questions generated the next highest percentage of matched responses (67%, and 60 to 77%). Personal opinion questions have the lowest percentage of matched responses (50%). In this section, let us take a closer look at the responses to these four types of questions.

Responses to general information questions

General information questions aim to gather information about respondents' overall impression of the survey materials under review in the cognitive interview setting, and to assess if respondents had basic understanding of the communicative intent of the survey materials. For example, this type of question asked if respondents knew the purpose of the survey letter they read or if they remembered any information from the letter. This type of question was usually asked first, prior to other types of questions. On the whole, the two Chinese respondents were able to produce matched responses to the general information questions by providing relatively relevant information. As indicated by Figures 8.1 and 8.2 above, most of the responses (67%) matched the proposition of the question asked in the interview.

The following example is a question-answer sequence for a general information question. In this example, the interviewer asked the respondent to read one survey letter and then asked him a general information question on what the letter was about.

Example 1. General information question and response [Case #2]

1. INT: 好，你觉得这封信是关于什么的？

2. R: 这里讲到美国社区调查， 所有信息都得到法律保护。 这个调查成功与否需要家庭的合作，联邦政府根据调查的信息制定计划，这些计划将影响到我们整个社区的保健， 教育和交通，如果你要了解进一步的情况，你可以到网站上去找。

1. INT: OK. What do you think this letter is about?

2. R: It talks about the American Community Survey. All data will be protected by law. The success of this survey depends on the cooperation from families. The federal government will make plans based on the data from the survey. These plans will affect our community's healthcare, education and transportation. If you need more information, you can go online to look for it.

As mentioned earlier, the intent of this question was to find out respondents' general impression of the survey letter under review in spite of its use of "what do you think," which may seem like a personal opinion question at the formal level. The question is really "What is this letter about?" The respondent answered that the letter talked about the American Community Survey and went on to give some details about the data collection effort, the legal protection for data security, and data uses. His response matched the question's proposition in that it provided direct and relevant information concerning what the question was asking.

However, there is one caveat in this case: the respondent was actually reading part of the letter back to the interviewer when he answered this question. In spite of this, data analysis shows that the two respondents were able to provide direct and relevant answers to the general information questions. In most cases, they relied on the materials under review and repeated some parts from the letter instead of using their own words to summarise the points. In addition, it is not likely that they would elaborate their responses (see Pan 2008 for more detailed discussion). In the next example, the respondent provided matched responses to the general information questions, but all her responses were brief.

Example 2. General information question and response [Case #1]

1. INT: 那您觉得这封信是关于什么的？

2. R:　 关于社区的服务啊，　医疗啊，　学校啊，　保健啊，　有什么新的好的建议啊。

3. INT: 还说了其他吗？

4. R:　 还说你们做这个调查到居民家里去。

5. INT: 好，　还有什么吗？

6. R:　 就这些了。

7. INT: 很好，　我们就想知道你看完这封信之后，哪些信息对你最有用，哪些东西你能马上记住。

8. R:　 对，　我感觉社区的医疗保险，学校，交通这些是最重要的。

1. INT: So, what do you think this letter was about?

2. R:　 It's about community services, medical, schools, healthcare, and if there are any new and good suggestions.

3. INT: Did it mention anything else?

4. R:　 (It) said that you will go to residents' homes to conduct the survey.

5. INT: OK, anything else?

6. R:　 That's all.

7. INT: Very good. We just wanted to know after you read this letter, what information is most useful to you and which parts you can remember right away.

8. R:　 Right, I feel that medical health insurance, schools and transportation in a community are most important.

In this excerpt, the interviewer first asked a general information question in turn 1 ("What do you think this letter was about?"). The respondent gave a relevant response that matched what the question asked for. However, her response was so brief that the interviewer probed further ("Did it mention anything else?") in turn 2. The respondent provided another short answer in turn 3. Obviously, the interviewer did not find the response adequate because she asked another question, trying to get more information in turn 5 ("OK, anything else?"). The respondent said no. The interviewer made another effort in turn 7, explaining the reason behind her questions. The respondent just repeated her first response without providing any more information.

These two examples indicate that although most responses to general information questions were direct and relevant, they were short. Chinese respondents were not likely to provide an elaborated response to this type of questioning.

Responses to specific information questions

In contrast with general information questions, specific information questions ask about specific facts included in the survey materials, or interpretation of a specific term or concept. Data analysis shows that the two Chinese-speaking respondents under study usually provided direct and relevant answers to this type of question. Their answers were explicit and often more elaborate and relevant.

Example 3. Specific information question and response [Case #2]

1. INT: 好，那在这段里提到 "统计目的"，这是什么意思呢？

2. R: 就是给你计划统计时用的资料啊，我提供的信息就是用作以后规划用的，这一段比较明白。

1. INT: OK. A phrase of "statistical purpose" is mentioned in this paragraph. What does that mean?

2. R: That means providing data for your planning and statistics, the information that I provide will be used for future planning. This paragraph is relatively clear.

In this excerpt, the respondent provided a response that exactly answered what the question asked for. In addition, the respondent not only gave a detailed account of his interpretation of the specific term 'statistical purpose,' but also offered an evaluative comment at the end of his response (这一段比较明白. "This paragraph is relatively clear."). His response was explicit in the sense that the respondent elaborated his impression and reaction when answering the question.

Responses to personal opinion questions

Compared with the other question types, personal opinion questions elicited the least amount of matched responses among the four question types. In other words, there are more responses to personal opinion questions that are either off topic or irrelevant to the proposition of a question (50%). For this study, the personal opinion questions asked in these interviews are about respondents' intention to participate in a survey ("If you were selected, would you participate in the survey?"), or their view of the survey ("Do you think it is important to participate in the survey?"). The pragmatic function of indirect answers to this personal opinion question may very well indicate a refusal on the part of the respondent.

The following is an example of indirect answer to a personal opinion question. The interviewer showed the respondent a survey advance letter and asked if the letter would make the respondent feel more or less likely to participate in the survey.

Example 4. Personal opinion question and response [Case #1]

1. INT:　如果你被抽中参加这个社区调查，你觉得这东西有没有让你觉得更愿意参加？或者有什么地方让你觉得不愿意参加？

2. R:　没有，　无所谓参不参加的。

3. INT:　我看你在考虑，　你在考虑什么呢？

4. R:　我没有什么很坏的想法啦，　我不会担心采访会怎么样，　美国的法律是可信的，　这个我不怕，　但我不希望被抽到，　因为我没有时间。

1. INT:　If you were selected to participate in this survey, do you think there were any parts in it (the letter) would make you feel more likely to participate, or less likely to participate?

2. R:　No. It doesn't matter to participate or not.

3. INT:　I can see you are thinking of something. What are you thinking about?

4. R:　I don't have any very negative thoughts. I don't worry about the interview. The US law is trustworthy. I'm not afraid of that. But I don't want to be selected because I don't have time.

In this extract, the interviewer asked a question designed to find out the respondent's opinion on whether she would participate in a survey after reading the survey advance letter. The respondent's first response in turn 2 is an off/opt out response. She did not provide any information to complete the question's proposition on whether she would be more likely or less likely to participate in the survey. It is not clear what her response (turn 2) refers to in this context. So the interviewer used a follow-up question to determine what the respondent was thinking. The respondent's first utterance in her second response (turn 4) did not reveal what she was thinking. She stated that she did not have any negative thoughts. Her real intention was only revealed in the last statement of her response: "I don't want to be selected because I don't have time." This response pattern is in line with the findings of previous studies (Günthner 1993, 1994; Young 1994) which show that the Chinese tend to put their main point toward the end of an argument for reasons of 'face'. This example illustrates that the respondent is not very direct in indicating her reluctance or unwillingness to participate in the survey. She provided two irrelevant answers in her responses. The interviewer had to probe and ask follow-up questions to discover her real intention. It can be argued that due to the Chinese cultural orientation to concerns about 'face', and emphasis on hierarchical order, Chinese-speaking respondents may find it hard to provide a direct refusal to a government-sponsored survey. This is an indication of indirectness that shows reluctance or even refusal on the part of the respondent.

The next example is from Case #2, in which the interviewer asked the same question about willingness to participate in the survey. We observe a similar pattern in the responses.

Example 5. Personal opinion question and response [Case #2]

1. INT: 看完之后，假设要你参加美国社区调查， 你觉得会不会参加呢？
2. R: 因为我英语不好， 很难参加的。
3. INT: 那如果提供中文的材料给你， 你会不会参加呢？
4. R: 我年纪大了， 精神各方面都不行啦， 语言也不行， 开车又不方便。
5. INT: 那如果我们把那些材料寄来你家呢？
6. R: 还是不行， 因为我有一些小孩子要带

1. INT: After you read it (survey brochure), if you were selected to participate in the American Community Survey, would you participate?
2. R: It is difficult to participate because my English is not good.
3. INT: If we provide you with Chinese materials, would you participate?
4. R: I'm old, and my energy is low. My language is not good, and I can't drive.
5. INT: Then what if we mail the materials to your house?
6. R: (I) still can't do it, because I have to take care of kids.

The question asked in this extract was intended to find out the respondent's opinion on his willingness or intention to participate in the government survey. As the interaction shows, the interviewer repeated the question three times in different formats (turns 1, 3 and 5). This is an indication that the interviewer did not get enough information from the respondent regarding his answer or intention in the first two utterances. Let us consider what types of response the respondent provided in each turn and how each response is coded under the current coding scheme.

In turn 1 in this excerpt, the first question is 'Would you participate?' It asks for personal opinion in stating one's intention to participate in the survey. However, the respondent's response emphasises the difficulty in participating ("It is difficult to participate because my English is not good") rather than his willingness to participate. The response provides partial information to the propositional content of the question 'Would you participate' by way of inference. The inference is 'Since it is difficult, I will not participate.' So the code is 'partial matching' of the response to the question. A partial matching response requires some inference processing on the part of the hearer.

In turn 3, the interviewer asked a second question to probe further: 'If we provide you with the Chinese materials, would you participate?' The question is still 'Would you participate?' The respondent provided a list of reasons in his response ("I'm old, and my energy is low. My language is not good, and I can't drive."), but did not touch upon his volition on whether he was willing to participate or not. So this response is coded as 'off'.

In turn 5, the interviewer asked a third question in response to the respondent's stated reasons: 'Then what if we mail the materials to your house?' At this time, the respondent said '(I) still can't do it because I have to take care of kids.' Notice that he gave a new reason for his refusal to participate in the survey. His response at this point matched what the question was asking. So it was coded as a matching response. As indicated by this example, it took three exchange turns for the respondent to provide a relevant response to the personal opinion question.

Responses to evaluation questions

Evaluation questions present another interesting finding. Although the rate of matching response to this type of question is high, the responses are not very informative as they were, in most cases, in agreement with the questions. That is, the respondents did not provide any evaluative comments that the questions aimed to elicit. Most comments were positive, for example "good", "easy", or "no problem" without further elaboration. The responses also tended to be very limited, consisting of just one word or one phrase. This pattern of giving only affirmative answers is similar to the pragmatic pattern of 'gratuitous concurrence' that Eades (2002, 2003) describes about the Australian Aboriginal English communicative style, which is characterised by the tendency to freely say "yes" in answer to questions regardless of whether or not the speaker actually agrees with the proposition. Following are two extracts from Case #2 that demonstrate this pattern:

Example 6. Evaluation question and response [Case #2]

[The interviewer showed the respondent a survey brochure and asked her to comment on the brochure]

1. INT:　你觉得这个小册子容不容易看懂？
2. R:　　容易。

…

…

3. INT:　这小册子里有没有什么地方让你产生顾虑？
4. R:　　没有。

1. INT: Do you think this brochure was easy or not easy to understand?

2. R: Easy.

...

...

3. INT: Was there anything in this brochure that caused you to be concerned?

4. R: No.

In this example, the interviewer asked two evaluation questions to get the respondent's reaction to the brochure under review. In both cases the respondent's answer consists of one word without much elaboration. Both responses focused on the positive aspect of the document (easy, no problem). In other words, evaluation questions tended to generate short and positive answers regardless of whether the respondent felt that way or not.

It should be noted that the two evaluation questions discussed in this example are closed questions which do not provide for open-ended responses, i.e. the format of the question makes it easy to elicit a simple answer (Schiffrin 1994). However, in the next excerpt from Case #2, the interviewer asked a series of evaluation questions in various formats, including the wh-question and yes/no question formats. In spite of the interviewer's efforts, and the fact that the respondent indicated something was bothering him (turn 7), the respondent did not offer many evaluative comments.

Example 7. Evaluation question and response [Case #2]

1. INT: 从中国语言和中国文化的角度来看，你觉得这封信写得如何？

2. R: 不错，简单明了。

3. INT: 有没有需要改进的地方？

4. R: 不需要了。我自己看觉得不错。

5. INT: 有什么词觉得不明白呢？

6. R: 没有。哦，这封信是局长写的，　不过 ...

7. INT: 刚刚你说 "不过"？

8. R: 哦没什么。

1. INT: From Chinese language and cultural perspective,
           how well do you think this was written?

2. R: Not bad. It's simple and clear.

3. INT: Were there any parts that need improvement?

4. R: No need. I myself think this is not bad.

5. INT: Were there any words that you found confusing?

6. R: No. Oh, this was written by the bureau director,
        but ...

7. INT: Did you just say "but"?

8. R: Oh, no, nothing.

In this excerpt, the interviewer asked a series of three evaluation questions and one follow-up question. The respondent provided positive responses to all three questions, stating that he thought the letter was well written, simple and clear, and there was no problem at all. Notice that he used a contrastive conjunction with a hesitating tone "不过 ..." (but ...) in turn 6. The interviewer asked a follow-up question, "Did you just say 'but'?", trying to get more information, but the respondent declined to elaborate on this seemingly negative reaction and dismissed this as an issue ("Oh, no, nothing"). This shows that the respondent was not willing to disclose any negative reaction to the interviewer.

Table 8.4 gives a summary of all responses to evaluation questions.

Table 8.4 Responses to evaluation questions

Case	Evaluation questions asked	Positive responses	Evaluative responses	Off-topic responses
#1	22	16	0	6
#2	20	12	4	6

Table 8.4 shows that the majority of responses to the evaluation questions were positive, stating that all translated materials were fine. A good number of responses in each case (6) were completely off topic and did not have any evaluative comments. There were a small number of responses (4) in Case #2 that offered some evaluation. This suggests that evaluation questions themselves do not necessarily generate much useful information because respondents tended to be acquiescent and stay away from any critical comments.

Discussion

Silverman (1997) critically raised the concept of an 'interview society' by pointing out that the 'interview society' has a set of presumptions for the act of interviewing. First it requires the emergence of the self as a proper object of narration. This means the person being interviewed can fully articulate him/herself in light of what is being asked. Secondly, it appeals to 'authenticity' and 'openness' in the interview interaction. That is, the interviewee is willing to reveal his/her true self and be authentic under scrutiny. Thirdly, it remains 'monologic' in that the interviewer and interviewee collaborate in the reconstruction of a common and unitary construction of the self (Silverman 1997: 248). Applying Silverman's concept to the survey interview setting, we can see that survey interviews operate on these assumptions of the 'interview society' which expects that each respondent is an individual 'self' that can be fully narrated and is open to the scrutiny of survey questions. The expected communication style in the interview setting is directness and openness, and each response can be clearly coded in the response options, if interview questions are carefully designed. Silverman (1997) further challenged the bias of data generated in interviews because not all societies fall into the category of 'interview society' or have the equivalent view or concept of 'self'. He cautioned researchers about the validity of data collected through interviews.

Along this line of argument, Chinese society can be categorised as a traditionally 'non-interview society' in the sense that interviewing was not a method of social science inquiry or a means of data collection in Chinese society until very recently. Moreover, the concept of self in the Chinese context has a different dimension or implication from that in Anglo-American culture. In a Chinese context, the individual self co-exists with others and is always in relation to others (Bond 1991, 1996). Thus a Chinese self is not an independent object whose opinions can be separated from others or reported individually. As I show elsewhere (Pan 2008; Pan et al. 2005), Chinese respondents did not have the same type of prior experience with civic engagement as their American counterparts. Actually, none of the Chinese respondents in our sample had participated in a survey interview or completed a survey questionnaire prior to this study. Due to their lack of civic engagement or survey experience, many interview questions may sound unnatural or awkward to Chinese respondents.

Based on the analysis of responses to four types of questions, we can see that several themes emerged. First, careful examination of how Chinese respondents respond to interview questions through the lens of discourse analysis can pinpoint exactly which type of questioning received the most indirect and irrelevant responses. Findings suggest that not all types of questions generated 'off/opt out' responses. Some types of questions worked better than others. For example, when responding to specific information questions, Chinese reports were more open and direct. This kind of analysis has furthered our understanding of Chinese indirectness in context and can help survey researchers better design interview questions.

Secondly, consistent with prior research (Pan 2008), results in this study suggest that Chinese respondents tended to be implicit, vague and off-track in their responses to personal opinion or evaluation questions. With this finding in mind, we can design interview questions that can generate the data the research is looking for. In this regard, the function of a question is a more important issue to consider than the structure of a question. For example, when trying to get at personal opinion responses, we can think about using a specific information question as a proxy for personal opinion questions.

Thirdly, the placement of questions is also crucial for eliciting the desired answers. We need to consider asking the personal opinion questions towards the end of an interview when respondents become more relaxed with interviewers or more comfortable with the interview event. We can also build in follow-up questions to get at the real answer to personal opinion questions. However, we need to be careful with the use of follow-up questions, because follow-up questions may seem pushy, and respondents can become offended by follow-up questions about their personal opinions.

Conclusion

The present study has examined the question-answer sequence in the context of survey interviews, and has demonstrated that Chinese-speaking respondents are not always implicit, indirect or vague in their answers to questions: it all depends on the types of questions asked in the interview. This research has contributed to the ongoing scientific inquiry into Chinese discourse and interaction in that it closely examined responses to questions in a certain speech event (survey interviews) and identified patterns of Chinese linguistic behaviour (directness vs. indirectness, relevance vs. irrelevance) in this particular setting.

Furthermore, findings from this study have practical implications for survey researchers and practitioners in terms of survey question development and evaluation. However, in order for us to understand the magnitude of the phenomenon identified in the current study, we need to consider other factors, such as demographic characteristics and socio-cultural factors, to determine how prevalent this linguistic pattern is with Chinese-speaking respondents. The coding method developed in this study should be applied to a larger sample size to examine the Chinese linguistic behaviour in combination with demographic characteristics. The next step is to continue this line of research and take into consideration demographic and sociocultural factors. The study reported in the next chapter (Chan, this volume) is an attempt to reach that goal.

Acknowledgements

I would like to express my gratitude to the US Census Bureau for their support of this research and for allowing me to access their Chinese interview data. I am thankful to Jessica Cox for her assistance in coding the data. I am very grateful to Anna Chan, Hao Sun and Kenneth Kong for reviewing an earlier version of the chapter and for providing constructive comments. Special thanks also go to Stephanie Sheffield and Marissa Fond for editing the manuscript. However any errors remain my sole responsibility.

Notes

1. *Disclaimer:* This chapter is released to inform interested parties of research and to encourage discussion of work in progress. The views expressed are the author's and not necessarily those of the US Census Bureau.
2. A large-scale study using the same coding scheme is applied in the subsequent study (see Chan, this volume).
3. It should be noted that while the phrase 'do you think' seems like a personal opinion question at the formal level, the intent of this question is to get at respondents' general impression of the survey letter under review. The question is really 'What is this letter about?'

References

Austin, J. L. (1962) *How to Do Things with Words.* Oxford: Oxford University Press.

Blum-Kulka, S., House, J. and Kasper, G. (eds) (1989) *Cross-Cultural Pragmatics: Requests and Apologies.* Norwood, NJ: Ablex.

Bond, M. H. (1991) *Beyond the Chinese Face: Insights from Psychology.* Hong Kong: Oxford University Press.

Bond, M. H. (1996) Chinese values. In M. H. Bond (ed.) *The Handbook of Chinese Psychology* 208–26. Hong Kong: Oxford University Press.

Brown, G. and Yule, G. (1983) *Discourse Analysis.* Cambridge: Cambridge University Press.

Brown, P. and Levinson, S. C. (1987) *Politeness: Some Universals in Language Usage.* Cambridge: Cambridge University Press.

Chan, A. and Pan, Y. (2009) Analysis of Chinese speakers' responses to survey interview questions in comparison to other language speakers. Paper presented at the 11th International Pragmatics Conference, Melbourne, Australia, 12–17 July 2009.

Chan, A. Analysis of Chinese Speakers' Responses to Survey Interview Questions in Comparison to Other Language Speakers. In Y. Pan and D. Z. Kádár (eds) *Chinese Discourse and Interaction.* London: Equinox.

Chen, R. (1993) Responding to compliments: A contrastive study of politeness strategies between American English and Chinese speakers. *Journal of Pragmatics* 20: 49–75.

Eades, D. (2002) Evidence given in unequivocal terms: Gaining consent of Aboriginal young people in court. In J. Cotterill (ed.) *Language in the Legal Process* 161–96. Houndmill: Palgrave Macmillan.

Eades, D. (2003) The politics of misunderstanding in the legal process: Aboriginal English in Queensland. In J. House, G. Kasper and S. Ross (eds) *Misunderstanding in Social Life: Discourse Approaches to Problematic Talk* 196–223. London: Longman.

Gao, G. (1998) 'Don't take my word for it': Understanding Chinese speaking practices. *International Journal of Intercultural Relations* 22: 163–86.

Günthner, S. (1993) German-Chinese interactions: Differences in contextualization, conventions and resulting miscommunication. *Pragmatics* 3: 283–304.

Günthner, S. (1994) Cultural differences in recipient activities: Interaction between Germans and Chinese. In P. Heiner et al. (eds) *Intercultural Communication: Proceedings of the 17th International L.A.U.D. Symposium, Duisburg, 23–27 March 1992* 481–502. Frankfurt am Main: Peter Lang.

Huddleston, R. and Pullum, G. K. (2005) *A Student's Introduction to English Grammar.* Cambridge: Cambridge University Press.

Kaplan, R. (1972) Cultural thought patterns in inter-cultural education. In K. Croft (ed) *Readings on English as a Second Language* 246–62. Cambridge, MA: Winthrop.

Levinson, S. (1983) *Pragmatics.* Cambridge: Cambridge University Press.

Li, X. (1999) *Chinese-Dutch Business Negotiations.* Atlanta, GA: Rodopi.

Ma, R. (1996) Saying 'yes' for 'no' and 'no' for 'yes': A Chinese rule. *Journal of Pragmatics* 25: 257–66.

Paltridge, B. (2006) *Discourse Analysis.* London: Continuum.

Pan, Y. (2000) *Politeness in Chinese Face-to-Face Interaction.* Stamford, CT: Ablex.

Pan, Y. (2008) Cross-cultural communication norms and survey interviews. In H. Sun and D. Kádár (eds) *It's the Dragon's Turn: Chinese Institutional Discourses* 17–76. Berne: Peter Lang.

Pan, Y. (forthcoming) Facework in refusal in Chinese survey interviews. *Journal of Politeness Research.*

Pan, Y. and Kádár, D. Z. (2011) *Politeness in Historical and Contemporary Chinese.* London/New York: Continuum.

Pan, Y., Landreth, A., Schoua-Glusberg, A., Hinsdale, M. and Park, H. (2010) Cognitive Interviewing in non-English languages: A cross-cultural perspective. In J. Harkness et al. (eds) *Survey Methods in Multinational, Multiregional, and Multicultural Contexts* 91–113. Berlin: Wiley.

Pan, Y., Craig, B. and Scollon, S. (2005) Results from Chinese cognitive interviews on the Census 2000 Long Form: Language, literacy, and cultural issues. *Statistical Research Division's Research Report Series (Survey Methodology #2005-09)*. Washington, DC: US Census Bureau.

Searle, J. (1966) *Speech Acts.* Cambridge: Cambridge University Press.

Schegloff, E. A. and Sacks, H. (1973) Opening up closings. *Semiotica* 7: 289–327.

Schiffrin, D. (1984) Jewish argument as sociability. *Language in Society* 13: 311–35.

Schiffrin, D. (1994) *Approaches to Discourse.* Cambridge, MA: Blackwell.

Silverman, D. (1997) Towards an aesthetics of research. In D. Silverman (ed.) *Qualitative Research: Theory, Method, and Practice* 239–53. London: Sage.

Sun, H. (2008) Participant roles and discursive actions: Chinese transactional telephone interactions. In H. Sun and D. Kádár (eds) *It's the Dragon's Turn: Chinese Institutional Discourses* 77–126. Bern: Peter Lang.

Tannen, D. (1981) Indirectness in discourse: Ethnicity as conversational style. *Discourse Processes* 3: 221–38.

Tannen, D. (1984) *Conversational Style: Analyzing Talk Among Friends.* Oxford: Oxford University Press.

Young, L. W. L. (1982) Inscrutability revisited. In J. Gumperz (ed.) *Language and Social Identity* 72–84. New York: Cambridge University Press.

Young, L. W. L. (1994) *Crosstalk and Culture in Sino-American Communication.* New York: Cambridge University Press.

Yu, M. C. (2003) On the universality of face: Evidence from Chinese compliment response behavior. *Journal of Pragmatics* 35: 1679–1710.

Watts, R. 2003. *Politeness.* Cambridge: Cambridge University Press.

Wierzbicka, A. (1985) A semantic metalanguage for a crosscultural comparison of speech acts and speech genres. *Language in Society* 14: 491–513.

Wierzbicka, A. (2003) *Cross-cultural Pragmatics: The Semantics of Human Interaction.* Berlin: Mouton de Gruyter.

Willis, G. (2005) *Cognitive Interviewing.* Thousand Oaks, CA: Sage Publications.

9

Discourse analysis of Chinese speakers' indirect and contrary-to-face-value responses to survey interview questions

Anna Yukyee Chan

Introduction

The motivation for the current research grew out of the need to understand the effect of communication styles on survey interviews and linguistic barriers in the administration of surveys to non-English speakers, including Chinese speakers (Pan 2008). Given that the United States is a multilingual country,[1] federal government statistical agencies, including the US Census Bureau[2] and survey research firms, find it necessary to provide informational brochures and/or questionnaires in languages other than English to survey participants. When conducting the Census and various census surveys, survey interviewers routinely encounter households that speak non-English languages (e.g. Spanish, Chinese, Korean, Russian and Vietnamese) at home.

Of relevance to this current study is the fact that, in 2007, there were over 2.5 million Chinese speakers in the United States and the Chinese language was the second most spoken non-English language spoken at home (Shin and Kominski 2010). In a series of studies examining survey interviews with Chinese respondents, Pan and her colleagues (Pan 2008, Pan et al. 2006, Pan et al. 2008, Pan et al. 2010) demonstrated that researchers met challenges and encountered problems with Chinese respondents providing responses that were irrelevant or off topic to interview questions. Pan (2008) examined the linguistic features of monolingual Chinese respondents in a structured cognitive interview setting and revealed that, consistent with prior literature on Chinese conversational style (described in greater detail in the following section), Chinese respondents showed a similar indirect style of communication when responding to interview questions. Unlike a regular conversation, survey interviews consist of a non-reciprocal flow of information where the survey interviewers are seeking information and the respondents are providing this. It is often assumed that survey respondents will provide direct responses to survey questions. If Chinese speakers use a communication style that masks their responses, it could have a direct effect on data quality. Therefore, a systematic study of the communication style of Chinese speakers and its effect on survey interviews may help shed light on these issues.

Communication styles of Chinese speakers

Prior research on the communication styles of Chinese speakers in their writing and conversations has shown that they tend to use *indirect* and *circular* styles in their interaction (Günthner 1993, 1994; Scollon and Scollon 1995; Young 1994). Young (1994) provided a detailed description of how the Chinese discourse and cultural tradition is an integrated system, and discussed the differences between Chinese and English based discursive practices and how these differences affect everyday conversation. Scollon and Scollon (1995) used a discourse approach, encompassing the concepts of ideology, forms of discourse, face system and socialisation, to intercultural communication and provided a comprehensive framework for the analysis of differences in communication style between East Asian speakers, including Chinese, and Anglo-North Americans. Other studies on Chinese pragmatics show that Chinese speakers engage in *contrary-to-face-value* (CTFV) communication style in their interactions. For instance, Ma (1996) identifies that CTFV communication can be other-serving or self-serving, and that there are two manifestations of CTFV communication: saying 'yes' for 'no' and vice versa. Ma defines CTFV communication as "any communication in which what is said is the opposite of, or different from, what the speaker believes to be true or what he or she is 'logically' expected to say" (*ibid.*: 258). According to Ma, the underlying principles governing Chinese CTFV communication is interpersonal harmony especially when it is other-serving, while CTFV messages can be "strategically conscious" and "manipulative" when it is self-serving. The ambiguity in responses is often a way to avoid direct confrontation. Ma asserts that within the Chinese culture, correct interpretation of the speech act depends on culture and context. The authenticity of a 'yes' or a 'no' message can usually be established through contextual and non-verbal cues. Other research has shown that Chinese communication tends to be other-oriented, with a heavy focus on face concern of the other and self. Self-denigration and other elevation in communication are held as the norms of Chinese politeness practice (Gu 1990; Pan and Kádár 2011). Chinese communication is also heavily hierarchical and makes a clear distinction between the insider and outsider (Pan 2000).

Theoretical framework: towards an understanding of Chinese communication styles

The works cited above discussed the traditional cultural norms and schemas for interpersonal relationships between Chinese people, which build on harmony and are other-oriented, with face and hierarchical concerns. These macro-level contextual factors are represented on the outer ring of the concentric circles in Figure 9.1. Based on this framework, Chinese speakers' communication styles are seen to be embedded in cultural norms and schemas, and Chinese politeness norms reflect and uphold the traditional values of interpersonal relationship. Indirect communication

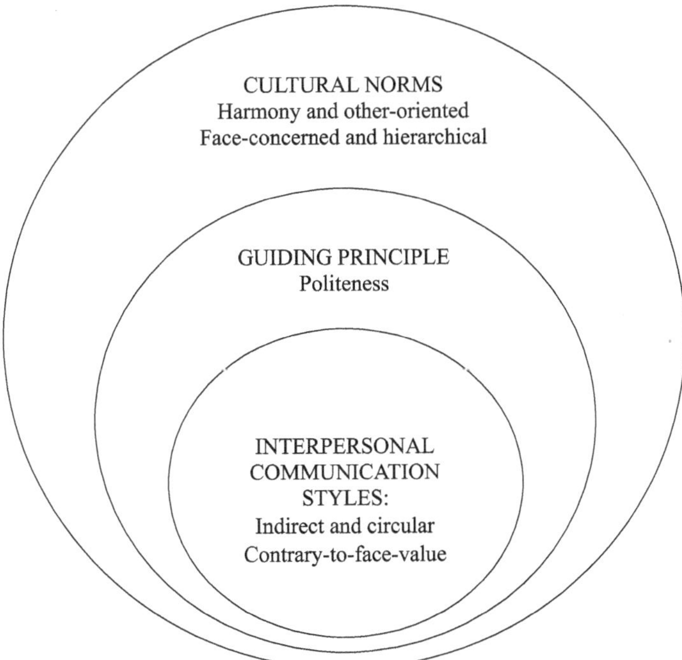

Figure 9.1 Theoretical framework: towards an understanding of the communication style of Chinese speakers

(or any communication that is the opposite of, or different from, what the speaker believes to be true or what he or she is 'logically' expected to say – contrary-to-face-value communication), is not deception but a reflection of the guiding principle of politeness and the traditional cultural concerns noted above regarding interpersonal relationship. These communication styles are 'normal' since the intention of wanting or not wanting others to know the real purpose of communication is based on the Chinese concept of politeness.

Research gap

In prior research studies involving the use of conversational data or interviewing type tools, much of the analysis of data gathered is of a qualitative nature. Such research requires painstaking detailed qualitative analyses of turn-by-turn conversations, and sometimes word-by-word analyses of sentences, which are generally provided in the form of language transcripts (e.g. Ma 1996; Young 1994). The analyses generally compare a detailed account of one case compared to another, such as a Chinese speaker or writer compared to a Western speaker or writer, and no control variables are examined. The issue with this type of analysis is that the researchers generally use text as evidence and do not examine a larger sample of subjects. Hence, the findings from these studies generally cannot be generalised beyond the specific study and individuals, and often lack representativeness. Moreover, this type of analysis is based on localised texts and requires a linguist specialised in the language to conduct the intensive data analysis, which would be labour intensive if survey researchers were to study behaviour in a large number of survey respondents.

To fill this research gap, it is necessary to develop a coding scheme where coders, not trained in the field of linguistics, could apply the tool to measure the communication style of a group of language speakers and allow the application of a quantitative analysis method. The research reported in this chapter is part of the ongoing research initiated by Pan (this volume) to systematically code and analyse the quality of survey responses provided by respondents. Based on linguistic theories, Pan developed a new approach to code and to analyse linguistic behaviours so that even a non-linguist could easily be trained to use the coding scheme. In this study, the coding scheme was applied to analyse and compare Chinese and English speakers' responses to one type of interview question (personal opinion questions) to fully explore the effect of communication styles on interview responses.

Study objectives

The primary objective of this study was to measure the communication style of a large sample of Chinese speakers so that the findings will be generalisable. The analysis focused on their responses to a personal opinion type question and expanded the scope of Pan's study (Pan, this volume) with a full set of Chinese and English cognitive interview data. By applying the new coding and measurement tool, this study compared the communication style of Chinese respondents to that of English-speaking respondents and performed statistical tests on any observed differences between the two sample groups. The second objective was to examine the internal validity of the survey question by analysing the contextual cues, provided by the respondents during the entire interview, that either support or contradict their face value response to the opinion question. This enables the coders to determine the meaning behind the response. A final objective was to explore the social and demographic factors associated with the communication styles of Chinese respondents to predict the scope of the phenomenon observed.

This research contributes to prior studies on Chinese discourse patterns and cross-cultural pragmatic differences between Chinese and native speakers of English by examining a larger study sample to enhance the external validity of the findings. It examines and controls for sub-group differences and the 'true' meaning of responses (internal validity of the survey question measure) for the Chinese speakers.

Findings from this research have practical implications for questionnaire development for Chinese speakers and will help evaluate an analytic tool developed for cross-cultural survey research.

Research questions

This study has three specific research questions in the design that correspond to its study objectives:

Q1. Are Chinese-speaking respondents more likely to use indirect and CTFV responses than respondents who speak only English at home?

Q2. Do Chinese speakers use indirect or CTFV responses to hide their lack of interest in participating in a future survey?

Q3. What type of social-demographic factors relate to the linguistic behaviours among Chinese speakers?

Methodology

Data

This research uses data collected as part of two multilingual research projects undertaken at the United States Census Bureau. The combined data set consists of 224 cognitive interviews conducted between 2006 and 2008 with five different language groups (Chinese, Korean, Spanish, Russian and English). Cognitive interviews are a commonly used qualitative method in survey research to pre-test survey questions. They are semi-structured interviews to "study the manner in which targeted audiences understand, mentally process, and respond to the materials" provided by survey researchers (Willis 2005: 3). Interviewers use think-aloud methods, cognitive probes and debriefing questions (Willis 2005) to elicit detailed and in-depth information about respondents' interpretations and mental processes when reacting to the material they are reading. In the two cognitive interviewing studies, participants were asked to review some survey documents and to provide their feedback regarding the survey documents. A series of questions were asked to ascertain their intention to participate in a survey called the American Community Survey (ACS) sponsored by the US Census Bureau.

Both projects recruited purposive samples in three metropolitan areas in the US with high concentrations of the target language groups, and a range of demographic characteristics to improve the representativeness of the sample.[3] For the purpose of this study, only the Chinese and English language groups were selected as the sample. Cognitive interview summary data (available in English only) and in-language transcripts (when available) of 46 Chinese and 33 English cognitive interviews were used in this study. Table 9.1 below shows the demographic characteristics of the two selected groups of language speakers.

Analysis

The key concept of interest for this chapter is the communication styles of the study sample when responding to a personal opinion survey question. Pan (this volume) defines personal opinion questions as those that "ask about respondents' views of an issue or intention of certain action". In this study, the analysis focused on examining respondents' communication style when responding to one such question, which asks respondents their intention to participate in a survey conducted by the US Census Bureau.

Table 9.1 Demographics of study sample

Characteristics	Chinese (total N=46)	English (total N=33)
Gender		
Female	28 (61%)	20 (61%)
Male	18 (39%)	13 (39%)
Age		
LT35	4 (9%)	9 (27%)
35–54	20 (43%)	17 (52%)
55 and over	22 (48%)	7 (21%)
Education		
Less than high school	25 (54%)	5 (15%)
High school	15 (33%)	14 (42%)
College	6 (13%)	14 (42%)
Year of Entry		
Before 1990	8 (17%)	Not
1990–1999	21 (46%)	Applicable
2000 or later	17 (37%)	
Preferred Chinese dialect		
Mandarin	30 (65%)	
Cantonese	10 (22%)	Not
Shanghainese	3 (7%)	Applicable
Fukienese	2 (4%)	
Shandonese	1 (2%)	

If you were selected, would you participate in the survey?

如果您被选中，您会不会参加这项调查？

This question was classified as a 'personal opinion question' according to Pan's coding scheme on interview question types because this question was designed a) to obtain information on whether respondents were willing to take the action of participating in the ACS and b) to predict their survey participation behaviour.

Personal opinion question and response types

The two major communication styles that will be measured in this chapter are (1) (in)directness of response; and (2) CTFV response.

Indirectness of response

This study defines and measures (in)directness of speech based on the (ir)relevancy of a participant's response to the interview question. To fully complete the proposition of the survey participation intention question, the interview question has a proposition with a key question word, functioning to elicit an expected 'yes/no' answer that matches the semantic content. Using discourse analysis methods, the types of responses were categorised based on their relevance to the proposition of the question. When the response fully answered the question, it was coded as 'match' and a matched response is defined as a direct response. A response that partly answered the question was coded as 'partial matching'. When a response was totally off track, or off topic, it was coded as 'off'. Any *don't know* response or resistance from a respondent to provide any answer was coded as 'opt out'. This study considers these three types of responses as indirect responses.

To ensure coders' reliability for this study, two sociolinguists (one native Chinese speaker and one non-native Chinese speaker) and another native Chinese social science researcher served as the coders. Using the coding scheme described above, they independently coded responses provided by the respondents during all exchange turns taken that related to a personal opinion type question asked by the interviewers; they obtained 237 codes for all 79 respondents. A very high inter-rater agreement between the coders was obtained (233 out of 237 codes received the same codes from all coders). To reach a consensus, the coders then convened to review and resolve the disagreement in coding. For the four items where there were disagreements, the coding that was identical for two of the three coders was used.

Contrary-to-face-value response

This study defines a CTFV response as saying 'yes' for 'no' and vice versa to the survey participation intention question. To determine whether a respondent has provided a CTFV response, other contextual cues and responses throughout the interview that provide contradictory evidences to their initial response were examined. For instance, imagine the following scenario. A respondent reported that she would probably participate in the survey when the interviewer asked the survey participation intention question (see excerpts from the interview below). However, after reviewing the entire interview summary (available in English only), clues and evidences suggesting that the respondent had provided a CTFV response were identified. For example, her response in another section of the interview shows that the respondent believed that only US citizens were required to participate in the survey. During one of the exchange turns, it became clear that the respondent, who was only temporarily staying in the US, was not a citizen; she did not believe she was included in the survey. If researchers only take the respondent's face value 'yes' response to the target question, the response may not be accurate. In this instance, the coder had a final interpretation of the meaning of the initial 'yes' response and changed the 'yes' response to a final 'no' response.

> Q: *If you received this letter at your household, what would you do next? Why?*
>
> R: *I will do according to what is being asked in the brochure. It says that it is required by the US law to answer the survey. … If you are an American citizen,* you have the duty to do this thing…
>
> Q: How about those who are here legally, such as green card holders, student visa or work visa holders?
>
> R: I don't know for sure, but *I feel I'm not included. I just stay here.* If the letter has my name on it, I would think it is for me. If it doesn't address me specifically, I don't feel it is for me…
>
> Q: So for those who live here for a few years, it is not for them.
>
> R: Yes, when you handed me this letter, I first looked at the address box of the envelope to see if it is for me, if it addresses me in the address. If it doesn't have my name, but just my address, I will think it's junk mail and will throw it into the trash.

These contextual cues helped determine the final meaning of the survey responses. When the final interpretation of the (true) response was contradictory to the initial response, the response was coded as CTFV.

Findings

This section addresses the three research questions in order. First, it reports the findings on the differences between the linguistic behaviours of Chinese and English speakers in their responses to the survey participation intention question. Then, it examines the relationship between the communication styles of Chinese respondents and their true intention to participate in the future survey. Finally it reports on the social factors that may be related to the communication style of Chinese speakers.

Indirect and CTFV responses

The first research question – '*Are Chinese-speaking respondents more likely to use indirect and CTFV responses than respondents who speak only English at home?*', is addressed in this section. First, the prevalence of the two linguistic behaviours (indirectness and CTFV response style) is presented, followed by a comparison of these behaviours between Chinese-speaking and native English survey respondents. A chi-square test was used to examine whether the observed differences between the groups, if any, were statistically significant.

Indirectness of response by language groups

A total of 46 Chinese and 33 English speakers were included in this analysis. Overall, the results show that the Chinese interviewees provided more indirect responses than the English interviewees in the study sample. Figure 9.2 shows the distribution of direct and indirect responses by Chinese and native English speakers. The first set of bars shows the percentage of respondents providing direct (matched) responses to the question asking about their intention to participate in the American Community Survey in the future. The first dark grey bar on the left shows that only 61 per cent of responses given by Chinese respondents matched the target question while the adjacent light grey bar shows that 97 per cent of responses provided by native English speakers matched the proposition of the target question.

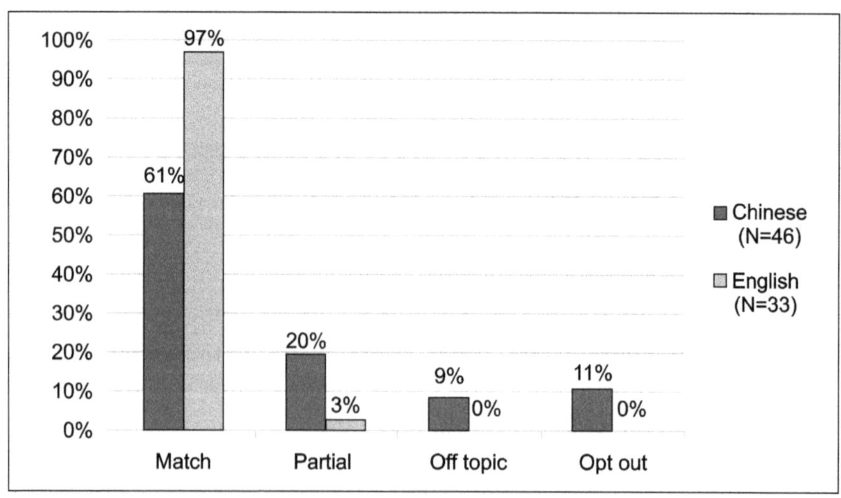

Figure 9.2 Percentages of direct and indirect response types by language groups

The next three sets of bars indicate the percentages of indirect responses (coded as 'partial', 'off-topic' and 'opt out') provided by the study sample. The dark grey bars show that Chinese speakers engaged in all three types of indirect responses: partially matching (20%), off (9%) and opt out (11%) responses. On the contrary, the English speakers only demonstrated one type of indirect responses – 'partially matching' – and at a much lower rate (3%). A binary variable was created to categorise all the responses into two categories: (1) direct responses and (2) indirect responses. The indirect responses comprise all three forms of indirect responses. Figure 9.3 shows that 39 per cent of Chinese speakers and 3 per cent of native English speakers in the study provided indirect responses to the question.

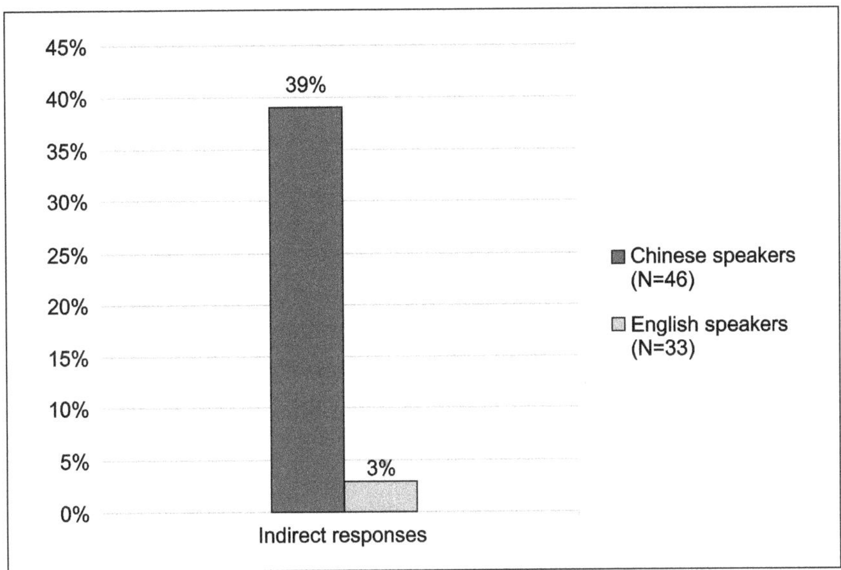

Figure 9.3 Percentages of indirect responses by language groups

Prior research suggests that there is a relationship between language and communication style. To test this hypothesis, a chi-square test was used and the observed group difference (39% versus 3%) is statistically significant (chi-square=13.7, p<.001; the same result was obtained using the Fisher Exact test, p<.001). The significant difference implies that there is a relationship between the language and the directness of expressed responses. Table 9.2 summarises the specified degree of confidence such that the estimated prevalence of indirect response behaviour of the sample can be given with more than 99 per cent confidence that the provided interval 0.20 to 0.59 contains the proportion of Chinese speakers that will use an indirect communication style. Similarly, the estimated prevalence of behaviour can be given with more than 99 per cent confidence that the provided interval 0 to 0.11 contains the proportion of English speakers that will use an indirect communication style. Note that the confidence intervals for the two language groups do not overlap, suggesting that there is a difference between the communication styles of the two groups.

Table 9.2 Confidence interval for estimated prevalence of indirect communication style by language groups

Language group	Mean (std dev.)	99% C.I. (low, high)	N
Chinese	0.39 (0.49)	0.20, 0.59	46
English	0.03 (0.17)	−0.05, 0.11	33

Initial face value responses and contrary-to-face-value evidence

This section presents the initial face value responses to the survey participation intention question, given by both the Chinese and English speakers in this study. Figure 9.4 summarises the face value responses of the two language groups. The first set of bars show that the percentage of English speakers who were willing to participate in the future survey was 94 per cent, whereas 74 per cent of the Chinese speakers said they were willing to do so. The second set of bars show that 3 per cent of English speakers and 11 per cent of Chinese speakers provided a 'no' response. Another revealed that 3% of English speakers and 15 per cent of Chinese speakers provided a response that suggested they 'may be' willing to participate in future survey responses. The chi-square statistical test shows that the difference in the willingness to participate in a future survey between the English (94%) and Chinese speakers (74%) is significant (chi-sq=5.9, p<.05). The English speakers in the study were significantly more likely to agree to participate in a future survey than the Chinese speakers.

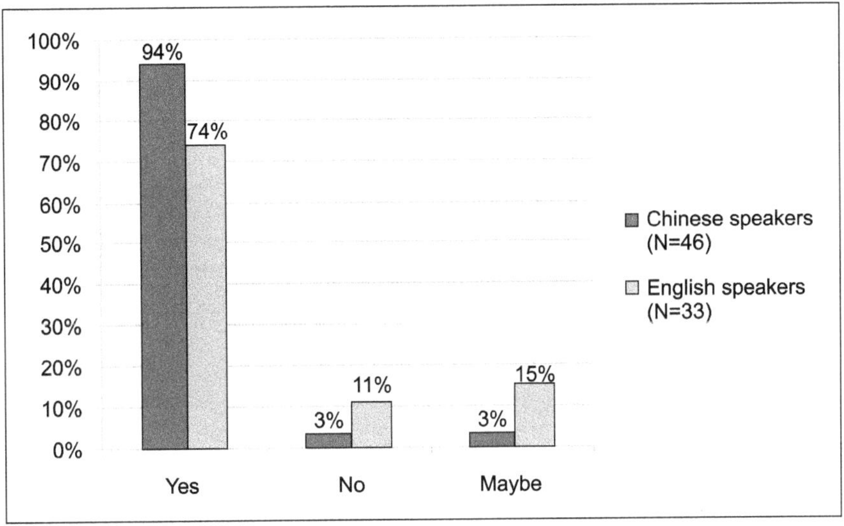

Figure 9.4 Initial face value responses by language groups

After the coders determined the (in)directness of responses to the survey participation intention question, the coders examined other responses in the interview that provided CTFV evidence in respondents' initial responses. The coders then made a final interpretation of the respondents' true intention to participate or not in a future survey. The results show that none of the English speakers provided contradictory evidence whereas 19 out of 46 (41%) of the initial responses provided by the Chinese speakers were contrary to face value. Among the 19 respondents who provided CTFV response, 18 of them provided a 'maybe' or a 'yes' initial response and they were reinterpreted as a 'no' response. The remaining respondent (1/19) had initially provided a 'no' response but was reinterpreted as a 'yes' response. Table 9.3 below provides the summary statistics for the estimated prevalence of the CTFV behaviour in the study sample. It can be presented with more than 99 per cent confidence that the provided interval – 0.22 to 0.61 – contains the proportion of Chinese speakers that will use CTFV communication style.

Table 9.3 Confidence interval for estimated proportion of CTFV communication style

Language group	Mean (std. dev.)	99% C.I. (low, high)	N
Chinese	0.41 (0.50)	0.22, 0.61	46
English	0 (0)	NA	33

Figure 9.5 shows both the initial face value and the final interpreted responses for the Chinese speakers in this study. The percentage of Chinese speakers who are willing to participate in the future survey drops from 74 per cent to 52 per cent while the percentage of those who have no intention to do so increased from 11 per cent to 44 per cent. This reinterpretation further increased the difference between the English (94%) and Chinese speakers (52%) in their willingness to participate in a future survey. Hence, this contrary-to-face-value response style can lead survey researchers to overestimate the proportion of Chinese respondents who are willing to participate in the future survey.

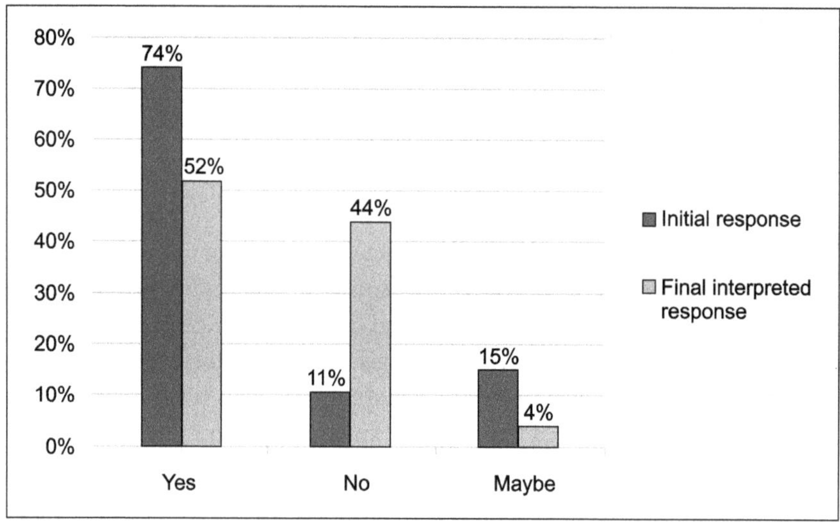

Figure 9.5 Percentages of initial and final interpreted responses to the survey participation intention question among Chinese speakers

Relationship between communication styles and survey participation among Chinese speakers

This section reports how Chinese respondents' communication style is related to their true intention to participate in a future survey. It addresses the second research question – *'Do Chinese speakers use indirect or contrary-to-face-value response to hide their lack of interest in participating in a future survey?'* Given that the normative style of Chinese communication is harmony-oriented, it is expected that Chinese respondents who do not wish to participate in the future survey will be more likely to provide indirect and/or CTFV responses than Chinese respondents who are willing to do so.

Figure 9.6 shows the proportion of indirect and/or CTFV responses that were provided by the Chinese respondents, based on their initial face value response. Overall, respondents with an initial face value 'yes' responses were much more likely to provide their responses directly, whereas those who had provided a 'maybe' or a 'no' initial response did so mostly indirectly. The first bar on the left of the graph shows the frequency distribution of the linguistic behaviours of Chinese respondents who provided an initial 'yes' response to the target question. About 68 per cent of them (23/34) provided the 'yes' response in a direct manner, where their answers matched the proposition of the survey question. Another 15 per cent (5/34) provided the 'yes' response indirectly, and 18 per cent (6/34) used both indirect and CTFV response styles. The middle bar shows that all Chinese speakers who provided a 'maybe' answer used both indirect and CTFV response styles – none did so directly. The last bar shows that all the respondents who responded 'no' initially did so indirectly.

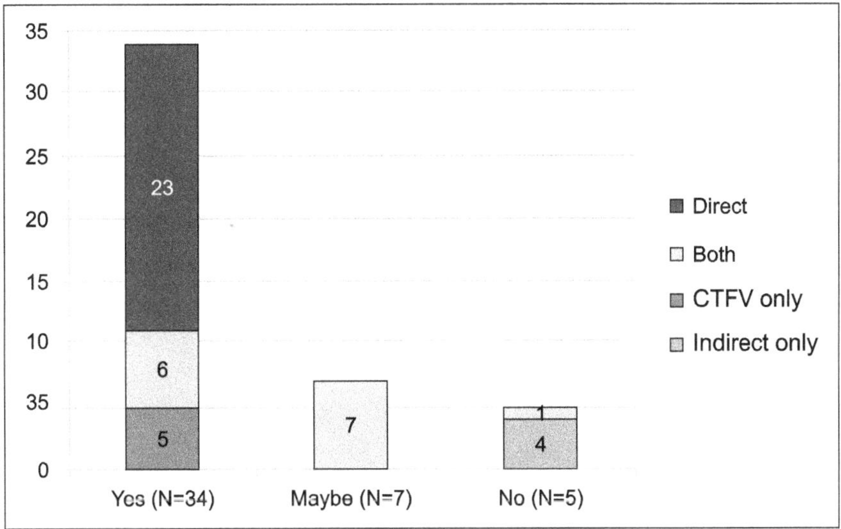

Figure 9.6 Chinese speakers' linguistic behaviours by initial face value responses

Figure 9.7 shows the final interpreted responses of the Chinese speakers. The key message from Figure 9.7 is that none of the true 'no' responses was provided in a direct manner. They were either provided indirectly and/or were CTFV responses. In contrast, the majority (23 out of 24 or 96%) of 'yes' responses were provided directly, and reinterpretation was not required for these genuine 'yes' responses.

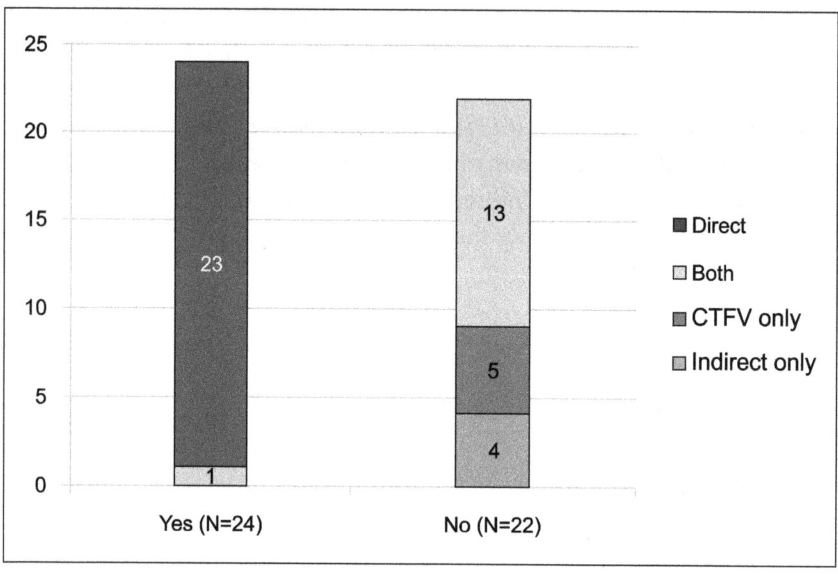

Figure 9.7 Chinese speakers' linguistic behaviours and final interpreted responses to participate in future survey

Chinese speakers' linguistic behaviour and its predictive value of responses to survey question

Earlier it has been shown that indirect responses are related to the final 'no' responses and that CTFV responses are mostly coded as final 'no' responses. Logistic regression has often been used in demography to estimate the probability of an event occurring, such as mortality (Singer and Willett 1991), and in this case to assess respondents' unwillingness to participate in a survey. This study used a logistic regression model to predict the final 'no' response (a binary dependent variable) as a function of the two observed linguistic behaviours. The findings indicate that both linguistic behaviours were significant in predicting a true 'no' response. The odds ratio estimates show that the Chinese speakers who provided indirect responses (p<.01) or those who gave CTFV responses (p<.01) were significantly more likely to have a final interpreted 'no' response to the survey participation question than their counterparts who did not use either one of these communication styles.

The same result is obtained when educational level was added to the model (results not shown), indicating that the relationship between communication style and true survey participation intention remains, regardless of the respondent's educational attainment. The identification of such linguistic behaviours may help identify problematic survey questions and help interpret the true meaning of an initial response for a survey question.

Social-demographic factors and how they relate to the linguistic behaviours among Chinese speakers

This section examines the relationship between social demographic factors and communication style among Chinese speakers, and addresses the third research question – '*What type of social-demographic factors relate to the linguistic behaviours among Chinese speakers?*' Associations were found between educational attainment and dialect preferences in communication style, but no statistically significant associations were found between gender and age. The next two sections describe the significant findings.

Educational attainment

Education is a formal way of socialising and reinforcing cultural norms, which are the expected behaviours within a society or group and indicate the approved and established norms of ways of doing things, of dress, of speech and of appearance (Scollon and Scollon 1995). It might be expected that Chinese respondents with higher educational attainment would demonstrate more culturally appropriate or prescribed behaviour than their counterparts with less education. The findings support this hypothesis. Figure 9.8 shows that 71 per cent of Chinese respondents with college education used an indirect response style while 43 per cent of those with high school and 28 per cent of those with less than high school educational attainment provided indirect responses. Similarly, Chinese respondents with college education had the highest percentage of using CTFV response style compared to high school (43%) and those with less than high school education (28%).

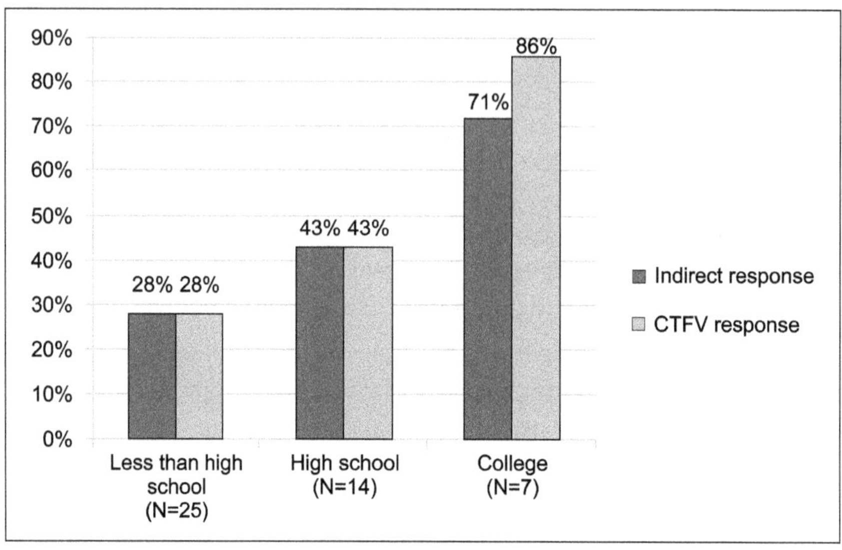

Figure 9.8 Percentages of indirect and contrary-to-face-value (CTFV) responses by educational attainment

Due to the small number of Chinese respondents with a college degree, the two groups of Chinese respondents with higher levels of educational attainment were combined into one group – at least high school education – so that a chi-square test could be conducted. The chi-square result shows that educational attainment is related to the use of indirect responses (chi-sq=2.8, p<0.1) and CTFV responses (chi-sq=4.0, p<0.05). Logistic regression analysis was used to examine whether the same binary education variable (at least high school versus less than high school) is predictive of Chinese respondents' communication style. The odds ratio estimates show that the Chinese speakers with at least a high school education are 2.8 times more likely than the other Chinese speakers to use indirect responses (p<.10) and 12 times more likely to use CTFV responses (p<.05) than their counterparts with less education.

Given the significant relationship between educational attainment and the use of indirect responses, a logistic regression model was used to predict the use of indirect communication as a function of the language group, and a control for respondents' educational attainment, to make sure the difference found between the two language groups was not because of educational attainment. The odds ratio estimate shows that regardless of educational attainment, respondents who were Chinese were 32 times more likely (significant at p<.01) to provide an indirect response to the survey intention question than those who were English speakers. Likewise, regardless of spoken language, respondents with at least high school education were three times more likely (significant at p<.10) to provide indirect responses than those with less educational attainment.

Dialect preference among Chinese speakers

Among the Chinese speakers in this study, about 65 per cent of them (see Table 9.1) spoke Mandarin or preferred to speak Mandarin, while the remaining spoke or preferred to speak a Chinese dialect other than Mandarin, such as Cantonese or Shanghainese. A significant association was found between dialect preference and indirect response style. Figure 9.9 shows that 69 per cent of Chinese respondents in this study whose preferred dialect was not Mandarin, used an indirect response style while 27 per cent of those who spoke or preferred to speak Mandarin did so. The difference is statistically significant (chi-sq=9.0; p<.01). The percentages of CTFV responses show a similar pattern for the two dialect groups – 56 per cent versus 33 per cent respectively. However, the chi-square test result was not statistically significant. It is possible that the sample size (n=46) is too small to detect any statistical significance for this factor.

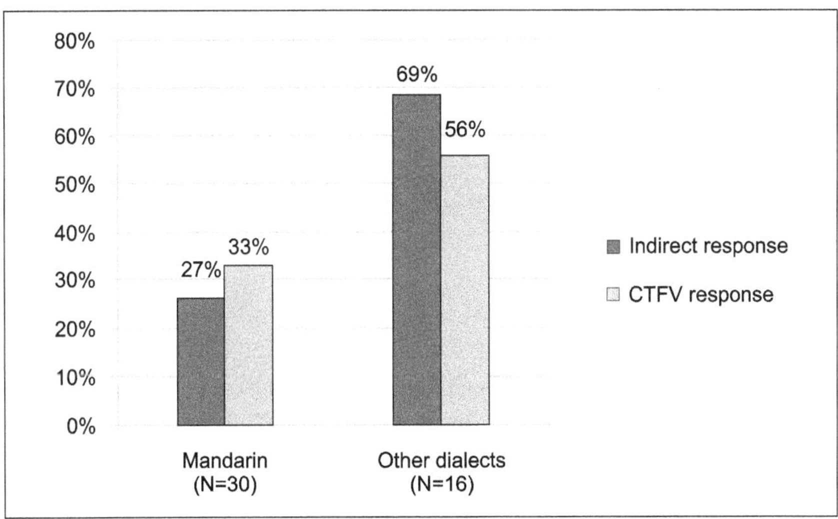

Figure 9.9 Percentages of indirect responses and dialect preferences among Chinese speakers

Summary

To summarise, the Chinese-speaking respondents in this study were significantly more likely to provide indirect responses that did not directly match the proposition to the survey questions than their English-speaking counterparts. More than 40 per cent of Chinese respondents demonstrated CTFV communication style, while none of the English respondents used this communication style. These findings addressed the first research question and showed that the use of indirect and CTFV response behaviours is more prevalent among Chinese-speaking survey respondents than among their counterparts who spoke only English at home, even after controlling for educational attainment.

The second research question, which hypothesised that Chinese speakers tend to use an indirect or CTFV communication style to hide their lack of interest in participating in a future survey, was supported by the study results. The use of these linguistic behaviours by the Chinese respondents is found to be highly associated with a true 'no' response. All but one of the respondents who had used either or both communication styles meant to say "no" to the survey question. The findings support the politeness theoretical framework that suggests Chinese respondents, who follow Chinese politeness norms and do not want to create disharmony, will use indirect and CTFV responses.

The third research question explores factors that may explain sub-group differences among the Chinese speakers. The results showed that educational attainment and dialect preferences are related to the use of indirect and CTFV responses among the Chinese speakers. Respondents who had at least completed high school were more likely to use indirect response style and CTFV responses than their counterparts with less than high school educational attainment. Respondents who spoke or preferred to speak a dialect other than Mandarin were more likely to use indirect response style than their Mandarin-speaking counterparts. It is possible that the sub-groups of Chinese speakers communicate differently when they are talking with people who speak other dialects because of the notion of insider and outsider.

Discussion

Based on the analysis of responses to one personal opinion question, and a comparison between the Chinese and English groups, several themes emerged. First, the new coding scheme, drawing from speech act theory, the discursive notion of question-answer sequences, and cross-cultural pragmatics to measure the level of indirectness in the Chinese discourse patterns, shows great promise and allowed the researcher in this study to analyse and quantify behaviour among a large group of respondents.

Second, the findings demonstrate that the use of quantitative data analysis methods is of great value to researchers who need to draw meaningful results from a large body of qualitative data. The quantitative approaches enable the researcher to estimate the prevalence of the indirect and CTFV communication behaviours identified by prior qualitative research with a group of Chinese speakers. Summary results provided in numerical terms can be presented with a specified degree of confidence, such that the estimated prevalence of behaviour can be given with more than 99 per cent confidence in this case that a certain percentage of Chinese speakers used indirect communication style in an interview. Similarly, any observed differences between two language groups can be accompanied by a statement giving the chance (probability) of error (say p=.01), that is, the chance that the conclusion is incorrect. The lower the chance of error the more confidence one can have that the observed difference is statistically significant. Thus the use of quantitative procedures in analysing qualitative information can lend greater credibility to the research findings. Finally, the main beneficial aspect of quantitative analytical approaches is that they provide the means to separate out a large number of complicating factors (e.g. education and dialect preference) that often obscure the main qualitative findings, such as in this study which examines the role of language (a measure of culture) on communication style.

Third, although a much higher proportion of the Chinese speakers in the sample provided indirect responses, compared to the English-speaking sample, it is important to note that such communication styles are used by both Chinese and English speakers in this study. Also, the use of an indirect communication style by Chinese respondents was not universal, and respondents tended to use this style to mask a refusal to participate in any future survey, which supports the assertions of the politeness theory.

Finally, the relatively high proportion of Chinese speakers who provided CTFV responses, compared to that of the English speakers (none), has significant implications for the quality of data collected from Chinese-speaking survey respondents. This finding is intriguing because it shows that a large portion of the CTFV responses were related to 'no' responses. It suggests that the interview question, which was asked in Chinese and was clearly understood by the Chinese respondents, may not be a valid tool of measurement if a large proportion of Chinese speakers who meant to provide a true 'no' answer used CTFV responses. Hence, it is important to design interview questions for Chinese speakers so that the questionnaire can collect the type of data that the research is seeking to generate. Moreover, it is necessary to analyse the responses of Chinese speakers throughout the entire interview, to look for cues and contextual information that are contradictory to the face value response.

Conclusion

While some discourse analysis studies use quantitative methods in analysing texts (Cheng, this volume; Jiang 2006), they often focus the analysis on variation using texts, such as the frequency count of language instances with a single case study rather than with a group of respondents. To expand on Pan's earlier work in this volume, this study used a relatively large data set, which allowed the researcher to examine the linguistic features of a group of respondents rather than just one case study, to relate these linguistics features to respondents' social contextual variables and to compare the group average with those of another language group. This validates the utility of discourse analysis and generalises the findings to a larger group of individuals. This research also links a discursive strategy (indirectness in responses to standardised questions in comparable interview settings) to demographic characteristics of the Chinese respondents under study. This analytical method resonates with the traditional sociolinguistic method of studying social class dialects (Labov 1972), and the analysis provides support to the findings and validates the conclusion of prior qualitative analysis research, such as those in Pan's chapter (this volume).

One major finding from this study is that the indirect speech style and CTFV responses provided by Chinese respondents may have far-reaching implications on survey data validity beyond the initial confusions it causes the interviewer. The findings are consistent with earlier qualitative research, and this study identifies the same differences in communication style with a larger sample of Chinese speakers, thus making the findings more readily generalisable. The comparisons between the Chinese and English groups provide strong evidence of the significant differences between the two groups. However, not all Chinese are implicit, indirect or vague in their answers when responding to the survey participation question.

Furthermore, the examination of demographic characteristics and sociocultural factors highlights the importance of within-group differences and variations of communication style among Chinese speakers. This study highlights why it is important to pay attention to the socio-demographic characteristics of survey participants and how these characteristics may affect the likelihood of collecting the type of direct and matched responses or data that survey researchers expect. This kind of analysis has furthered the understanding of Chinese linguistic behaviours in context, and will help survey researchers' design and improve questionnaires for survey interviews.

Although the sample in this study was not randomly selected, the demographic characteristics of this sample were carefully matched to those of the survey respondents to the 2006 American Community Survey, to enhance the representativeness of the sample so that the results may be generalisable to the larger Chinese-speaking population. Future study should apply the new metric used for this study to a random sample, and control for social demographic factors identified in this research. This will enhance the external validity of the current study by strengthening the findings from the current study and allowing an estimation of the extent of certain Chinese linguistic behaviour to be generalised beyond the cognitive laboratory sample.

Acknowledgements

I would like to express my gratitude to the US Census Bureau for supporting this research and for its permission to use its cognitive interview data. I am grateful to Dr. Yuling Pan for her support of this research by allowing me to use the data that she has collected and by providing invaluable comments on an earlier draft of this manuscript. Special thanks to Rolando Rodriguez and Dr. Katherine Condon who reviewed and provided constructive comments, which improved this chapter. I appreciate the comments from Dániel Z. Kádár and from anonymous reviewers, which have made this manuscript better. Special thanks to Jessie Cox for coding the data, and Stephanie Sheffield and Sarah Wilson for editing earlier drafts of this manuscript. However, any errors remain my sole responsibility.

Notes

1. Based on Census Bureau data, over 55 million US residents (about one in five) aged five and older reported regularly speaking a language other than English at home (Shin and Kominski 2010).
2. The United States Census Bureau serves as the leading source of quality data about the US nation's people and economy (www.census.gov) and is one of the largest data collection agencies in the world. These demographics and economic data are collected mainly in the form of survey questionnaires.
3. For more details of the two research projects, please see Pan et al (2006, 2008).

References

Cheng, W. (2011) The pragmatics of Q&A interactions in public media discourses. In Y. Pan and D. Z. Kádár (eds) *Chinese Discourse and Interaction*. London: Equinox.

Gu, Y. (1990) Politeness phenomena in modern Chinese. *Journal of Pragmatics* 14: 237–257.

Günthner, S. (1993) German-Chinese interactions: Differences in contextualization, conventions and resulting miscommunication. *Pragmatics* 3: 283–304.

Günthner, S. (1994) Cultural differences in recipient activities: Interaction between Germans and Chinese. In P. Heiner et al. (eds) *Intercultural Communication: Proceedings of the 17ᵗʰ International L.A.U.D. Symposium, Duisburg, 23–27 March 1992* 481–502. Frankfurt am Main: Peter Lang.

Jiang, X. (2006) Cross-cultural pragmatic differences in US and Chinese press conferences: The case of the North Korea nuclear crisis. *Discourse and Society*, 17(2): 237–257.

Labov, W. (1972) *Sociolinguistic Patterns*. Philadelphia, PA: University of Pennsylvania Press.

Ma, R. (1996) Saying 'yes' for 'no' and 'no' for 'yes': A Chinese rule. *Journal of Pragmatics* 25: 257–266.

Pan, Y. (2000) *Politeness in Chinese Face-to-Face Interaction*. Stamford, CT: Ablex.

Pan, Y. (2008) Cross-cultural communication norms and survey interviews. In H. Sun and D. Kádár (eds) *It's the Dragon's Turn: Chinese Institutional Discourses* 17–76. Berne: Peter Lang.

Pan, Y. (2011) What are Chinese respondents responding to? A close examination of question-answer sequences in survey interviews. in Y. Pan, and D. Z. Kádár (eds) *Chinese Discourse and Interaction*. London: Equinox.

Pan, Y. and D. Z. Kádár (2011) *Politeness in Historical and Contemporary Chinese*. New York: Continuum.

Pan, Y., Landreth, A., Schoua-Glusberg, A., Hinsdale, M. and Park, H. (2010) Cognitive interviewing in non-English languages: A cross-cultural perspective. In J. Harkness et al. (eds) *Survey Methods in Multinational, Multiregional and Multicultural Contexts* 91–113. Berlin: Wiley.

Pan, Y., Hinsdale, M., Schoua-Glusberg, A. and Park, H. (2008) Cognitive Testing of ACS Multilingual Brochures in Multiple Languages. *Research Report Series* (Survey Methodology – #2008-6), Statistical Research Division, US Census Bureau Washington, DC 20233.

Pan, Y., Schoua-Glusberg, A., Hinsdale, M., and Park, H. (2006) Cognitive Testing of Translations of ACS CAPI Materials in Multiple Languages. *Research Report Series* (Survey Methodology – #2006-9), Statistical Research Division, US Census Bureau Washington, DC 20233.

Scollon, R. and Scollon, S. W. (1995) *Intercultural Communication: A Discourse Approach*. Oxford: Blackwell.

Shin, H. B. and Kominiski, R. A. (2010) *Language Use in the United States: 2007 American Community Survey Reports, ACS-12.* US Census Bureau, Washington, DC.

Singer, J. D. and Willett, J. B. (1991) Modeling the days of our lives: Using survival analysis when designing and analyzing longitudinal studies of duration and the timing of events. *Psychological Bulletin* 110 (September 1991): 268–290.

Young, L. W. L. (1994) *Crosstalk and Culture in Sino-American Communication.* New York: Cambridge University Press.

Willis, G. (2005) *Cognitive Interviewing.* Thousand Oaks, CA: Sage Publications.

10

Customer-employee interaction from a diachronic perspective

Hao Sun

Introduction

Approaching discourse analysis from a diachronic perspective, the research described in this chapter examines Chinese telephone interactions between customer callers and employee recipients. Built on the author's previous research (Sun 1998, 2004, 2008), the current study compares data obtained recently with a comparable set collected over a decade ago, aiming to identify and characterise shifts and changes in business employees' discourse as observed recently in customer-employee telephone discourse interactions in mainland China.

This situated discourse analysis contributes to the fields of discourse analysis, sociolinguistics, pragmatics and cross-cultural studies in that it provides an up-to-date, detailed account of Chinese discourse interactions based on customer-employee telephone interactions. It enriches the field of institutional discourse from a cross-cultural perspective, as interlocutors in the Chinese interactional contexts assume designated institutional roles. In addition, it makes important contributions to studies in sociolinguistics in general with valuable insights obtained from a diachronic analysis of discourse practice over time. Although the current study is not focused on historical pragmatics, a newly established field that has gained growing recognition (Arnovick 1999), it shares a similar concern in uncovering and elucidating changes in language use. Comparing two sets of comparable discourse data collected in the same linguistic community at two points of time, it adds to scholarship in sociolinguistics with regard to language change and variation as well as how language and society interact at the level of discourse and pragmatics in particular communities. As pointed out by Eckert and McConnell-Ginet, "neither language nor the social world is static" (2003: 52), and they are maintained mutually as well as changing mutually.

This study is intended to contribute to an increasing body of research examining changes in various aspects of language due to external social factors. Focusing on the diachronic development of linguistic landscape, namely types of signs in Tokyo, Backhaus (2005) reports an increase in linguistic heterogeneity in terms of the number of languages and scripts, the amount of multilingual information, foreign language proficiency and proportion of languages and scripts. Thomaj (2006) examines the impact of historical and sociological changes on the Albanian language, in particular the lexical development, describing the adoption of many foreign words as well as making a distinction between justified and unjustified borrowings. Discussing the interaction between globalisation and language, Coulmas (2005) addresses issues of overall language situations, policies and outcomes at both national and global levels in globalising environments. In addition, scholars conducting research in the area of call centres have investigated the issue of linguistic globalisation (e.g. Sonntag 2009) through the examination and comparison of global language practices and perceptions.

The current study was undertaken in light of observed changes in discursive practice in China during the past decade or so, and these shifts are closely connected to changes in economic and social structure in the Chinese society. In general, China's economic transformation has been recognised as a remarkable success. According to a recent report (Barboza 2010), China has surpassed Japan to become the second largest economy in the world behind only the US. At the same time, the Chinese government has shown a general policy of active engagement towards globalisation during the past few decades. According to Wu (2003), marketisation and globalisation are "entangled processes". Since the 1990s, globalisation as a paradigm of change has become "a kind of discourse and social imagination in China and has become a substitute for 'modernization' there" (Bao 2008: 557).

The rapid economic growth and the government's policies embracing globalisation have led to significant urban development and infrastructure transformation of the metropolis Shanghai into an emerging world city. As part of the strategy in the early 1990s for closer integration with the world economy, the Chinese central government designated Shanghai to be made one of the international economic, financial and commercial centres, which led to preferential policies towards its development especially during the decade 1990–2000. The municipal government responded actively and in a timely way to these historic opportunities and their efforts have resulted in many local initiatives and significant changes.

Among other factors, foreign investment is a central force underlying the rapid rise of the Chinese economy and the transformation of Shanghai into one of the world's leading emerging global cities (Wu 2003). For example, foreign investment in Shanghai in 2000 was three times that of 1992. In addition to the massive inflow of foreign investment, Shanghai's development zones have become the most favoured places for foreign investors. These development zones implement special policies for foreign ventures and enterprises, where key tenants are typically multinational enterprises, for example, GM, IBM, Volkswagen, Sharp and Philips (Wei and Leung 2005). By 2002, about 299 companies from the Global 500 corporations had investments or offices in Shanghai, among which 166 firms had direct investment; over 60 had set up China headquarters there (Wei and Leung 2005). Meanwhile, the infusion of foreign direct investment (FDI) and the great potential for regional headquarters has been accompanied by increasing growth in finance, banking and service sectors. According to Wei and Leung (2005), as of 2000, there were 45 foreign banks with branches in Shanghai, including City Bank, Bank of American and HSBC among others, providing important financial services to foreign firms in Shanghai. The concentration of banking services further underlines the role of the metropolis of Shanghai as the most important financial centre in China.

The combined effects of opening up and marketisation have fundamentally altered the role of Shanghai in China's development. Between 1990 and 2000, per capita GDP (in US dollar terms) has more than tripled for the city of Shanghai (Zhang 2003). More recent urban developments have been further accelerated by the World Expo held recently in Shanghai as well as efforts in making the city a financial centre of Asia. The metropolis of Shanghai currently has a population of approximately 19 million including both residents and a work force in transit; there were also over 150,000 resident foreigners working and living in Shanghai in 2009 (Statistical Yearbook 2010). Cited as a city which, by international standards, "represents one of the most successful cases of urban economic development in the 1990s" (Zhang 2003: 1550), Shanghai is continuing its growth, seeking to make itself more cosmopolitan in terms of commerce, information technology and service in various dimensions.

In addition, rapid economic development, market economy, globalisation and continued opening up to other countries have also led to changes in values, ideology and the development of consumerism. "Consumerism is indispensable to globalization" (Bao 2008: 563). At the same time, the status of customers has changed, or raised to be exact, as a result of the market economy and other economic and social changes. Nowadays consumers, including customers, are appealed to, sought or even competed for, and the quality of the services provided to customers has improved in many respects accordingly. In addition, there seems to be a push for promoting civility and etiquette as reflected in the showing of short video programmes on city buses advocating the use of courteous expressions and behaviour for office and social interaction. Along with observations of changes in various dimensions discussed above, telephone interactions between customers and employees seem to manifest a shift as well, which will be examined in detail below.

Before our discussion proceeds further, a note of explanation is in order. The term 'employee' is used in this chapter as a broad term to refer to any employee who answered customers' calls on behalf of the business or service by which each of them was employed, whether it was a restaurant, department store, company or telephone directory service. The term 'representative' is used in this chapter as well, but it refers to staff members whose only duties consist of providing customer service over the telephone without attending to customers face-to-face on the premises. In addition, representatives might receive specific customer service training for telephone interactions while this may not be the case for employees.

In spite of the fact that the term 'business telephone calls' is often used in analysis of business communication, as well as in telephone interactions, none of the calls in this study falls into this category since all the calls involve a customer and an employee rather than interactions between two representatives from two different companies. In this chapter, the term 'customer-employee telephone interactions' (CETI for short) is used for the sake of convenience to refer to discursive interactions over the telephone between customers and employees of businesses, services or city government offices.

Primary findings discussed in this chapter are centreed on observed differences in the closing phase of employees' discursive patterns. For comparison purposes, the chapter follows a similar organisation pattern to that of the author's previous publication (Sun 2008). The section immediately below focuses on *Data and Methodology*. Some differences between the two sets of data are described in the section '*Customer-employee telephone interactions*' which provides descriptions of two CETI in their entirety, as well as providing background information for the focused analysis. The section '*Revisiting closings*' follows up with a detailed analysis of closings, and presents the most salient differences between the two sets of data. The *Discussion* section is followed by a *Conclusion*.

Data and methodology

Examining customer-employee telephone interactions in the same linguistic community as my earlier research (Sun 2004, 2008), this study takes a diachronic approach to discourse analysis, comparing employee recipients' discursive practice across time. Focusing on the same linguistic community renders a diachronic comparison meaningful. Examining similar communicative events further underlines the comparability of such interactions as well as the relationship between the two parties involved.

This study uses two sets of telephone calls in Chinese recorded in Shanghai, China more than a decade apart: the first set (data A) was collected in the mid-1990s while the current set (data B) was obtained in the spring of 2009. Both sets consist of naturally occurring telephone interactions, and each set constitutes part of a larger set of telephone recordings. For this chapter, the focus of my analysis is on data B while data A serves as the baseline for comparison.

Data A (collected in the mid-1990s) is comprised of 16 calls to businesses, services or institutions. These calls were recorded by four female native speakers of Chinese, aged between 35 and 50 at the time data A was collected. The current set of calls (data B) consists of 22 telephone calls recorded by three of the four female participants who took part in the earlier study over a decade ago. All three women are high school graduates, and two of them obtained associate degrees. Their job titles include technical assistant, administrator and administrative staff. All of them had extensive experience with the use of the telephone both at work and at home. Each of the participants kept the recording devices with them for about a week and they did not make any phone calls for the sake of recording, only when there was a real need to call a service, store or company.

Although all the participants who provided data B also took part in data A collection, the various places the phone calls reached were not necessarily the same across the two sets of data due to several factors. First, all the calls occurred naturally and they were made based on the specific needs of the callers at the time of the recording. Secondly, there were changes in the establishment and development of various businesses and services. In addition, the types of services available over the phone increased significantly for data B. For example, calling restaurants to make reservations is a common reason for recorded calls in data B, but it is not observed in data A at all, as most restaurants did not have reservations over the telephone available at that time. Finally, considerable changes also took place in city residents' living standards and life styles. Therefore there was no intended match of the businesses or services called between the two sets of data. Also, none of the names used in this article is in the original form in order to maintain the anonymity of both participants and enterprises.

Methodologically, the fact that the new data were provided by the same participants who recorded telephone calls earlier adds rigour to the findings of this study. Due to technical difficulties in recording good quality telephone interactions using cellular phones, only landline telephone calls were used for this study, even though the cellular phone was already extremely common in Shanghai when data B was collected.

This situated discourse analysis is informed by several theoretical frameworks. The model of Communities of Practice, as outlined by Wenger (1998) and Eckert and McConnell-Ginet (1992), and discussed in Holmes and Meyerhoff (1999), provides important theoretical guidelines for this study. A Community of Practice, as defined by Eckert and McConnell-Ginet (1992), differs from the notion of a speech community in that it is "defined simultaneously by its membership and the practice in which that membership engages" (1992: 95). Therefore, the concept of practice connotes doing, but it is doing "in a historical and social context that gives structure and meaning to what we do" (Wenger 1998: 47). Situating discourse interaction in its social context, this theory assumes that discourse constitutes a type of social practice in which individuals are neither completely free nor without any control. Therefore, linguistic behaviours are not individual and disconnected phenomena. As the authors point out, the notion of Community of Practice explores and articulates the link between social practice and individual place. It enables us not to view the individuals as disconnected entities but as actors participating in social events in various Communities of Practice. Most importantly, this theory assumes change, and that such practice is dynamic (Eckert and McConnell-Ginet 2003). This is central to the current analysis with a focus on identifying and characterising differences and changes in discursive patterns.

The businesses and services to which calls were made in this study include a variety of enterprises including the municipal telephone directory service, banks, restaurants, department and retail stores, utility services and government offices. While most store employees serve customers on their premises as well as answering telephone calls when needed, telephone directory service representatives do not need to attend to customer callers on site. They receive training and their interactions with customers might also be observed more closely, as indicated by the voices of other representatives communicating with customers simultaneously in the background on the recordings. Sometimes, there are also customer satisfaction surveys included at the end of telephone interactions between customer callers and telephone operators or representatives of major banks and large corporations. Therefore, the employees whose discursive interactions are under examination in this study in fact work in different environments and belong to different Communities of Practice. For example, employees who perform various duties in stores or restaurants may only answer customer calls when such needs arise. Their daily working experience will be different from representatives whose job requirements consist of primarily serving customers over the telephone with few other responsibilities or little face-to-face contact with customers.

In fact, it is useful to view the different enterprises for which the employees work as belonging to 'constellations of practices', adopting the notion from Wenger (1998). A constellation is "a particular way of seeing" (1998: 127) entities as related, although they may not be particularly close to one another. Characteristics of a constellation, according to Wenger (1998), can include facing similar conditions, overlapping styles or discourses being located in proximity or having interactions. As all the enterprises described in this study are situated in the same city, serve the same population in general and are embedded in a similar historical, cultural and social context, each individual Community of Practice is not isolated from the practice of other communities; they are somehow connected in a broader sense. "Interactions among local communities can affect their practices without an explicit sense of participation in a constellation" (Wenger 1998:128). Their individual, specific discourse practice may mutually and collectively influence and shape the practice of other communities as well. Such a configuration enables us to see continuities that define broader configurations as well as variations among the different communities. In addition, individuals participate in multiple Communities of Practice; they do not simply belong to one community exclusive of other groups, and they may even assume different roles.

In addition, I draw on analytical concepts from conversation analysis to examine particular aspects of closings in the telephone interactions, as closings in the data constitute one of the most salient observed differences between the two sets of data. Outlined in Schegloff (1968) and Schegloff and Sacks (1973), Conversation Analysis focuses on organisational issues of interaction, examining the interactive and collaborative nature of conversation (Eckert and McConnell-Ginet 2003). Schegloff and Sacks (1973) point out that "conversational closings converge from a diverse range of conversations-in-their-course to a regular common closure with 'bye bye' or its variants" (*ibid.*: 291). Two components are crucial, the authors state, regardless of how other aspects may differ in telephone conversation closings – an initiation of closing and a terminal component. One of the most important notions for Conversation Analysis is adjacency pairs, which constitutes a basic unit as well as an important structure of conversational interaction (Schegloff and Sacks 1973), and it is 'at work' in both the beginning and closing of telephone conversations (Schiffrin 1994). Examples of an adjacency pair include apology and response, invitation and acceptance, thanking and reply, and reciprocal leave-taking. As proposed by Schegloff and Sacks (1973), adjacency pairs exhibit five characteristics: two-utterance length, adjacent positioning of component utterances, different speakers producing each utterance, relative ordering of parts, and discriminative relations. Interactional features examined in this study show interesting phenomena in terms of the functions and positions of the two parts of an adjacency pair.

In order to further capture and shed light on the described changes in discursive practice, frequency of distribution of the features being examined is incorporated in the current analysis of discourse. Combined qualitative and quantitative analyses, an approach that has been adopted by an increasing number of scholars (e.g. Fitzmaurice and Taavitsainen 2003), provide evidence of the differences between the two sets of data under comparison, thus strengthening the observations and analyses presented.

A key to transcript conventions is included as an appendix to this chapter. In the transcript, the letter 'C' stands for customers, who in all cases are callers, while the letter 'E' refers to employees who respond to customer calls. The short form 'LT' is used to represent leave-taking expressions such as *zaijian* 再见 'Goodbye' or 'Bye'.

Customer-employee telephone interactions

For the purpose of comparison, we start with the presentation of two telephone calls from beginning to end; both interactions took place between a customer and an employee. The depiction of a communicative event (Hymes 1972; Saville-Troike 2002) in its entirety enables us to view "the ways in which speech activity is embedded in situations – how a particular activity is initiated, how it is structured, how it ends" (Eckert and McConnell-Ginet 2003: 103). More importantly, this format is similar to the descriptions of an earlier study (Sun 2008) and provides an overview of the communicative events, their discursive features as well as the structural components of the interactions, such as closing.

Excerpt 1 is taken from data set A (Sun 2008), which was recorded in the mid-1990s. The call as shown in Excerpt 1 was made to a dental clinic. It is presented here only to provide a basis for comparison with Excerpt 2.

Excerpt 1 (data A)

01 E: 请 讲
    qing jiang
    'How can I help you?'

02 C: 喂. 是 不 是 都 市 牙 防 所 啊
    wei shi bu shi du shi ya fang suo a
    'Hello. Is this the Municipal Dental Clinic?'

03 E: 嗳
    Ai
    'Yes.'

04 C: 谢 谢 你. 请 问 一下
    xie xie ni   qing wen yi xia
    'Thank you. May I please ask

05   你们 这 儿牙科 拔 牙齿 有 沒 有 专 家 门 诊 啊
    ni men zher ya ke ba ya chi you mei you zhuan ja men zheng a
    if you have appointments by specialists for tooth extraction?'

06 E: 有 的
    you de
    'Yes.'

07 C: 大概 是 什 么 時 间 啊
    da gai shi shen me shi jian a
    'Roughly when are these appointments?'

08 E: 一四
    yi si
    'Mondays and Thursdays.'

09 C: 一四啊
    yi si a
    'Mondays and Thursdays?'

10 E: 嗳
    Ai
    'Yes.'

11 C: 是 全 天 呢//还是 半 天
    shi quan tian ne hai shi ban tian
    'For the whole day or just half of the day?'

12 E: //全天
    quan tian
    'The whole day.'

13 C: 全 天 是 嗎?
    Quan tian shi ma
    'The whole day, right?'

14 E: 嗳
     Ai
     'Right.'

15 C: 你 们 下 午 几 点 挂 号 啊
     ni men xia wu ji dian gua hao a
     'When does check-in begin?'

16 E: 一 点   钟
     yi dian zhong
     'One o'clock.'

17 C: 上   午 呢
     Shang wu ne
     'How about in the morning?'

18 E: 八 点   钟
     Ba dian zhong
     'Eight o'clock.'

19 C: 哦. 謝謝 你哦
     o xie xie ni o
     'OK, thanks a lot.'

20 E: 不要緊
     bu yao jin
     'No problem.'

21 C: 哦
     o
     'OK.'

Excerpt 2 below is from data set B, which was collected in 2009. It is a call made to a restaurant to check on a reservation the caller made a few days earlier. This example is selected for several seasons. First, several features evident in this call are representative of other calls in the current data (data B). Therefore, it serves as a clear example of contrast, reflecting differences compared with data A. Another important reason for the selection of this example is that the transcription of the entire discourse is complete as every utterance is audible.

Excerpt 2 (data B)

01 E: 你 好 玉园 请 讲
     ni hao yuyuan qing jiang
     'Hello. Jade Garden. How can I help you?'

02 C: 哎 玉 园 对吗=
     ei yu yuan dui ma
     'Hello. Jade Garden right?'

03 E: =欸
         yes
         'Yeah.'

04 C: 你 是 城 市 公 园 里 面 的 玉 园 对 吗   =
         ni shi cheng shi gong yuan li mian de yuyuan dui ma
         'This is the Jade Garden in the City Park, correct?'

05 E: =对的
          dui de
         'Yes.'

06 C: 我 想 问 问. 我 明 天 中 午 订 的   餐. 房 间 给
         我 看 看.
         wo xiang wen wen wo ming tian zhong wu ding de can fang jian gei wo
         lankan
         'I'd like to check on my reservation for lunch tomorrow. Do you know which
         room it would be?'

07   查 查 是 不 是 订 好 了
         Cha cha shi bu shi ding hao le
         'Just to check on the reservation.'

08 E: 贵 姓 啊
         Gui xing a
         Surname RF
         'Your (respected) last name please.'

09 C: 我 姓 李. 木子 李
         wo xing li mu zi li
         'It's Li, with the radical wood plus son.'

10 E: 全 名. 请 问
         quan ming qing wen
         'Your full name please.'

11 C: 嗯李婷=
         n li ting
         'Uh Ting Li.'

12 E: =订 好 了 订 好 了
         ding hao le ding hao le
         'It's done. It's done.'

13 C: 订 好 了 对 吧
         ding hao le dui ba
         'OK, it's done, right?'

14 E: 对 的
         dui de
         'Yes.'

15 C: 明 天 中 午 对 吧=
    ming tian zhong wu dui ba
    'Tomorrow for lunch, correct?'

16 E: =对 对 对//好吧
    dui dui dui hao ba
    'Yes, that's right. OK?'

17 C: //哪个 房 间 啊
    na ge fang jian a
    'Which room would it be?'

18 E: 到 时 候 我 报 上 你 的名 字.房 间 号 现 在 不
    能 确 定
    dao shi hou wo bao shang ni de ming zi fang jian hao   xian zai bu
    neng que ding
    'I'll just find your name then, but we don't know which room at this point.'

19 C: 哦 好 的=
    O hao de
    'Oh OK.'

20 E: =好 谢 谢 您 /// 再 见 啊
    hao xie xie ni   zai jian a
    'OK, thank you very much. Bye-bye.'

21 C: / //好 的. 谢 谢 再见
    hao de xie xie zai jian
    'OK. Thanks. Bye.'

Comparing Excerpt 2 with Excerpt 1, we note several differences. First, as can be seen in Excerpt 1, there was no self-identification provided by the clinic. The caller therefore initiated a check in line 2 to ensure that this was indeed the clinic she intended to reach. In Excerpt 2, it is different. The employee provided the name of the restaurant as part of her opening (line 1) in addition to the greeting: "Hi, Jade Garden. How can I help you?" What is interesting is that, in spite of the employee's identification of the restaurant in line 1, there were two repairs initiated by the customer caller, first in line 2 and then in line 4, to ensure that she had indeed reached the right number before she explained the purpose of her call. Repair (Schegloff et al. 1977), one of the mechanisms at work for conversation interactions, refers to correction of an utterance, which can be initiated and completed by either oneself, the current speaker, or others in the conversation, an interlocutor. These two other-initiated repairs indicate that the self-identification provided was not heard clearly; at least the customer was not able to determine the name of the business based on the utterances provided in line 1. Examination of the recorded interaction indicates that the three phrases "Hi, Jade Garden. How can I help you" in line 1 were indeed uttered in a manner with no obvious pauses in between the phrases so that they might very well be heard as a single phrase instead of three separate ones. In spite of the repairs observed in Excerpt 2, business self-identification is a feature exhibited in many other calls in data B, thus reflecting a change in the discursive practice of the businesses and services.

The second observed difference in Excerpt 2 involves the employee's choices of words and phrases. As shown in the transcript, the language used seems fairly courteous, including the use of the polite form 贵姓 *guixing* '(respected) last name please' and the use of the honorific pronoun 您 *ning* 'you' in thanking. On the other hand, while the use of a hedger such as 'Thank you' preceding the purpose statement was observed in line 4 of Excerpt 1, the customer in Excerpt 2 stated the purpose of her call in a rather straightforward manner without a prefacing modifier, beginning with the phrase 我想问问 *wo xiang wen wen* 'I was wondering' to indicate a request for information. The different discursive choices used indicate a slight shift in terms of how both parties aligned themselves vis-à-vis each other. Compared with findings observed in data A, the employee in Excerpt 2 used more courteous word choices in the brief interaction while the customer seemed somewhat more assertive and straightforward.

In the closing section, three features are of interest here: first, each of the two turns actually consists of three different moves: a response, a token of appreciation and then leave-taking (LT). The employee's utterances include 'OK', 'Thank you very much', and 'Bye-bye'. Similarly, the customer caller's expressions consist of three tokens of 'OK', 'Thanks' and 'Bye', a very interesting feature of interaction. Secondly, compared with other calls, this is a fairly short closing, which is completed in two turns (not counting the pre-closing in line 18). Thirdly, the fact that there is both 'signature thanking' (Schegloff and Sacks 1973) and leave-taking extended by both parties forms a sharp contrast with the pattern of a lack of reciprocity on the part of the employees evident in data A. Here the employee's participation in closing projected her as an interlocutor who manifested a similar level of involvement in interaction to that of the customer. Such interaction behaviour is very different from the patterns observed in the earlier study, as is further elaborated on in the section *Revisiting closings*.

Comparing Excerpt 2 with Excerpt 1 in terms of communicative purpose, outcome and manner of interaction, we observe that the customer caller in Excerpt 2 obtained the information she needed and the restaurant staff member provided the information requested. The customer stated her purpose fairly clearly; similarly, the employee answering the phone replied to the questions directly and unequivocally, thus fulfilling the customer's request.

Having presented an overview of one telephone interaction in data B in its entirety compared with an example from a decade ago, we now move on to the examination of closings in detail, as most salient differences are shown in patterns of closing, compared with data set A. It is to closing that our discussion now turns.

Revisiting closings

One of the most striking contrasts between data A and data B is that while 50 per cent of the calls in data A end with a single turn for closing, the number of calls following this pattern decrease drastically to one call (4%) in data B. Meanwhile, the current data also show a variety of new patterns not observed in data A, which will be presented below in detail. It is also striking that about 59 per cent (13 out of 22) of the calls in the current data exhibit leave-taking, whether it is initiated by the customer, the employee, both parties in an overlapping manner, or realised with repetitions of LT. These features form a clear contrast with data set A, considering the fact that only less than one-third of the calls in data A involve LT.

In order to establish a point of departure, salient patterns from an earlier study (Sun 2004, 2008) with regard to closing are briefly summarised here. There are five patterns of closing: (I) one-turn closing, (II) three-turn closing with LT from the customer, (III) three-turn closing with LT from both parties, (IV) two-turn closing (acknowledgement) and (V) two-turn closing (expression). The distribution of these patterns is shown in Table 10.1 below.

Table 10.1 Distribution of closing patterns: data A**

Types	I *One-turn*	II *Three-turn* *(LT by C)*	III *Three-turn* *(LT by C&E)*	IV *Two-turn* *(acknowledge-ment)**	V *Two-turn* *(expression)*	Total *(data A)*
Numbers of calls	8	4	1	2	1	16
Percentage	50%	25%	6%	13%	6%	100%

* The term acknowledgement (category IV) refers to a reply such as "uh hum" in response to a signature thanking while an expression (category V) refers to phrases such as "No problem".

** The percentages for both the total and the subtotal in all the tables in this chapter are rounded up or down.

Two important observations can be made about data A from Table 10.1 above. First, approximately 69 per cent of the calls (Type I, IV and V) do not involve leave-taking at all; these calls end with signature thanking only. Secondly, 50 per cent of the calls (Type I) terminate with the customers' single utterance of 'thank you'; there is no reciprocal reply from the addressee, an overwhelming pattern of lack of reciprocity.

Closings observed in data set B exhibit quite different, as well as more diversified, patterns. If we use the categories already established based on data A, only 6 out of the 22 calls can be properly categorised, accounting for less than 28 per cent of the total, as shown in Table 10.2 below.

Table 10.2 Distribution of closing patterns: data B (I–V)

Types	I One- turn	II Three- turn *(LT by C)*	III Three- turn *(LT by C&E)*	IV Two- turn *(Acknowledge- ment)*	V Two- turn *(Expression)*	I–V *Subtotal* turn	Total *(data B)* *I–XI*
Numbers of calls	1	3	0*	2	0	6	22
Percentage	5%	14%	0%	9%	0%	28%	100%

*   Variant forms of pattern III are separately identified as Types VIII and IX respectively in Table 10.3.

The remaining 16 calls (72 % of the total) of data B show new, different as well as more complicated patterns, which are presented in Table 10.3. It is to patterns VI, VII, VIII and IX that the discussion in this section next turns.

Table 10.3 Distribution of closing patterns: data B (VI–XI)

Types	VI *Voice recording*	VII *Repeated LT*	VIII *Over- lapped LT*	IX *E initiated LT*	X *Three turns*	XI *N/A**	VI–XI *Sub- total*	*Total (data B)*
Numbers of calls	4	2	2	6	1	1	16	22
Percentage	18%	9%	9%	27%	4.5%	4.5%	72%	100%

*   This 'N/A' category refers to a call of which the ending cannot be accurately deciphered/described.

In the following section, descriptions of new patterns observed are provided, followed by an example for each new category identified.

Voice recording (Type VI)

The category called 'voice recording' refers to telephone interactions which end with the requested phone number being provided by an automated system. There are four calls in data set B that fit into this category. Excerpt 3 below provides an example.

Excerpt 3

01 E: 电 话. 你 记　　一下
　　　telephone you note once
　　　'The phone number (is), please make a note.'

02 (Recording) 美食　餐 饮　有 限　公　司
　　　　　　　mei shi meal drink limited company
　　　　　　　'Mei Shi Food Corporation.'

03 E: 请　稍　等
　　　please a bit wait
　　　'Hold on please.'

　(Recording)

04　　工　号 xxxx 为　您　服务
　　　　work number for you service
　　　　'Employee number xxxx is providing service for you.'

05　　请　记录. 3345 777
　　　　please note
　　　　'Please make a note, 3345777.'

06　　请记录. 3345 777
　　　　please note
　　　　'Please make a note, 3345777.'

Calls with such endings in this set of data were all made to the municipal telephone directory service, and feature a distinctive way of closing. What stands out in terms of closing is that there is no more verbal communication between the customer and the human agent following the 'Hold on please' phrase (line 3). After the name of the requested place is stated as shown in line 2 and a phrase for holding on in line 3, customers then hear the recording of the employee number first (line 4), followed by a prompt to get ready, and then the recording of the specific telephone number requested is played twice, as shown in lines 5 and 6. This type of closing manifests a closure unlike other categories in the data, as the automated service assumes the role of the representative in providing the requested phone number. As voice recording in fact constitutes the last turn of the interaction, typical collaborative closing between the two interlocutors is irrelevant in such interactional contexts.

A further point of interest is that, as can be seen from Excerpt 3 above, identification (line 4) of the staff member who is providing the service has also become part of the procedure for telephone interactions between customer representatives and customers in some contexts (such as the directory service), and this is achieved by reference to an employee number rather than personal names. This practice suggests a particular way of identifying staff members in the Chinese context, and it constitutes a major difference from practices in other cultures in which employees often identify themselves by names, for example, Denmark (Have 2002), UK (Cheepen 2000) and the US (Sun 1998). In Chinese culture, identifying oneself to unfamiliar interlocutors using one's name is uncommon. The example discussed in Pan et al. (2002) of Chinese-speaking sales representatives' unwillingness and even resistance to identify themselves in their telemarketing practices in the US (in spite of their excellent performances in other aspects of communication) well illustrates an important difference between the two cultures in this respect. The use of an employee number for staff identification may reflect partly the need to strike a balance between customer service quality control and the need to maintain Chinese culture in a growing market economy under the impact of globalisation. In a sense, it marks the interactional context as institutional or transactional (Brown and Yule 1983) rather than personal or purely socially oriented. However, from a different cultural perspective, such a practice may not be perceived in a positive light, as identifying an employee by number may have negative implications. Such a difference in discourse and business practice is clearly the result of difference in cultural norms.

Repeated leave-taking (Type VII)

The closing pattern identified as repeated leave-taking refers to calls with the presence of more than one extended LT. The following example shows how and when the caller in this case extended leave-taking three times.

Excerpt 4

```
01 E:  嗯.//知道 了
       OK know ASP
       'Uh hum, I understand.'
02 C:  //好    吧
       good SFP
       'OK.'
```

03 E: 这　边　去尽量　　帮　你　问　一下. ///好　　吧
  this side go try best help you ask once good SFP
  'We'll try our best to request the way you want, OK?'

04 C: ///好　的　　好　　的. 麻烦　你　　了
  good PT good PT trouble you ASP
  'OK all right, thank you very much.'

05 E: 欸. 不　客　气
  Yes no guest
  'Oh, you're welcome.'

06 C: 哦. 好. 再　　见　　哦
  OK good again see SFP
  'OK, all right, bye-bye.'

07 E: 嗯. //(xxxx 都市佳话)
  metropolis excellent speak
  'Uh hum (xxxx Super Communication).'

08 C: //再　　见
  Again see
  'Bye.'

09 E: 张　　　小姐再　　见
  zhang Miss again see
  'Bye Ms Zhang.'

10 C: 再　　　见
  again see
  'Bye.'

This is one of the calls made to a reservation hotline provided by the municipal telephone directory service. As can be seen, the caller's LT occurred in lines 6, 8, and 10 respectively. In line 6, the caller said "Bye-bye" to the representative, following his acknowledgement (line 5) in response to her thanking in line 4. In line 7, the representative responded to the caller's first verbalised LT with an "uh hum", followed by an expression presumably thanking the caller for using Best Tone, although the first part of this utterance cannot be determined exactly due to the overlap of the utterance of the customer. The caller's second LT was verbalised in an overlapping manner with the latter part of the representative's utterance in line 7.

Although the caller had already extended her first LT in line 6, the representative continued to verbalise the remaining part of the whole expression "(xxxx) Super Communication", instead of simply responding with a LT on his part. It is possible that this verbalised expression, which was not heard clearly, due to overlapping speech, was part of the routine the service representatives were required to go through before closing each call.

Therefore, the representative's "uh hum" in the first part of line 7 was uttered in response to the caller's initial LT in line 6, after which he continued with the verbalisation of thanking in the same turn. This overlapped with the caller's second uttered LT. When the representative finally extended his LT in line 9, he also added the specific mention of 'Ms' along with the caller's last name. In return, the caller responded with her third LT.

The discursive and interactional features manifested in this call underscore the courteous and responsive manner in which this representative interacted with the caller and handled her request, which seems to have contributed to the caller's appreciation as a customer and partly resulted in her repeated LT. The fact that there is an overlap, as shown in line 7 and line 8, between the caller's second LT and the agent's presumably signature thanking contributed to the need for her to do a repeated LT in line 8. The agent's formal LT in line 9 leads to another, perceived, needed reply on the part of the customer due to the cultural pattern and dynamics of closing in Chinese, as discussed in Sun (2005), with regard to multiple turns of LT. Repeated LT, in fact, is a fairly common phenomenon for interactions between familiar friends and acquaintances, as observed in Sun (2005). The fact that it is observed in this customer-employee interaction reflects the customer caller's level of satisfaction and pleasant feelings about the interaction she experienced.

Overlapped LT (Type VIII)

The sub-category entitled 'overlapped' LT refers to calls in which both parties verbalised LT in an overlapping manner. In the following excerpt, the caller made an inquiry to a store about whether the type of florescent light she needed to purchase was available.

Excerpt 5

01 E:　把灯管带着. 因为不一定　　　　　好用的
　　　　Ba deng guan daizhe. Yin weibuyi ding haoyong de
　　　　Marker light tube bring PT because not sure good use PT
　　　　'Bring the light tube along as the ones we have may not be the right kind
　　　　　for you.'

02 C:　哦. 好　的　好　的
　　　　O. Hao de hao de
　　　　OK good PT good PT
　　　　'OK. sure.'

03 E: 好　吗
       Hao ma
       good Qtg
       'OK?'

04 C: 哦. 谢谢你=
       O. Xiexieni
       OK thank you
       'All right, thanks a lot.'

05 E: = 不要紧//再会
        Bu yaojinzaihui
       not matter again meet
       'No problem. Bye.'

06 C: //再会哦
       Zaihui o
       Again meet OK
       'Bye-bye.'

As can be seen from Except 5 above, participation in closing from both parties is evident. In line 3, the employee initiated a pre-closing in the form of an inquisitive "OK" awaiting confirmation from the customer, intended to check with the customer to make sure that she had no other questions. The customer's reply and her signature thanking in line 4 indicated her confirmation and readiness to close the call. In response, the employee replied in line 5 with "No problem", which linked to the caller's thanking. In the same turn (line 5), the employee continued his closing move with "Bye", which then overlapped with the customer's LT (line 6).

It is worth pointing out that it is the customer caller who uttered "Thank you" first, although the employee's tentative "OK" in line 3 could be seen as a pre-closing. The interaction indicates that both parties were actively involved in the assessment of each other's readiness for closing.

Employee-initiated leave-taking (Type IX)

Closing patterns identified as Type IX constitute a group of calls that feature LT initiated by employees. Given that most calls in data A do not even exhibit LT, this is a salient phenomenon, indicating a sharp contrast in interaction behaviours of employees between data A and data B. In addition, with a total of six calls belonging to this category out of 22, it accounts for 27 per cent of the total number of interactions in data B. Excerpt 5 above fits this category and Excerpt 6 below provides another interesting example.

Excerpt 6

```
01  E:  对　的
        Dui de
        Right PT
        'Right.'

02  C:  哦. 好　的
        O. Hao de
        OK good PT
        'Oh, OK.'

→ 03  E:  嗯. //再　见
        En. Zaijian
        OK again see
        'Uh hum, bye.'

04  C:  //位子是有　的. ///是吗
        Wei zishi you de shi ma
        seat be have PT   be Qtg
        'There is no problem with seating, right?'

→ 05  E:  ///有　的
        You   de
        have PT
        'No problem.'

06  C:  哦 好 的. 那. ［谢谢　你
        O  hao de   naxiexieni
        OK, good PT then thank you
        'OK all right, then. Thank you.'

→ 07  E:  [好　再　见. 没　关系
        Haozaijianmei guan xi
        good again see  no matter
        'OK bye. You're welcome.'

08  C:  好 好好. 再　见
        Haohaohao.Zaijian
        good again see
        'OK. Bye'
```

This call was also made to a restaurant. The employee answering the phone was responsive, and her tone was friendly as well. When she offered affirmative replies to the customer's questions, her utterances include the particle 的 in both line 1 and line 5. The particle 的 is typically unstressed, thus often produced very briefly. In this case, however, it was verbalised with similar length and stress as the preceding content words 对 *dui* 'right' in line 1 and 有 *you* 'have' in line 5. Such prosodic characteristics of the particle are not original features of mainland Mandarin. These are relatively recent discursive phenomena, according to the participants, largely due to influences of discursive styles from Hong Kong and Taiwan through mass media and pop culture such as commercials, songs, movies and TV programmes, although no published study seems to have focused on this phenomenon. Affirmative replies, as shown in line 1 and line 5, with the particle 的 in each case given the same length and stress as the preceding content word, render a softened response as well as a friendly tone compared with potential replies consisting of only one character, leaving room for further interaction.

There are interesting issues surfacing in this case as well. In this call, there are two attempts by the employee to end the call, as shown in lines 3 and 7 respectively. In line 3, after her verbalised backchannel 嗯 "uh hum", the employee extended LT in the same turn after a brief pause, and her LT overlapped with the caller's re-stated question about the seating in line 4. Furthermore, while the caller was double checking the status of her reservation in line 4, the employee started to respond to the caller again before the customer had completed her utterance, thus the employee's conformation 有的 *you de* 'no problem' in line 5 overlapped a second time with the caller's tag question 是吗 *shi ma* 'right?' In line 6, while the caller was taking a short pause after the word 'then', the employee started her turn in line 7 by first responding with 好 *hao* 'OK', followed by LT, which resulted in a simultaneous utterance produced in an overlapping manner with the caller's thanking. Although the employee had already extended LT a second time, on hearing the customer's thanking, she followed up with 'no problem' in response to the customer's 谢谢你 *xie xie ni* 'Thank you'.

The above observations indicate that the employee did not always wait for her turn, as can be seen from both her overlapped (lines 3 and 5) and simultaneous (line 7) utterances with the customer. It is also clear that she initiated LT twice in both line 3 and line 7, and her first attempt for leave-taking (line 3) was made before the caller had the chance to convey appreciation. Furthermore, her second LT, in line 7, was extended before the caller's utterance was verbalised completely. Previous findings of both Chinese and English calls between customers and employees, however, indicate that, typically, it is the customer caller who first indicates one's readiness to end the call (Sun 1998).

On the other hand, the employee could have terminated the interaction without the follow-up 'You're welcome', if she had chosen to, as far as the closure of the conversation is concerned since leave-taking, which is typically the last utterance in closing, has been verbalised in line 7. The fact that she did add the 'You're welcome' expression (which I will call a post-LT-response to the customer's token of appreciation), seems to indicate her courtesy, although the phrase 'You're welcome' (line 7) might sound out of sequence from a strict structural point of view. I argue that her last utterance is significant at two levels. It is important from an *interaction perspective* because, as a participant, she did not leave an interactional move un-responded to; her reply provided the customer with an acknowledgement so that the first part of the exchange in the form of thanking was accompanied by its second part 'You're welcome' although it was not necessarily in the adjacent position structurally. From a *pragmatic view*, it adds a last touch to the customer-employee relationship, or a warming gesture which is tantamount to reinforcing the idea that 'I am glad to have assisted you' however brief the interaction might be. It is due to such consideration that her overlapped utterances (in line 5 and 7) are not perceived as reflections of intentional rudeness in the current analysis.

Discussion

Compared with patterns of interactions observed in a similar set of data collected more than a decade ago, the discursive practice of employees exhibits several differences. First, employees exhibit similar levels of involvement in interaction, in particular for closing, which is very different from the salient pattern of lack of reciprocity shown by the employees observed in the earlier data. In addition, many of the employees state the name of the enterprises at the beginning of the call. Furthermore, employees in the current data use polite expressions more, reflecting a higher level of courtesy and responsiveness to customers.

These perceived differences seem to reflect shifts at different levels. First, there are undoubtedly institutionalised changes that have taken place, enforced presumably by the management or administration of the various enterprises or institutions concerned. A clear indication of such changes is the provision of self-identification by the businesses or services. As is shown in Excerpt 2, the employee recipient of the call stated the name of the business along with a greeting expression in the first turn as part of the opening routine. Considering the fact that self-identification was not provided by most businesses and services a decade or so ago, self-identification by many businesses and services observed in data B constitutes an important change. This observed change in discursive practice must have resulted from decisions by the management or the administration of the businesses or services, as it is certainly beyond the authority and discretion of any individual employee to implement changes at the institutional level. Therefore, the establishment of business self-identification for many enterprises is one of the most telling pieces of evidence of change in discursive practice for businesses and institutions.

Apart from institutionalised changes, a shift in interactional behaviours and discursive patterns of individual employees is evident as well. These changes are manifested in individual employees' verbal responsiveness, in the choices of words and routine expressions used, and in the increase in the number of closings accomplished with reciprocal participation from employees – a sharp contrast with the patterns observed before. It is also likely that the observed interactional behaviours of individuals are affected by changes in institutionalised discursive practices as well, since discursive practice is shaped and constrained by individuals' institutional roles in particular sociocultural and interactional contexts.

More importantly, as telephonic practices for businesses and services are not isolated linguistic phenomena, observed changes in discursive practice reflect broader changes in Chinese society, including significant economic reform as well as the effect of globalisation. For the past three decades, China's economic reform and the implementation of the Open Door policy has brought about rapid growth and tremendous economic changes in the country. Initiated in 1979, China's economic reform includes incremental expansion of the role of the market and a reformist approach concerning ownership (Zhang 2003). Numerous State-owned enterprises have been closed or privatised with the restructuring of the economy and the introduction of the market economy.

In view of the transformation in various dimensions of the economic, cultural and social contexts discussed above, the observed changes in discursive practice mirror the results of the economic reform and globalisation taking place in the local context. Specifically, several factors might have contributed to the changes in discursive practice including the market economy, establishment of multinational enterprises and foreign ventures in the city, increased business opportunities and contact with businesses, organisations and people from other cultures, a change in the status of customers, and an increasing population of non-Chinese residents working and living in Shanghai.

The discursive analysis presented in this chapter reflects changes in business culture and communication practice in contemporary China. It also captures the interconnectedness of language, culture and society. The observed changes consist of institutional regulations and individual discursive choices, taking place in response to the larger environment in which discourse occurs, including economic reform, social changes and globalisation, all of which constitute an important part of the social, cultural and historical reality of the context of the discursive phenomenon under discussion. In this sense "the contents and the forms of globalization have a partly discursive character" (Fairclough 2006: 163). In addition, the linguistic practices of individual members are also constitutive of the practice of the community.

Conclusion

The nature of the customer-employee interactions examined in this study has not changed from that of comparable events examined a decade ago, and the participants' roles in the communicative situations remain the same, with the customer caller on one end of the telephone line and the employee recipient on the other. However, a shift has taken place in the discursive practice of business and service employees, as manifested in a more customer-friendly style of interaction. Salient differences exhibit most clearly in interlocutors' participation structure for closing. Differences were observed in the ways enterprises identify themselves, as well as in employees' choice of words and expressions.

Discursive practice reflects its time; it also continues to evolve in response to the larger historical, cultural and social contexts of the discursive communities. Observed differences in discursive patterns are significant as they mirror the realities of the society that is undergoing socio-economic and cultural changes, under the impact of economic reform and globalisation. This study demonstrates that analysis of discursive practice provides insight into the social and cultural dimensions of the discursive communities. At the same time, discursive practice becomes part of the changed and changing society. The changes in discourse interaction depicted in this chapter constitute and contribute to the shaping and reshaping of social realities.

Appendix: Transcription symbols

C   customer caller

E   employee recipient

LT   Leave taking

.   brief untimed pause

            = latch   no obvious interval between turns

e.g. C: wake you up=

            A: =no problem

            A's 'No problem' follows C's last word 'up' without a perceivable pause.

// (or ///) beginning of overlap between two utterances

      e.g. A: Thank you // Bye-bye

         C: // Bye-bye

      In this case, A's 'Bye-bye' overlaps with C's 'Bye-bye.'

      '///' is used to differentiate different instances of overlaps.

::   stretched sound

[simultaneous talk

      e.g. A: [Hi

         C: [How are you

      In this case, A and C talk at the same time. For differentiation purpose, '[[' and '[[[' simply refer to different instances of overlapped utterances when there is more than one simultaneous talk in the same excerpt.

(xxxx)   utterances not being able to be determined

-->   feature referred to in discussion

( )   author's explanation

Acknowledgements

I wish to express my sincere appreciation to the anonymous reviewers as well as to the editors Yuling Pan and Dániel Z. Kádár for their helpful comments and suggestions on an earlier version of the manuscript. All errors remain my own.

References

Arnovick, L. (1999) *Diachronic Pragmatics: Seven Case Studies in English Illocutionary Development.* Amsterdam/Philadelphia, PA: John Benjamins.

Backhaus, P. (2005) Signs of multilingualism in Tokyo: A diachronic look at the linguistic landscape. *International Journal of the Sociology of Language* 175/176: 103–121.

Bao, Y. (2008) Shanghai Weekly: Globalization, consumerism, and Shanghai popular culture. *Inter-Asia Cultural Studies* 9: 557–567.

Barboza, D. (2010, August 15) China surpasses Japan as second-largest economy. *New York Times.* Retrieved from www.nytimes.com

Brown, G. and Yule, G. (1983) *Discourse Analysis.* Cambridge: Cambridge University Press.

Cheepen, C. (2000) Small talk in service dialogues: The conversational aspects of the transactional telephone talk. In N. Coupland (ed.) *Small Talk* 288–311. Harlow, Essex: Pearson Education.

Coulmas, F. (2005) Changing language regimes in globalizing environments. *International Journal of the Sociology of Language* 175/176: 3–15.

Eckert, P. and McConnell-Ginet, S. (1992) Communities of practice: Where language, gender, and power all live. In K. Hall, M. Bucholtz and B. Moonwoman (eds) *Locating Power: Proceedings of the Second Berkeley Women and Language Conference* 89–99. Berkeley, CA: Berkeley Women and Language Group, Linguistics Department, University of California.

Eckert, P. and McConnell-Ginet, S. (2003) *Language and Gender.* Cambridge: Cambridge University Press.

Fairclough, N. (2006) *Language and Globalization.* London: Routledge.

Fitzmaurice, S. and Taavitsainen, I. (2003) *Methods in Historical Pragmatics.* Berlin: Mouton de Gruyter.

Have, P. T. (2002) Comparing telephone call openings: Theoretical and methodological reflections. In K. K. Luke and T. Pavlidou (eds) *Telephone Calls: Unity and Diversity in Conversational Structure across Languages and Cultures* 233–248. Amsterdam: John Benjamins.

Holmes, J. and Meyerhoff, M. (1999) The community of practice: Theories and methodologies in language and gender research. *Language in Society* 28:173–183.

Hymes, D. (1972) Models of the interaction of language and social life. In J. Gumperz and D. Hymes (eds) *Directions in Sociolinguistics: The Ethnography of Communication* 35–71. Oxford: Basil Blackwell.

Pan, Y., Scollon, S. W. and Scollon, R. (2002) *Professional Communication in International Settings.* Malden, MA: Blackwell.

Saville-Troike, M. (2002) *The Ethnography of Communication.* 3rd ed. Malden, MA: Wiley-Blackwell.

Schegloff, E. A. (1968) Sequencing in conversational openings. *American Anthropologist* 70: 1075–1095.

Schegloff, E. A. and Sacks, H. (1973) Opening up closings. *Semiotica* 8: 289–327.

Schegloff, E. A., Jefferson, G., and Sacks, H. (1977) The preference for self-correction in the organization of repair in conversation. *Language* 53: 361–382.

Schiffrin, D. (1994) *Approaches to Discourse.* Malden, MA: Blackwell.

Sonntag, S. K. (2009) Linguistic globalization and the call centre industry: Imperialism, hegemony or cosmopolitanism? *Language Policy* 8: 5–25.

Statistical Yearbook 2010. Retrieved from www.stats-sh.gov.cn/tjnj/nj10. htm?d1=2010tjnj/C0214.htm

Sun, H. (1998) Telephone conversations in Chinese and English: A comparative study across languages and functions. Unpublished doctoral dissertation, University of Arizona, Tucson.

Sun, H. (2004) What does non-reciprocal term[inal] exchange index? In C. Hallen (ed.) *Selected Proceedings of the Deseret Language and Linguistic Society 1997 Symposium* 33–36. Provo, UT: Brigham Young University.

Sun, H. (2005) Collaborative strategies in Chinese telephone conversation closings: Balancing procedural needs and interpersonal meaning making. *Pragmatics* 15: 109–128.

Sun, H. (2008) Participant roles and discursive actions: Chinese transactional telephone interactions. In H. Sun and D. Z. Kádár (eds) *It's the Dragon's Turn – Chinese Institutional Discourses* 80–136. Berne: Peter Lang.

Thomaj, J. (2006) The Albanian language: Developments in the lexicon under the new social and political order. *International Journal of the Sociology of Language* 178: 103–112.

Wei, Y. H. D. and Leung, C. K. (2005) Development zones, foreign investment, and global city formation in Shanghai. *Growth and Change* 36: 16–40.

Wenger, E. (1998) *Communities of Practice: Learning, Meaning and Identity*. New York: Cambridge University Press.

Wu, F. (2003) The (post-) socialist entrepreneurial city as a state project: Shanghai's reglobalisation in question. *Urban Studies* 40: 1673–1698.

Zhang, L. Y. (2003) Economic development in Shanghai and the role of the state. *Urban Studies* 40: 1549–1572.

11

Chinese prenatal genetic counselling discourse in Hong Kong: Healthcare providers' (non)directive stance, or who is making the decision?

Olga Zayts, Virginia Wake Yelei and Stephanie Schnurr

Introduction

In this chapter we take a discourse analytic perspective and examine the Chinese institutional discourse of prenatal genetic counselling (henceforth, PGC) in Hong Kong. We focus on the interactions between Chinese healthcare providers and patients[1] and examine how the notion of non-directiveness, which has historically been adopted as the guiding principle in the genetic counselling profession, is challenged in this sociocultural context. Our interest in the Hong Kong context is twofold: first, the genetic counselling profession is still establishing itself in the region (Lam 2006); therefore the tenets guiding the profession are also being established and negotiated by the professionals. In addition, compared to other countries (e.g. the US and the UK), there are very few discourse and conversation analytic studies of genetic counselling in Hong Kong (Zayts and Kang 2009, 2010; Zayts and Schnurr 2011). This chapter contributes to this emerging body of research by examining Chinese interactional data.

Participants of PGC include healthcare providers and patients who are pregnant and over the age of 35 – considered to be of advanced maternal age and at increased risk of having a baby with Down syndrome (Tang et al. 1991). In these encounters healthcare providers inform patients about this risk and available testing options for Down syndrome, and offer social and emotional support to patients and their families. A non-directive approach in PGC refers to the value neutral stance healthcare providers take in PGC encounters. This approach falls within patient-centred healthcare in that it postulates that only patients know what is in the best interests of their families and that their autonomy in decision making should be respected (Kessler 1997).

Recently, however, the non-directive approach has been questioned in both its ideology and practice in terms of its professional goals and feasibility (Anderson 1999; Bosk 1992; Clarke 1991; Gervais 1993; Pilnick 2002; Shiloh 1996). It has been argued that "it potentially requires both complete suspension of expert professional judgment and an orientation to what may be *heard* as directive even if it is not produced or intended as such" (Pilnick and Zayts 2011). In our own previous work on counselling non-native English-speaking patients in Hong Kong, in particular Filipina patients (Zayts and Kang 2009), we have highlighted that the principle of non-directiveness may pose particular challenges to healthcare providers working in contexts where patients may have different expectations as to the degree of their autonomy due to different social and cultural norms of communication in medical encounters.

In this study we broadly define non-directiveness as refraining from steering patients towards one decision over another regarding prenatal testing, and directiveness as engaging in and influencing patients' decision making. We demonstrate that in the PGC encounters between Chinese healthcare providers and patients in Hong Kong, the discourse of the healthcare providers is characterised by a directive approach. We suggest that in Hong Kong the institutional and the sociocultural contexts in which these encounters are situated have a crucial impact on how these interactions unfold – in particular, in ways that challenge the principle of non-directiveness.

Background

(Non)directive discourse practices in genetic counselling contexts

Much of the work of genetic counselling professionals is done through the use of language. Despite abundant research on non-directiveness (e.g. Weil 2003; Weil et al. 2006; Wertz and Fletcher 1988), there is a certain disjuncture between the theoretical endeavours and the practicalities of providing genetic services. As Benkendorf et al. (2001) note, many genetic counsellors are not sure how non-directive counselling is *actually* enacted in practice and conflate it with the use of indirect speech in language (see also Zayts and Kang 2009).

Conflating indirect speech with non-directiveness may lead to undesirable outcomes and hinder the patients' understanding of the provided information. For example, when counsellors use generic nouns, such as 'some people' or 'most people', patients may face difficulties in inferring which utterances apply to them (Benkendorf et al. 2001). On the other hand, the overt use of indirect speech does not preclude genetic counselling professionals from steering their patients in the direction of a particular decision. Pilnick (2008) identifies several means by which the interactional context may influence the conceptualisation and reception of potential decisions, despite the healthcare professionals being non-directive in the delivery of information. For example, the sequential location of talk about genetic tests immediately following the discussion of other, more routine tests may lead to conflation of two different groups of tests by patients. Another example that Pilnick (2008) discusses is taking the lack of overt refusals to undergo genetic testing as implying consent to testing.

Some studies have noted specific linguistic means that healthcare providers may draw on in their pursuit of non-directiveness. More specifically, Sarangi and Clarke (2002) analyse the recycled use of past events mutually known by healthcare providers and patients. And in another study Sarangi et al. look at the question format healthcare providers employ to initiate what they call 'reflective frames' to invite patients "to adopt introspective and self reflective stances towards their own experiences" (2004: 135). In these cases healthcare providers adopt the role of 'active listeners' and let patients reflect on their decision-making process.

In this chapter we build on these studies and examine the discursive means by which the healthcare providers in Hong Kong enact their (non)directive stance in the PGC encounters.

Prenatal genetic counselling in Hong Kong

An important aspect of the PGC encounters is ensuring that decisions that patients take regarding prenatal testing[2] are informed, that is, that they are based on good quality medical information that patients fully understand (Bekker et al. 2004; Dormandy et al. 2006; Marteau and Dormandy 2001). In Hong Kong this is achieved through a number of PGC-specific activities. At the first appointment in a prenatal hospital eligible patients[3] are introduced to the PGC service through information leaflets and a 15-minute video outlining what Down syndrome is and what tests are available. A part of the video also discusses support for families with Down syndrome children. Following this, an appointment is made for a face-to-face consultation with a healthcare provider. According to the interviews with the healthcare providers, they see the face-to-face meetings as an important component of PGC as it allows them to tap into and ensure patients' understanding of provided information.

Noteworthy is the fact that there are very few board certified genetic counsellors in Hong Kong, and the role of genetic counsellors is often taken up by obstetricians and midwives. Some (but not all) of them may have received additional training in counselling. There are several implications of this situation. First, it leads to a relatively short time, 15 minutes on average, allocated to each patient, since the healthcare providers are also responsible for the provision of other routine prenatal services. Second, the lack of formal training is compensated by observing more senior and experienced colleagues and consulting institutional documents, such as extensive guidelines regulating PGC activities. In addition, when medical personnel are involved in the provision of PGC services, this may lead to a situation when routine prenatal services are conflated with PGC, and the 'medical' agenda (i.e. providing tests) rather than the 'counselling' agenda (i.e. facilitating the decision making and providing psychological and emotional support) may take a prevailing role. In the analysis to follow we take these specifics of PGC in Hong Kong into consideration and discuss their impact on the (non)directiveness of these encounters.

Data and methodology

This chapter is based on the data from a large interactional study of PGC in Hong Kong which has been ongoing since 2006 and involves the close collaboration between a linguistic research team and a public hospital.

In the hospital 2602 patients received PGC services in 2007–2009. The majority of them (85%) were Chinese. At the moment the data comprises video-recorded consultations with ten Chinese patients (recruitment ongoing). In the extracts that we have selected for this chapter, two healthcare providers participate (who are referred to as HP1 and HP2 in the transcripts) who are Hong Kong Chinese. The language of the consultations is Cantonese. The overall recording time is more than three hours. Other data used for the analysis include written counselling guidelines of the hospital and qualitative semi-structured interviews with the healthcare providers and the patients prior to and after the consultations. We believe that employing such a multi-method approach enriches the analysis of the discourse data.

Following the video recording, the consultations were transcribed and analysed using the approach of interactional sociolinguistics which takes into account both the sociocultural context and the local context in which an interaction takes place in order to understand and interpret how meaning is negotiated between participants (Schiffrin 1994).

Data analysis

Our analysis of (non)directive discourse in the PGC context in Hong Kong focuses on two levels: on the global level, we discuss the sustainability of the principle of non-directiveness in the designated sociocultural context of Hong Kong; and on the local level, we examine how this is constructed discursively.

As mentioned above, the PGC in the hospital where we collected our data is regulated by institutional guidelines. An extensive review of these documents has revealed an interesting picture. Despite the fact that the healthcare providers refer to what they are doing as 'genetic counselling' (and this is also reflected in the name of the department where they work), the counselling component is absent in the guidelines. In all reviewed documents the word 'screening' (rather than 'counselling') is used. This lexical choice has an important implication as the process of screening presupposes a provision of tests. The workflow for the healthcare providers outlining what they should do during a PGC encounter also contains the description of 'medical' rather than 'counselling' activities, for example, an explanation of the risks of having an infant with Down syndrome and different methods of screening, and outlining available options if a fetus is confirmed to have Down syndrome. Therefore, these documents indicate the prevalence of the 'medical' agenda in these encounters. This observation is crucial for analysing the (non)directive practices of the healthcare providers in PGC: while non-directiveness is important in counselling, it may not be in provision of medical treatments. What we may be observing in the PGC context in Hong Kong, then, is the conflation of two different activities, counselling and screening, and the professional principles of one activity may not be directly transferrable to another activity. Therefore, the directiveness of the healthcare providers' discourse may be due to the institutional agendas they are pursuing.

In addition to the institutional context, another important factor to consider is the sociocultural context of Hong Kong in which these encounters are situated. Research has noted that in social interactions displaying a hierarchical relationship participants assume on different roles: those in a higher position are predominantly the speakers, while those in a lower position are the listeners (Gao and Ting-Toomey 1998). Moreover, in these encounters, interlocutors in a higher position tend to use directive expressions (Lee-Wong 1999) while those in a subordinate position use indirect language (Gao et al. 1995; Young 1994). In the PGC context this hierarchy may impact the directiveness of the healthcare providers' discourse and their engagement with the decision making. The specific sociocultural norms and values of Hong Kong in their turn will impact on how this directiveness is perceived by the participants of these interactions. Previous research on counselling discourse in Asia, for example, has noted that patients of Asian background tend to expect a more directive treatment and be told what to do (Johnson and Nadirshaw 2002).

To examine the participants' perception of PGC encounters in this study, the patients were asked by the research team about their expectations of the consultation before seeing the healthcare provider, and about their satisfaction with the consultation after having seen the healthcare provider. The interview data have revealed that a large number of patients (around 40%) did not have any expectations of the consultation (this high number may be partly attributed to the fact that many of them were first time mothers with no previous experience of PGC), and some patients (around 10%) displayed an orientation towards the counselling agenda, which is evidenced by such answers as "[I expect to discuss] the impact of the positive and negative screening result." However, around 50 per cent of the patients expressed overt orientation to the healthcare providers' roles as the 'medical experts' and 'advisors'. This is evidenced in, for example, answers like "[I expect to] confirm whether everything is OK with my baby", or "[I expect] help in solving my problems." Therefore, the interview data suggest that the patients perceive having a Down syndrome infant as a 'problem' and the healthcare providers as being in the position to solve that problem. The interview data after the consultations have revealed that the patients were, overall, satisfied with the consultations. These expectations by the patients also allow for a certain degree of directiveness on the part of the healthcare providers. The interview data are consistent with what we observed in the interactional data, namely the various degrees of directiveness in the healthcare providers' discourse as they routinely engage in the decision-making process and express their own judgements and values. Our finding is in contrast to the previous studies of genetic counselling which have suggested that the healthcare providers are at pains to maintain a non-directive stance in counselling (e.g. Benkendorf et al. 2001; Pilnick 2008). In Extracts 1–4 below we discuss different degrees of directiveness of the healthcare providers' discourse ranging from most explicit to implicit.

Explicit suggestion of a specific testing option

The most directive examples found in our data are instances where the healthcare providers make direct suggestions to the patients to pursue specific testing options. Extract 1 demonstrates an explicit discursive construction of a suggestion in which the healthcare provider advocates one specific option that she favours.

Extract 1

Context: This is the patient's (P) first experience of PGC. Before the consultation she and her husband (H) opted for a screening test. However, they were unaware of the different screening options available. Therefore, in the consultation they are facing difficulties in making a decision.

1　HP1:　[宜家係十二週既.(.)吓.最遲要兩三個禮拜啦即係.(.)一係就今日度住頸
　　　　　皮先啦:度住頸皮，然之後再決定er:就抽驗血呀，定係:(.)下個禮拜塭
　　　　　一日返嚟驗血呀(.)一或十六週，erer十八週返嚟做抬水[囉:

2　P:　　　　　　　　　　　　　　　　　　　　　　　　　　　　　[°唔.°

3　HP1:　[咁其實度咗先[啦:=

4　P:　　　　　　　　[°唔.°

5　HP1:　=咁之後你嗰　d 慢慢諗囉:，我今日突然同你講咁多嘢，你需要　時間
　　　　　去消化嫁嗎:

6　P:　　唔.好呀.

7　HP1:　<好唔好呀?>

8　P:　　[唔.

9　HP1:　[咁你今日度住頸皮先[啦.

10　H:　　　[即係呢兩個分別唔多，只不過一個早一個遲[啫:

11　HP1:　係呀:，嚟一次嚟[兩次囉:

12　H:　　　　　　　　　[係.( )

13　HP1:　依個係一-一次過塭定囉: [譬如=

14　H:　　　　　　　　　　　　[°唔.°

15　HP1:　=話:你今日決定得到既，咪今日囉.咁呢，下個禮拜就有報告[囉.

16　H:　　　　　　　　　　　　　　　　　　　　　　　　　　　　[哦:°

17　HP1:　但係如果呢個呢，就:你慢慢等吓等吓都得呀嗎:你可以容許你再等到
　　　　　十六週，先返嚟驗血呀.或者到時你先返嚟, .h驗血[或者驗=

18　H:　　　　　　　　　　　　　　　　　　　　　　　　　　　　[°哦:°

19　HP1:　=胎水都得.>如果你做A呢個.<

20 P: 唔:

21 H: 唔.

22 HP1: 咁但係，如果你好急既.我今個禮拜決定得到喇，即克做喇，咁你咪打個電話返嚟，我哋同你抽返個血囉:

23 H: [唔.

24 P: [唔.

25 HP1: 咁點都今日度住頸皮先[啦.

26 H: [唔.

27 HP1: 好呀.

28 H: 唔.好呀.

1 HP1: [Now it is 12 weeks on-(.) ly. The latest time is in two or three weeks that is. (.) How about doing the nuchal translucency today:, do the nuchal measurement, and then make a decision later er: to have a blood test, or: (.) next week find a date to come back and have the blood test (.) or come back in the sixteenth week, eh-eh the eighteenth week for amniocentesis all right? That's it.

2 P: [°um°

3 HP1: [So go ahead and do the measurement first [alright :?=

4 P: [°um.°

5 HP1: =then you can take your time to think about the others, alright:? Today I suddenly told you a lot, and you need some time to digest the information

6 P: Um. All right.

7 HP1: <alright?>

8 P: [um.

9 HP1: [so today you have the nuchal translucency first, alright.

10 H: [that is the difference between the two is not great it is only just that one is earlier and one is a little later

11 HP1: Yes: it's to come once or [come twice

12 H: [right. ( )

13 HP1: This takes a- one time to complete [for example=

14 H: [°um.°

15 HP1: =if you can decide today, then you have it done today. Then, next week you will have the report [lor.

16 H: [°oh:°

17 HP1: But if it's this one, then: you can wait patiently wait and wait and it's fine. You could allow yourself to wait till the sixteenth week, to come back to

have the blood test done. Or until then you come back, .h to have your
blood tested [or having=

18 H: [°oh:°

19 HP1: =amniocentesis will do.>if you choose this A.<

20 P: Um:

21 H: Um.

22 HP1: But, if you are very eager. I can make a decision in this week, would like
to do it immediately, then you can make a phone call back, and we could
make up by giving you the blood test, alright?

23 H: [um.

24 P: [um.

25 HP1: No matter what today do the nuchal translucency first [alright.

26 H: [um.

27 P: Okay.

28 H: Um. Okay.

In turn 1, the healthcare provider makes a suggestion that the patient should
take a nuchal translucency test. Note the use of the suggestive expression
'一係就……啦' (*Jat hai zau …… laa*, "how about" or "what if") which
constructs the healthcare provider's active directive role. Following a
minimal response from the patient, the healthcare provider repeats an
explicit suggestion for the nuchal translucency (turn 3). Her directiveness
is mitigated by an account of why she is making this suggestion: the couple
has received a lot of information and they need some time to think it over
(turn 5). The healthcare provider's suggestion elicits the patient's agreement
唔.好呀 (*Ng. Hou aa*, "Um. All right") (turn 6) and a minimal acknowledgement 唔 (*ng*, "um") (turn 8). However, it becomes apparent that the
husband is not entirely clear about the differences in the screening tests: he
tries to paraphrase those differences in terms of the time frames when the
tests can be performed. His utterance serves as a request for clarification
from the healthcare provider (turn 10).

The healthcare provider's response 係呀:嚟一次嚟兩次囉 (*Hai aa:
lai jat ci lai loeng ci lo*, "Yes: it's to come once or come twice") (turn 11)
is not a direct answer to the husband's question. Instead of clarifying that
there are other differences between the two options besides the time frame
when they can be performed, the healthcare provider draws attention to
the convenience of having the nuchal translucency test (turns 13 and 15)
that can be performed on the day of the visit. She mentions that, for the
other tests, the couple would need to come again. She also highlights that
the results will be available quicker in comparison to other tests (turns 15

and 17). This information receives minimal responses from the patient and her husband.

In turn 25 the healthcare provider steps up to settle the decision by repeating her suggestion of taking the nuchal translucency test. The phrase 咁點都 (*gam dim dou*, "no matter what (what option you choose)"; "anyway") indicates that she interprets the question raised by the husband as irrelevant to her suggestion of having the nuchal translucency.

Thus in this interaction the healthcare provider's directive stance is evidenced by her explicit suggestion to pursue a particular course of action. She persists with and reiterates this suggestion, despite the question raised by the husband and his misunderstanding of the provided information that his question points to. Throughout this interaction the directiveness of the healthcare provider's discourse is mitigated by the use of the Cantonese particles 啦 (*laa*, "la") and 囉 (*lo*, "lo") (which are conventional downtoners). On the other hand, when used by a person of a higher social status the particles convey an authoritative undertone.

Throughout this interaction it is the healthcare provider, not the couple, who talks most and makes a decision. However, the directiveness of the healthcare provider's talk is conjointly constructed by all participants in this interaction: the patient's and husband's responses are confined to minimal acknowledgements and they do not appear to object to the healthcare provider taking the lead. In the interview after the consultation, the couple expressed their satisfaction with the consultation, and noted that the healthcare provider was very informative and 'helped' them (rather than directed them) in making a decision.

Healthcare providers' less explicit directive strategies

Highlighting the tests of the healthcare providers' preference and delaying the decision about tests that they do not favour

In the interviews the healthcare providers have noted that they prefer screening tests over alternative options (diagnostic tests or taking no test). Taking screening tests has been described as pursuing 'a woman's best interests.' This rather strong preference for screening tests by the healthcare providers can also be observed in their behaviour in the actual counselling sessions. However, as found in our corpus, Chinese patients routinely opt for diagnostic tests. Therefore, these consultations often present a tension between the preferred choices of the healthcare provider and the patients. The screening tests that the healthcare providers prefer are considered to be safe for the mother and the fetus but they only provide the probability of having an infant with Down syndrome, whereas the diagnostic tests that the Chinese patients often prefer offer a higher detections rate (nearly 100%) but carry a risk of miscarriage (0.5 to 1%) (Leung et al. 2004).

Extract 2 is an example of how the healthcare provider and the patient negotiate this tension in the PGC session.

Extract 2

Context: This is the patient's (P) second pregnancy and with the first one she underwent amniocentesis. The extract presents the decision-making stage of the consultation, after the healthcare provider (HP1) has delivered the information about available tests. The husband (H) is present at the consultation.

1   H: 唔唔。

2   P: °咁點呀°?

3   H: 唔?羊水.

4   P: 吓?

5   H: 羊水. 抽羊水.

6   P: 有機會無嫁.

7   H: 唔?一次過做呀嗎:

8   P: 吓?

9   H: 一次過做呀嗎:

10   P: 有機會[無嫁.

11   H: [既然-既然你頭咁講啦,你-即係你做完之後，你可能最後又擔心剩返嗰可能10零個percent，都有機會有既話呢,吓,我就覺得就直頭唔好做依個喇,無為即係攪兩次喇第一樣野,同埋你就算做咗你-你都擔心嗰10幾個percent嗎:

12   P: 唔唔.

13   H: 咁意義唔太大.

14   P: °唔: 咁[做羊水啦:°

15   HP1   [°你點睇呢.°

16   P: [.hhh ((P laughs))

17   HP1: [.hhh ((laughs))

18   H: This one, [of course.

19   HP1: [你好似,太太好似有d想做篩查係咪呀?

20   P: 我做羊水啦,其實一開始$都係諗住$做羊水嫁啦:

21   HP1: 你嚟之前,頭先你同我講過你想做羊水.=

22   H: =係呀.

23 HP1: 咁啦:因為依家依家到um做羊水都有段時[間啦.

24 H: [唔.

25 HP1: 咁你返去諗吓囉,如果真係想改既，咁你咪話返比[我哋聽囉.

26 H: [Okay.

27 HP1: 你都仲有幾日時間.

28 H: Um um.

29 HP1: .h 咁我當你做住羊水先啦:如果你真係返去諗過，真係想改你咪打電話返嚟.頭先我哋有張卡比你既.

1   H: Um um.

2   P: So what should we do?

3   H: Eh? Amniocentesis. ((pointing to the paper))

4   P: Eh?

5   H: Amniocentesis. Do the amniocentesis.

6   P: But it would carry a risk of miscarriage.

7   H: Um? Because it gets done at one time.

8   P: Eh?

9   H: Because it takes one time to complete:

10 P: But it carries a risk of [miscarriage.

11 H: [Since-since you said just now, you- that is after
        doing it, you may finally worry about the remaining ten odd per cent of
        having Down syndrome, I feel it'd better not to do this one, no need to
        test twice for the same thing. And even though you have done it, you are
        worried about the ten odd per cent.

12 P: Umum.

13 H: So it doesn't make much difference.

14 P: °Um: Then [do the amniocentesis.°

15 HP1:   [°What do you think?°

16 P: [.hhh ((P laughs))

17 HP1   [.hhh ((laughs))

18 H: This one, [of course.

19 HP1:   [You seem- Mrs seems a bit like to have screening test, is that
        right?

20 P: I'll do amniocentesis then. Actually at the very beginning, I hehe thought
        of hhh amniocentesis anyway.

21 HP1: Before you came, previously you told me that you'd like to have the a
        amniocentesis.=

22 H: =Yes.

23 HP1: How about this: Because from now-now till the time for amniocentesis,
        there is still [time.

24 H: [Mhm.

25 HP1: So you'd go home and think about it. If you really want to change, then
        you can [tell us.

26 H: [Okay.

27 HP1: You still have time.

28 H: Um um.

29 HP1: .h so I'll take you as choosing the amniocentesis first:, if you go home and
        really think that you really want to change, then you can give us a call. I've
        already given you a card.

In this extract, the patient is torn between wishing to get the assurance
from the amniocentesis and the fear of losing her baby as a result of the
amniocentesis. She asks her husband for his opinion in turn 2. Contrary
to his wife the husband is certain about the amniocentesis (turn 5). The
patient points to the downside of the invasive test, namely the risk of
miscarriage 有機會無嫁 (*Jau gei wui mo gaa wo*, "But it would carry a risk
of miscarriage") (turn 6). Turns 6–10 demonstrate interesting repetitions
between the patient and her husband. The husband first responds to the
patient's concern about the risk of miscarriage by providing an account
for his choice and highlighting the efficiency of the test 一次過做呀嗎: (*Jat
ci gwo zou aa maa*, "because it takes only once"). In turn 8, the woman
only gives a minimal response with 吓 (*haa*, "eh (what)") to question her
husband's rationale. The repetition that follows presents an inverted pattern
of the previous exchange: the husband repeats his reason for opting for
the amniocentesis and the patient repeats her concern about the risk of
miscarriage (turn 10). The patient's exact repetition highlights her concern
and indicates that she is not convinced that the amniocentesis is the best
choice. It is only after her husband brings up another reason, namely the
uncertainty they would have to deal with by having the screening test, that
the patient agrees with her husband.

Following that, the healthcare provider, who has not taken a speaking
turn up to this moment, overlaps with the patient and directly addresses
a question to her, °你點睇呢° (°*Nei dim tai nei*°, "°What do you think?°")
This shift in participant structure (Rosenfeld 1996) enables the patient
to re-address her uncertainty. She responds to the healthcare provider's
question with laughter (turn 16). The patient's laughter may suggest that the
healthcare provider has identified her uncertainty and concerns. By recip-
rocating the patient's laughter the healthcare provider signals her alignment

with the patient (Haakana 1999). In the next turn the participant structure changes again as the husband issues a response for his wife, "This one, of course." In striking contrast to the rest of the interaction, this utterance is in English, the official language used in formal settings in Hong Kong. This code switch constructs the husband's seriousness and determination in the decision. Nevertheless, the healthcare provider ignores the husband's utterance and in turn 19 brings up the patient's perspective 你好似, 太太好似有滴想做篩查係咪呀 (*Nei hou ci taai taai hou ci jau dik soeng zou sai caa hai mai aa*, "You seem- Mrs seems a bit like to have the screening test is that right?"). By bringing up the patient's preference for the diagnostic testing (gleaned from the previous exchange between the couple), the healthcare provider signals her own preference for the screening test and expresses her alignment with the patient.

When the patient states that she was originally planning to have the amniocentesis, the healthcare provider employs another strategy, namely suspending the couple's final decision by asking them to think about their choice when they get home (turn 25). Note also that, following the healthcare provider's suggestion to take more time to think about their choices, the husband only issues minimal acknowledgements and the wife does not say anything. This interaction demonstrates that, although the couple is active in the decision-making process and appears to have taken an autonomous decision, the healthcare provider manages to engage in the decision-making by aligning herself with the patient's uncertainties regarding the amniocentesis and delaying the decision to pursue this option that she does not favour.

Assuming prenatal testing as the patients' choice

The choices that patients make regarding prenatal testing and how these choices are negotiated have been the foci of much research in recent years (e.g. Heyman et al. 2006; Markens et al. 1999; Pilnick 2008; Reminnick 2006; Weinans et al. 2000; Williams et al. 2005). Available research has indicated that often pregnant women do not feel they are in a position to make an autonomous choice, experiencing constraints from the healthcare providers and the sociocultural context in which they live. It has also been noted that the woman's right to refuse the prenatal testing is not always explicitly brought up or highlighted in the consultation (for a more detailed discussion see Pilnick and Zayts 2011), as Extract 3 below illustrates.

Extract 3

Context: The extract comes from the second consultation which has been scheduled following a positive screening result that put the patient (P) at a higher risk (1 in 244) of having a baby with Down syndrome. The patient is 37 years old and this is her first pregnancy. The extract comes after the healthcare provider (HP2) has delivered the positive screening result. The husband (H) is present at the consultation.

1   HP2: 咁變左睇下你同先生:覺得 (.) 擔唔擔心。想唔想進一步做抽羊水既檢查。抑或我地可以照超音波，睇下如果大致上 (..) eh:: 睇唔到一啲咩特別，

2   P: 唔。

3   HP2: 咁 (.) 就 (.) 唔抽羊水。(..) 咁但係超音波嗰度，攞黎驗bb唐氏綜合症就唔係 (.) 百分之一百既。

4   P: 唔。

5   HP2: 五成到準啦。

6   P: 唔。

7   HP2: 四五成到。

8   P: 唔唔。

9   HP2: 咁如果睇到啲:結構呀 ((P clears her throat)) 各樣都係ok既話呢，咁就都拉低左有事個機會囉。

10 P: 唔唔，唔唔。

1   HP2: So this depends on whether you and your husband: feel (.) if you are worried. If you'd like to go for amniocentesis testing. Or we can have an ultrasound, to see if roughly (..) eh:: we don't see anything special,

2   P: Um.

3   HP2: Then (.) we won't go for amniocentesis. (..) But it is not 100 per cent accurate for ultrasound, to see whether the baby has Down syndrome or not.

4   P: Um.

5   D: It is 50 per cent accurate.

6   P: Um.

7   D: About 40, 50 per cent.

8   P: Um hmm.

9   D: If we see the structure ((P clears her throat)) and everything is OK, it will lower the risk.

10 P: Um hm, um hm.

In turn 1 the healthcare provider outlines two options to the couple: having an amniocentesis or an ultrasound. The directiveness of the healthcare provider's discourse lies in the assumption that the couple will pursue further testing and in 'brushing off' the possibility that the couple may choose not to pursue any testing. The directiveness of the healthcare providers' discourse may be partly attributed to the fact that the couple have received an initial positive screening result. However, having a positive screening result does not necessarily lead to further testing, and the decision whether to pursue it or not should lie with the couple.

In the interaction the healthcare provider constructs the patient and her husband as the main decision makers, stating that the choice depends on whether they are worried or not. The utterance 咁變左睇下你同先生：覺得（.）擔唔擔心。(*Gam bin zo tai haa nei tung sin saang gaaau dak daam ng daam sam*, "So this depends on whether you and your husband: feel (.) if you are worried") (turn 1) is tentatively constructed. However, at the end of the turn the healthcare provider switches to the all-inclusive pronoun 'we' that connotes that she is also part of the decision-making process. She goes on to provide statistical information about the two testing options thereby steering the discussion around the decision making. However, these statistics do not prove crucial for the couple in making their decision. As revealed later in the consultation (this part of the consultation is not included in the extract), the patient's concern lies with the risk of miscarriage associated with the procedure of the amniocentesis. In this consultation, despite the healthcare provider highlighting the tests, the patient manages to postpone the final decision until after having consulted her mother, which could be interpreted as an indirect refusal of the healthcare provider's directive approach. The patient thus manages to take the lead in the decision-making process. However, examples like this, where the patient manages to resist the healthcare provider's directive approach, are not typical in the Chinese data in our study.

Discussion and conclusion

In this chapter we have examined the Chinese institutional discourse of PGC in Hong Kong. We have demonstrated that the discourse of the healthcare providers is characterised by directiveness as they routinely engage in the activities that have an impact on the patients' decision making regarding prenatal genetic testing.

In our analysis of how this directive talk is constructed discursively, we have discussed a number of discursive strategies on which the healthcare providers draw, ranging from explicit engagement in the decision making (Extract 1) to more implicit examples of directiveness, such as highlighting the tests the healthcare provider prefers and delaying the decision about the test that the healthcare provider does not favour (Extract 2), as well as assuming that the patients will pursue genetic testing rather than choose not to find out about any abnormalities that the baby may have (Extract 3). This directiveness of the healthcare providers' talk in PGC in Hong Kong contrasts with the previous studies of genetic counselling in other countries where the healthcare providers are said to strive to attain a non-directive stance (e.g. Pilnick 2008; Sarangi and Clarke 2002; Sarangi et al. 2004). We have suggested that the sociocultural and the institutional contexts in which the PGC interactions are situated play a crucial role in how directive healthcare providers are. The principle of non-directiveness has been endorsed in Western contexts where egalitarian patient-centred relationship between healthcare professionals and patients are promoted; however, as our findings suggest, this may not be unquestionably applicable to other sociocultural contexts (see also Roberts 2006). As we have shown in our analysis, in Hong Kong a more directive approach by the healthcare providers is perceived and interpreted by the participants as a norm of the genetic counselling interactions. In addition, conducted by obstetric doctors and nurses on the premises of a hospital, and regulated by the guidelines stressing screening rather than the counselling agenda, these interactions are bound to display a greater degree of directiveness by the healthcare providers.

In the analysed data we have also observed that the healthcare providers dominate and control the interactional floor. The patients' participation is confined to mainly minimal acknowledgements, and except for Extract 3, there is no evidence in the analysed data of the couples objecting to the healthcare providers taking an active role and influencing the decision making. Therefore, the directiveness of the healthcare providers' discourse is, to some extent, co-constructed by all participants in these interactions. The patients and their husbands orient themselves as listeners and recipients of the healthcare providers' directives. This observation is also supported by the interviews with the couples before and after the consultations in which they have stated their expectations to receive advice and help from the healthcare providers, and where they have expressed their satisfaction with the PGC services that they have received. These findings lend support to the previous research on Chinese interactions among participants in hierarchical relationships, including in medical settings, that have highlighted the directive nature of the discourse of participants in a higher social position.

To conclude, this is an exploratory study. Clearly, there is a need for further research to focus on the impact of the sociocultural and institutional context on genetic counselling in the context of Hong Kong.

Acknowledgements

The research reported here was fully supported by a grant from the Hong Kong Research Grants Council of the Hong Kong Special Administrative Region, China (project no. HKU 754609 H).

We would like to thank the research assistants, in particular Alice Yau and Kitty Ho, for assisting with transcribing the data.

Notes

1. While pregnant women are typically referred to in the literature as 'women' or 'clients,' we use the term 'patients' in line with the practices at the hospital where the data were collected. Similarly, we use the term 'Down syndrome' as opposed to 'Down's syndrome.'
2. In the hospital the following tests are available to the patients: direct invasive (or diagnostic) tests such as CVS or amniocentesis; indirect non-invasive (or screening) tests such as nuchal translucency and a maternal blood test; or having no test.
3. At the time of recording, women over the age of 35 years were eligible for the PGC services. From July 2010 a new programme has been implemented: now prenatal screening tests are offered to patients of all ages. Diagnostic tests are no longer offered in the public health sector for women of 35 years of age or under.

References

Anderson, G. (1999) Nondirectiveness in prenatal genetics: Patients read between the lines. *Nursing Ethics* 6: 126–136.

Bekker, H. L., Hewison, J. and Thornton, J. G. (2004) Applying decision analysis to facilitate informed decision making about prenatal diagnosis for Down syndrome: A randomised controlled trial. *Prenatal Diagnosis* 24: 265–275.

Benkendorf, J. L., Prince, M. B., Rose, M. A., De Fina, A. and Hamilton, H. E. (2001) Does indirect speech promote nondirective genetic counselling? *American Journal of Medical Genetics* 106: 199–207.

Bosk, C. (1992) *All God's Mistakes: Genetic Counselling in a Paediatric Clinic.* Chicago, IL: University of Chicago Press.

Clarke, A. (1991) Is non-directive genetic counselling possible? *Lancet* 338: 959–1026.

Dormandy, E., Michie, S., Hooper, R. and Marteau, T. M. (2006) Informed choice in antenatal Down syndrome screening: A cluster-randomized trial of combined versus separate visit testing. *Patient Education and Counselling* 61: 56–64.

Gao, G. and Ting-Toomey, S. (1998) *Communicating Effectively with the Chinese.* Thousand Oaks, CA: Sage.

Gao, G., Ting-Toomey, S. and Gudykunst, W. (1995) Chinese communication process. In M. H. Bond (ed.) *The Handbook of Chinese Psychology* 280–293. Hong Kong: Oxford University Press.

Gervais, K. G. (1993) Objectivity, value neutrality, and nondirectiveness in genetic counseling. In D. M. Bartels, B. LeRoy and A. L. Caplan (eds) *Prescribing Our Future: Ethical Challenges in Genetic Counseling* 119–130. New York: Aldine de Gruyter.

Haakana, M. (1999) Laughing matters: A conversation analytical study of laughter in doctor-patient interaction. Unpublished doctoral dissertation, Department of Finnish Language, University of Helsinki.

Heyman, B., Hundt, G., Sandall, J., Spencer, K., Williams, C., Grellier, R. and Pitson, L. (2006) On being at higher risk: A qualitative study of prenatal screening for chromosomal anomalies. *Social Science and Medicine* 62: 2360–2372.

Johnson, A. W. and Nadirshaw, Z. (2002) Good practice in transcultural counseling: An Asian perspective. In S. Palmer (ed.) *Multicultural Counselling: A Reader* 119–128. London: Sage.

Kessler, S. (1997) Psychological aspects of genetic counseling. XI. Nondirectiveness revisited. *American Journal of Medical Genetics* 72: 164–171.

Lam, S. (2006) *CGS: 25 Years of Clinical Genetic Service.* Hong Kong: Clinical Genetic Service Department of Health.

Lee-Wong, S. M. (1999) *Cross-Cultural Communication: Politeness and Face in Chinese Culture.* Frankfurt am Main: Peter Lang.

Leung, T. N., Chau, M. M. C., Chang, J. J., Leung, T. Y., Fung, T. Y. and Lau, T. K. (2004) Attitudes towards termination of pregnancy among Hong Kong Chinese women attending prenatal diagnosis counselling clinic. *Prenatal Diagnosis* 24: 546–551.

Markens, A., Browner, C. H. and Press, N. (1999) 'Because of the risks': How US pregnant women account for refusing prenatal screening. *Social Science and Medicine* 49: 359–369.

Marteau, T. M. and Dormandy, E. (2001) Facilitating informed choice in prenatal testing: How well are we doing? *American Journal of Medical Genetics* 106: 185–190.

Pilnick, A. (2002) There are no rights and wrongs in these situations: Identifying interactional difficulties in genetic counseling. *Sociology of Health and Illness* 24: 66–88.

Pilnick, A. (2008) 'It's something for you both to think about': Choice and decision making in nuchal translucency screening for Down's syndrome. *Sociology of Health and Illness* 30: 511–530.

Pilnick, A and Zayts, O. (2011) 'Let's have it tested first': Directiveness, circumstance and decision-making following positive antenatal screening in Hong Kong. In N. Armstrong and H. Eborall (eds) *Sociology of Health and Illness: The Sociology of Screening.* doi: 10.1111/j.1467-9566.2011.01425.x

Reminnick, L. (2006) The quest for the perfect baby: Why do Israeli women seek prenatal genetic testing? *Sociology* 28: 21–53.

Roberts, C. (2006) Continuities and discontinuities in doctor-patient consultations in a multilingual society. In M. Gotti and F. Salager-Meyer (eds) *Advances in Medical Discourse Analysis: Oral and Written Contexts* 177–195. Bern: Peter Lang.

Rosenfeld, Elif T. (1996) Participant structure in therapeutic discourse: An analysis of dyadic discourse in marital therapy. PhD dissertation, Georgetown University, Washington, DC.

Sarangi, S. and Clarke, A. (2002) Zones of expertise and the management of uncertainty in genetics risk communication. *Research on Language and Social Interaction* 35: 139–171.

Sarangi, S., Bennert, K., Howell, L., Clarke, A., Harper, P. and Gray, G. (2004) Initiation of reflective frames in counselling for Huttington disease predictive testing. *Journal of Genetic Counselling* 13: 135–155.

Schiffrin, D. (1994) *Approaches to Discourse.* Oxford: Blackwell.

Shiloh, S. (1996) Decision-making in the context of genetic risk. In T. Marteau, M. Richards and A. Hunt (eds) *The Troubled Helix: Social and Psychological Implications of the New Human Genetics* 82–103. Cambridge: Cambridge University Press.

Tang, M., Ghosh, A. and Chan, F. Y. (1991) Genetic counselling in prenatal diagnosis. *Journal of the Hong Kong Medical Association* 43: 75–77.

Weil, J. (2003) Psychosocial genetic counseling in the post-nondirective era: A point of view. *Journal of Genetic Counseling* 12: 199–211.

Weil, J., Ormond, K., Peters, J., Peters, K., Biesecker, B. B. and LeRoy, B. (2006) The relationship of nondirectiveness to genetic counseling: Report of a workshop at the 2003 NSGC annual education conference. *Journal of Genetic Counseling* 159: 85–93.

Weinans, M. J., Huijssoon, A. M., Tymstra, T., Gerrits, M. C., Beekhuis, J. R. and Mantingh, A. (2000) How women deal with the results of serum screening for Down syndrome in the second trimester of pregnancy. *Prenatal Diagnosis* 20: 705–708.

Wertz, D. C. and Fletcher, J. C. (1988) Attitudes of genetic counselors: A multinational survey. *American Journal of Human Genetics* 42: 592–600.

Williams, C., Sandall, J., Lewando-Hundt, G., Heyamn, B., Spencer, K. and Grellier, R. (2005) Women as moral pioneers? Experiences of first trimester antenatal screening. *Social Science and Medicine* 6: 1983–1992.

Young, L. W. L. (1994) *Crosstalk and Culture in Sino-American Communication.* New York: Cambridge University Press.

Zayts, O., Kang, M. A. (2009) 'So, what test do you prefer?' Negotiating politic behavior in an L2 prenatal genetic counselling setting in Hong Kong. *Journal of Politeness Research: Language, Behaviour, Culture* 5: 33–52.

Zayts, O. and Kang, M. A. (2010) Information delivery in prenatal genetic counseling: On the role of initial inquiries. *Journal of Asia Pacific Communication* 20: 243–259.

Zayts, O. and Schnurr, S. (2011) Laughter as a medical providers' resource: Negotiating informed choice in prenatal genetic counseling. *Research on Language and Social Interaction* 44(1): 1–20.

12

The pragmatics of Q&A interactions: Public discourses in Hong Kong

Winnie Cheng

Research in questions and responses

Questions and their responses are ubiquitous and have been "a crucial locus of research" (Enfield et al. 2010: 2615) in various fields, including the philosophy of language, anthropology, grammar, conversation and discourse analysis, and pragmatics (*ibid.*). Widdowson (1979: 138) argues for the importance of considering the interactive aspect of questions and responses, as they are social activities that relate to the world outside the discourse. Similarly, Stenström (1994: 38) suggests that a question "is an interactive element which can only be interpreted by what it does 'here and now' in a particular conversation". Questions are "utterances which require a verbal response from the addressee" (Carter and McCarthy 2006: 424), and yet Tsui (1992) considers the possibility of a non-verbal response by defining questions as 'elicitations' that function "to elicit an obligatory verbal response or its non-verbal surrogate" (p.101).

Question-response sequences and patterns have been examined in a wide range of spoken interactions, such as academic discourse (Piazza 2002), American television talk shows (van Rees 2007), British debate interviews (Emmertsen 2007), conversation (Cheng and Warren 2001; Enfield et al. 2010; Steensig and Drew 2008), medical consulting rooms (Boyd and Heritage 2006), news interviews (Clayman and Heritage 2002), press conferences (Clayman et al. 2006), public discourses (Cheng 2004), and a performance appraisal interview (Adams 1981).

Ilie (1999) compared semi-institutional talk shows to institutionally rule-governed discourses such as news interviews and courtroom interrogation, and found that talk shows are characterised by less predictable and less conventionalised question-response adjacency pairs. The talk show hosts use institutionally functioning standard questions, that is, *'information-eliciting, confirmation-eliciting,* and *answer-eliciting* questions' (Ilie 1999: 996), to exert the authority of the institutional roles assigned to the questioners. However, the hosts also use '*mixed types of questions* that fulfill several functions simultaneously', particularly three types of non-standard questions, namely expository questions, rhetorical questions and echo questions, that co-occur or overlap with each other frequently, and "function argumentatively in relation to their responses" (*ibid.*: 996). In another study, Piazza (2002) analysed the pragmatics of conductive questions in academic discourse when tutors and students "try to convey their preference for a given answer from their hearer/s" (*ibid.*: 509). Findings show that the degree of conduciveness of questions, for example "form, prosody, repetition and topic maintenance or change, hearer's answer to the question itself, speaker's dominance, relationship to the source of authority (i.e. the assigned reading)" (*ibid.*: 526) depends on the interaction of different textual and contextual elements. Léon (2004) examined the semantic structure of question-answer pairs in French news interviews of political personalities, and found that "agreeing answers are preferred second pair parts" (*ibid.*: 1916), hence supporting Sacks (1973/1987) notion of preference for agreement. Other studies have examined public discourses. Emmertsen (2007), for instance, examined challenging questions in British debate interviews and found that the interviewers initial challenging questions polarise interviewees' positions, and that asking hostile challenging questions shows the interviewers adhering to the demands for formal neutrality in news interviews.

Speech acts of question and answers

In pragmatics, studies of questions and their responses have been "a route into the theory of speech acts" (Enfield et al. 2010: 2615). Speech acts are "the basic or minimal units of linguistic communication" (Searle 1969: 16) and are produced "in actual situations of language use, by people having something 'in mind'" (Mey 2001: 93). Speakers use directives (Searle 1979) that "embody an effort on the part of the speaker to get the hearer to do something, to 'direct' him or her towards some goal (of the speaker's mostly)" (Mey 2001: 120). Questions are a sub-class of directives, because by questioning we are trying to get the speaker to do something, namely to perform a speech act (Searle 1979: 13). Questions "appear quite frequently in everyday conversational discourse" (Weber 1993: 20). Answering, a speech act in the category of assertives (Searle 1979) functions as a possible and prospective response to a question (Sinclair 1992).

In classifying question functions, both Stenström (1984) and Tsui (1987, 1992) adopt the term 'elicitation' (Sinclair and Coulthard 1975) with a focus on the elicitative force the questions have in a discourse. In Stenström's (1984) study of questions and responses, questions are classified into ten different elicitative functions in terms of "what type of R (response) is required" (Stenström 1984: 152), namely acknowledge, action, clarify, confirm, identify, offer, permit, polar, react and repeat. However, some of the elicitative functions of questions, namely action, offer and react, are actually indirect requests, rather than questions that function to elicit information (*ibid.*: 149). Apart from elicitative force, questions also have different degrees of conduciveness. A conducive question is one which favours one response over another (*ibid.*: 47), and this depends on how the hearer interprets the utterance in a particular situation. Stenström (1984) describes three types of conducive questions: exclamatory questions, rhetorical questions and suggestions. Tsui (1992) identifies six functions of questions, namely inform, confirm, agree, commit, repeat and clarify. Later, Piazza (2002) develops a model for the analysis of conducive questions with reference to four aspects: (1) the questioner's old belief underlying the question, (2) the new assumption the questioner formulates in her/his mind, (3) the expected answer, and (4) the formal aspect of the question itself.

In the discussion about the responses to questions, it is important to consider the function of the response, particularly whether the utterance following a question is an answer. In discourse analysis, Sinclair and Brazil (1982: 42), for instance, suggest that whatever follows a question could be classified as an answer, a diversion, or anything else. In conversation analysis, adjacency pairs show not only the ordering of pair parts but also discriminative relations between the parts, and so 'question-answer', 'greeting greeting', 'offer-acceptance/refusal' are instances of pair types (Schegloff 1984: 33). Halliday and Hasan (1976) classify responses to questions into direct and indirect responses. To them, a direct response is an utterance which answers the question; indirect responses are (1) "commentary" which is an utterance that comments on the question, (2) "disclaimer" that denies the relevance of the question, and (3) "a supplementary response" that gives supplementary information or implies but does not express the answer (Halliday and Hasan 1976). Joshi (1983) identifies three types of cooperative responses that are desirable in the question-answer (Q-A) systems in his study: corrective indirect responses, supportive indirect responses and suggestive indirect responses.

The present study

The vastness of studies of question-answer patterns and functions in English reviewed above shows a range of participants and cultural and interactional contexts. Nevertheless, studies of Chinese language in public discourses in Asia, particularly in Hong Kong, have not been conducted. In order to contribute to this important but lacking area of research, the present study aims to conduct a speech act analysis of question-answer pairs (Schlegloff and Sacks 1973) in Chinese (Cantonese) that occur immediately after public discourses such as public speeches, seminars, media briefings, forum discussions and media interviews. The research goal of the study is to understand how the participants make discursive and pragmatic choices in the questions and answers, as embedded in the local organisational and institutional peculiarities of the discourses and the broader sociocultural and political contexts of interactions in the Hong Kong Special Administrative Region (hereafter 'Hong Kong') (Mey 2001).

In spoken professional and public discourses such as presentations, legislative council meetings, forum discussions and press conferences, the Q&A interactions are, typically, in marked contrast to the highly planned monologic presentations and speeches that precede them, and so require the speakers to adopt very different discursive and pragmatic strategies. While the preceding presentations are typically highly planned, frequently written, either in full or in note form, and therefore very much under the control of the presenter in terms of content, structure and language, the interactions involving questions and answers are typically unrehearsed and unplanned in terms of the exact content and functions. They also very often require the speaker to depart from his or her script or notes and engage in a more spontaneous dialogue with questioners who may range from the supportive to the hostile. Although, of course, in political Q&A interactions involving politicians and government officials, their staff, or ghost-writers, will have provided them with potential questions and model answers in advance, in a relatively open society such as Hong Kong these events can never be fully controlled. The questions in these contexts can be regarded as "warranted" (Borge 2007: 1691) in the sense that "S stands in and S believes S stands in a relation R to H such that S can demand or expect H to sincerely answer S's question" (*ibid.*: 1691).

In Biber's (1995) analysis of the linguistic features of different dimensions of variation across spoken and written genres, public conversations, which are similar to the Q&A interactions in the public contexts examined in this study, are found to be an involved production lying between prepared speeches and face-to-face conversations. The public conversation is characterised as a non-narrative discourse having a non-abstract style and being neutral in the dimension of situation-dependent vs. elaborated reference, overtly argumentative, and high in on-line informational elaboration marking stance (Biber 1995).

The study investigates the pragmatics of the questions and answers in the domain of public discourses in Cantonese in order to address the following research questions:

1. What are the pragmatic functions of the questions?
2. What is the relative distribution of the different functions of questions?
3. What are the pragmatic functions of the answers?
4. What is the relative distribution of the different functions of answers?
5. What are the relations between different question functions and answer functions?
6. What is the relation between context of interaction and the pragmatics functions of questions and answers?

When classifying the pragmatic functions of questions and answers, the study draws on the typologies of Webber (2002) and Stenström (1994). Webber's (2002) typology of questions consists of five pragmatic functions:

Type 1a: information eliciting: facts
Type 1b: information eliciting: opinions
Type 2: criticism or attack
Type 3: suggestions
Type 4: comments
Type 5: more than one pragmatic function

Regarding the pragmatic functions of answers, according to Stenström (1994), not all answers to questions are 'proper' in the sense that they really answer the question. Stenström (1994: 114–115) identifies five sub-categories of answers, namely <comply>, <imply>, <supply>, <evade> and <disclaim>, which are ordered from most appropriate to least appropriate, as described and illustrated in the following:

<comply> – gives adequate information explicitly
A: when is it
B: four thirty tomorrow

<imply> – gives adequate information implicitly
A: do you want people to come to the registry office
B: not many

<supply> – gives inadequate information
A: was he a personal friend of yours or
B: erm (.) well (.) er (.) he used to be my tutor

<evade> – avoids answering a 'question' (consciously)
A: erm well have you any other suggestions
B: well he didn't give me any

<disclaim> – declares that the 'answer' is unknown
A: what happens if anybody breaks in and steals it are are is
      are we covered or
B: erm (pause) I don't know quite honestly
(Stenström 1994: 114–115)

In an interaction, speakers are concerned with how to do things with words, that is, speech acts (Austin 1962), and an utterance is classified into an locutionary act that is made via the illocutionary force of the utterance, that is, the communicative force or intention behind the words that are uttered (Searle 1969). The study examines the utterances in the public discourses collected in the Hong Kong in terms of the illocutionary force of questions and answers in the Q&A interactions in various public contexts of situation (Halliday and Hasan 1989). Through the initial analysis of the illocutionary acts of the utterances in the Q&A interactions, question-answer pairs were identified and then analysed.

Data for the study

The study collected spoken Q&A interactions (34,430 words) from the websites of some Hong Kong government offices. The data were genuine face-to-face spoken interactions for public communication, including consultation forums, seminars and legislative council meetings. The recordings of the Q&A interactions downloaded from the websites were transcribed verbatim and then translated into English. The data set consisted of 11 Q&A interactions, all in Cantonese (Table 12.1). The speakers (S) who asked questions were reporters in Contexts 1, 2, 4–9, business people in Context 3, the general public in Context 10, and legislative councillors in Context 11. Across all the Q&A contexts, the hearers (H) are government officials.

Table 12.1 Frequencies of Cantonese question-answer pairs in public contexts of interaction in Hong Kong

Context of interaction (Cantonese)	*Word count*
1. Government officials and professionals gathered in a forum to discuss the economy of Hong Kong, 9 January 2003. At the end government officials answer reporters' questions about the topic of the meeting.	1,559 (4.53%)
2. Mr Henry Tang, Chief Secretary for Administration, Hong Kong answers reporters' questions after a ceremony, 25 March 2003.	728 (2.11%)
3. Forum on Closer Economic Partnership Arrangement (CEPA) and Hong Kong River Delta economic integration, 2 October 2003 and 3 November 2003. Representatives from the Hong Kong Trade Development Council answer questions from business people.	3,130 (9.09%)
4. Mr Henry Tang, Chief Secretary for Administration, Hong Kong, answers reporters' questions at a hotel lobby in Shanghai, before returning to Hong Kong after a meeting with the Major of Shanghai, 27 April 2004.	584 (1.70%)
5. Mr Thomas Tso, Deputy Secretary for Housing, Planning and Lands, Hong Kong answers reporters' questions after the submission deadline of West Kowloon cultural district development proposals, 19 June 2004.	1,523 (4.42%)
6. Mr Justice Woo Kwok-hing, Chairman for the Electoral Affairs Commission, Hong Kong answers reporters' questions after the announcement of the results of the Legislative Council Election, 13 September 2004.	608 (1.77%)
7. Dr Sarah Liao, former Secretary for Environment, Transport, & Works, Hong Kong answers reporters' questions after a radio broadcast, 8 November 2004.	1,857 (5.39%)
8. Prof. K. C. Chan, Secretary for Financial Services and the Treasury, Hong Kong answers reporters' questions after the seminar, 6 August 2007.	1,313 (0.04%)
9. Mr Ambrose Lee, Secretary for Security, Hong Kong answers reporters' questions regarding the situation in Thailand, 13 April 2009.	1,138 (3.31%)
10. Ms Anissa S. Y. Wong, Permanent Secretary for the Environment, Hong Kong answers questions from the public regarding the air quality in Hong Kong, 13 January 2008.	5,441 (15.8%)
11. Mr Donald Tsang, Chief Executive, Hong Kong answers questions from legislative councillors, 14 May 2009.	16,549 (48.6%)
TOTAL	34,430 (100%)

Findings

Pragmatic functions of questions in Q&A interactions

The Q&A interactions were first analysed using Webber's (2002) typology of five pragmatic functions of questions. Table 12.2 presents the frequencies of the pragmatic functions of the questions in each of the 11 public contexts of Q&A interactions.

Table 12.2 Frequencies of pragmatic functions of questions in Q&A interactions

Q&A context	Type 1a	Type 1b	Type 2	Type 3	Type 4	Type 5 (combination of types)	Total
1						2+4+3 (1) 1a+4 (1)	2 (1.56%)
2	5						5 (3.93%)
3	28						28 (22.04%)
4	4						4 (3.15%)
5	10	1					11 (8.66%)
6	4						4 (3.15%)
7	7					1a+4 (1)	8 (6.3%)
8	5	3					8 (6.3%)
9	5					1a+2 (2) 1a+4 (8) 1a+2+3+4 (1) 1a+1b+2 (1)	17 (13.4%)
10	5	1					6 (4.72%)
11	13	1	3			1a+2+3 (1) 1a+2 (5) 1a+3 (2) 1a+4 (6) 1b+2 (1) 1b+2+4 (1) 2+3 (1)	34 (26.77%)
TOTAL	86 (67.7%)	6 (4.7%)	3 (2.4%)	0	0	32 (25.2%)	127 (100%)

Table 12.2 shows that across the 11 contexts of public Q&A interactions, the greatest number of questions is found in Context 11 (26.77%). This is not surprising as Context 11 has the greatest number of words, constituting 48.6 per cent of the total number of words in the data set. Context 11 was

recorded at a Legislative Council meeting when the Chief Executive of Hong Kong received questions from the councillors. Among the 127 Cantonese question-answer pairs in the 11 public contexts, the most frequent question types are Type 1a (information eliciting: facts) (67.7%) and Type 5 (more than one pragmatic function) (25.2%). Type 1b (information eliciting: opinions) (4.7%) and Type 2 (criticism or attack) (2.4%) occur very infrequently, and Type 3 (suggestions) and Type 4 (comments) do not occur alone, but these two types are used in combination with Type 1a (information eliciting: facts) and Type 2 (criticism or attack) to form Type 5 (combination of types) questions. Type 1a questions are found in all but the first context of public Q&A interactions; Type 1b in Contexts 5, 8, 10 and 11; and Type 2 only in one of the 11 interactions (Context 11).

The following (Examples 1–4) illustrate and discuss the different pragmatic functions of questions found in the 127 question-answer pairs. Example 1 shows a reporter asking a question to Dr Sarah Liao, former Secretary for Environment, Transport and Works, Hong Kong who answers reporters' questions after a radio broadcast, 8 November 2004.

Example 1 (Q&A context 7)

Type 1a: information eliciting: facts

> 記者：你剛才表示，如果用天然氣發電，減少用煤減少排放，電費可能增加，可否再詳 述一下？

> Reporter: You just said that if natural gas is used to produce energy, to reduce the use of coal and to reduce emissions, electricity bills may increase. Can you elaborate on that?

The question makes an attempt to elicit further information about what the government official has just said about the effect of the use of natural gas on electricity bills.

Example 2 is an extract from an interaction in a hotel lobby in Shanghai where Mr Henry Tang, Chief Secretary for Administration, Hong Kong, answered reporters' questions on 27 April 2004 before he left for Hong Kong after having a meeting with the Major of Shanghai.

Example 2 (Q&A context 4)

Type 1b: information eliciting: opinions

> 記者：現時關於人大所作決定，很多港商表示結束了政爭，可以專心「搞好」經濟，是否這樣？

> Reporter: Regarding the decision made by the Standing Committee of the National People's Congress, many local businessmen in Hong Kong said that

political conflict has been resolved, (they) can focus on 'the development' of the economy. Is it the case?

The Chief Secretary for Administration is asked by a reporter about what he thinks about what many Hong Kong businessmen have said regarding the decision made by the Standing Committee of the National People's Congress.

The Type 2 question in Example 3 below is one of the three of this type in the whole Q&A interaction data set. It was addressed to Donald Tsang, Chief Executive of Hong Kong, by a Legislative Council Member at a council meeting, 14 May 2009.

Example 3 (Q&A context 11)

Type 2: criticism or attack

梁國雄議員:你用了一億元搞國民教育,為何教科書內將六四的血痕用墨掩蓋。

Leung Kwok-hung, Legislative Council Member: You have spent 100 million dollars on civil education. Why have textbooks covered up the June 4 blood traces with ink?

The question was interpreted as a criticism against the Hong Kong Government by the Legislative Council Member. It begins with a declarative asserting a fact – that Hong Kong has spent HK$ 100 million on civil education – followed by an interrogative that criticised the government of an action that seems to counteract the effort made, in monetary terms, to promote civil education.

Example 4 is taken from the same context of interaction as that in Example 3.

Example 4 (Q&A context 11)

Type 5: more than one pragmatic function

張宇人議員:特首,其實我剛才問,是他們希望停收牌費及百分百擔保低息貸款,其實這些是他們希望你立即做。似乎這個豬流感,就不只 是中國,剛才你說遊客來,剛才我說跌了六、七成,其實我看不到是短線,以及昨日又有事發生,未來還會比之前兩星期辛苦。雖然我知道財政司聽到,其實你會不會覺得需要真的跟財政司說這個行業你要幫手,除了我的飲食行業外。

Tommy Cheung Yu-yan, Legislative Council Member: Chief executive. In fact what I just asked was that they hope to stop charging license fees and (to have) fully guaranteed low-interest loans. In fact they hope that you will immediately do this. Apparently this Swine flu is not only found in China. Just now you said tourists come. Just now I said (the arrivals) have dropped by sixty seventy percent. In fact I do not see it as short-term. And yesterday things happened. In the future (things) will be tougher than the past two weeks. Although I know the Financial Secretary has heard, in fact wouldn't you think there was a need to really talk to the Financial Secretary that you have to help this industry, besides my catering industry?

The question shows a combination of Type 3: suggestions and Type 2: criticism or attack. Tommy Cheung Yu-yan is a member of the Legislative Council of Hong Kong, representing the catering industry in the functional constituency seat. He asks the Chief Executive of the Government of the Hong Kong for a response about 'this industry', hoping or suggesting that the government will stop charging license fees and will provide them with fully guaranteed low-interest loans. In the same turn, he criticises the government for not having provided assistance and support not only to catering but also to the tourism industry.

Pragmatic functions of answers in Q&A interactions

Following the pragmatic functions of questions, what follows is a discussion of the findings relating to the pragmatic functions of the answers in the Q&A interactions in the public contexts of communication, which were classified according to Stenström's (1994) five sub-categories of answers, namely <comply>, <imply>, <supply>, <evade> and <disclaim>, ordered from the most appropriate to the least appropriate.

Table 12.3 shows the frequencies of pragmatic functions of answers in the 127 question-answer pairs in the 11 public contexts.

Table 12.3 Frequencies of pragmatic functions of answers in Q&A interactions

Q&A context	<comply>	<imply>	<supply>	<evade>	<disclaim>	TOTAL
1	1	1				2 (1.57%)
2	2		1	2		5 (3.94%)
3	23	1	2	1	1	28 (22%)
4	1	1		2		4 (3.15%)
5	5		1	1	4	11 (8.66%)
6	2		2			4 (3.15%)
7	6		1		1	8 (6.3%)
8	4	2		2		8 (6.3%)
9	9		6	2		17 (13.4%)
10	4			2		6 (4.72%)
11	12	4	7	10	1	34 (26.8%)
TOTAL	69 (54.3%)	9 (7.09%)	20 (15.75%)	22 (17.32%)	7 (5.6%)	127 (100%)

Across all the Q&A interactions, the frequencies of occurrence of the pragmatic functions of answers are in descending order of <comply>, <evade>, <supply>, <imply> and <disclaim>. The <comply> function constitutes more than half (54.3%) of the 127 answers. It is interesting to note that <evade>, avoiding answering a <question> (consciously) (Stenström 1994: 114), ranks second (17.32%) among the five answer functions.

The examples below illustrate different pragmatic functions of answers in the Cantonese Q&A interactions. Example 5 shows a reporter asking a question of the Former Secretary for Environment, Transport and Works, Hong Kong, Dr Sarah Liao after a radio broadcast, 8 November 2004.

Example 5 (Q&A context 8)

<comply> (gives adequate information explicitly)

> 記 者:除了向海南島引入天然氣外，還有什麼地方可引入天然氣？
> 環境運輸及工務局局長：我們可以購買天然氣，不一定需要管道引入，例如澳洲及印尼都有天然氣輸出。

> Reporter: Apart from importing natural gas from South China Island, where else can (we) import natural gas from?

> Secretary for the Environment, Transport and Works, Dr Sarah Liao: We can purchase natural gas, not necessarily importing in via pipelines, for instance Australia and Indonesia have natural gas to export.

The answer by Dr Sarah Liao to the reporter's question for information is one of <comply>. She provides the answer requested, namely the two countries from which natural gas could be purchased. In fact, the answer provides more information than required by explaining that the government does not just pipe in natural gas, they import natural gas via shipments.

In Example 6, the Hong Kong government officials and professionals had a discussion about the Hong Kong economy on 9 January 2003.

Example 6 (Q&A context 2)

<imply> (gives adequate information implicitly)

> 記 者 ： 現 時 關 於 人 大 所 作 決 定 ， 很 多 港 商 表 示 結 束 了 政 爭 ， 可 以
> 專 心 「 搞 好 」 經 濟 ， 是 否 這 樣 ？
> 財 政 司 司 長 ： 這 個 意 見 我 從 多 方 面 都 聽 到 ， 今 次 人 大 常 委 作 了 一
> 個 決 定 後 ， 其 實 對 於 投 資 者 而 言 是 有 一 個 穩 定 性 ， 因 為 對

投 資 者 是 否 投 資 、 或 是 否 繼 續 投 資 ， 都 取 決 於 經 濟
效 益 和 穩 定 的 投 資 環 境 ， 所 以 今 次 有 助 投 資 者 在 這
一 方 面 的 考 慮。

Reporter: Nowadays about the decision of The Standing Committee of the National People's Congress, many Hong Kong businessmen remark that having ended political conflict (Hong Kong/Hong Kong Government) can focus on 'improving' the economy. Is this the case?

Financial Secretary: This opinion I have heard from various (sources/people). Since the Standing Committee of the National People's Congress has made the decision, in fact for the investors there is a degree of stability; because whether the investors invest or whether (they) continue to invest depends on economic efficiency and a stable investment environment, so this time (it) helps investors' consideration in this aspect.

The Financial Secretary does not explicitly respond to the reporter's question about whether the Hong Kong Government is to focus on 'improving' the economy, now that the political disputes have been settled. He only gives the answer implicitly, by implying that political stability has a positive impact on investors' decisions about whether to continue investing in Hong Kong. The term 'political conflict' is, however, not mentioned.

Example 7 is taken from the Q&A session after Mr Justice Woo Kwok-hing, Chairman for the Electoral Affairs Commission, Hong Kong has announced the results of the Legislative Council Election, 13 September 2004.

Example 7 (Q&A context 7)

<supply> (gives inadequate information)

記者：今次點票不如估計中快，會否檢討在日後 選舉 是否 繼續 使用 投票站轉點票站的方式點算選票？

胡國興法官：我們會盡量檢討，因為方法的問題包括好多方面，如票箱的設計等，我們會全面作出檢討，然後才會提議日後的選舉安排怎樣去做。而我們作出有關建議之前是會首先諮詢市民的，然後才決定作出甚麼安排。

Reporter: The ballot paper counting was not as quick as expected. Would (you) review that in future elections to see whether to continue to use the practice of turning polling stations into ballot counting stations?

Judge Woo Kwok-hing: We will review that as far as possible, as the question about methods involves many aspects, for example, the design of the ballot boxes. We will conduct a comprehensive review, and then will suggest arrangements for future elections. But before we make suggestions, we will first consult the citizens, and then decide what arrangements to make.

Mr Justice Woo Kwok-hing does not answer the reporter's 'yes-no' question adequately, as he does not say whether or not there will be a review of the current ballot counting method in order to determine 'whether to continue to use the practice of turning polling stations into ballot counting stations'. Instead, he only gives an answer that there will be 'a comprehensive review' and consultations with the citizens.

Example 8 is a question-answer pair when Mr Henry Tang, Chief Executive for Administration, Hong Kong, responded to reporters' questions after a ceremony in Hong Kong, March 2003.

Example 8 (Q&A context 2)

<evade> (avoids answering a <question> consciously)

記者: 是否有時間表，例如何時再開會、會面？他們會否來香港？

財政司司長: 我們都是採取一個實事求是的方式，在一些具體的事情方面，我們希望可以加快和深化。

Reporters: Will they come to Hong Kong? If yes, when?

Financial Secretary: We have always been doing our jobs in a practical way. We know exactly what needs to be done and we are very efficient.

My Tang is evasive about whether there is a timetable or timeline for the next meeting with the counterparts in China, and whether the Chinese officials will come to Hong Kong again. Instead, the answer, which is about the working style, practice and efficiency of the Hong Kong Government, is not related to the questions.

Example 9 is taken from the Q&A interaction in which Mr Thomas Tso, Deputy Secretary for Housing, Planning and Lands, Hong Kong answers reporters' questions after the submission deadline of West Kowloon cultural district development proposals, 19 June 2004.

Example 9 (Q&A context 6)

<disclaim> (declares that the answer is unknown)

記者：現在涉及多少公司或財團？

房屋及規劃地政局副秘書長：現在我沒有這方面的資 ，因為仍未打開該建議書。

Reporter: Right now how many companies or financial groups are involved?

Deputy Permanent Secretary for Housing, Planning and Lands: Right now I don't have the information on this because (we) have not yet opened those proposals.

Example 9 shows that when being asked about the number of companies and financial groups that are involved, Mr Thomas Tso simply says "I don't have the information on this", followed by giving a reason that they "have not yet opened those proposals".

Patterns of Q&A pragmatic functions

To address the fifth research question, all the 127 question-answer pairs were examined to identify the question and answer patterns. Fifteen patterns were identified (Table 12.4).

Table 12.4 Patterns of pragmatic functions of question-answer pairs in Q&A interactions

Question pragmatic function + answer pragmatic function	*Frequencies of occurrence*
1. Type 1a + <comply>	52 (41%)
2. Type 1a + <imply>	6 (4.72%)
3. Type 1a + <supply>	11 (8.66%)
4. Type 1a + <evade>	11 (8.66%)
5. Type 1a + <disclaim>	6 (4.72%)
6. Type 1b + <comply>	4 (3.15%)
7. Type 1b + <evade>	2 (1.57%)
8. Type 2 + <imply>	1 (0.79%)
9. Type 2 + <supply>	1 (0.79%)
10. Type 2 + <evade>	1 (0.79%)
11. Type 5 + <comply>	13 (10.23%)
12. Type 5 + <imply>	2 (1.57%)
13. Type 5 + <supply>	8 (6.3%)
14. Type 5 + <evade>	8 (6.3%)
15. Type 5 + <disclaim>	1 (0.79%)
TOTAL	127 (100%)

As described above, the frequent occurrence of Type 1a questions (information eliciting: facts) in public interactions indicates that this is the predominant discursive feature characteristic of Q&A interactions in public contexts of situation. It also reveals the institutional role assigned to the questioners, who were primarily media reporters but also included the general public, legislative council members and people from business.

As shown in Table 12.4, Type 1a questions are most frequently responded to with <comply> (41%), followed by <supply> and <evade> (both 8.66%), and then <imply> and <disclaim> (both 4.72%). Type 1b questions (information eliciting: opinions) are responded to with only two functions: <comply> (3.15%) and <evade> (1.57%). The three instances of Type 2 criticism or attack questions are responded to with one instance of <imply>, one <supply> and one <evade>. This shows that a question which has the communicative function to criticise or attack is not responded to with a <comply>. Type 5 questions with more than one function are more likely to receive a <comply> (10.23%) answer, followed by <supply> and <evade> (both 6.3%), with <imply> and <evade> only occurring twice (1.57%) and once (0.79%) respectively.

Findings of the study show that the answer <evade> (avoids answering a <question> (consciously)) is more frequent when responding to questions that elicit facts (Type 1a, 8.66%) than questions that elicit opinions (Type 1b, 1.57%), showing that facts, compared to opinions, can be more sensitive and hence interviewees are found to be more cautious about providing them. As discussed above, Type 3: suggestions and Type 4: comments are not found at all in the data set.

The performance of speech acts presupposes the interaction of "human agents, whose *intentions* are relevant and indispensable to the correct understanding and description of their utterances" (Mey 2001: 93). The speech acts uttered are "entirely dependent on the context of the situation in which such acts are produced" (*ibid.*: 94), and more specifically, any particular act of speaking is "highly dependent, as to its interpretation, on the cultural context in which it is performed or 'uttered'", and that any act of speaking needs "a proper context of utterance to be validly performed [and] doesn't properly make sense unless it is *situated*, as to both its linguistic and its cultural context … it is the context of culture and language which 'sets up' the language user to deal with a particular act of speaking (or non-speaking, as the case may be)" (*ibid.*: 279). It is, therefore, important that the question-answer pairs are examined and discussed as they occur in each public context of interaction (Table 12.5).

Table 12.5 Question-answer pairs in each public context of interaction

Q&A Context	1a+ <C>	1a+ <I>	1a+ <S>	1a+ <E>	1a+ <D>	1b+ <C>	1b+ <E>	2+ <I>	2+ <S>	2+ <E>	5+ <C>	5+ <I>	5+ <S>	5+ <E>	5+ <D>
1											1	1			
2	2		1	2											
3	23	1	2	1	1										
4	1	1		2											
5	4		1	1	4	1									
6	2		2												
7	5		1		1						1				
8	2	2		1		2	1								
9	3		2								6		4	2	
10	3			2		1									
11	7	2	2	2			1	1	1	1	5	1	4	6	1
TOTAL	52	6	11	11	6	4	2	1	1	1	13	2	8	8	1

Table 12.5 clearly shows the breakdown of question-answer types in terms of functions specific to each public context of communication. Some cases of interest include Q&A Context 3 where the businessmen attending the forum on CEPA ask primarily Type 1a questions to elicit facts which are responded to with <comply> answers, and Q&A Context 11 where a wide range of question types are found with a correspondingly a wide range of answers. The phenomenon indicates the open and free-flowing proceedings of council meetings where legislative councillors and the Chief Executive of the Hong Kong Government engage in Q&A interactions that serve different communicative functions.

Summary of findings

Eleven Q&A interactions in Cantonese in public contexts of situation in Hong Kong with 127 question-answer pairs have been analysed to identify the patterns in the pragmatic functions of the questions, the relative distribution of the different functions of questions, the pragmatic functions of the answers, the relative distribution of the different functions of answers, and the relations between different question functions and answer functions. The high frequencies of fact-eliciting and opinion-eliciting questions across all the Q&A interactions support the institutional goals of the interactions as well as the institutional roles assigned to the speakers (i.e. questioners).

Regarding answers, the relatively high level of <comply> is probably the result of the politicians being asked 'friendly' questions as there are very few critical 'unfriendly' questions in the data set examined. While the Q&A patterns can be seen as largely "institutionally functioning" (Ilie 1999: 996), unlike Ilie's (1991) semi-institutional talk show questions, "non-standard questions" (*ibid.*: 996) are not found in the public discourses examined in this study. Similar to Ilie's (1999) findings, both institutionally functioning standard questions, in this case only one type, i.e. "information eliciting: facts [and] *mixed types of questions* that fulfill several functions simultaneously" (*ibid.*: 996) are found to be used in this study.

Findings also show patterns of the semantic structure of question-answer pairs. Compared to Léon (2004) who found that "agreeing answers are preferred second pair parts" (*ibid.*: 1916), the present study shows a predominant question-answer pattern of 'information eliciting: facts' and <comply> (41%), the occurrence of which outnumbers the second frequent patterns, namely 'information eliciting: facts' and <supply> (giving inadequate information) and 'information eliciting: facts' and <evade> (avoiding answering a question) (both 8.66%). The top three response types, from <comply> to <supply> to <evade>, hence vary in the extent of cooperativeness in terms of giving a satisfying response to the question (Joshi 1983).

Conclusions and directions for future studies

The present study, which has quantitatively and qualitatively analysed Q&A interactions in public contexts of interaction, primarily at forum discussions, seminars, legislative council meetings and after government press briefings, exemplifies "real cases of question-answer dialogue [that] exist as real cultural and institutional practices" (Walton 1989: 11). Different from non-institutional talk shows, which seem to fulfill both informational and entertainment functions (Ilie 1999), Q&A interactions in the public domain of interaction between guest speakers or government officials and journalists and reporters constitute institutional dialogues that assign institutional goals and roles to speakers, with speakers assuming interactional roles relative to other participants (Ilie 1999: 976). The question-answer pairs examined in this study can be compared to the questioning patterns in news interviews and courtroom interrogation which are more "predictable" and "conventionalized" (*ibid.*: 995).

The study reported in this chapter focuses on the frequencies and patterns of question-answer pairs in Cantonese public discourses. Lin

(2008), in her study of questions and responses in business communication in Hong Kong, concludes that the pragmatic functions of a question and its corresponding response can be described with confidence if the factors of "discourse intonation, discourse structure, situational context, institutional identities and roles of the participants, goals and communicative purposes of the interactions and so on are taken into consideration" (Lin 2008: 346). Future studies could include an analysis of discourse intonation (e.g. Cheng et al. 2008). The present study of spoken public discourses has only focused on the linguistic text, that is, the words that are uttered, but not the communicative value of discourse intonation (Brazil 1997) which is concerned with the choices that speakers make and their reactions to the ongoing task of making sense to their hearers in context in real time (Cauldwell 2002). With regard to discourse intonation, a meaningful research focus could be the relationship between the question types (e.g. *yes/no* question, tag question, declarative question, *wh*-question and alternative question), the use of intonation and their expected responses (Biber et al. 1999; Quirk et al. 1985).

This study underscores the relationship between the communicative purposes, roles of participants and communicative context and the realisations of the speech acts of questions and responses in Q&A interactions. Future studies could analyse instances of question-answer pairs with reference to other pragmatic theories, constructs and phenomena such as politeness phenomena (Brown and Levinson 1987), impoliteness (Culpeper 1996), conversational implicatures (Grice 1975), and (in)explicitness, (in)directness and vagueness (Cheng and Warren 1999, 2003). A bald-on-record answer, for instance, is one that is stripped of any redressive action, that is, an answer without use of any politeness linguistic devices (Brown and Levinson 1987). The questions and answers could also be examined in terms of the ways in which speakers structure discourse information, which can be accounted for by the use and perception of messages in communication, clarity and topics in conversation, social relations orientation and self orientation (Gudykunst 1998; Gudykunst and Ting-Toomey 1988; Hall 1977; Hofstede 1983), and the notions of face and (im)politeness (Brown and Levinson 1987: Culpeper 1996).

Another area that could be studied is the syntactic structures of questions and their corresponding responses (Wintergerst 1993), either 'expected' or 'expectable' responses (Bublitz 1988). Previous studies have focused on the mismatch of form and function in an utterance and the potential communication breakdown or misunderstanding (Du Bois 1992; Geluykens 1992; Weber 1993). Finally, future studies could also examine the Q&A interactions that occur in other 'large' and 'small' cultural contexts (Holliday et al. 2004). Large culture refers to the received view of culture, which sees it as national, racial or ethnic, while small culture pertains to "any cohesive grouping" (Holliday 1999: 237). The findings of studies of other large or small cultures could be compared with those of the Chinese Q&A interactions in the public and professional domains described in the present study.

Acknowledgement

The work described in this chapter was substantially supported by a grant from the Research Grants Council of the Hong Kong Special Administration Region (Project No. 87S1).

Note

As examples from Cantonese Q&A were transcriptions downloaded from various publicly available institutions, the original discourse markers in Cantonese have been converted to written Chinese, which is essentially modelled on Mandarin in speech.

References

Adams, K. (1981) Question-answer adjacency pairs in a performance appraisal interview. *Journal of Applied Communication Research* 9: 72–84.

Austin, J. L. (1962) *How to do Things with Words*. London: Oxford University Press.

Biber, D. (1995) *Dimensions of Register Variation: A Cross-linguistic Comparison*. Cambridge/New York: Cambridge University Press.

Biber, D., Johannson, S., Leech, G., Conrad, S. and Finegan, E. (1999) *Longman Grammar of Spoken and Written English*. Harlow: Pearson Education Limited.

Borge, S. (2007) Unwarranted questions and conversation. *Journal of Pragmatics* 39: 1689–1701.

Boyd, E. and Heritage, J. (2006) Taking the patient's medical history: Questioning during comprehensive history-taking. In J. Heritage and D. Maynard (eds) *Communication in Medical Care: Interactions between Primary Care Physicians and Patients* 151–184. Cambridge: Cambridge University Press.

Brazil, D. (1997) *The Communicative Role of Intonation in English*. Cambridge: Cambridge University Press.

Brown, P. and Levinson, S. C. (1987) *Politeness: Some Universals in Language Usage*. Cambridge; New York: Cambridge University Press.

Bublitz, W. (1988) *Supportive Fellow-speakers and Cooperative Conversations: Discourse Topics and Topical Actions, Participant Roles and 'Recipient Action' in a Particular Type of Everyday Conversation*. Amsterdam/Philadelphia, PA: John Benjamins.

Carter, R. and McCarthy, M. (2006) *Cambridge Grammar of English: A Comprehensive Guide – Spoken and Written English Grammar and Usage*. Cambridge: Cambridge University Press.

Cauldwell, R. (2002) The functional irrhythmicality of spontaneous speech: A discourse view of speech rhythms. *Apples* 2: 1–24.

Cheng, W. (2004) 'Well thank you David for that question': The intonation, pragmatics and structure of Q&A sessions in public discourses. *The Journal of Asia TEFL* 1: 109–133.

Cheng, W., Greaves, C. and Warren, M. (2008) *A Corpus-Driven Study of Discourse Intonation*. Amsterdam/Philadelphia, PA: John Benjamins.

Cheng, W. and Warren, M. (1999) Inexplicitness: What is it and should we be teaching it? *Applied Linguistics* 20: 293–315.

Cheng, W. and Warren, M. (2001) 'She knows more about Hong Kong than you do isn't it': Tags in Hong Kong conversational English. *Journal of Pragmatics* 33: 1419–1439.

Cheng, W. and Warren, M. (2003) Indirectness, inexplicitness and vagueness made clearer. *Pragmatics* 13: 381–400.

Clayman, S. and Heritage, J. (2002) *The News Interview*. Cambridge: Cambridge University Press.

Clayman, S., Elliott, M., Heritage, J. and McDonald, L. (2006) Historical trends in questioning presidents 1953–2000. *Presidential Studies Quarterly* 36: 561–583.

Culpeper, J. (1996) Towards an anatomy of impoliteness. *Journal of Pragmatics* 25: 349–367.

Du Bois, J. W. (1992) *A New Approach to English Grammar, On Semantic Principles*. Oxford: Clarendon Press.

Emmertsen, S. (2007) Interviewers' challenging questions in British debate interviews. *Journal of Pragmatics* 39: 570–591.

Enfield, N. J., Stivers, T. and Levinson, S. C. (2010) Question-response sequences in conversation across ten languages: An introduction. *Journal of Pragmatics* 42: 2615–2619.

Geluykens, R. (1992) *From Discourse Process to Grammatical Construction: On Left Dislocation in English*. Amsterdam: John Benjamins.

Grice, P. (1975) Logic and conversation. In P. Cole and J. Morgan (eds) *Syntax and Semantics, 3: Speech Acts*. New York: Academic Press.

Gudykunst, W. B. (1998) *Bridging Differences: Effective Intergroup Communication*. 2nd ed. Thousand Oaks, CA: Sage.

Gudykunst, W. B. and Ting-Toomey, S. (1988) *Culture and Interpersonal Communication*. Newbury Park, CA: Sage.

Hall, E. (1977) *What Context? Is It in Use? R & D Report No. 3041*. Austin, Texas: Texas University, Austin. Research and Development Center for Teacher Education.

Halliday, M. and Hasan, R. (1976) *Cohesion in English*. London/New York: Longman.

Halliday, M. and Hasan, R. (1989) *Language, Context, and Text: Aspects of Language in a Social-Semiotic Perspective.* Oxford: OUP.

Hofstede, G. (1983) Dimensions of national cultures in fifty countries and three regions. In J. Deregowski, S. Dziurawiec and R. Annis (eds) *Explications in Cross-Cultural psychology* 335–355. Lisse, the Netherlands: Swets & Zeitlinger.

Holliday, A. (1999) Small culture. *Applied Linguistics* 20: 237–264.

Holliday, A., Hyde, M. and Kullman, J. (2004) *Intercultural Communication: An Advanced Resource Book.* London: Routledge.

Ilie, C. (1999) Question-response argumentation in talk shows. *Journal of Pragmatics* 31: 975–999.

Joshi, A. K. (1983) Varieties of cooperative responses in question-answer systems. In F. Kiefer (ed.) *Questions and Answers* 229–240. Dordrecht: D. Reidel.

Léon, J. (2004) Preference and 'bias' in the format of French news interviews: The semantic analysis of question-answer pairs in conversation. *Journal of Pragmatics* 36: 1885–1920.

Lin, I. (2008) Questions and responses in business communication in Hong Kong. Unpublished PhD dissertation, Department of English, The Hong Kong Polytechnic University, Hong Kong.

Mey, J. (2001) *Pragmatics: An Introduction.* 2nd ed. Malden, MA: Blackwell.

Piazza, R. (2002) The pragmatics of conductive questions in academic discourse. *Journal of Pragmatics* 34: 509–527.

Quirk, R., Greenbaum, S., Leech, G. and Svartvik, J. (1985) *A Comprehensive Grammar of the English Language.* London: Longman.

Sacks, H. (1973/1987) On the preference for agreement and contiguity in sequences in conversation. In G. Button and J. R. Lee (eds) *Talk and Social Organization* 54–69. Clevedon: Multilingual Matters.

Schegloff, E. A. (1984) On some questions and ambiguities in conversation. In J. Atkinson and J. Heritage (eds) *Structures of Social Action* 28–52. Cambridge: Cambridge University Press.

Schegloff, E. A. and Sacks, H. (1973) Opening up closings. *Semiotica* 8: 289–327.

Searle, J. R. (1969) *Speech Acts: An Essay in the Philosophy of Language.* London: Cambridge University Press.

Searle, J. R. (1979) *Expression and Meaning. Studies in the Theory of Speech Acts.* Cambridge/New York: Cambridge University Press.

Sinclair, J. McH. (1992) Priorities in discourse analysis. In M. Coulthard (ed.) *Advances in Spoken Discourse Analysis* 79–88. London: Routledge.

Sinclair, J. McH. and Brazil, D. (1982) *Teacher Talk.* Oxford: Oxford University Press.

Sinclair, J. McH. and Coulthard, M. (1975) *Towards an Analysis of Discourse.* London: Oxford University Press.

Steensig, J. and Drew, P. (2008) Questioning. *Discourse Studies* 10: 5–133.

Stenström, A.-B. (1984) *Questions and Responses in English Conversation* (Lund Studies in English 68). Malmö, Sweden: Liber Verlag.

Stenström, A. B. (1994) *An Introduction to Spoken Interaction.* London/New York: Longman.

Tsui, A. (1987) On elicitations. In M. Coulthard (ed.) *Discussing Discourse* 80–106. Birmingham: ELR.

Tsui, A. (1992) A functional description of questions. In M. Coulthard (ed.) *Advances in Spoken Discourse Analysis* 89–110. London: Routledge.

van Rees, M. A. (2007) Discourse analysis and argumentation theory: The case of television talk. *Journal of Pragmatics* 39: 1454–1463.

Walton, D. (1989) *Question-Reply Argumentation.* New York: Greenwood.

Webber, P. (2002) The paper is now open for discussion. In E. Ventala and S. Thompson (eds) *The Language of Conferencing* 227–253. Frankfurt am Main, Germany: Peter Lang.

Weber, E. (1993) *Varieties of Questions in English Conversation.* Amsterdam/ Philadelphia, PA: John Benjamins.

Widdowson, H. G. (1979) *Explorations in Applied Linguistics.* London: Oxford University Press.

Wintergerst, A. (1993) Why-questions in classroom discourse. *College ESL* 3: 70–79.

13

On the positive formation of Chinese group identity

Dániel Z. Kádár

> *According to the tradition there are many ambitious yet*
> *disappointed men of letters in the area of the capital.*
> 慷慨悲歌士，相傳燕趙多。
>
> Huang Zunxian 黃遵憲 (1848–1905): *Kangkai* 慷慨 (*Sad Song*)

Introduction

Background

The aim of this study is to explore the discursive ways in which group identity was formed in a historical Chinese Community of Practice (Wenger 1998).

This discursive topic is not only relevant to sinological research but also to discourse studies and historical pragmatics. While in recent years extensive research has been devoted to the discursive formation of individual and group identities, Chinese discourse identity formation has been left behind. In fact, some studies examine the relationship between Chinese identity and discourse, but most of them focus on the formation of Chinese national political identity (e.g. Flowerdew 2004; Nyíri 2001; Tsu 2005), that is, the Communist Party's efforts to unite the People's Republic of China (PRC) by means of ideological practices in, for example, media.

This lack of interest as regards in-group identity issues is surprising because in 'mainstream' sinology many works are devoted to identity research, even though most of these studies approach identity from literary and historical perspectives (e.g. Ma and Cartier 2003, and several sections of Befu 1993). The interest of sinologists in how Chinese identity is formed is not coincidental: group identity is a key issue in China, due to the importance placed upon interpersonal relationships. While it would be over-stereotyping to represent the Chinese as 'social beings' (indeed, human beings are social by nature and there is no reason to exoticise the Chinese), traditionally, 'networking' or *guanxi* 關係 building has a unique culture and practice in China (Yang 1994). While in recent years it has been demonstrated that the role of 'networking' is often overemphasised in order to mystify China (Chan 2008), it can be argued, nevertheless, that such practices have special importance in traditional Chinese culture. In more concrete terms, Chinese are traditionally socialised to get things done by giving and receiving favours; to ensure the smoothness of favour transaction, a great deal of energy is invested in the enforcement of in-group relationships (once a favour is done/ accepted, the two parties involved are in-group people).

The present study fills an important knowledge gap: it addresses identity formation in a closed Chinese group or 'Community of Practice' in a modern sense (see more below). From a theoretical perspective, this is a pilot study in the sense that it connects current socio-pragmatic theories with the research of Chinese data, instead of treating identity formation in a traditional, sinological way. Along with this theoretical stance, the present chapter contributes also to historical pragmatics due to the fact that in diachronic studies the formation of discursive identity is somewhat neglected.

The second part of the analysis in this chapter approaches identity formation discourse from the perspective of politeness research: it devotes special attention to politeness as a "discursive resource" (Thornborrow 2002) in group-identity formation activities. It is argued that along with fulfilling its primary discursive function, politeness can also serve the secondary goal of reinforcing (in-)group relationships. That is, forms of politeness can contribute to the formation of group identity as meta-messages (Tannen 2006). By arguing in this way the present chapter aims to demonstrate the applicability of Chinese politeness beyond the conventional interpersonal communicative level, hence contributing to the voluminous research on identity and politeness, which began with the publication of Brown and Levinson's (1987) seminal work and has become a thoroughly studied field (see for example Spencer-Oatey and Ruhi 2007).

The case study

The present study explores the discursive identity formation practice of a southern Chinese group/Community of Practice: inhabitants of the Shaoxing 紹興 area in Zhejiang Province who lived in northern China. This southern Chinese group was chosen because in China there has been a long-standing southern vs. northern nationalistic and ideological opposition (see Eberhard 1965; Friedman 1995). This opposition originates in Chinese history: there were significant linguistic and social differences between the southern and northern parts of the Chinese Empire, and these areas were ruled by different dynasties during several periods. As a result of socio-cultural barriers, the populations of the southern and northern areas have different stereotypes. Inhabitants of the north regarded, and often continue to regard, southern Chinese as 'feminine', 'profit-oriented' and 'improper/non-standard in speech' (in reference to the fact that most of the southern Chinese are 'dialect' speakers and speak standard Chinese with a 'heavy' accent; cf. Chan 1998). Southerners are often referred to by the northern Chinese as the 'barbaric southerners', or *nanman(zi)* 南蠻子. On the other hand, the southern Chinese consider their northern compatriots 'provincial' and 'servile' (in reference to the northerners' inclination to follow the central government, traditionally located in Peking). Southerners often describe the people of the north as 'country bumpkins', using degrading terms such as *tubaozi* 土包子 ('rube').

Contexts in which southern Chinese form their identities in contrast to their northern counterparts, and vice versa, provide noteworthy data with which to study identity formation. Therefore, this chapter analyses the correspondence of a closed circle of expatriated southern Chinese men of letters who lived in the north. It can be claimed that this corpus is particularly illuminating because it shows Chinese identity formation in an 'accelerated' form due to the 'alien' setting. As the epigraph from the famous politician Huang Zunxian 黃遵憲 demonstrates, southern Chinese living in the north regarded themselves as people in 'exile', and this circumstance necessitated stronger reliance upon in-group native relationships, that is, collaboration with others from the Shaoxing area.

Structure

The present study consists of the following sections: an overview of the methodology and corpus; a discussion of the main discursive topics of identity formation in the corpus, that is, a survey of the discursive topics that aided members of the Shaoxing group to form their in-group identity; and an analysis of the linguistic manifestations of *identity formation* discourse from the perspective of politeness. As argued, along with the choice of certain discursive topics, members of the Shaoxing group made use of unique forms of politeness such as ritualised rudeness (cf. Kádár 2010b) in order to differentiate themselves from the northerners and shape their identity as a group.

Methodology and corpus

Methodology

The present chapter relies on the notion of Communities of Practice (henceforth CofP), which was developed by education specialists (Lave and Wenger 1991) and was incorporated into linguistics by Eckert and McConnell-Ginet (1992, 1998). As Bucholtz (1999) points out, CofP is particularly suitable for the analysis of identity formation, since unlike the Labovian (1966) notion of 'speech community', the analysis of CofP makes it possible to focus on the individual, along with the group. As Bucholtz (1999: 209) argues,

> The traditional model's [i.e. speech community's] strong preference for structure over agency means that individual variation, or style, is interpreted as the mechanical outcome of structural forces such as situational norms. A more agentive view locates style in personal choices concerning self presentation [...]

This shift in focus is possible because in the analysis of CofP one analyses community as an entity constituted by practices (in line with sociological notions, cf. Bourdieu 1978), rather than a spatially located group. Among the linguistic and social practices that form a CofP, a most paramount one is identity formation, that is, the ways in which individuals form their relationship with and role within a CofP.

As Bucholtz (1999: 211–212) argues, identity-forming practices manifest themselves in two ways on the level of language use:

> Negative identity practices are those that individuals employ to distance themselves from a rejected identity, while positive identity practices are those in which individuals engage in order actively to construct a chosen identity. In other words, negative identity practices define what their users are not, and hence emphasize identity as an intergroup phenomenon; positive identity practices define what their users are, and thus emphasize the intragroup aspects of social identity.

Using Bucholtz's definition, the present chapter approaches *positive* identity-formational practices, that is, cases when individuals engage in discourse in order to construct their identities as group members – hence the label 'positive' in the present chapter title. Following Bucholtz's theorisation it is argued that this practice has different linguistic layers, that is, it can be expressed on phonological, lexical, syntactic, etc. levels. Since this chapter studies historical data, which lacks several observable features of contemporary audio-recorded data (see more on this problem in Jacobs and Jucker 1995), the focus is on (a) lexical and (b) discursive manifestations of identity-forming practices. In other words, this study explores the way in which identity is (re-)constructed through the choice of certain linguistic forms and discursive topics. In the first part of the analysis, in the section *Discursive topics of positive identity formation*, I examine the formation of identity on a more general level, by studying positive identity-forming practices on a discursive level. In the section *Im/politeness in positive identity formation* I explore the interaction between lexical forms and discursive strategies in the case of positive identity formation, by focusing on the politeness practices of the Shaoxing group.

It can be claimed that the present chapter is a relevant addition to studies on CofP. This is because few historical pragmaticians have ever tried to exploit the notion of CofP in the analysis of historical data (but see some studies in Culpeper and Kádár 2010).

Corpus

The present study explores a corpus of 60 letters (see Kádár 2009), selected from the epistolary collection *Xuehong-xuan chidu* 雪鴻軒尺牘 (*Letters from Snow Swan Retreat*), written between ca. 1758 and 1811[2] by the office clerk Gong Weizhai 龔未齋 (1738–1811; Weizhai was Gong's 'study-name' and his birth name was E 萼). This edited collection, containing 186 private letters of varying length, written to various addressees by Gong, is claimed to be one of the most stylistically representative collections of late imperial Chinese letter writing (Zhao 1999). Furthermore, it is one of the most 'popular' historical Chinese letter collections (Kádár 2010a), and was used as an 'epistolary textbook' during the 19th and early 20th centuries. In fact, it is often referred to as an epistolary 'model work' (*chidu mofan* 尺牘模範) by scholars of Chinese.

In general, epistolary discourse is significant for the scholar involved in identity research, for the following reason. As Nevalainen (2007: 1) notes, "Letter writing has always been a situated activity." Epistles cannot and should not be studied 'hermetically', that is, as texts only. In spite of their potential literary value, letters are fundamentally practical writings that serve the conveyance of information between the writer and the addressee in a certain time and so they are of interest to scholars involved in the analysis of social interactions. Consequently, epistolary corpora reveal a great deal of information about social discourse, in particular if they are considered from the viewpoint of Fairclough's (1992: 73) analytic theory that describes the production of texts as a three-dimensional phenomenon, that is:

1) The basis of a letter is *text*: vocabulary, grammar, cohesion, text structure, speech acts, intertextuality, as well as coherence.
2) Text is produced by *discursive practice*. In the case of epistolary activity, discursive practice may include amongst other things the production, distribution and consumption of letters (see Wood 2007: 51), as well as the writing of specific epistolary genres.
3) Finally, discursive practice is formed by a wider *social practice*.

In the exploration of the corpus studied, the present chapter relies on the three-dimensional model. It is claimed that the social practice of group identity formation made it necessary to reinforce group identity through the discursive practice of writing 'socialising' letters (see below), and this discursive practice manifested itself in the text of the letters in the corpus.

The present corpus is significant from the perspective of studying identity formation because, as was already touched upon in the introduction, along with their concrete goals (such as request, apology, invitation), many of the letters of Gong Weizhai fulfil an important major social function, namely, the formation of camaraderie among a group of Shaoxing clerks who lived and worked in the north, mostly in Peking and its neighbouring areas.[3] This region was traditionally regarded by southern literati as a distant and often hostile place. However, for many of these southern literati, moving to the capital was the best way to develop a career, and they often complained about their lives as expatriates as an unpleasant necessity.[4] This antagonistic situation was also a basic problem for the members of the Shaoxing literati who usually found positions in the capital as office clerks (see Zhu and Yong 2007). As becomes evident from the correspondence of Gong Weizhai, as well as that of his friend Xu Jiacun 許葭村 (his exact dates are unknown), these men of letters formed a closed CofP in the capital: they rarely made connections with 'out-group' (wai 外) people, except a few personal relationships with, for instance, courtesans. In order to manage their lives in this 'alien' setting, the members of this group, struggling in relatively poor circumstances in the capital, aided each other by means of favours and gifts.[5]

While it is not a standard practice to use the notion of CofP in historical pragmatic studies, the Shaoxing group can be rightly characterised using this modern notion, rather than as a 'speech community'. This is not only because the members of this group were dispersed geographically (hence the importance of written correspondence in their identity-forming communication) and did not engage in speech with each other on a daily basis, but also because they were united by discursive *practices*. That is, as mentioned previously, the main goal of the Shaoxing correspondence was to maintain close interpersonal relationships between correspondents, and from this perspective many letters can be defined as 'social' or 'socialising' letters. In other words, the CofP characteristic of the Shaoxing group also manifests itself in the formation of unique linguistic group practices (see the section below on im/politeness in positive identity formation), that is group 'myths', to use Bourdieu's (1991: 223) term.

A theoretical and methodological issue that should be addressed here is the present chapter's reliance on a corpus that was written by a single author. Since the letters were produced by an individual, their reliability as sources representing the style of a whole CofP can be questioned. In order to resolve this problem, the corpus studied was compared with the other most important epistolary corpus of the Shaoxing group, namely Xu Jiacun's (see above) *Qiushuixuan-chidu* 秋水軒尺牘 (*Letters from Autumn Water Retreat*; cf. Kádár 2010a), with particular attention devoted to the letters between Gong and Xu. This comparative research has shown that most unique features of the letters studied are not Gong's individual preferences or idiosyncrasies but rather they represent the in-group style of the Shaoxing CofP.

Before beginning the analysis it should be noted that in the present study the extracts cited from the corpus studied are denoted by numbers such as V.4; these are identical to the number of texts in the English translation of the corpus (Kádár 2009).

Discursive topics of positive identity formation

If we survey the choice of discursive topics by means of which group identity was formed in the corpus studied, we can identify the following major, and somewhat stereotypical, themes:

1. Difficulties of the author's and his addressee's lives as office assistants
2. Southern literati in the north
3. Letter writing.

In what follows, I analyse these discursive topics.

Difficulties of the author's and his addressee's lives as office assistants

In Gong Weizhai's correspondence a popular theme is lamentation for the difficulty of his life as an office assistant, as well as the expression of sympathy for the addressees who struggle with the same problems. Complaining about official life is, to some extent, a typical theme of historical Chinese literati. However, Gong's lamentation and expression of sympathy for others in fact originates in the actual harsh circumstances of underpaid clerks living in the alien surroundings of the capital, as becomes evident from the corpus. In other words, these individuals struggled with and lamented the 'trivial' difficulties, such as financial and existential problems, rather than complaining about the officials' life in relation to more sophisticated ideals. For instance, the traditionally 'shameful' discursive topic of financial difficulty[6] often occurs in Gong's correspondence. As the following extract cited from letter VIII.4 illustrates, it often proved to be difficult for Gong and his addressees to cover even their fundamental needs, due to their low salary as office clerks:

(1) 孟浪棲枝，徒留笑柄。為今之計，只好借鄉試名色，決意旋歸。惟是行李蕭條，不獨旅人減色，還祈毋忘季布一諾，踐省城傳述之言，使不至流落他方，得以老死牖下。是皆君子周急之賜也。

And now, if I were to linger here in my current predicament I would be a laughing-stock. For this reason I can do naught but use the triennial province examination as a pretext to leave and return home. However, I have faced difficulties in covering my travel expenses, and, apart from the journey, have had the additional worry of being forced to respectfully ask you to remember my need and recall the promise you made to me in the provincial capital to aid my return home.

Thus, the discourse on the difficult life of office clerks is rooted in the difficult existential situation of the Shaoxing group in the northern area of the capital.

In light of the Shaoxing clerks' aforementioned problematic situation in the capital, it is no wonder that discourse on this issue is common throughout Gong Weizhai's correspondence. As Gong and most of his addressees were office clerks,[7] complaining about and expressing sympathy for an issue that was a common concern for the group must have fulfilled an efficacious positive identity-forming function. In fact, this discursive topic became such a common issue in the correspondence of this group that in a number of letters it is referred to by the author in order to attain a secondary communicative goal.[8] For example, as the following excerpt cited from letter XV.3 illustrates, the author laments his own difficulties in order to admonish his nephew:

(2) 余惟以碌碌終生，不能自立為愧。吾姪當求其所以自立者，貧不足為憂，且斷不可憂焉！

I have spent my life carrying out menial tasks and I am ashamed that I was unable to achieve independence. My nephew should seek to stand on his own two feet, and not be held back by the fear of poverty, which itself is nothing to fear.

The fact that the hardship of the author's life as a clerk became part of his discursive practice shows that it was involved in the (sub-)cultural 'script' (Yule 2002: 86) of the CofP of the Shaoxing men of letters. That is, in such interactions the author's reference to this discursive topic must have served the ritual and implicit confirmation of camaraderie between himself and his addressees.

Yet, in many cases the difficulty of a clerk's life is the very topic of Gong's correspondence, as illustrated by the following two extracts, cited from letters I.2 and VI.2:

(3) 聞足下憂貧頗甚，想旬日以來，能減得幾分否？吾輩生長儒素之家，貧固其常也。[...] 但士可貧而不可窮。[...] 願與足下共勉之。

I have heard that you, sir, are very much afraid of poverty and cannot but think about whether the next tenday will bring more poverty or mayhap some fortune. However, both of us were raised in the families of righteous officials where poverty is always lurking. [...] It is only a Confucian scholar who can endure poverty without losing heart. [...] Would that we were to encourage each other to follow this path, sir.

(4) 人生六十曰衰，吾輩神為形役，其衰更易。弟年未六十，而齒豁頭童，鬢髮早白，平時壯志，早已消磨。祇以苦債未完，猶作場中傀儡。秋風短笛，粉墨登場，此更桑榆景迫，所黯然神傷者，蓋亦心憐之，而不得不作如是云耳！

足下一生游歷，未染世情，獨往獨來，不與時賢為伍。此弟二十年來，亦以此 硜硜自守者。坐是四壁仍空，一貧如故。

When one reaches his sixtieth year he is called weak. However, our spirit has great influence on our body and its suffering makes one grow weak all the faster. This younger brother of yours has not yet seen his sixtieth winter, but my face has already grown old and my beard and hair have turned grey, and my ideals, once so loftily held, have long since disappeared. It is only because my bitter responsibility demands it that my role as a puppet on the stage has not yet ended. With sorrow in my heart I must continue my work like a doll in the theatre, which makes my person – already suffering the approach of decline – all the more dejected, and I can do naught but complain in this woeful manner.

> You, sir, wandered throughout your life and remained unstained by the ugly nature of the world. You follow your own path and disassociate yourself from worthless people praised as sages in their generation. This younger brother of yours has also obstinately adhered to this principle in the last twenty years – hence I still abide amongst my empty walls with nothing, as poor as before.

In the first example, in order to raise the spirits of the addressee, the author refers to the financial difficulty of office clerks. Obviously, the act of encouragement fulfils the function of building camaraderie (cf. Limaye 1987) and Gong's closing words "Would that we were to encourage each other to follow this path, sir" also reinforce this function via the proposal of mutual encouragement. In the second example the author, in a depressed manner, describes his own difficulties. In a similar way to the previous excerpt, the author makes an explicit act to reinforce their in-group bond, as well as implicitly strengthening camaraderie with the addressee via emphasis on an issue that is a common concern for the addressee and himself. That is, he mentions that he followed the author's moral principles, and hence he (just as the addressee) "still abide[s] amongst [...] empty walls with nothing, as poor as before." In other words, the author forms group identity with the addressee when he contrasts the addressee and himself with a larger group of greedy and worthless officials and office assistants (non in-group people).

It should be noted that the author regularly emphasises the financial difficulties of office clerks, as the above examples illustrate. Nevertheless, complaints about the office assistants' tiring and uninteresting tasks also play an important role in his identity-forming discourse, usually in tandem with the previous discursive topic; see for example the following excerpt cited from letter XIV.4:

(5) 老尚依人，雞肋蠅頭，不遑餬口，其窘況有難為知己告者。

> I have grown old but still must rely on others in order to earn my living, and have to undertake monotonous tasks in order to earn my paltry wages, and I cannot even find time to eat.

Southern literati in the north

As previously noted, opposition between the southern and northern parts of China is one of the central discursive topics in Gong Weizhai's correspondence. In fact, there has been a long-running stereotypical cultural difference between these two regions and traditionally many literati from both areas wrote disparagingly about each other (see Eberhard 1965). To some extent, Gong's discourse on this discursive topic belongs to this stereotypical theme.

However, in Gong Weizhai's letters the formation of the Shaoxing CofP identity has an importance beyond the emphasis of the traditional attitudes of the southern literati. Considering the fact that the Shaoxing circle lived in alien surroundings, where they had to rely on each other in order to attain some success, discourse on the south vs. north opposition must have fulfilled a group-identity-forming function. This claim is also supported by the fact that, besides emphasising the cultural superiority of south China over the north, which is a more typical discursive topic in the interaction of southern literati, in his correspondence Gong Weizhai emphatically described, often in quite negative terms, the difficulties of his and his addressees' lives in the north (capital), as well as his desire to abandon his position as an office assistant and return to the south.

In the present corpus, the south vs. north dichotomy occurs in different contexts. A typical discursive topic is the author's description of his difficulties in the north, as well as his expression of sympathy for the addressees' similar struggles. In order to illustrate the author's discussion of this discursive topic, we cite the following excerpt:

(6) 西人之子，竟為吾輩意計所不能料。行路之難，眞難於上青天矣，可懼哉！長安居大不易，有就須曲就之。即如僕逗遛此間，亦非得已，然終無可如何耳。

It is indeed hard for us to understand the mind of the people of Peking. Thus, for strangers like us attaining our goals is as difficult as ascending into the blue sky and this is a dreadful matter! It is very difficult to live in the capital: even if one manages to find a post here he must force himself to undertake it, no matter what it is. One need but look at my humble self: I remain here as I have no alternative and am unable to find a better path.

This excerpt from letter XV.4 (a response to the recipient's previous complaints about his difficulties) illustrates that the description of the author's and his addressees' difficult circumstances in an alien setting were meant to form emotive ties between them, and so contributed to the formation of group identity. This is also shown by the fact that the description of this discursive topic in some instances co-occurs with the author's discourse on the difficulties of office clerks, as illustrated by the following excerpt cited from letter VIII.4:

(7) 惟是行李蕭條，不獨旅人減色，還祈毋忘季布一諾，踐省城傳述之言，使不至 流落他方，得以老死牖下。

However, I have faced difficulties in covering my travel expenses, and, apart from the journey, have had the additional worry of being forced to respectfully ask you to remember my need and recall the promise you made to me in the provincial capital to aid my return home. In this way *I will be able to avoid wandering destitute in foreign lands* [my emphasis] and return home to live my insignificant life devoid of accomplishment. And indeed, I can now finally return home [...]

Examples of this kind reveal that in fact the identity formation of the Shaoxing literati as a group of office assistants and officials and as southerners living in the north often merged together.

Another related discursive topic is the author's description of his yearning to return to the south, as illustrated by the following excerpts cited from letter VI.2:

(8) 惟足下先賦歸與，弟須三四年後始能踐約。耕山釣水之樂，請先獨得之。

You, sir, decided to return home first, and this younger brother of yours must wait three or four years before being able to do the same. Hence I beg you, sir, to enjoy the pleasure of ploughing the land and fishing the rivers yourself till my return.

A similar discursive topic is the author's melancholy when he, having managed to abandon his office in order to return south, had to say farewell to his friends who would continue to work in the north. The author's discussion of this discursive topic is illustrated by the following excerpt cited from letter VIII.1:

(9) 茲已決意南旋，臘初買車起程。惟與知己遠違，未免悵快。

Now, at last I am resolved to return to the South, and at the beginning of the Twelfth Month I will prepare my carriage and embark on my journey. All that troubles me is the distance that shall stand between us, my friend, and I cannot suppress feelings of melancholia at this prospect.

It is evident that the final goal of the members of the Shaoxing group was to return home after they built a career in the capital. Therefore, discourse on this wish – as well as the expression of sorrow when a group member finally attained this goal but hence had to leave the others – fulfilled a group-identity-forming function, similar to the aforementioned discursive topic of the antipathy toward northern life.

A pivotal discursive topic is the expression of homesickness. This discursive topic is arguably not a peculiarity of the Shaoxing group; it is sufficient to cite the renowned Tang dynasty poet Li Bai's 李白 (701–762) famous couplet 舉頭望明月， 低頭思故鄉 ('Lifting myself to look, I found that it was moonlight. Sinking back again, I thought suddenly of home.'),[9] to illustrate that this was a widely applied emotive discursive topic in historical Chinese literature. Yet, in Gong Weizhai's correspondence this discursive topic also fulfils a group-identity-forming function, as illustrated by the following excerpt:

(10) 雲雨寺前，一泓清水，兩岸垂楊。明日同往，聽黃鸝數聲，以消客悶，正不必雙柑斗酒也。

> In front of the Yunyu Temple there is a clear river, on its two shores the willows weep into the water. Let us go thither on the morrow: the song of the orioles will banish our homesickness.

As this citation from letter II.1 makes clear, the expression of longing for his homeland has a cohesive power in Gong's discussion.

Finally, a discursive topic related to the south vs. north dichotomy is the nationalistic comparison between these areas, to the advantage of the south, as illustrated by the following citation:

(11) 松竹梅為歲寒三友。而北地松竹不多見，梅更無之。惟夭桃穠李，每燦爛於豐臺芍藥之間。然轉眼而成為黃土矣，增花落春殘之感。南冠而北游者，亦往往為習俗所移，貴春花而忘秋實。致歲寒之盟，與松竹梅同其廖落，殊為唧嘆。

> The pine, the bamboo and the sour plum are the three friends of winter. However, here in the North there are very few pines and bamboos, and the sour plum is even rarer. It is only the beautiful peach and plum tree blossoms amongst the peonies of Fengtai that attract the eye during winter. Yet, in the twinkle of an eye they fall to the earth and the sorrow at their passing and the longing for spring becomes even stronger. The men of the South who come hither are gradually changed by the land – just like the peach and plum which bloom beautifully once a year, but lose their flowers in an instant, they tend to value appearance and not intrinsic worth. Thus, it is as difficult here to find lasting friendship as it is to behold the pines, the bamboo, and the sour plum, and this is deeply regretful.

As this excerpt, cited from letter I.3, illustrates, there is an explicit evaluative description of the south vs. north dichotomy in Gong's correspondence, southern culture and identity appearing to be more valuable than their northern counterparts.

Letter writing

The office assistants of the Shaoxing group were expert letter writers: they were regarded as a distinguished group of epistolary experts, or Shaoxing-shiye 紹興師爺 (lit. 'Revered Masters from Shaoxing'). Therefore, discourse on epistolary activity fulfilled a fundamental group-identity-forming function in the correspondence of Gong Weizhai, as illustrated by the next excerpt cited from letter XII.3:

(12) 惟三十餘年，客窗酬應之札，自攄胸膈，暢所欲言。雖於尺牘之道，去之千里，而性情所寄，似有不忍棄者，遂於病後錄而集之。內中惟僕與足下酬答為獨多。惜足下鴻篇短製，為愛者攜去，僅存四六一函，錄之於集。借美玉之 光，以輝燕石，並欲使後之覽者，知僕與足下乃文字之交，非勢利交也。

Nevertheless, for more than thirty years, in service far from home, I have written extensive correspondence in which I narrated my feelings with artless words. Although these writings are a thousand miles distant from what one would call the art of letter writing, they record my various dispositions and I feel reluctant to throw them away. Therefore, after recovering from my illness I have copied and collected my correspondence. Amongst my letters, those which this humble servant wrote to you, sir, are by far the most numerous. It is regretful to me however, that most of your outstanding letters of various length are no longer in my possession, my friend, and I have only one letter of forty six sentences left, which I have copied into my collection. Thus, I would like to ask you, sir, to lend me your refined works and let them illuminate my worthless collection, like shiny jades enlightening worthless stones. In this way the readers of my work will know that the relationship between you, sir, and my humble self was a true friendship between men of letters and not the snobbish and greedy connection of some of the literati.

This letter serves socialisation, which is proved by the fact that the author requests the recipient to lend him his letters: edited collections of historical Chinese letters were single authored (Kádár 2010a), and so the author's request is symbolic and it primarily serves to elevate the other and hence to reinforce the relationship. The social function of this letter is 'wrapped' in discourse on letter writing. Quite understandably, discourse on an activity in which a CofP has special skill (see for example Bucholtz's 1999 discussion on the intellectual discourse of female nerds) fulfils a strong positive-identity-formation function. Psychologically, emphasis of a group's strength reinforces myths (cf. Bourdieu 1991 above) of group identity, which aid members to regard their group as a distinguished one.

Summing up, the present section has overviewed different discursive topics chosen by the Shaoxing literati in order to form their identity as a group. In what follows, we analyse the style of discourse within this circle, more precisely the interaction between certain forms and discursive activity, with special focus on forms of politeness.

Im/politeness in positive identity formation

Analysis of the Shaoxing corpus, in particular letters written to power-equals, has revealed another noteworthy means of identity formation besides strict-sense discourse, namely, the application of 'unusual', or more precisely distinctive, forms of politeness. Many of these forms have been analysed in Kádár (2010b), and so the present analysis is restricted to the exploration of their role in group identity formation.

In the Gong Weizhai corpus there are some cases when the author, by using certain linguistic forms, symbolically defies the norms of deference but in fact expresses a polite meaning. Such utterances work in a similar way to 'mock impoliteness', as defined in Culpeper (1996: 352), that is,

> Mock impoliteness, or banter, is impoliteness that remains on the surface, since it is understood that it is not intended to cause offence.

It can be argued that in the correspondence of the CofP studied, mock impoliteness is a *politeness* 'strategy', in a Brown and Levinson (1987) sense.

Such manifestations are not only noteworthy because they represent a unique aspect of discursive politeness, but also because they seem to have a group-identity-formational function. As the corpus studied demonstrates, members of the Shaoxing group made use of tools of politeness that are somewhat unconventional in order to differentiate themselves as a distinct group from the inhabitants of the capital. In a sense, these linguistic practices are quite similar to the intellectual 'word coinage' of the female nerds in Bucholtz's (1999: 212) study: exactly as female nerds coin new terms as part of an identity formational activity, Shaoxing men of letters made innovations in traditional forms of deference.

Importantly, when focusing on this phenomenon I do not intend to suggest that the choices of politeness register made by the author and his correspondents were always intentional. In accordance with Mills' (2003) work, I would argue that the choice of discursive register or 'politeness' is often, from a cognitive perspective, an unconscious process. Yet, it could be argued that, in cases of innovation, choice of register requires intellectual work, and in such marked cases it aims to reconstruct the group ethos (or 'myths', see above) shared by members of the Shaoxing CofP. That is, the Shaoxing clerks probably used these forms as they shared the belief that they were a distinguished group of expert letter writers who led their lives beyond conventions.

While in historical research it is impossible to peer into the interactants' minds and reconstruct the reason why certain linguistic forms are chosen, there is indirect evidence indicating that the members of the Shaoxing CofP shared a heroic group ethos. This ethos can be observed, for example, in the way in which Gong represents his recipient in letter VIII.2:

(13) 曾憶雲雨寺前，坐柳陰而聽黃鳥，足下縱酒肆談，解衣磅礴，有不可一世之概，今尚得如當年豪邁否？

> I recall the old times when we were sitting in front of the Yunyu Temple in the shadow of the willows listening to the song of the orioles: you, sir, drank plenty of wine and spoke openly, loosening your jacket and talking without ceremony, and your spirit indeed surpassed our whole generation. Do you still preserve the heroic spirit you possessed in those days?

The piquancy of this heroic description of the recipient as a blunt and brave person is that it is made in a deferential and highly sophisticated way, that is, it would be difficult to imagine the recipient or the author talking in a truly blunt and heroic manner. In other words, this claimed bluntness was sophisticated and in fact meant to be the in-group manifestation of the Shaoxing CofP's cultural superiority.

This ethos manifested itself in their in-group language use, in particular in the use of mock impoliteness: 'sophisticated bluntness' appealed to the addressee's face needs on the one hand, and also served as a form of self representation, on the other. On the level of linguistic forms, the members of the Shaoxing group applied several types of 'irregular' manifestations of 'mock impoliteness' (Culpeper 1996), including idioms and historical references, as well as linguistic humour. In order to illustrate the function of these expressions, we cite the following extracts:

(14) 陳遵尺牘，名震當時。然高自位置，惜墨如金，不肯輕投一札，足下殆亦有此癖！

> Chen Zun [of old] gained a great reputation amongst his generation for [his expertise in] letter writing. However, he formed an overtly high opinion of himself and he spared his ink as if it was gold, not willing to send a letter to anyone [if it were not necessary]. [I wonder,] sir, whether you are not on the edge of falling into the error of his conceit? (XIII.1)

(15) 豈可以牛溲馬勃，溷充其數？想亦足下阿其所好，而觀察公謬採虛聲也。

> Now, why should he invite a useless fellow like me to fill a position [when I hold not the merits to do so]? I am afraid that you, sir, are partial due to our friendship and [that you have unintentionally misled] His Excellency to form a false image of this person. (XII.2)

(16) 先錄此文，順馬遞上，作蓮幕之傳單何如？呵呵！

> [Yet,] first I record this poem and entrust a courier to respectfully present it to you. Is it fit even to be used as [an artless and functional] note [to keep you abreast of my experiences here]? Hah-hah! (VI.1)

In (14)–(16) one can observe some 'cooperation' between lexical and discursive manifestations of politeness (more precisely, mock impoliteness), that is, in line with Bucholtz's (1999) theorisation, identity formation manifests itself on different linguistic levels.

In extract (14), written to a close friend, the author makes an analogy between the behaviour of Chen Zun 陳遵 (his exact dates are unknown), a renowned Han dynasty (206 BC–AD 220) man of letters, and that of the addressee. This historical reference expresses a seemingly 'negative' (impolite) meaning. That is, the author, longing for the correspondent's letter, symbolically reprimands him for sparing his ink like Chen Zun, and wonders whether the correspondent does not 'fall into the error of Chen's conceit' (*yi you ci pi* 亦有此癖, lit. 'also have this craving'). However, at the same time the author emphasises the great expertise of Chen in epistolary art by using the conventional expression *ming zhen dang shi* 名震當時 (lit. 'one's name shakes his age'), and so by symbolically scolding the addressee for behaviour that resembles that of Chen Zun, he conveys a secondary elevating meaning by comparing the correspondent's talent to that of Chen.

Extract (15) is cited from a letter written to a colleague and friend who recommended the author to the Chief Provincial Judge who decided to employ him, but the author had to decline the invitation. In the present extract the author symbolically reprimands the correspondent, by using the idiomatic expressions *e-qi-suo-hao* 阿其所好 (lit. 'flattering one's favourite') and *miucai-xusheng* 謬採虛聲 (lit. 'erroneously gathering false reputation', trans. 'form a false image of this person'). However, this symbolic reprimand, another manifestation of mock impoliteness, conveys a self-denigrating meaning, that is, it not only conveys the message that the correspondent is in fact a good friend of the author but also denigrates the author's skill by claiming that it does not warrant the correspondent's approbation.

Finally, in (16) the author applies the onomatopoeic word *hehe* 呵呵 ('hah-hah'); such an onomatopoeic word would sound somewhat rude in other contexts but here it conveys a humorous self-denigrating meaning. This onomatopoeic form, in this case the manifestation of mock impoliteness, 'collaborates' with the discursive practice of the author who tries to reconfirm the aforementioned group ethos of 'unconventional and heroic literati'.

It should be noted that in some cases Gong uses idioms that are semantically even ruder than the ones above. For example, in some letters the idiom *shijia-zhi-pi* 嗜痂之癖 (lit. 'the depraved taste of eating scabs') is applied in order to decline the correspondent's appraisal of the author's work through an act of polite self-denigration. That is, in these contexts by using *shijia-zhi-pi* symbolically Gong claims that the correspondent who likes the author's work has depraved taste, and hence the secondary self-denigrating meaning of this expression.

In sum, members of the Shaoxing group made use of mock impoliteness in some in-group discussions, in order to express their cultural superiority and excellent skills in letter writing.

Summary

This chapter has explored identity formation in historical China via the case study of the Shaoxing CofP. This exploration has contributed to Chinese discourse studies, which have neglected identity formation beyond the nationalistic level. Furthermore, it has contributed to politeness research by demonstrating the applicability of linguistic politeness (and impoliteness) beyond the maintenance of interpersonal relationships.

The present study has left negative identity-forming practices unexamined. The reason for this thematic choice/limitation, apart from a limitation of space, is that while the Shaoxing correspondence provides some instances of negative practices, such as the avoidance of explicitly northern Chinese lexical items, these practices are relatively vague. Negative identity-forming practices would be more observable if we were to study CofP practices in relation to other CofPs, which is a difficult task if one relies on historical correspondence.

Whilst the present enquiry is rather limited in scope, it is hoped that it will generate future research on Chinese identity formation, which addresses identity-forming practices of different CofPs, and studies both positive and negative practices.

Notes

1. I would like to express my gratitude to Yuling Pan for her invaluable comments on this work. I would also like to express my gratitude to the anonymous referees for their constructive input. I am indebted to Ben Mousley for reviewing the style of the present chapter. It is needless to say that all the remaining errors are my responsibility. I would like to express my gratitude to the following organisations whose generous support made it possible to carry out the research that has led to the development of the present chapter. The long-term Research Grant (RG003-U-07) of the Chiang Ching-kuo Foundation, ROC, has provided the necessary support for the acquisition of materials necessary for this research. The three-year Postdoctoral Research Grant (PD 71628) of the Hungarian Scientific

Research Fund (OTKA) has provided the necessary institutional and financial background for the second phase of the present research.

2. Historical Chinese epistolary collections, unlike their European counterparts (e.g. Fitzmaurice 2002), usually do not include subscriptions (nor superscriptions), and so it is usually difficult to date them.

3. Most of the Shaoxing correspondents lived in smaller townships in the capital province of Zhili 直隸.

4. It should be noted that in the present discussion the expression 'south' is not applied in a strict geographical sense. In fact, from a geographical perspective Zhejiang Province, and so Shaoxing, belongs to east China and not south China. However, in traditional Chinese thinking (see Eberhard 1965) the territory that lays south of the Yangtze River is determined as southern China, and so from a cultural perspective the Shaoxing Group is a typically southern intellectual circle.

5. On the importance of favours and gifts in Chinese social life see Yan (1993). It should be noted that in the present collection there is also evidence for the importance of gifts in the Shaoxing community; see for example letter XI.4.

6. Historical Chinese men of letters, unlike their Western counterparts (see for example Valle's 2007 discussion on Paston family letters), avoided mentioning financial issues in their correspondence as far as it was possible. This was due to the fact that according to traditional Confucian prescriptions talking about money does not fit the role of a noble person (*junzi* 君子) (see Kádár 2005).

7. It should be noted that some of Gong's letters in the present corpus were written to superiors who were supposedly of Shaoxing origin (see for instance letter IX.3); however, as a matter of course in such letters the author does not touch upon the issue of office assistants' difficulties.

8. There are 11 such letters in the translated corpus, which are the following: II.3; IV.1; IV.2; V.1; VII.4; VIII.1; VIII.3; X.1; XIII.2; XV.2; XV.3.

9. See this poem in the famous collection *Tangshi sanbai shou* 唐詩三百首 (*Three Hundred Tang Dynasty Poems*) VII.1. 233.

References

Befu, H. (1993) *Cultural Nationalism in East Asia: Representation and Identity*. Berkeley, CA: Institute of East Asian Studies, University of California.

Bourdieu, P. (1978) *Outline of a Theory of Practice*. Cambridge/New York: Cambridge University Press.

Bourdieu, P. (1991) *Language and Symbolic Power*. Cambridge: Polity Press.

Brown, P. and Levinson, S. C. (1987) *Politeness: Some Universals in Language Usage*. Cambridge: Cambridge University Press.

Bucholtz, M. (1999) 'Why be normal?' Language and identity practices in a community of nerd girls. *Language in Society* 28: 203–223.

Chan, B. (2008) Demystifying Chinese guanxi networks. *Business Information Review* 25: 183–189.

Chan, M. K. M. (1998) Gender differences in Chinese: A preliminary report: In H. Lin (ed.) *Proceedings of the Ninth North American Conference on Chinese Linguistics* 35–53. Los Angeles, CA: University of South California.

Culpeper, J. (1996) Towards an anatomy of impoliteness. *Journal of Pragmatics* 25: 349–367.

Culpeper, J. and Kádár, D. Z. (eds) (2010) *Historical (Im)politeness*. Berne: Peter Lang.

Eberhard, W. (1965) Chinese regional stereotypes. *Asian Survey* 5: 596–608.

Eckert, P. and McConnell-Ginet, S. (1992) Communities of practice: Where language, gender, and power all live. In K. Hall, M. Bucholtz and B. Moonwoman (eds) *Locating Power: Proceedings of the Second Berkeley Women and Language Conference* 89–99. Berkeley, CA: Berkeley Women and Language Group.

Eckert, P. and McConnell-Ginet, S. (1992) Think practically and look locally: Language and gender as community-based practice. *Annual Review of Anthropology* 21: 461–490.

Eckert, P. and McConnell-Ginet, S. (1998) Communities of practice: Where language, gender and power all live. In J. Coates (ed.) *Language and Gender: A Reader* 484–494 Oxford: Blackwell.

Fairclough, N. (1992) *Discourse and Social Change*. Cambridge: Polity Press.

Fitzmaurice, S. (2002) *The Familiar Letter in Early Modern English: A Pragmatic Approach*. Amsterdam/Philadelphia, PA: John Benjamins.

Flowerdew, J. (2004) Identity politics and Hong Kong's return to Chinese sovereignty: Analysing the discourse of Hong Kong's first chief executive. *Journal of Pragmatics* 36: 1551–1578.

Friedman, E. (1995) *National Identity and Democratic Prospects in Socialist China*. New York: M. E. Sharpe.

Jacobs, A. and Jucker, A. H. (1995) The historical perspective in pragmatics. In A. H. Jucker (ed.) *Historical Pragmatics. Pragmatic Developments in the History of English* 1–33. Amsterdam/Philadelphia, PA: John Benjamins.

Kádár, D. Z. (2005) Power and profit: The role of elevating/denigrating forms of address in pre-modern Chinese business discourse. In F. Bargiela-Chiappini and M. Gotti (eds) *Asian Business Discourse(s)* 21–56. Bern: Peter Lang.

Kádár, D. Z. (2009) *Model Letters in Late Imperial China – 60 Selected Epistles from 'Letters of Snow Swan Retreat'*. Munich: Lincom.

Kádár, D. Z. (2010a) *Historical Chinese Letter Writing*. London/New York: Continuum.

Kádár, D. Z. (2010b) Exploring the historical Chinese polite denigration/elelvation phenomenon. In J. Culpeper and D. Z. Kádár (eds) *Historical (Im)politeness* 117–145. Bern: Peter Lang.

Labov, W. (1966) *The Social Stratification of English in New York City*. Washington, DC: Center for Applied Linguistics.

Lave, J. and Wenger, E. (1991) *Situated Learning: Legitimate Peripheral Participation.* Cambridge: Cambridge University Press.

Limaye, M. R. (1987) Pragmatics, 'situated' language and business communication. *Journal of Business and Technical Communication* 1: 68–88.

Ma, L. J. C. and Cartier, C. L. (2003) *The Chinese Diaspora: Space, Place, Mobility, and Identity.* Plymouth: Rowman and Littlefield.

Mills, S. (2003) *Gender and Politeness.* Cambridge: Cambridge University Press.

Nevalainen, T. (2007) Introduction. In T. Nevalainen and S. K. Tanskanen (eds) *Letter Writing* 1–11. Amsterdam/Philadelphia, PA: John Benjamins.

Nyíri, P. (2001) Expatriating is patriotic? The discourse on 'new migrants' in the people's republic of China and identity construction among recent migrants from the PRC. *Journal of Ethnic and Migration Studies* 27: 635–653.

Spencer-Oatey, H. and Ruhi, S. (eds) (2007) *Identity, Face and (Im)politeness.* Special Issue of *Journal of Pragmatics* 32/4.

Tannen, D. (2006) Language and culture. In R. W. Fasold and J. Connor-Linton (eds) *An Introduction to Language and Linguistics* 343–372. Cambridge: Cambridge University Press.

Thornborrow, J. (2002) *Power Talk: Language and Interaction in Institutional Discourse.* London: Longman (Pearson Education).

Tsu, J. (2005) *Failure, Nationalism, and Literature: The Making of Modern Chinese Identity, 1895–1937.* Stanford, CA: Stanford University Press.

Valle, E. (2007) 'The pleasure of receiving your favour': The colonial exchange in eighteenth-century natural history. In T. Nevalainen and S. K. Tanskanen (eds) *Letter Writing* 131–153. Amsterdam/Philadelphia, PA: John Benjamins.

Wenger, E. (1998) *Communities of Practice: Learning, Meaning and Identity.* Cambridge: Cambridge University Press.

Wood, J. (2007) Text in context. A critical discourse analysis approach to Margaret Paston. In T. Nevalainen and S. K. Tanskanen (eds) *Letter Writing* 46–71. Amsterdam/Philadelphia, PA: John Benjamins.

Yan, Y. (1993) *The Flow of Gifts: Reciprocity and Social Networks in a Chinese Village.* Cambridge, MA: Harvard University Press.

Yang, M. M. (1994) *Gifts, Favours, and Banquests: The Art of Social Relationships in China.* Ithaca, NY: Cornell University Press.

Yule, G. (2002) *Pragmatics.* Oxford: Oxford University Press.

Zhao, S. 趙樹功 (1999) *Zhongguo chidu wenxue shi* 中國尺牘文學史 (*The History of Chinese Epistolary Literature*). Shijiazhuang: Hebei renmin chubanshe.

Zhu, Z. 朱志勇 and Yong, Y. 李永鑫 (2007) *Shaoxing shiye yu Zhonggzo mufu wenhua* 紹興師爺與中國幕府文化 (*The Masters of Shaoxing and the Chinese Office Assistant Culture*). Beijing: Renmin chubanshe.

14

'Polysemous' politeness: Speaker self-referring forms in *Honglou Meng*

Xinren Chen

Introduction

Research background

Address forms in Chinese have been under some investigation in relation to politeness. Following Brown and Levinson (1987), pronouns of deferent other-address and self-reference would be universally treated as a strategy of negative politeness. Contrary to their view, Gu (1990) argues for culture-specificity in investigating politeness. To this end, Gu proposed four Chinese-specific maxims. Of Gu's four maxims, based on the socially sanctioned belief in and expectations for respectfulness, modesty, attitudinal warmth and refinement, both the Self-denigrating Maxim and the Address Maxim relate to the use of address terms (the other two maxims being the Tact Maxim and the Generosity Maxim). In Gu's opinion, Chinese linguistic politeness is not just instrumental (in Brown and Levinson's sense of mitigating face threat) but normative as well, as shown by the use of Chinese address terms. Thanks to Gu and other Asian scholars (e.g. Ide 1989; Matsumoto 1989), who effectively demonstrated that the universality argument did not work well in accounting for Chinese or other Asian language politeness, research of linguistic politeness in Asian languages has gained attention in pragmatic studies.

Gu's model, while it has generated wide interest since its publication, has been subject to some criticism. Among other scholars, Dániel Kádár (2007a) argues against Gu's over-generalised application of traditional Chinese denigrating/elevating terms, claiming that these terms are scarcely used in modern colloquial language. In his opinion, Gu's use of historical data to support synchronic arguments obscures the essential difference between modern and pre-modern Chinese (im)politeness systems; rather, a demarcation line must be drawn between them (Kádár 2007a: 21). In addition, Kádár points out that Gu obscured the relation between the Address Maxim and Self-denigrating Maxim on the grounds that the two maxims can be unified in pre-modern Chinese politeness as "traditional Chinese polite terms of address compulsorily express denigrating/elevating meaning" (*ibid.*: 23).

On the whole, Kádár's reasoning and demonstration fit in with the Chinese data, pre-modern and modern. However, the data he used for illustration purposes cover hearer-oriented address terms and speaker-targeted address forms at the same time, rather than systematically focus on one type only. A richer and more subtle picture of linguistic politeness in pre-modern China can be gained if either self-reference or other-reference is systematically examined alone. In addition, the exploration of the use of speaker-targeted address forms, or more exactly speaker self-referring forms (henceforth SSFs) (like "I" in the utterance "I like the film" and "Mom" in the utterance "Mom is tired" when Mom is the actual speaker) in their dynamic context – which is somewhat inadequate, although Agha (2007) and Kádár (2007b) have touched upon the issue of how the use of address terms can be a strategic act – will help to characterise it as an intentional choice driven by multiple purposes.

For this reason, drawing on data from the vernacular novel *Honglou Meng* 红楼楼 (*A Dream of Red Mansions*), also referred to as *Shitou Ji* 石头记 (*The Story of the Stone*), a vernacular Chinese novel written in the Qing dynasty, this study examines the ways in which speakers referred to/ addressed themselves in pre-modern Chinese society. Its goal is to context-ually analyse the circumstances under which characters in the novel employ the expressions for self-reference and reveal the possible motivations behind their choice, so as to more fully exhibit the complexities of politeness behind the use of Chinese address forms.

Data

The source studied, *Honglou Meng* 红楼梦 was (mostly), compiled by a man of letters, Cao Xuqin 曹雪芹 (1715–1763). This work of 120 chapters, composed around 1749, is perhaps the best-known vernacular Chinese novel. As a portrayal of the fortune of four big families (Jia, Wang, Shi and Xue), the novel revolves around the tragic love and marriage of Jia Baoyu, Lin Daiyu and Xue Baochai.[1] Imitating spoken language in the daily life of pre-modern Chinese society and involving interaction on a large variety of topics such as daily events and conflicts in and across various social groups, it has been used as a suitable source by many studies including the afore-mentioned book by Kádár (2007).

In the course of data collection, the present researcher focuses on the way the characters in the novel, including those mentioned above, use SSFs, as well as the conversational episodes involving the use of SSFs. While discussing the data, this study considers the pragmatic identities of and social relations between the interactants, in an effort to arrive at a fairly thorough analysis of the SSFs, especially the non-deictic SSFs.

In presenting the data, the author couples the Chinese examples from *Honglou Meng* with their English version, which is rendered on the basis of Yang Xian-yi and Dai Nai-die's translation of the novel (Yang and Yang 1994), so as to highlight the presence and function of the SSFs, while facilitating the understanding of the text.

Linguistic realisations of speaker self-reference in *Honglou Meng*

After examining the whole text of *Honglou Meng*, we categorise the SSFs used into the following major types, each with their frequency counts, as reported in Table 14.1.

Table 14.1 Occurrences of SSFs in *Honglou Meng*[2]

Category	SSFs	Frequency	%
A	First person pronouns (including *wo* 我, *wu* 吾 and *an* 俺)	6163	93.7%
B	Self-denigrating SSFs (including *xiaoren* 小人, *xiaode* 小的, *nucai* 奴才, *fanguan* 犯官, *qie* 妾, *xiaguan* 下官, *xiaowang* 小王)	218	3.3%
C	Modesty-featuring SSFs (including *wansheng* 晚生, *xuesheng* 学生, *pindao* 贫道 and *xiaodao* 小道)	104	1.6%
D	Kinship terms (including *zhi-er* 侄儿, *xiongdi* 兄弟, *xiaodi* 小弟, *di* 弟, *ni qin shenzi* 你亲婶子 and *Rong-er* 蓉儿)	80	1.2%
E	Other forms {including official titles (*faguan* 法官), third person quasi-pronoun (*renjia* 人家) and "ben+an official title" (*ben jue* 本爵)}	9	0.2%
	Total	6574	100%

First person pronouns

In *Honglou Meng*, there are three forms of the person pronoun that speakers use for self-reference, namely, *wo* 我, *wu* 吾 and *an* 俺, as exemplified respectively below:

(1) 士隐听得明白，心下犹豫，意欲问他来历。只听道人说道："你我不必同行，就此分手，各干营生去罢。三劫后我在北邙山等你，会齐了同往太虚幻境销号。"（第1回）

   Shiyin ting de mingbai, xin xia youyu, yiyu wen ta laili. zhi ting daoren shuo dao: 'ni wo bubi tongxing, jiu ci fenshou, ge gan yingsheng qu ba. san jie hou wo zai beimangshan deng ni, hui qi le tong wang taixu huanjing xiaohao.'

   Shiyin, hearing this clearly, wondered what it meant. Before he could ask, the Taoist told the monk: 'This is where you and I (*wo* – first person pronoun) part. Each must go about his own business. Three rounds of suffering from now I (*wo* – first person pronoun) shall wait for you at Mount Beimang, and together we can go to the Land of Illusion to have this affair expounded.' (Chapter 1)

(2) 宝玉见是一个仙姑，喜的忙来作揖，笑问道："神仙姐姐，不知从那里来，如今要往那里去？我也不知这里是何处，望乞携带携带。"那仙姑道："吾居离恨天之上灌愁海之中..."（第5回）

   Baiyu jian shi yige xiangu, xi de mang lai zuoyi, xiao wen dao: 'shengxian jiejie, bu zhi cong nali lai, rujin yao wang nali qu? wo ye bu zhi zheli shi he chu, wang qi xiedai xiedai.' na xiangu dao: 'wu ju Lihentian zhi shang Guanchouhai zhi zhong, [...]'

   Overjoyed by the apparition of this fairy, Baoyu made haste to greet her with a bow. 'Sister Fairy,' he said with a smile, 'do tell me where you are from and where you are going. I have lost my way. May I beg you to be my guide?' 'I (*wu* – historical first person pronoun) live above the Sphere of Parting Sorrow and in the Sea of Brimming Grief,' she answered. (Chapter 5)

(3) 张王氏哭禀："... 那一天晌午，李家店里打发人来叫俺，说："你儿子叫人打死了..."（第86回）

   Zhangwangshi ku bing: '[...] na yi tian xiangwu, Li jia dian li dafa ren lai jiao an, shuo: 'ni erzi jiao ren da si le, [...]"

   Mrs. Zhang, weeping, testified, '...That afternoon, someone from the inn came and said to me (*an* – dialectal first person pronoun), 'Your son has been killed ...' (Chapter 86)

In (1), *wo* 我, which is the canonical form that speakers use for self-reference in modern Chinese, is almost exclusively used when characters in the novel make self-reference. Neither *wu* 吾 in (2), which is a historical or archaic form, nor *an* 俺 in (3), which is particular to some dialects, are scarcely used today, though.

From Table 14.1, it is evident that in the pre-modern Qing dynasty, of all the SSFs as employed in *Honglou Meng*, first person pronouns (*wo* 我, *wu* 吾 and *an* 俺) were the dominant ones[3] (with a total of 6163 times of occurrence, accounting for 93.7% of all the SSFs), which is plausibly the same as the situation in modern Chinese. The preponderance of first person pronouns, which are deictic by nature, suggests that person deixis also demonstrates pre-emptive usage like time deixis (e.g. Levinson 1983). In other words, by default, the speaker gives priority to the use of deixis in the form of first person singular pronoun ('I' in English, '*je*' in French, and '*wo*' in Chinese) when referring to himself or herself, instead of any non-deictic expressions, such as his or her name and self-denigrating terms. Also as in the case of time deixis, the pre-emptive requirement of person deixis can be violated deliberately or non-deliberately in communication, yielding what is called the anti-preemptive usage (Zhang 1994).

As shown in the novel, *wo*, as a pre-emptive deictic SSF, can be used by all the addressers for self-reference; thus, it is identity-neural and has nothing to do with politeness: it only serves to mark the role of the addresser, without indexing the communicator's social identity.

It is worth pointing out that in *Honglou Meng*, *wo* is used both in situations when the interactants are equal and in those where the interactants are socially unequal, as exemplified in (4).

(4) 略待半刻，见王夫人无话，方欲退出去，薛姨妈忽又笑道："你且站住。我有一件东西，你带了去罢。"说着便叫："香菱！"帘栊响处，才和金钏儿玩的那个小丫头进来，问："太太叫我做什么？"(第7回)

> *lue dai ban ke, jian Wang furen wu hua, fang yu tui chuqu, Xue yima hu you xiao dao: 'ni qie zhanzhu. <u>wo</u> you yijian dongxi, ni dai le qu ba.' shuo zhe bian jiao: 'Xiangling!' lianlong xiang chu, cai he Jinchuan'er wan de nage xiaoyatou jinlai, wen: 'taitai jiao <u>wo</u> zuo shenme?'*

> It seemed Lady Wang had no further instructions for her, and she was on the point of leaving when Aunt Xue stopped her. 'Wait a minute,' she said with a smile. '<u>I</u> (*wo* – first person pronoun) have something for you to take back.' She called for Xiangling and the portiere clacked as in came the girl who had been playing with Jinchuan. 'Did you call <u>me</u> (*wo* – first person pronoun), madam?' she asked. (Chapter 7)

Xue Yima and Xiangling, who are from different social classes, both use *wo* for self-reference in this conversation. Thus, in this context, no social gap between them can be deduced from the self-referring *wo* they use. Nor can we see any effort on the part of the inferior girl to address the lady with socially appropriate politeness. This might suggest that in the pre-modern Qing dynasty period, the sense of equality and self-awareness was already very noticeable (this can probably be further testified if compared with the use of SSFs in earlier dynasties).

Self-denigrating terms

Self-denigrating terms as the most frequently used non-deictic SSFs (with a proportion of 3.3%) involve the denigration or depreciation of oneself. The following are examples extracted from *Honglou Meng*:

(5) 三姐从那边来了，一手捧着鸳鸯剑，一手捧着一卷册子，向湘莲哭道：
    "妾痴情待君五年，不期君果冷心冷面。..."（第66回）

   Sanjie cong nabian lai le, yi shou peng zhe yuanyang jian, yi shou peng zhe yijuan cezi, xiang Xianglian kuo dao: 'qie zhiqing dai jun wu nian, buqi jun guo leng xin leng mian. [...]'

   Third Sister came in, with the 'duck and drake' swords in one hand, and a book in the other. With tears in her eyes, she told Xianlian: 'I (*qie* – a denigrating term) waited five years for you, my lord, not knowing you would prove so cold-hearted. ...' (Chapter 66)

(6) 凤姐儿道："你二爷在外头弄了人，你知道不知道？"旺儿又打着千儿，
    回道："奴才天天在二爷门上听差事，如何能知道二爷外头的事呢？"
    （第67回）

   Fengjie'er dao: 'ni erye zai waitou nong le ren, ni zhidao bu zhidao?' Wang-er you da zhe qian er, hui dao: 'nucai tiantian zai erye men shang ting chaishi, ruhe neng zhidao erye waitou de shi ne?'

   'Did you know that your Second Master had bought a house and married a concubine outside?' Xifeng demanded. 'I (*nucai* – a denigrating term) am on duty all day long at the inner gate,' stammered Lai Wang. 'How could I (the first person pronoun takes zero form in Chinese) know about the Second Master's business?' (Chapter 67)

In (5), while You Sanjie is confiding her feelings to Liu Xianglian, she uses a chain of *qie* 妾 (lit. 'concubine') for self-reference. The term *qie*, which in Chinese literally denotes a woman who is a concubine of a man, is used self-referentially by You Sanjie as a token of self-abasement to signal her inferiority to the addressee. This was common among ancient Chinese women speaking to their husbands, although they were not their concubines. Likewise, *nucai* 奴才 (lit. 'slave') in (6), which originally denotes the servants in a Manchu family, is used by Wang Er for self-reference to signal his inferiority to his master. Other such self-abasing SSFs used in *Honglou Meng* include *xiaode* 小的 (lit. 'worthless person'), *xiaoren* 小人 (also lit. 'worthless person'), *xiao wang* 小王 (lit. 'worthless lord'), *xia guan* 下官 (lit. 'worthless official') and *fanguan* 犯官 (lit. 'convicted official'). Basically, these forms are formulaic and, according to the social hierarchical system during the Qing dynasty, their use was almost compulsory.

The use of self-denigrating terms in *Honglou Meng* implies that during the pre-modern Qing dynasty, self-denigration was a general conversational practice, stipulated by social conventions in the historical period when an inferior person (like a servant or a wife) made self-reference before his or her superior (like a master or a husband). The formulaic SSFs are social-indexes (Kasper 1990), conveying normative politeness or technically something like a "societal meta-message" (Kádár 2007a: 24). This embodies the impact on communication exerted by the unequal positions in the hierarchical social structure in the Qing dynasty, rather than instrumental politeness or, as Kasper (1990) puts it, "strategic politeness", where choices are dependent upon situational variables and intentions (as discussed in the following section, *Use of non-deictic SSFs as a strategic polite act*). Underlying such expressions of self-denigration is the social need of the addresser to recognise the difference in social position relative to the addressee. For instance, in (5), the use of *qie* 妾 (lit. 'concubine') reflects the addresser's awareness of her position in the marriage, revealing women's inferior position in the then society. Likewise, *nucai* 奴才 ('servant in a Manchu family') in (6) reflects the addresser's recognition of the addressee's nobility and his own inferiority. It should be noted that in modern Chinese, some SSFs, such as *qie* 妾 and *nucai* 奴才 have almost vanished. This change may partly reflect the change of Chinese social system; in particular, the Chinese social structure has evolved from the mould that placed stress on social hierarchy into one that gives more weight to equality, at least in some domains of social life. According to Gu (1990, 1992), one of the ways to express politeness in Chinese is self-denigration. However, the claim is not true of modern Chinese society because almost all the truly self-denigrating terms have ceased to be used as SSFs today.

Modesty-featuring terms[4]

As the second most frequently used non-deictic SSFs, modesty-featuring terms refer to those linguistic forms that speakers use with the purpose of showing modesty by lowering their own position so as to yield a sense of superiority to the addressee. Consider the following examples:

(7) 张先生道："晚生粗鄙下士，知识浅陋。…"贾珍道："先生不必过谦。…"
（第10回）

Zhang xiansheng dao: 'wansheng cubi xiashi, zhishi qianlou, [...]' Jia Zhen dao: 'xiansheng bubi guoqian, [...]'

'I (*wanshan* – a modesty-featuring term) am simply an ignorant layman, ...'
replied Dr. Zhang. 'You are too modest, sir. ...' (Chapter 10)

(8) 雨村听说出'贾'字来，益发无疑，便从新施礼，道："学生自蒙慨赠到都，
托庇获隽公车，受任贵乡。..."（第103回）

Yucun ting shuo chu 'Jia' zi lai, yifa wu yi, bian congxin shili, dao: <u>xuesheng</u>
zi meng kai zeng dao du, tuopi huo jun gongche, shouren guixiang, [...]'

The word *jia*, a homonym for Yucun's surname, confirmed his conjecture.
He bowed again and said, 'Since you generously helped me to go to the
capital, I (*xuesheng* – a modesty-featuring term) was lucky enough to pass the
examination and was assigned to your honorable district. ...' (Chapter 103)

In effect, *wansheng* 晚生 (lit. 'a later-born person') used by Mr Zhang in (7)
and *xuesheng* 学生 ('student') used by Jia Yucun in (8) are both indicators
of modesty because there is no junior-senior or student-teacher relation
between the two interactants in the exchanges concerned. By claiming
oneself to be born later than the addressee, the speaker implies that the
addressee has some seniority as opposed to him/herself. Similarly, by
referring to oneself as a student, the speaker gives the privilege of a teacher to
the addressee and suggests that he/she is willing to learn from the addressee.
In *Honglou Meng*, other such self-referring expressions include *pindao* 贫道
(lit. 'poor Taoist') and *xiaodao* 小道 (lit. 'worthless Taoist').

Unlike the self-denigrating terms, the modesty-featuring terms[5] in
Honglou Meng (accounting for 1.6% of all the SSFs) were not used to
convey normative politeness, in that they were not compulsory and the
speakers concerned could have used the stylistically and socially neutral
deictic first person pronouns without causing socially defined rudeness.
Nevertheless, the use of these terms did sound polite because of the
deference involved and was more or less anticipated (Haugh 2003) among
those who were educated or had some social rank. Their use, which is
neither absolutely normative nor highly strategic, could help to construct
the socially approved image of a polite or decent speaker for their users,
although it might not be intended as immediately useful to their current
goal of communication.

Kinship terms

Another non-deictic category of forms that speakers employ for self-
reference has to do with those terms indicating the kinship relationship
between the addresser and the addressee, as shown by *xiongdi* 兄弟 ('young
brother') in (9).

(9) 贾琏便推门进去，说："大爷在这里呢，兄弟来请安。" 贾珍听是贾琏的
声音，唬了一跳，见贾琏进来，不觉羞惭满面。（第65回）

Jia Lian bian tui men jinqu, shuo: 'daye zai zheli ne, <u>xiongdi</u> lai qing'an.' Jia Zhen ting shi Jia Lian de shengyin, hu le yi tiao, jian Jia Lian jinlai, bujue xiucan manmian.

Jia Lian opened the door and went in. 'So you're here, sir,' he said with a smile. 'I (*xiongdi* – a kinship term) have come to pay my respect.' Frightened at the voice of Jia Zhen, Jia Zhen was too embarrassed to speak. (Chapter 65)

This category has a variant form in the novel, which is realised by prefacing a term of address with *ni (de)* 你（的） ('your'), as exemplified by *ni qin shenzi* 你亲婶子 (lit. 'your true sister-in-law') in (10).

(10) 话说那柳家的听了这小么儿一席话，笑道："好猴儿崽子！你亲婶子找
野老儿去了，你不多得一个叔叔吗？"（第61回）

huashuo na Liu jia de ting le zhe xiao me er yi xi hua, xiao dao: 'hao hou'er zaizi! <u>ni qin shenzi</u> zhao ye lao'er qu le, ni bu duo de yige shushu ma?'

'You monkey!' chuckled Mrs. Liu. 'If I (*ni qin shenzi* – second person pronoun plus a kinship term) go to find a lover, doesn't that mean one more uncle for you?' (Chapter 61)

There is yet another form that a speaker uses for self-reference, namely *er* 儿 ('child'), which has just the same self-referring function although it is found in a poem in the novel rather than in a conversation:

(11) 〔分骨肉〕一帆风雨路三千，把骨肉家园，齐来抛闪。恐哭损残年，爹
娘休把儿悬念。（第5回）

(fen gurou) yi fan fengyu lu san qian, ba gurou jiayuan, qi lai pao shan. kong ku sun can nian, dieniang xiu ba <u>er</u> xuannian.

Three thousand *li* she must sail through wind and rain,
Giving up her home and her own flesh and blood;
But afraid to distress their declining years with tears
She tells her parents: 'Don't grieve for <u>me</u> (*er* – a kinship term).'
(Chapter 5)

A more complex way of making speaker self-reference under this broad category is to use the addresser's first name plus a kinship term. For example:

(12) 贾蓉旁边笑着劝道："好婶娘！亲婶娘！以后蓉儿要不真心孝顺你老人家，
天打雷劈。"（第68回）[6]

Jia Rong pangbian xiao zhe quan dao: 'hao shenniang! yihou <u>Rong-er</u> yao bu zhenxin xiaoshun ni laorenjia, tian da lei pi.'

> Jia Rong pledged smilingly, 'Dear aunt! Dear aunt! I (*Rong-er* – first name of the speaker plus a kinship term) will be truly obedient to you. May a thunderbolt strike me if I don't!' (Chapter 68)

Rong-er 蓉儿 here refers to the addresser Jia Rong. Compared with the full name (Jia Rong), *Rong-er*, with *er* 儿 ('child') indicating that the addresser is of the junior generation relative to the addressee, sounds much more cordial.

The use of the kinship expressions appears polite as they convey the sense of familiarity. Although familiar terms are not normatively required, their use, a typical interactional practice in pre-modern as well as modern Chinese society, may serve to establish emotional affinity between the interactants in contrast with the modesty-featuring terms that serve to express deference.

Compared to the deictic self-referring expressions in Category A in Table 14.1, the SSFs in other categories (Categories B–E in Table 14.1) used in *Honglou Meng* are non-deictic, accounting for 6.3 per cent. It is natural to query why these non-deictic expressions are employed in place of the deictic ones, which are generally expected.

We assume that, compared with the deictic forms, the non-deictic SSFs may convey specific information about the speakers' social identities. From the frequent non-use of person pronouns or the use of the non-deictic SSFs, we can learn that in the pre-modern Qing dynasty, the individuals still consciously rely on social relations to define their identities. For example, the self-referring expression *xiongdi* 兄弟 ('young brother') in (9) is determined with reference to the addressee (brother), which indicates the kinship between the addresser and the addressee. When Jia Lian uses *xiongdi* 兄弟 for self-reference before Jia Zhen, the information about their kinship is immediately conveyed. In the Chinese culture, kinship has a binding power. People in a lower family position should respect and comply with those of a higher position; a person in a higher position has some control over the one in the lower position, and at the same time s/he also has the obligation to show concern and care to the one in the lower position. This was especially true in pre-modern China.

From the non-deictic SSFs used, we can infer that Chinese society in the pre-modern Qing dynasty was a hierarchical one and the hierarchy was linguistically and pragmatically marked. Thus, the investigation of the choices of SSFs can in a sense help understand the social orientation of the Chinese people in that period.

Use of non-deictic SSFs as a strategic polite act

The variationist theory of language use (e.g. Labov 1972), especially the study of social dialects, might lead people to simply assume that a person of a specific social identity will choose corresponding linguistic expressions. However, pragmatic studies, especially those based on the analysis of dynamic contexts (like Thomas 1995 and Grundy 1995), have shown that the use of language does not invariably exhibit a one-to-one correspondence between language form and language function or between identity and language. According to the Theory of Linguistic Adaption proposed by Verschueren (1999), the use of language is a process of constant choice at different linguistic levels on the basis of contextual correlates, with the purpose of accomplishing certain communicative goals and/or achieving some special communicative effect. If the addresser overly flouts a certain convention or maxim (like the appropriateness of using address terms relative to the speakers' identity) as specified by certain contextual factors (including the physical world, the social world, the mental world and the linguistic context), it must be due to the desire to facilitate the realisation of some illocutionary end or achieve some special communicative effect.

In general, the use of the non-deictic SSFs in *Honglou Meng* as discussed above reflects the speakers' adaptation to the well-established social norms in pre-modern China. However, as we shall demonstrate through contextualised analysis, some instances of the SSFs used in the novel are unconventional (in that the speakers opt out from the default identity relations and construct an ad hoc identity through deliberate choice of specific SSFs). This represents strategic politeness[7] or, in Watts' terms, marked politeness (Watts 2003), because the chosen SSFs can convey interpersonal affect that might facilitate the achievement of some special communicative effects.

Enhancing the chances of achieving a current illocutionary goal

Possessing certain facilitative identity information, kinship terms used as non-deictic SSFs may contribute to the fulfilling of the speaker's illocutionary goal. For example:

(13) 贾珍不肯坐，因勉强陪笑道：“侄儿进来有一件事要求二位婶娘、大妹妹。”邢夫人等忙问：“什么事？”（第13回）

Jia Zhen buken zuo, yin mianqiang peixiao dao: '<u>zhi-er</u> jinlai you yijian shi yao qiu er wei shenniang, da meimei.' Xing furen deng mang wen: 'shenme shi?'

Jia Zhen would not take a seat. Forcing a smile he announced, 'I (*zhi-er* – a kinship term) have come to ask a favor of you (*shenniang* and *da meimei* – two kinship terms)' 'What is it?' inquired Lady Xing and others. (Chapter 13)

Here, when asking for a favour from his interlocutors (his aunts and cousins), Jia Zhen not only replaces *nimen* 你们 (plural second person pronoun) with *shenniang* 婶娘 ('aunt') and *da meimei* 大妹妹 (lit. 'big sister', which actually refers to cousins) but also substitutes *wo* 我 (first person pronoun) with *zhi-er* 侄儿 (a kinship term meaning 'nephew + child') at the beginning of the talk, so as to highlight the kinship. Considering the kinship relation, Lady Xing would probably give a hand to Jia Zhen since it is her *nephew* who is turning to her for help. The non-compulsory choice of the kinship term as an SSF thus reflects Jia Zhen's considered effort to take advantage of the shared Chinese social cultural background – kinship. Here is another example:

(14) 贾琏连忙走上，跪下禀说："这一箱文书既在奴才屋里抄出来的，敢说不知道么？只求王爷开恩。奴才叔叔并不知道的。"（第105回）

Jia Lian lianmang zou shang, gui xia bing shuo: 'zhe yi xiang wenshu ji zai <u>nucai</u> wu li chao chulai de, gan shuo bu zhidao me? zhi qiu wangye kai'en. <u>nucai</u> shushu bing bu zhidao de.'

Jia Lian hastily stepped forward and knelt to report, 'Since those documents were found in <u>my</u> (=*nucai*'s) humble house, how can I deny knowledge of them? I only beg Your Highnesses to be lenient to my uncle who knew nothing about this.' (Chapter 105)

The term *nucai* 奴才 ('slave') was originally a self-referring expression for servants to address themselves in conversation with their masters in Manchu families. This expression was later extended beyond the Manchu families when the relationship between the interlocutors was not necessarily that of servants and master. Unlike the case in (6), in (14) Jia Lian uses *nucai* 奴才 for self-reference (not in the subject or object position, though) because he has made a mistake and wishes to be forgiven by the prince. Although he is not really a servant of the prince, he deliberately uses this self-referring expression for self-denigration to undermine his own positive face (Brown and Levinson 1987) in the hope of gaining sympathy and forgiveness from the prince.

Bridging interpersonal distance

Some non-deictic self-referring expressions may serve to establish rapport and affinity between the interlocutors or to impress the addressees favourably in order to bridge the gap between them, which can be regarded as positive politeness in Brown and Levinson's terms. In *Honglou Meng*, a character may use a kinship term as an SSF, although the relationship between the current interlocutors is not what the term denotes (thus, it is different from the use of *xiongdi* 兄弟 in (9)). For example:

(15) 雨村最赞这冷子兴是个有作为大本领的人，这子兴又借雨村斯文之名，故二人最相投契。雨村忙亦笑问："老兄何日到此？弟竟不知。今日偶遇，真奇缘也。"（第2回）

> *Yucun zui zan zhe Leng Zixing shi ge you zuowei da benling de ren, zhe Zixing you jie Yucun siwen zhi ming, gu err en zui xiang touqi. Yucun mang yi xiao wen: 'laoxiong he ri dao ci? di jing buzhi. jinri ouyu, zhen qiyuan ye.'*

> As Yucun admired his enterprise and ability while Zixing was eager to cultivate one of the literati, they had hit it off well together and become good friends. 'When did you arrive, old brother?' asked Yucun cheerfully. 'I (*di* – a kinship term) had no idea you were in these parts. What a coincidence, meeting you here.' (Chapter 2)

As we know, Jia Yucun and Leng Zixing are not blood brothers in *Honglou Meng*, yet Jia Yucun not only calls Leng Zixing *laoxiong* 老兄 (lit. 'old elder brother') but also uses the kinship term *di* 弟 (lit. 'younger brother') as an SSF. By strategically setting the brotherhood social relationship, Jia Yucun uses positive politeness to narrow the emotional distance from Leng Zixing and promote interactional harmony. In *Honglou Meng*, such strategic use of kinship terms as SSFs is very common. Both Jia Yucun and other male characters used them although the interlocutors were not true blood brothers. As kinship terms, their strategic use is noteworthy because their original meaning has been extended and, what is more, this use is also retained in modern Chinese. Here is another example from the novel:

(16) 且说次日午间，门上人回道："请的那张先生来了。"贾珍遂延入大厅坐下。茶毕，方开言道："昨日承冯大爷示知老先生人品学问，又兼深通医学，小弟不胜钦敬。"（第10回）

> *qie shuo cirri wujian, menshangren hui dao: 'qing de na Zhang xiansheng lai le.' Jia Zhen sui yan ru dating zuo xia. cha bi, fang kaiyan dao: 'zuori cheng Feng daye shi zhi laoxiansheng renmin xuewen, you jian shentong yixue, xiaodi busheng qinjing.'*

> The next day at noon the doctor was announced. Jia Zhen conducted him into the reception hall and made him take a seat. When they had drunk tea he broached the subject, saying, 'Yesterday I (*xiaodi* – 'little' plus a kinship term) was overwhelmed with admiration by all Mr Feng told me of your character, learning and profound knowledge of medicine, sir.' (Chapter 10)

In the above example, there is no true brotherhood relationship between Jia Zhen and Mr Zhang. The strategic use of *'xiaodi'* (lit. 'little younger brother') in (16) as a token of positive politeness is to reduce the social distance between them. Therefore, it can be seen that the choice of SSFs is not always a mechanical process based on the real social relationship; sometimes its use is likely to be a discourse strategy driven by certain communicative goals. By resorting to kinship, an essential element in the Chinese social culture, the speaker can aspire to establish a harmonious social relationship with the addressee so as to pave the way for future interactional affairs. In other words, the use of non-deictic kinship terms as SSFs is often an endeavour at positive politeness whose goal is to create harmonious communication.

Indicating respect to the communicator

This strategic function is realised by the use of the modesty-featuring forms rather than the self-denigrating terms because the use of the latter was compulsory – the speakers had no freedom not to use them. Take a previous example, (8), repeated as (17):

(17) 雨村听说出 "贾" 字来，益发无疑，便从新施礼，道："学生自蒙慨赠到都，托庇获隽公车，受任贵乡。..."（第103回）

 Yucun ting shuo chu 'Jia' zi lai, yifa wu yi, bian congxin shili, dao: '<u>xuesheng</u> zi meng kai zeng dao du, tuopi huo jun gongche, shouren guixiang, [...]'

 The word *jia*, a homonym for Yucun's surname, confirmed his conjecture. He bowed again and said, 'Since you generously helped me to go to the capital, <u>I</u> (*xuesheng* – a modesty-featuring term) was lucky enough to pass the examination and was assigned to your honorable district. ...' (Chapter 103)

Clearly, the strategic use of the modesty-featuring SSFs to show one's respect to the addressee occurs when the two participants in the interaction are comparable in social status. The use is strategic because the social relationship between the interlocutors is generally not the type depicted by the modesty-featuring term used. In (17) *xuesheng* 学生 ('student') semantically refers to a student and sometimes also to a person who learns something from a senior. In the context of example (17), Yuncun is not a student of his interlocutor (a Taoist); in effect, Yuncun's use of this expression can lower his own social status, which will result in the elevation of his interlocutor's position. For this reason, Yuncun's speaker-based mode of deference is also a type of negative politeness.

Indicating the addresser's power or authority, commanding the addressee's awe and submission

Very infrequently adopted in *Honglou Meng* (possibly as there are very few episodes involving interaction between officials and servants in the novel), 'ben + an official title' ('this official') as an SSF may perform this type of function. The speaker adopting this kind of self-referring expressions is generally empowered to make this choice by certain institutions; their inter-actants are their subordinates or any other people within their jurisdiction. The choice is strategic because the speaker could have used the default deictic first person pronoun. Consider (18) below:

> (18) 王爷喝命："不许罗唣，待本爵自行查看！"（第105回）
> *wangye he ming: 'buxu luozao, dai <u>ben jue</u> zixing chakan!'*
> 'No disorder now!' called the prince sternly. '<u>I</u> shall come in person to supervise the search!' (Chapter 105)

In Example 18, the prince uses the term *ben jue* 本爵 (lit. 'this official') to highlight his identity as someone in power and with authority, which runs counter to politeness, either normative or strategic. Probably, the interactants, out of fear of his authority, will submit to his command.

Conclusion

Regarding the relationship between address forms and politeness, the latter can be approached from both how speakers address others and how they refer to themselves (as indicated by the use of SSFs). This chapter focuses on the latter. In the novel *Honglou Meng*, we have found that there exist at least four major types of SSFs. Apart from the dominant default *wo* 我 (first person pronoun), there is widespread use of self-denigrating and modesty-featuring SSFs, partly verifying the claims about the politeness phenomena in the Chinese culture formulated by Gu (1990, 1992). The claims are only *partly* confirmed because many forms, especially self-denigrating SSFs, have ceased to exist in modern Chinese discourse, as pointed out by Kádár (2007a). Nevertheless, the practice of using non-deictic self-referring expressions is still prevalent in modern Chinese, which will be testified by the data of modern Chinese corpora in the future. In addition, the finding also partly endorses Kádár's view that politeness use in pre-modern and modern China needs to be divided into appropriate stages and that in the former stage there used to be plenty of socially imposed formulaic or normative politeness as opposed to instrumental politeness, in Brown and Levinson's sense, or strategic politeness as discussed in this study.

Whereas speakers tend to use the default deictic first person pronoun (*wo* 我 and its variants like *wu* 吾 and *an* 俺) for self-reference in Chinese, as in other languages, a prominent feature in the language is that the speakers also adopt some non-deictic self-referring expressions to indicate their identity relative to the addressees to achieve some special communicative effects. This feature, rare in English, Japanese and probably many other languages, reflects a unique element of the Chinese social culture, notably, the emphasis on the identity relationship and on the practice of positioning oneself so as to see things from the interlocutor's perspective. This feature is grammaticalised as formulae of politeness in the pre-modern Chinese self-referring system which is evolving with the change of social life.

By researching the use of SFFs in *Honglou Meng*, the present study enriches the understanding of the complexity of politeness forms in Chinese culture. Specifically, in *Honglou Meng*, when someone in an inferior social position uses self-denigrating terms for self-reference, which is virtually socially required, his or her purpose is to convey normative politeness to the communicator in a superior position. When someone uses modesty-featuring SSFs to a person of equal social status, which is socially encouraged but practically optional, his or her purpose is to convey politeness by way of speaker-based deference. When someone uses a kinship term for self-reference, which is open to free choice, his or her purpose is to convey politeness by establishing rapport and narrowing social distance, which in turn will promote the realisation of the speaker's illocutionary goal. By contrast, people at the higher level rarely seem to position themselves in the place of their interlocutors (this is based on initial observation of the interactions in *Honglou Meng*, which awaits further confirmation). When they do opt for this strategy, their purpose is, contrary to showing politeness, to highlight their authority, and command the interlocutor's subordination and submission to their will. Thus it is clear that the use of non-deictic self-referring expressions, except for the self-denigrating terms, is more or less pragmatically motivated, especially manifested by the deliberate construction of a marked identity through the use of SSFs, rather than made randomly or by passively following the identity relationships involved. To achieve the special communicative effects, the users of these non-deictic SSFs strategically take advantage of the Chinese social and cultural elements (like kinship and social hierarchy).

Future research on this topic can further investigate what factors may contribute to the addresser's choice of self-referring expressions. In addition to the power relationship and emotional distance, other factors like age, gender and the type of speech act being performed by the addresser may also play a role.[8]

Notes

1. Jia Baoyu was the hero or protagonist of the story while Lin Daiyu was the heroine. Jia fell in love with Lin at first sight when she came to live with the Jia family after her parents died. However, their love failed to develop into a marriage because Jia's parents intended to have, and succeeded in having, Xue Baochai marry him. As a result, Lin died in misery and Jia was very sad and in the end became a monk.

2. The terms in this survey only involve the self-referring expressions in the subject and object positions, thus not including the relevant terms used as attributives.

3. It is worth mentioning that the historical form *wu* 吾, which occurs ten times in *Honglou Meng*, had almost dropped out of use in pre-modern Chinese. But it is equally noteworthy that in that period, *wo* 我 and *wu* 吾 may co-occur even in the same sentence, such as the case below. This indicates that the Qing period might be the last stage for the transition from *wu* to *wo*:

   那僧道："正合吾意。… 待这一干风流孽鬼下世，你我再去。如今有一半落尘，然犹未全集"（第1回）

   na sen dao: "zheng he wu yi. [...] dai zhe yi gan fengliu niegui xiashi, ni wo zai qu. rujin you yiban luochen, ran you wei quan ji."

   "Exactly the same as what I (*wu* – historical first person pronoun) was thinking. … After all these romantic souls have gone down, you and I (*wo* – first person pronoun) can follow. So far only half of them have descended to earth." (Chapter 1)

4. One referee suggested that this category be integrated into Category B. Likewise, Gu Yueguo considers modesty as "another way of saying self-denigration" (1990: 239). His Self-denigrating Maxim, which consists of two clauses: (a) denigrate self and (b) elevate other, absorbs the notions of respectfulness and modesty. However, this author maintains the distinction between the two categories because Category C concerns modesty but does not involve defaming or smearing one's own image, and many forms in this category like '*xuesheng*' and '*wanbei*' survive in modern Chinese to a large extent, whereas those forms in Category B have almost entirely gone into extinction as SSFs today. In addition, unlike the use of modesty-featuring terms, the use of self-denigrating terms by a supposedly socially inferior person to someone superior does not necessarily make the addressee feel his/her own position is elevated.

5. It is worth mentioning that while some modesty-featuring terms in *Honglou Meng* like *xuesheng* 学生 (student) are still widely used in modern China, some other modesty-featuring expressions, such as *wansheng* 晚生 (lit. 'a later-born person') and *xiaguan* 下官 (lit. 'worthless official'), are generally not used any longer as SSFs today.

6. Yang's translation missed this sentence and this author makes up for it here.

7. It is worth mentioning, though, that the use of plural first person pronoun, like 'we' in English, can also be strategic, as documented in Brown and Levinson (1987) and Levinson (1983). We focus on the strategic use of non-deictic SSFs here because they are less studied on the one hand and they offer most cases of strategies in *Honglou Meng* on the other.
8. This study is funded by a NJU '985' project (NJU985JD05) and the Priority Academic Program Development of Jiangsu Higher Education Institutions.

References

Agha, A. (2007) *Language and Social Relations*. Cambridge: Cambridge University Press.

Brown, P. and Levinson, S. C. (1987) *Politeness: Some Universals in Language Usage*. Cambridge: Cambridge University Press.

Cao, X. and Gao, E. (1987) *A Dream of Red Mansions*. Beijing: Renmin Wenxue Press.

Grundy, P. (1995) *Doing Pragmatics*. London: Arnold.

Gu, Y. (1990) Politeness phenomena in modern Chinese. *Journal of Pragmatics* 14: 237–257.

Gu, Y. (1992) Politeness, language use and culture. *Foreign Language Teaching and Research* 4: 12–17.

Haugh, M. (2003) Anticipated versus inferred politeness. *Multilingua* 22: 397–413.

Ide, S. (1989) Formal forms and discernment: Two neglected aspects of linguistic politeness. *Multilingua* 8: 223–248.

Kádár, D. Z. (2007a) *Terms of (Im)politeness: A Study of the Communicational Properties of Traditional Chinese (Im)polite Terms of Address*. Budapest: Eötvös Loránd University Press.

Kádár, D. Z. (2007b) On historical Chinese apology and its strategic application. *Journal of Politeness Research* (Special Issue on *Apologies*) 3: 125–150.

Kasper, G. (1990) Linguistic politeness: Current research issues. *Journal of Pragmatics* 14: 193–218.

Labov, W. (1972) *Sociolinguistic Patterns*. Philadelphia, PA: University of Pennsylvania Press.

Levinson, S. (1983) *Pragmatics*. Cambridge: Cambridge University Press.

Matsumoto, Y. (1989) Politeness and conversational universals: Observations from Japanese. *Multilingua* 8: 207–221.

Thomas, J. (1995) *Meaning in Interaction: An Introduction to Pragmatics*. London: Longman.

Verschueren, J. (1999) *Understanding Pragmatics*. London: Arnold.

Watts, R. (2003) *Politeness*. Cambridge: Cambridge University Press.

Yang, X. and Yang, G. (tr.) (1994) *A Dream of Red Mansions*. Beijing: Foreign Language Press.

Zhang, Q. (1994) The pre-emptive usage of deictic words. *Journal of Modern Languages* 2: 8–14.

15

Epilogue: What makes Chinese unique in discourse and interaction?

Kenneth Kong

This volume is a timely and welcome addition of scholarship at this critical moment when 'cultural' interpretation of language is in crisis. In the past, national or ethnic culture seemed to be a final explanation when no better explanations could be found. When an American has communication problems with a Chinese, whatever is misunderstood, even the small hitches that occur in any interaction, is most likely to be attributed to cultural differences. Communication studies, which is more interested in theorising and generalising, is a good example of a tendency to over-generalise the influence of culture and downplay the individualistic and intracultural differences:

> To the Chinese, who value the non-confrontational style of interaction, verbal language is too direct to express disapproval and disdain, especially in the face-to-face context. It would not only induce conflicts, but also make the verbal critic lose face because he or she has used an inappropriate means of indicating disapproval (words in the face-to-face context), which has caused the wrongdoer to lose face again. (Jia 2007: 56)

Does this mean all Chinese are indirect and avoid conflicts at all cost? Using a broad-brush approach and labels such as 'Chinese' and 'American' cultures has proven to be problematic in both application and further testing of a theory. Even if communication difference does exist in conflict avoidance behaviour between Chinese and Americans in the US, what about the mainland Chinese and Hong Kong Chinese? Obviously one's behaviour is governed by many other factors in addition to one's national culture. If culture is simply reduced to a nation, what of all those sub-cultures which play an increasingly important role in our daily life? This is what Holliday calls the distinction between 'large culture' and 'small culture'. Large culture is "essentialist in that it relates to the essential differences between ethnic, national and international entities" (Holliday 1999: 240). The main objective of large culture analysis is prescriptive, that is, to identify what is desirable or acceptable in a certain culture. In contrast, small culture is non-essentialist in that it does not relate to the notions of ethnic, national or international entities but to "any cohesive social group which is not necessarily subordinate to large cultures. To Holliday, large cultures are reified small cultures, taking up from the idea of Berger and Luckmann (1966). Small cultures are everyday constructions which are independent of what is prescribed as normal and unmarked values in mainstream social culture grouping.

The strength of an etic orientation, usually adopted in communication studies, is to provide an overview of culture from a position outside a system and compare it with other systems using a structure created by the analyst (Berry 1980). However, the most obvious weakness is that fuzzy concepts such as culture cannot be easily pinned down, categorised and classified. This is why theories and macro-categories have to be examined and verified from an emic perspective. Chang and Haugh (this volume) are especially interested in the role of emic interpretation of 'face' and distinguish emic concepts and practices in the study of face-threatening acts which can be strategically employed.

Instead of taking a broad-brush or etic approach to culture, all the chapters in this volume take a linguistic approach to the issue, assuming the importance of the fine-grained or moment-by-moment nature of language. This allows us to be more careful about over-generalisation and at the same time to understand what is unique about being a Chinese.

Meanwhile, any comparison of language underscores an important debate about what has been called 'linguistic relativity': the influence of one's language on the thinking or belief system (see Gumperz and Levinson 1996 for a review of the notion). There can be at least three positions in relation to linguistic relativity. First, the language one speaks does not influence how he or she perceives things. The second position is that the language of one's belonging will 'determine' the thinking patterns of the person, making it almost impossible to perceive like the speakers of other languages do. The third position strikes the middle ground by positing that the language someone can use only has some influence in thinking and perception. Most recent research tends to go for the middle position in which language and thinking have a certain degree of influence but the degree is debatable and contested. In some spheres of communication, the influence tends to be weaker especially with our styles of thinking increasingly globalised and homogenised. For example, in a study comparing the women's magazine *Cosmopolitan* in different countries (Machin and van

Leeuwen 2007) it was found that different countries tend to capitalise on the similar cultural resources of portraying social problems facing women in different countries all over the globe, although the solutions suggested are different, implying that cultural values remain intact. In other spheres of communication which are less subject to globalisation, such as institutional meetings or family gatherings, the influence of language on culture seems to be stronger and has a more lasting and durable effect on how entities are perceived. However Sun (this volume) tends to align with the strong influence of globalisation in her comparison of service calls recorded recently and a decade ago in China, with evidence of a more customer-friendly style of interaction, salient differences exhibited in forms, how enterprises identify themselves, employees' choice of words and expressions, and participation structure in closing sequences. The discrepancy in the degree of influence could be explained by the contexts where the data was collected. Journalistic discourse is more subject to institutional control than business discourse which mainly aims at profit-making.

While all the chapters use the Chinese language as data of analysis, they are committed to different issues or interests. This is not to deny the value of this important volume, far from it. Interest in Chinese discourse and interaction is a relatively new endeavour that needs exploration in different directions. Some chapters (Sun for example) are more interested in how Chinese discourse responds to the global influence of journalistic practice and consumer culture. Some take Chinese data as an example, showing more universal features of language, without focusing on the influence of the Chinese language per se (He, for example). Some use Chinese data to make arguments about what is unique about Chinese discourse (Cheng, for example). The range of paradigms and positions embodied in this single monograph is understandable given the contested nature of language, culture and context. In brief, in addition to the influence of globalisation on Chinese discourse practice as mentioned above, the chapters in this volume have three other threads: exploration of an interactional feature using Chinese examples, the scale or extent of influence of Chinese culture and the unique linguistic realisation in Chinese.

Exploration of an interactional feature by using Chinese examples

Some chapters in this volume (e.g. He, Kádár and Chen) lay their focus on the more universal nature of interaction which is applicable not only to

Chinese but also to other languages. In her chapter, He argues that modality might not be encoded in modal verbs but that it can be realised through the sequential organisation of turn-taking. Kádár (this volume) highlights the role of classical Chinese discourse in the formation of the Chinese identity. Chen (this volume), by studying the non-deictic self-referring expressions in a vernacular Chinese novel, *Honglou Meng* (*A Dream of Red Mansion*), underscores both the normative and strategic dimensions of politeness, supporting the notion that it can be incorporated under a broader framework of relational work (Locher and Watts 2005) or rapport management (Spencer-Oatey 2005). The arguments above are relatively easier to make because there has been a common consensus that meaning is not necessarily derived from words but through dynamic negotiation in interactions. Nevertheless, researchers are still faced with a difficult question of what distinguishes Chinese from other languages in terms of 'how' an interactional resource such as modality is acquired, used and distributed in different ways. But this task is not an easy endeavor given the multiplicity of Chinese as a culture, nation and just a notion, as Pye (1990: 58) argues: "... China is not just another nation-state in the family of nations. China is a civilisation pretending to be a state."

Whether China should be regarded as a nation or a civilisation is out of the scope of this brief closing, but what concerns us is whether people who speak the same language, Chinese, have the same belief systems and communication styles. To deal with this issue, one must be prepared for a set of even more perplexing questions concerning the complex picture Chinese presents as a language with many branches and sub-branches of dialects. At best, one can only make informed *predictions* of the influence of Chinese on discourse and interactional patterns. Mandarin speakers may demonstrate different language use than Cantonese speakers although they are both Chinese. This is especially problematic when one tries to relate the so-called Chinese belief or thought system to intercultural communication, assuming certain behaviour must be manifest among Chinese speakers. Some of the chapters in this volume provide important insights in this area. Zhang and Chan (this volume) identify the different use of repair in Mandarin and Cantonese speakers in casual conversations and news interviews. Kádár also touches on the issue of the differences between northern and southern Chinese. Yet there is still a large gap to be filled in the different patterns of behaviour among the Chinese in different dialect and geographic groups.

The scale or extent of influence

Some chapters in this volume have an explicit interest in how Chinese values or norms influence interaction patterns. Pan (this volume) argues that Chinese informants tend to be evasive in answering survey questions related to personal opinions and evaluation of certain issues. The tendency to give a partial answer and unwillingness to take stance are related to the Chinese culture of indirectness and face. In the same vein, in her study of respondents' responses to survey questions, Chan (this volume) argues that Chinese-speaking respondents tend to provide more indirect and/or contrary-to-face-value responses than English-speaking respondents. This is echoed in Cheng's (this volume) argument that Chinese speakers tend to avoid questions of criticism in public domains. On the other hand, Gu (this volume) contends that power is the dominating feature of Chinese interactional patterns. How can one balance the concerns of power and face needs in a culture where both are equally important? The interesting interplay of indirectness and power is illustrated by Zayts et al. (this volume) in their study of prenatal genetic counselling sessions in Hong Kong. Prenatal genetic counsellors in Hong Kong tend to take a more 'directive' stance with their clients compared with the counterparts of Western countries because healthcare receivers in Hong Kong expect to be 'told' what to do instead of being 'advised' what to do. Besides, the non-directive approach advocated in the mainstream Western medical culture can be overridden by the powers invested in the healthcare providers, that is, genetic counselling nurses in Chinese institutional contexts.

To some extent, the complex interaction of interpersonal factors in Chinese discourse and interaction is not surprising, and Chinese is in no way the only culture marked by such dilemmas and concerns. For example Leetch (2007) aptly points out that the East-West divide in politeness behaviour is misleading. There is a universal concern across different cultures or languages over similar interactional factors. The 'universal' factors identified by Leetch include the vertical distance between speaker and hearers (in terms of status, power, role and age); horisontal distance (e.g. strangers vs. friends); imposition weight and value/cost (e.g. a request for money vs. a request to switch on a light); socially defined rights and obligations (e.g. the legitimate right of a citizen to government medical service vs. a salesperson's obligation to help; socially defined territory (in-group vs. out-group). To Leetch's list we can add socially recognised role expectations, in other words, what role a particular participant is expected to assume in a certain situation and whether the relationship is expected to be long-term or just a transient one.

To a large extent, these factors are present in any culture and differ only in their degree of influence and linguistic realisations. Chinese may attach higher value to vertical distance in a situation than Japanese do but Japanese may attach higher value of socially defined rights and obligations in others. Chinese may also be more prone to the concern of socially defined territory; but this does not mean it is unique to Chinese culture, as Leetch argues:

> There is little doubt that the Eastern group-orientation and the Western individual-orientation are felt to be strong influences on polite behaviour. But do the East and the West need a different theory of politeness? I would argue that they do not, because the scales of politeness can be used to express such differences in values, both qualitative and quantitative. (Leetch 2007: 201)

In fact, a separate theory of politeness, or any other interaction phenomenon, would make any comparison across languages even more difficult or impenetrable. Imagine a separate theory for Chinese, Japanese, British, Indian and so on, not to mention a separate theory for southern Chinese and northern Chinese or for West-coast Americans and East-coast Americans. Having said this, the intercultural complexity has to be addressed but it has to be done in a more systematic way in order to generate useful and 'applicable' findings. In what situations will Chinese place more emphasis on factor X, in what situations will Americans place more emphasis on factor Y? By doing this, we can gain a better understanding of the complex relationship between culture and interactional phenomena. For example, Pan et al. (2002) found that the participants of Chinese meetings are more concerned with the issue of power which can manifest in different forms at different stages of meetings. In the case of foreign language teaching or communication training, transparent formulation of any intercultural difference is especially important. As much as possible, off-putting terms which carry cultural values should be avoided. As Wierzbicka (2006) argues, explanations of cross-cultural differences can be biased and 'culture-bound' especially if terms such as 'independence strategies' and 'symmetrical solidarity' are used. Instead, as she argues, these differences can be introduced in universally teachable terms such as 'good' or 'bad', 'when' and 'if'.

Unique linguistic realisations

Another important concern shared by a number of chapters in this volume is how the same linguistic phenomenon is realised differently in Chinese. For example, as Leetch (2007: 195) argues, the different manifestations of politeness, "the values of politeness are *encoded* mainly through the differing morphological, syntactic and lexical resources of languages". Added to politeness are other interactional resources such as repair (Zhang and Chan, this volume). The different use of particles *De* (in Madarin) and *Ge* (in Cantonese) as a repair strategy is echoed in the Zayts et al. study in which the Cantonese particles 啦 [la] and 囉 [lo] have the dual functions of mitigating the force of a statement on one hand and accelerating its force on the other, depending on the nature of interactions and the participants' role expectations. Endo's study of *wo juede* (this volume) takes up a similar argument. Although having a similar function of marking epistemic stances like English discourse markers, the Chinese *wo juede* (I think) seems to have different functions according to the position it appears in: turn-medial position marking uncertainty about a claim, therefore distancing the speaker from it; turn-initial position marking signalling mitigation of disagreement between participants; and turn-final position for soliciting response, therefore promoting turn-transition.

Understanding of the different linguistic realisations across languages is important in understanding the relationship between form and function. While the same form can perform different functions in different languages, the same function can be realised by different forms. There is never a one-to-one matching relationship, even in a single language. The problem is even greater when comparing linguistic realisations in different languages. Does the same linguistic feature in language A have the same functions in language B? Even if it does, the meaning may vary according to when it is used and whom it is used for (as demonstrated by Zayts et al. in this volume). This form-function mismatch is one of the most problematic areas, especially for foreign language learners. Most of the chapters in this volume focus on micro-linguistic realisations, leaving to future studies a more macro-level analysis of linguistic realisations, such as different stages of a meeting or a report in Chinese.

Future directions

The insightful chapters in this monograph about Chinese discourse and interaction have mapped some interesting future directions, including:

- What differences exist between Chinese speakers of different dialects or from geographical regions in terms of their discourse and interaction practices?

- What is the value or importance attached to sociocultural assumptions in different situations and contexts involving Chinese speakers?
- What are the micro-linguistic differences between Chinese and other languages? In other words, what are the unique linguistic and interactional resources (such as modality, evaluation, politeness, repair, turn-taking) available in Chinese discourse?
- What are the macro-linguistic differences between Chinese and other languages? In other words, what are the differences of moves and staging in Chinese discourse? How do they reflect their cultural and social assumptions?
- What are the important multi-modal resources in Chinese discourse?
- What are the important genres or genre repertoires available in Chinese? What purposes do they serve? In what ways are they different from other languages?
- What are the emerging features of the Chinese language in the age of globalisation?

These questions underscore the need to study Chinese discourse and interaction with a more diversified approach. Most of the chapters in this volume adopt conversational analysis as their main analytic frameworks. While this is a perfectly legitimate focus, the reality of 'Chinese-ness' in discourse and interaction may lie far beyond what is found in conversation. In recent research, there is a split, as it were, in the direction of discourse analysis. On the one hand, analyses can be limited only to linguistic realisations without enough consideration of the specific context. This is especially true in the developing field of corpus linguistics, which tends to generalise thus losing insights from the specific contexts in which those concordance lines are situated. On the other hand, there has been an increasing call for the need to study discourse-in-action, in contexts where discourse needs to be understood in relation to other meditational tools and social practices which are not at all linguistic. Mediated Discourse Analysis (MDA) which "takes mediated action as the unit of analysis" (Scollon 2008: 233) is the most recent approach to discourse that acknowledges the importance of specific moments where different social practices converge. The diversity of methodologies in discourse analysis reflects not only the interdisciplinary nature of the field (as the editors point out in the Introduction) but also the multitude of the problems facing discourse analysts.

While chapters in this volume have a more 'practical' take on identifying Chinese-specific features in discourse and interaction, they are all shadowed by some more theoretical concerns underlying their practical analyses. These concerns include 'indexicality', 'inflexivity' and 'performativity' of discourse, all of which are fairly well established in the literature of linguistic and cultural anthropology (Agha 2006; Duranti 1997; Hanks 1996). Indexicality refers to the provoking or pointing of language to various contextual variables and vice versa, for example the use of a linguistic variety to index power or solidarity. There is need for more systemic studies identifying the different ways in which Chinese can be used as an indexical of power, social relations and ideology. The second more theoretical concern is cultural reflexivity. There are two meanings of reflexivity. The first refers to the linguistic utterances themselves and the second meaning refers to the wider web of social practices in which utterances are embedded. At the level of utterances, language can be used to structure, organise and classify language itself; as Agha (2006) maintains, linguistic signs can be used to typify other linguistic signs. Meta-discourse, using discoursal devices to make comment on other discourse, is an example of linguistic reflexivity. At a level higher than utterances, reflexivity refers to the unconscious action of human agents to respond to situational demands, underscoring the notion of performativity, the production of our social and cultural identities through creative use of contextual and interactional resources. Chinese identity is not a fixed notion but an ongoing projection of being. All the issues above have an important bearing on being Chinese and on what makes Chinese discourse and interaction unique.

Finally I would also like to make a brief comment on the methodology of identifying 'Chinese-ness' in discourse. While intercultural comparison has to be made, analysis can easily fall into the danger of what Blommaert (2005) calls 'synchronization', which refers to ignorance of time-scale differences or historicity and to "the reduction of overdetermination to just one single (clear, transparent) meaning, resulting in images of continuity, logical outcomes, and textual coherence" (*ibid.*: 136). Intercultural studies in discourse are especially prone to this tendency because of their need to make generalisations about different cultures and, at the same time, to address the important issue of identifying historical links in different cultures. For example, directness can be synchronised simply as indexical of hierarchical orientation in Chinese culture, and of egalitarian orientation in American culture, but this comparison ignores the "different simultaneous layers" (*ibid.*) of context and historicity, of directness vs. indirectness, markers used at different levels, places and time in the two cultures. Another difficulty in drawing any definite conclusions from intercultural comparison is what difference and how much of it can support an argument. For example, if a Chinese speaker of English tends to apologise more when interacting with an American, to what extent can the difference be attributed to Chinese Confucianism or just to the strategic use of language which is not his/her mother tongue? Obviously there is still some way to go before we can finally establish what count as unique features in Chinese discourse and interaction in a more systematic way, and the chapters in this volume make an important step on this journey.

Acknowledgement

The work described in this chapter was supported by a grant from the Research Grants Council of Hong Kong Special Administrative Region (Project No: HKBU/242308).

References

Agha, A. (2006) *Language and Social Relations*. Cambridge: Cambridge University Press.

Berger, P. L. and Luckmann, T. (1966) *The Social Construction of Reality: A Treatise in the Sociology of Knowledge*. Garden City, NY: Anchor Books.

Berry, J. (1980) Introduction to methodology. In H. C. Triandis and J. Berry (eds) *Handbook of Cross-Cultural Psychology*, Vol. 2, 1–28. Boston: Allyn and Bacon.

Blommaert, J. (2005) *Discourse: A Critical Introduction*. Cambridge, MA: Cambridge University Press.

Duranti, A. (1997) *Linguistic Anthropology*. Cambridge: Cambridge University Press.

Gumperz, J. and Levinson, S. (eds) (1996) *Rethinking Linguistic Relativity*. Cambridge: Cambridge University Press.

Hanks, W. F. (1996) *Language and Communicative Practices*. Boulder, CO: Westview Press.

Holliday, A. (1999) Small cultures. *Applied Linguistics* 20(2): 237–264.

Jia, W. (2007) The Chinese conceptualizations of face: Emotions, communication, and personhood. In L. A. Samovar and R. E. Porter (eds) *Intercultural Communication: A Reader*. Shanghai: Shanghai Foreign Language Education Press.

Leetch, G. (2007) Politeness: Is there an East-West divide? *Journal of Politeness Research* 3: 167–206.

Locher, M. A. and Watts, R. (2005) Politeness theory and relational work. *Journal of Politeness Research* 1(1): 9–33.

Machin, D. and van Leeuwen, T. (2007) *Global Media Discourse*. Abingdon: Routledge.

Pan, Y., Scollon, S. and Scollon, R. (2002) *Professional Communication in International Settings*. Oxford: Blackwell.

Pye, L. (1990) China: Erratic state, frustrated society. *Foreign Affairs*. 69(4): 56–74.

320   *Chinese Discourse and Interaction*

Scollon, R. (2008) Discourse itineraries: Nine processes of resemiotization. In V. K. Bhatia, J. Flowerdew and R. H. Jones (eds) *Advances in Discourse Studies.* 233–44. London/New York: Routledge.

Spencer-Oatey, H. (2005) (Im)politeness, face and perceptions of rapport: Unpacking their bases and interrelationships. *Journal of Politeness Research* 1(1): 95–119.

Wierzbicka, A. (2006) *English: Meaning and Culture.* Oxford: Oxford University Press.

Authors Index

CPSIA information can be obtained
at www.ICGtesting.com
Printed in the USA
BVHW042331181119
564238BV00006B/27/P